ENOUGH TO BE SHARED: A PURPOSE-DRIVEN NAME

A VIVID LIFE STORY APPLICATION OF GEORGE APPIAH-SOKYE

DR. GEORGE APPIAH-SOKYE

authorHOUSE

AuthorHouse™
1663 Liberty Drive
Bloomington, IN 47403
www.authorhouse.com
Phone: 833-262-8899

Published by AuthorHouse 06/03/2021

ISBN: 978-1-6655-2622-7 (sc)
ISBN: 978-1-6655-2621-0 (hc)
ISBN: 978-1-6655-2620-3 (e)

Library of Congress Control Number: 2021910076

FOREWORD

By
MBANYANE MHANGO (PhD)

AS PRESIDENT OF A SEMINARY tasked with theological education of ministers and laity, I take seriously stories of academic and professional success. This is why I am drawn to the academic and professional success of Dr. Appiah-Sokye. This autobiography is quintessential to a portrait of success that has potential to birth or jumpstart someone's aspirations towards academic and professional success. His story shows that academic and professional success is possible even in the face of difficulties. Notably, adversity is the bedrock of creativity because it unleashes the power of human ingenuity. Dr. Appiah George appeals to the reader to regard adversity as an opportunity in disguise. Re-imagining life challenges courts academic and professional success.

By reading this book, readers especially students and young professionals from diverse socio-economic backgrounds will learn that success begins in one's mind before it finds concrete expression in life. The wisdom and scholarly insights Dr. Appiah-Sokye shares within the thirty chapters of this book will embolden you to dream big and to realize your destiny. Though time is critical, the story of Dr. Appiah-Sokye partly suggests that a late start in a career is not invariably a liability or disadvantage. Informed by experience, a person who gets an opportunity to study at a relatively old age, is likely to value such opportunity and therefore work hard towards success. In this light, the author stresses the need to embrace every event in life as a learning curve. Given that challenges are endemic to life, it is imperative to expect twists and turns and to trust God.

To appreciate the value of the treasure hidden in the fabric of this book, allow me to provide you with a brief testimony of my dear friend, Dr. Appiah-Sokye. There are not many people who are both academically accomplished but also humble. I can truly attest that Dr. Appiah-Sokye is such a person. It is in this sense that I consider myself fortunate to have Dr. George Appiah-Sokye as a friend. As someone that I have known for over 15 years, I am impressed by his expertise, ethics, humility, and concern for posterity. In many ways, this autobiography is rooted in a deep concern for posterity. Dr. Appiah-Sokye's character traits undergird the truthfulness of this autobiography. As such, the readers should approach his story with a hermeneutic of trust not of suspicion. His is truly a life enough to be shared by all.

Dr. Appiah-Sokye rightly states that academic and professional success is not a mystical feat but demands commitment and determination. Notwithstanding this, he accents the role of the grace of God in one's success. The author maintains that success in life is neither an accident nor a coincidence. Rather, it is identified with those who conceive triumphant and tragic experiences of life as an invitation to learn. This is not to dismiss the pain that may be associated especially with experiences of lament. On the contrary, it is re-conceived challenges by re-framing them in a larger context. This way, one is likely to embrace challenges as an enrollment to further learning.

Towards this end, appropriate disposition is indispensable for learning and success in life. Dr. Appiah-Sokye enlists us to view all life experiences as relevant to one's learning curve. This thinking relates to his personal conviction that education is not an end in itself. Rather, it is what one does with education that counts the most. True value of academic and professional success is subject to the impact one has both within and outside his or her immediate family. The academic and professional success of Dr. Appiah-Sokye likewise reflects in the lives of many people that he has impacted over the years, both in Ghana and elsewhere.

Moreover, he elucidates that meaningful learning demands networking and continuous search for growth. Although his academic and professional qualifications relate to business administration, accounting, and tax, readers from other disciplines will find the principles and philosophy that he espouses as readily adaptable. It is partly in this sense that the wiring of this book itself is a testament to the appropriateness of his name 'enough to be shared.' Dr. Appiah-Sokye's story shows that parents reveal their aspirations for their children's future by naming them in ways that reflect such aspirations. Of course, a name does not work as a magic wand. Instead, it serves as a guiding post especially as one encounters diverse vicissitudes of life.

To conclude, Dr. Appiah-Sokye demonstrates that share resolve and responsibility are intricately linked to academic and professional success. Despite stiff competition for admission into university in his early days in his native nation of Ghana, Dr. Appiah-Sokye was one of few students that were given opportunities to study at the University of Ghana both at undergraduate and graduate levels. Unsatisfied by his accomplishments in Ghana, he continued his studies in the US and earned a doctorate in Business administration and other professional qualifications. I now invite you to read for yourself the life defining and challenging story of Dr. Apiah-Sokye.

PREFACE

THIS BOOK IS A DOCUMENTATION of my life account from birth to April 15, 2021. The book's publication is to commemorate my 57th birthday. The title of the book is appropriate because it adequately encapsulates the theme of my story. While the name *George* is a common first name, the compound last name *Appiah-Sokye* has African origin; yet the name *Sokye* (Enough to be shared) resonates with several people. For that reason, most people prefer to call me by that name because of the virtues the name represent. The need to write my life story arose as a result of continuous requests by young people especially those interested in accounting and finance; as well as, those from the church for mentorship. Life is a journey that can be broken down into milestones and benchmarks-some life experiences are negative and others are positive, presenting useful lessons and teaching moments. While positive life experiences can be emulated by others; negative aspects of life can be avoided, circumvented, or mitigated by many. A true-life story goes beyond the details portrayed in typical resumes and curriculum *vitae* because there is equally important information that is beyond the scope of profiles provided on individuals. Unlike film shows that tell the story in few hours, life lessons are for the long haul. For that reason, resumes and curriculum vitae do not tell all the story. Life experiences can be shared by the very person recounting the story and feedback can also be received by the same person whose life is being discussed. Consequently, the more additional information is shared, the more people get to know the person better. I am excited to present to you my life story account, backed by appropriate life applications for your reading pleasure. Ladies and gentlemen- *Enough to be Shared: A Purpose-Driven Name- A Vivid Life Story Application of George Appiah-Sokye.*

A Request to User

I have tried to cover several topics; nevertheless, new developments will be presented in future, involving ambiguities, controversies, divergence and convergence in knowledge in this area despite my attempt to provide you with detailed information from both feedback and self-disclosure. Likewise, it is impossible that all aspects of an argument would be stated at all times. Dear reader, my request to you is to contact me for more explanation if specific need arises. In this case, this life story will be beneficial to all.

DEDICATION

THIS BOOK-*ENOUGH TO BE SHARED: A Purpose Driven Name-A Vivid Life Story Application-* is dedicated to all who have impacted my life through motivation and education. I like to dedicate this work to all young people who have looked up to me for mentorship. I thank God for their lives.

CONTENTS

LIST OF TABLES

INTRODUCTION

THE SIGNIFICANCE ATTACHED TO NAMES and naming in Ghanaian society is remarkable (Abarry, December 1991); it is strikingly different from what obtains in Euro-American cultures; because names of people...tend to emanate from the interplay of religious, mythical, social, and historical realities (Abarry, 1991; Abraham,1962). For this reason, proper names exist in all languages; though, differences abound, there is broad, systematic and cross-cultural constancy to many name-giving practices (Jeshion, August 2009). The name *George Appiah-Sokye* can be explained as follows:

> *One*, George is a Western name given to me at birth by my parents. *George* is a Greek Baby Name, meaning *a farmer* or *tiller of the soil* (www.sheknows.com -accessed on 02/25/2020).
>
> In African societies, individuals are named based on the cultural expectations and the proper identification of the personality named in association with status, birth order and circumstance, a particular clan or genealogical groups' beliefs, and attributes (Abarry, 1991; Quartey-Papafio, 1913).
>
> *Two*, the meaning of the name- *Appiah* is not clear but two people have offered in sight as follows: (a) a user in South Sudan has attributed the name *Appiah* to Arabic origin, meaning-*forgiveness*; and (b) another user in Virginia in the United States of America has stated that the name-*Appiah* is of African Origin, meaning *"Prince"* (Retrieved from www.names.org -accessed on 02/25/2020).

Three, the name-*Sokye*- contemplates-either-(i) *enough to be shared*, or (ii) literally, *a hat-carrier*. One of the supporters of this School of thought is the late Elder Osei Kwaku, who explains that there were two *Appiahs* in Asante Mampong (Ghana) but the one who became the Asante *Mamponghene* (traditional ruler) was often seen wearing a hat (*ekye*). For that reason, the name *Osokye*-literally means- a hat carrier, implying responsibility- is more of a description that became a name. One of the adherents of the other School of thought is Elder David Antwi Boakye, who is of the view that "enough to be shared" encapsulates the virtue of the name-*Osokye*.

The virtues that are implicit in my name encompass the following: *(1) farmer or tiller of the soil, (2) forgiveness or prince, (3) enough to be shared or carrier of responsibility.* Jeshion (August 2009) elaborated that proper names are given to people; and as a result, *"we form a singular thought because utterances with proper names straightaway cause us to accord significance, prima facie, to the referent (or supposed referent) of the proper name, and taking that individual to have significance causes us to form a name-labeled mental file"* (p.x).

I prefer that friends and family call me-*Nkonimdi* (meaning Victory) to remind me that victory over situations and circumstances can be accomplished with determination, hard work, assiduity, dedication, and tenacity of purpose. Typically, the good deeds of people are told at death in tributes and biographies, when their virtues and legacies are shared. The question is: *Why should we wait for people to die before their legacies can be shared?* Life is a *journey* with an origin and destination-birth and death; but characterized by peaks (ups) and valleys (downs), as well as, meanders (winding).

As one advances in age, there tends to be a decay of memory

traces and so directly reported life experience becomes challenging; nevertheless, there is the need to preserve oral history through written formats to benefit posterity. Life experiences and perspectives can be examined, explored, or explained to illicit worldviews, legacies, ethos, and reflection to sharpen life skills. Likewise, written life histories allow for the role of people who have made impact to be celebrated to provide opportunity for people to make input into future editions and updates.

In this book, the themes to be covered will include but not limited to the following: background and new beginnings, focus on academic and professional education, experiences from work and extra mural activities; as well as, what has gotten done, including credit unionism, deploying technology in teaching, and accomplishments. Similarly, acknowledgment of contribution of others, legacies, and lessons learned to be applied as springboard of success for others to emulate.

CHAPTER 1

THE HUMBLE BEGINNINGS

EICHSTELLER (2019) ASSERTED THAT BIOGRAPHICAL narrative research has a complicated genealogy and rooted in history and analysis of everyday document, biography provides an account of the life lived and experienced. George Appiah-Sokye is my name and I was born in Ghana on Wednesday, April 15, 1964 to George Emmanuel Appiah-Sokye, alias Kofi Appiah (a native of Krobo-Ashanti) and Christiana Oppong Kontoh Appiah, alias Akua Asuako or Kontoh (a native of Asaam-Ashanti), both of blessed memory. A brief background of Ghana is as follows:

> *Ghana, a small African country located on the beautiful Atlantic coastline just north of the Equator, was called the "Gold Coast" until 1957, when she gained her independence from Great Britain. There was good reason for the name; the country's gold deposits were among the world's largest, putting her in the league with South Africa. And, as in South Africa, the billions of dollars earned from Ghana's gold deposits did not improve the lives of her indigenous people. Yet, another hope for prosperity was on the distant horizon* (Owusu, 2017, p.1).

I started my elementary education at the Saint Monica's Primary School in 1969 and continued at the Anglican Middle School at Mampong-Ashanti in Ghana. I gained admission to the Pentecost Secondary School in 1977 in Kumasi and later on transferred in 1978 to the Juaben Secondary School from 1978 to 1983, where I obtained the

General Certificate of Education (G.C.E) Ordinary Level certificate in 1983. The courses offered encompassed the following: *English Language, Modern Mathematics, and Biology; Principles of Accounting, Commerce, Economics, French, Geography, and Oral English.* I proceeded to the Saint Peter's Secondary School in Nkwatia-Kwahu in the Eastern region of Ghana from 1983-1985, where I obtained the G.C.E. Advanced Level certificate in *Accounting, Economics, Geography*, and *General Paper.*

After High School or Secondary School, I gained admission to the School of Administration of the University of Ghana, Legon in 1986, and completed in 1989; with a Bachelor of Science (BSc) degree in Business Administration, with a concentration in Accounting. A decade after undergraduate studies, I returned to the University of Ghana School of Business Administration for my Master of Business Administration (MBA) degree in Accounting from 1999 to 2001. In January 2012, I commenced my Doctor of Business Administration (DBA) degree, with a concentration in Advanced Accounting and completed in October 2016.

I have the following certifications: (a) Certified Public Accountant (CPA) since 2010 (b) Certified Internal Control Auditor (CICA) since 2009, (c) Chartered Accountant (CA) since 2006, and Chartered Tax Practitioner (MCIT, FCIT) since 1995 and 2011 respectively. Consequently, I am an active member of the American Institute of Certified Public Accountants (AICPA) and the Institute for Internal Controls, Delta Mu Delta, and Golden Key International Honour Society; as well as, inactive membership in the Institute of Chartered Accountants, Ghana and fellowship in the Chartered Institute of Taxation, Ghana.

I trace the beginning of my working life to the Mampong District Hospital over thirty-five years ago; as a National Service personnel in 1985 and also a second year National Service with Pomadze Poultry Enterprise Limited in 1990. I have worked in Ghana and the United

States of America in different capacities, including: accounting, auditing, property management, teaching, and many more. I have worked for the following organization: *first*, (i) Youth Connection Charter School in Chicago (January 2013 to date), (ii) Adjunct Faculty with the Southern New Hampshire University (SNHU) from January 2015 to date; (iii) The Church of Pentecost U.S.A., Inc from February 2008 to August 2009; *second*, (iv) The Ghana Internal Revenue Service (April 1991 to October 2001); (v) Ghana Institute of Professional Studies (IPS), now University of Professional Studies, Accra from January 2004 to January 2012.

Third, (vi) CTI-Tech Limited (December 2003 to April 2004); (vii) Premier Resource Management Limited (March 2002 to December 2003); Osei Kwabena and Associates, Chartered Accountants (August 2001 to February 2002); and Albert Academy Limited (1990-1991). *Lastly*, I served as a Partner/Consultant with SMME Consult Limited from January 2005 to December 2011 and also served the Ghana Co-operative Credit Unions (CUA) Association Limited from 1992 to 1998.

I am a man of faith, and I make no apologies that I am a Christian. I was born into the Pentecostal heritage but I made a personal decision to accept the Lord Jesus Christ as my personal savior on December 30, 1979. I have held several appointments and position in the church. My passion is to develop the next generation of Christian leaders. I enjoy traveling, social work, reading, writing, and listening to music.

On family life, on January 2, 1993 I got married to Patience Olivia Asafo-Adjei (daughter of Frank Asafo-Adjei and Comfort Appiah-Twum, both of blessed memory) in Kumasi at the Methodist Church, Ayigya, UST in Kumasi. The officiating ministers were Reverend Kofi Amponsah (Principal of the Wesley College in Kumasi), Reverend Dr. Sarfo Kantanka (UST), Apostle B.K Swanzy (Area head of Mampong Church of Pentecost), and Reverend Richard Amankwah (Resident

Minister of Ayigya Methodist Church). However, Patience joined the silent majority in August 2000 and I re-married Maame Yaa on March 20, 2005 at the Church of Pentecost, Madina. The officiating minister was Reverend Emmanuel K. Apea. Together, my wife and I have four children-One lady and four gentlemen, including Edith, Geopat, Orgetience, and Emmanuel; as well as, two awesome grand-children: Adepa and Nkyira. Kingsley Appiah-Sokye (Paa Kay) is my grandson, named after me by my nephew-Johnny Essah-Mensah.

ANCESTRY

The name- *Appiah-Sokye* can be traced to the *Mamponghene* (the traditional ruler of Mampong-Ashanti in Ghana), who was taken together with Nana Prempeh I (the king of the Asante kingdom) to the Seychelles in 1896 at the time he was advanced in age but never returned. Nana Appea Osokye ruled Asante Mampong in the 1800s. The name of my paternal grandfather is Kwadwo Appau and one of his characteristics is that he had several children from different parts of Ghana, including Mampong and Effiduasi in the Ashanti region; as well as, Yeji in the Brong Ahafo region. The common names that are linked to Grandpa Appau encompass the following: Addae, Appau, Serwaa, Nkansah, Nonno, and many more. In addition to my father and some of his brothers, other children of his could be traced to *Konkonhene's*(a sub-chief) house and Opanin Appiah's (blacksmith) line, and so on.

My father has relationship with the Jamasi-Asante stool (Right wing to the Silver stool) of Asante Mampong. The late Nana Brobbey of Jamasi was a kinsman of my father and his nephew Yaw Yaw Frimpong (deceased) of the Jamaica Poultry Farms was a cousin of my father. I knew both Nana Brobbey and his nephew very well when they were alive because we met at family funerals. Uncle Yaw Frimpong used to pay courtesy calls on my father on Wednesday (market days of Mampong Ashanti in Ghana), when he came to town to conduct regular business and visits. The late Nana Brobbey married the elder daughter of my late Grand-father-George John Echie, with whom he had several children who are known to me. My father named me after his uncle-George John Echie.

The Asantehene (Nana Agyemang Prempeh) refused to pay 50,000 ounces of gold as stated in the treaty of *Fomena* but he offered to pay 600 ounces of gold or £2000; and as a result, the Governor of the Gold Coast did not accept the amount because the King managed to sponsor a delegation to England (Edward A. Ulzen Memorial Foundation, February 1, 2018). Consequently, he ordered the arrest of Nana Akwasi Agyemang Prempeh (King of Asante-listed as Number 1) and *fifty-four* listed persons including *Nana Appea Osokye* (the Chief of Mampong-listed as Number 3) and also listed were *Yaa Boatemaa* (Mamponghene's wife-listed as number 27), *Kwaku Fokuo* (Mamponghene's servant-listed as number 28) and *Kwame Ware* (Mamponghene's son-listed as number 29).

After the arrest they were sent to the Cape Coast Castle on February 1, 1896 (Edward A. Ulzen Memorial Foundation, February 1, 2018). Per Asante historical account, "the Asantehene Prempeh was deposed and arrested, and he and other Asante leaders (including Nana Appiah-Osokye) were sent into exile in the Seychelles in 1896" (Retrieved from en.wikipedia.org -accessed on 02/24/2020;www.pfsr.org/history-of-Seychelles -accessed on 02/25/2020). Joseph K. Adjaye, writing on *Asantehene Agyemang Prempeh I, Asante History, and the Historian* in 1990 postulated that "the history is the most important known single source of primary information on genealogical history of the Asante kingship" (p.22). ...So, they finally allowed Prempeh to return and to be reinstated as Asantehene in 1926" (Kreol International Magazine, June 4, 2012). Nevertheless, Nana Appiah-Osokye never returned with some of his children. My father's daily journal stated: "On January 31, 1985- Attended the 50th anniversary of the formation of the Ashanti Confederacy "the Golden Jubilee"

On the maternal side, I trace my ancestry to the Asona clan that is believed to have migrated from *Denkyira* in the Central region, and led by the old lady, *Ofori Nana*; who carried the stool at her back and later on settled at *Atwampumah*. The descendants were associated with the *Krontihene* stool of Asante Mampong. The names of *Nana Ampratwum* and *Nana Akwasi Asuako (both of blessed memory)*, who released land for Mampong Zongo. *Nana Akwasi Asuako* was deposed by the Convention Peoples Party (CPP) government but I grew up to see him. Written history shows that three of the high-ranking chiefs in the Asante state of Mampong, included (1) *Nana Asuako Peprah*-Krontihene of Mampong, (2) *Nana Owusu Brempon Sarpong*- Amaniehene of Mampong, and (3) *Nana Afrifa Nsiah*- Nsumankwahene of Mampong; had been interviewed to cover the history of Mampong, genealogy of Mampong kings, the role of the office of the Mampong Nsumankwahene, and Islamic influence in Mampong (Akyeampong, n.d.).

CHAPTER 2

PARENTAL ETHOS AND VALUES

THE ASSOCIATIONS BETWEEN WRITTEN EVENTS concerning family members, produce knowledge about the relations between the members (Hanssen, 2019, p.311). My father was a practicing Pentecostal from the Apostolic Church in the *1950s* and my mother joined the Apostolic Church on marrying my father in 1952. Later on, the name of the church became the Church of Pentecost in 1962. As with Iuliu-Marius in 2019, who was grateful to the role played by his mother and father in his formation, but also to the richness of images that remained in his memory which explains, at least partially, his predilection for poetry, metaphor, and Biblical theology...remains today, as he confesses, deeply related with his native village (p.220). The role played by my parents have significant impact on my upbringing and who I am today.

THE LIFE HISTORY OF MY FATHER

The late George Emmanuel Appiah-Sokye (Senior) alias Opanin Kofi Appiah was born on the September 23, 1922 at Asokore near Effiduasi in the Ashanti region of Ghana. Even though, his parents were natives of Ashanti Mampong. Both deceased parents were from Krobo-Ashanti and while his mother (Madam Ama Agyenkwa) was from the *Bretuo* clan; his father (Opanin Kwadwo Appau) was from the *Aduana* clan. My paternal grand-parents gave birth to seven children. The first was still born, my father was the second, the third died when he was fifteen years of age, the fourth was stillborn, the fifth one survived, the sixth one also survived. The seventh died at age seven.

Additionally, the mother had two children with another man; a son and a daughter. My father and his siblings have passed on as of March 17, 2020.

George Emmanuel Appiah-Sokye received his education at the Presbyterian Junior and Senior Schools in Mampong-Ashanti from 1931 to 1941. After schooling, he engaged himself in the buying and selling of eggs and groundnuts to and from Takoradi for a period of one year. Likewise, he left home for Bibiani in Western North region of Ghana in 1944 and stayed with Opanin Kwabena Agyei, Madam Adwoa Nkyira's husband (all blessed memory); and it was there and then that he took to his electrical profession. Later on, he had his practical work at the Bibiani 1927 Limited (a mining company) from 1944 to 1946. Subsequently, he returned home and became a *pupil teacher* at Sekodumasi-Ashanti and Basa in Brong-Ahafo in the Krachi Area from 1946 to 1948.

He opened a store in Mr. B.E. Adwetoa's house in Mampong-Ashanti and later became a soap manufacturer from 1949 to 1952. Moreover, worked on his uncle George John Echie's farm in Ahafo and returned in 1952, and in 1956, was then transferred to Mampong Maternity Hospital, where he worked until 1971.

On marriage life, he married one lady from Benim near Asante Mampong from 1944 to 1949. He later married my mother Christian Oppong (Akua Kontoh) from Asaam-Ashanti. The life of my mother has been covered below in this chapter. I must confess that; throughout my father's Christian life he did not achieve things on a silver platter. To this end, I must state that the course was full of spiritual warfare throughout his Christian life. He separated from my mother and married another woman (name withheld), a Midwife and fell from the Pentecostal *faith* but through the *Prayer Tower* of Pastor Isaac Kwasi Adu Mensah, he had a new revelation of heaven and became a devout and staunch member of the Church of Pentecost. Additionally, he had his right hand first finger cut off by a machine at Maternity Hospital in 1968. Similarly, he fell from the top of roof in 1969; and in 1971, he had a terrible bicycle accident on the Maternity Hospital -Bonkrong Road near Mampong-Ashanti and was admitted at the Komfo Anokye Teaching Hospital (KATH) in Kumasi, where he was unconscious for two weeks.

The achievements of my father include but not limited to the following: *first*, he managed to build a compound-house with the house number T.87 in Tunsuom in Mampong-Ashanti, containing 13 rooms, 2 kitchens, 2 bathrooms, a store and 2 toilet rooms. *Second*, he looked after one of his younger brothers through elementary and secondary education; *three*, he sent one of his brothers to Ahafo for cocoa cultivation in 1969 and engaged two farm labourers (names withheld). *Four*, he built three bedrooms for his mother on plot and house number T.20 in Tunsuom in Mampong-Ashanti. Lastly, he was enstooled the *Apentenhene* of Krobo-Ashanti in 1969 by Nana Yaw Sarfo (the Krobohene, deceased). All-in-all, throughout his life time he engaged himself in God's ministry until his untimely death. He was prayerful, a counselor, a teacher, a preacher and an indispensable elder of the Church of Pentecost. Elder George Emmanuel Appiah-Sokye joined the silent majority on the September 23, 1986, which marked his *64th birthday* (*Extracted from the Funeral Brochure of the Late George Emmanuel Appiah-Sokye dated 25/9/86*).

LEGACIES

I have learned proper record-keeping from my father and that has served me well. A review of my father's daily journal showed: (1) **Grace of Giving**:

February 6, 1983–OFFERING IN AID of the Chapel was held on this day. I offered four hundred ¢400.00+¢200.00 as a promise. My wife offered

¢200.00+¢1,000.00 as a promise. Mirriam offered ¢100.00+¢400.00 as a promise. MAY GOD RAIN UPON OUR DESERT...AMEN!!

August 17, 1983-Paid my February Promise today-17ᵗʰ August 1983.

January 1, 1984 – Presented, my wife and I, Christmas gift of four hundred cedis to Pastor (name withheld).

August 10, 1984-Planted my seed of one thousand cedis, away from myself to learn to rely on my source. (2) **Teaching Gift**-I have examined the writings of my father on topical Christian issues through document review and want to share one on-<u>How to break a fast</u>, as follows:

> *"After a long fast a number of days treat yourself as you a baby, because your stomach will become tender and delicate. Never overeat when coming off even a short fast. Do not give vent to your appetite. I hear some people who can drink juice when breaking a fast. If you cannot take juice on a weak stomach; however, then, take cereal with milk with NO sugar. You may take broth a short interval with a little cooked rice added. The length of the fast determine how slowly you should get back to solid food. The Scriptural texts to support the power of Biblical fasting includes but not limited to the following: Matthew 17:21; Mark 9;29;Exodus 34:30;I Kings 19:1-8;Daniel 10:2-3;Esther 4:16;Jona 3:5-10;Luke 4:1-2,18;Acts 13:2;Acts 9:9-17; II Corinthians 11:27;I Corinthians 7:5;Matthew 6:16-18"* (Notes from the writings of G. E. Appiah-Sokye).

THE LIFE HISTORY OF MY MOTHER

The name of my mother is Christiana Oppong Kontoh Appiah (a.k.a Akua Kontoh) and was born in 1925 to Opanin Kwadwo Oppong of Asaam-Ashanti and Obaa Panin Afia Fofie of Asaam, all of blessed memory. She was the second of four siblings, three female and one male. She did not have formal education but received informal education from the environment she found herself in such as the church, association with the Anglican missionaries. She was taught by the husband to memorize most of the names of the human anatomy. Earlier in her working life as a young adult, she accompanied her late uncle (Kwadwo Owusu) to Mim in the Brong-Ahafo region of Ghana. While her uncle farmed, she kept her uncle's store- selling provisions, hardware, and gold dust, among others. Per her own narratives: *"she did not know the value of the gold dust at the time because families bought the gold dust to smear on dead bodies of loved ones"*

Later on, in her adult live, she endeared herself as a woman of *many parts*, as follows: *One*, Madam Akua Kontoh as a *fish monger*- she dealt in different assortment of fishes as her main pre-occupation, buying her inventory such as herrings from Mankessim and Cape Coast in the Central region of Ghana, Accra; and fresh fish from Kumasi. Arguably, she was the first Ashanti to sell smoked fish in Mampong-Ashanti, Ghana. Therefore, her association with her *Ga* and *Fante* friends (Maame Kaa and Esi Mansah, both of blessed memory) provided her with the needed expertise. While some of the *stock-in-trade* were sold in fresh state, others were smoked for resale. She plied her trade in Mampong, Kofiase, Sekodumasi, Ejura, Nsuta, and Agona in the Ashanti region and Atebubu and Amantin in the Brong Ahafo region.

Two, Maame Kontoh as a *farmer*- she maintained farms at Akranpah, Katinga, Hintado, and Owuo Bourho; where she planted maize, yam, vegetables, and so on. She also reared sheep for some period of time. She took to farming during the lean season for the fish business. *Third*, Maame Akua Kontoh as *a trader*: she traded in plantain from *Tepa*, *Mim*, and *Dadiesoaba* in the Brong and Ahafo regions of Ghana. She sold tomatoes and kenkey along the line.

She supported the church financially even in her old age through tithes, offering, and special offerings. She was called to the office of a deaconess in the church and was duly retired at her old age. She worked with the following Pastors who were posted to Mampong: Pastor Bimpong, D. Y. A Owusu, T. A. Addo, Amponsah, Isaac Kwasi Adu Mensah, Samuel Opoku Adipah, F. T. Obuobi, Prophet J. E. Ameyaw, and so on. She joined the Apostolic Church in the Gold Coast in the 1950s, when she got married to her late husband-*George Emmanuel Appiah-Sokye*. She was baptized on June 7, 1953 by Pastor Ankomah (the father of Elder James McKeown- a.k.a *A good one there* in New Jersey, U.S.A.).

Her spiritual ministry focused on: (a) intercession, praying daily for the church, family, those charged with governance, and so on. (b) She was a woman of service; and for that reason, catered for ministers of the Gospel such as: Apostle Joseph Egyir Painstil, Pastors: Emmanuel Parker, J. R. K. Mensah (Ejura-Ashanti), Pastor Mante (Effiduasi-Ashanti), Elders: J. K. Asante, Clottey, Gyimah, and so on. She was the lead caterer for major conventions, where she cooked for ministers and also hosted elders who came to preach at Mampong on Sundays from other towns and villages. She also hosted church visitors and strangers. She supported the family when the need arose and also accommodated family members in the household.

My mother survived spiritual attacks, survived lorry accident, survived lightning/thunder strike in the 1980s, and also survived 29 years of widowhood. Nevertheless, the provision of God was manifest in her life. By way of illustration, (a) the late Apostle Dr. Emmanuel Owusu Bediakoh supported her financially for over 20 years with periodic financial contribution of five hundred thousand cedis (equivalent GH¢50) or one million cedis (or GH¢100). (b) There is one important thing that cannot be spared mentioning in that in 1993 when the family was rendered homeless arising out of protracted litigation, the late Maame Amaniampong absorbed the entire household into hers; even though, during this time, her house was under construction and she did not have enough space, yet she offered the family warmth and comfort for eight (8) months. This gesture would forever be remembered.

The association between *the Kyei* and *the Amaniampong* families was developed in the church from the 1950s. (c) Several Mampong Area Heads of the Church of Pentecost, including Apostles: B. K. Swanzy, *Kwaku* Asare, Emmanuel Kwame Apeah, and a host of others have also assisted her during her life time. (d) The late Elder F. K. Atuah (Esq) and wife also provided legal service to the family virtually on *probono* basis. *Lastly*, there is no space to mention all who have in diverse ways been a blessing to my mother, their contribution is acknowledged. May God richly bless them all. My mother's favorite Scriptural texts were: (i) *"Praise the Lord: for He is good and His mercies endures Forever"* (Psalm 118, Psalm 136, I Chronicles 16:34, and Psalm 107:1); and (ii) *"the lines have fallen unto me in pleasant places"* (*Me hye hama afa dee eye ama me-* Psalm 16:6).

Maame Kontoh (alias Kofiase Mma kuo Panin) was preceded in death by her husband, George Emmanuel Appiah-Sokye (September 23, 1922 to September 23, 1986), sisters (Akosua Konadu and Mary Boampong); as well as, two inseparable Christian sisters- Maame Kyei (alias Dadease Mmaa Kuo Panin) and Maame Amaniampong (alias Daaho Mmaa Kuo Panin). On June 5, 2016 she passed on peacefully and joined the silent majority. She remained a widow for 29 years until her untimely death (*Extracted from the Funeral Brochure of the Late Christian Appiah dated 15/10/2016*).

FAMILY TREE

The contribution of my parents together toward the global population is 89, as of October 2016. The names of the children according to order of birth are as follows: (1) Adwoa Saka (Mampong-Ashanti);

(2) Akosua Nyamekye (Asaam-Ashanti); (3) Samuel Asiako Appiah (Mampong-Ashanti); (4) Alex Kofi Appiah (France); (5) Mrs. Freda Appiah Agyaaning (formerly of Pentecost Hospital, Accra); (6) Miriam Appiah (Accra); (7) William Appenteng Appiah (Belgium); (8) George Appiah-Sokye (U.S.A.); and (9) Majorie-Rant Akosua Serwaa Appiah (Accra). The pictures of my siblings are provided in Chapter 22.

MY FATHER'S HOUSE

On our nuclear family, my father's daily journal elaborated, as follows:

December 4,1982–My wife and I renewed our marriage today, it was confirmed by Pastor F.T. Obuobi, the District Pastor in charge of Mampong Ashanti.

December 14, 1982–THY WILL BE DONE OH GOD– signed for me by two Pastors on the 14th day of December 1982 at Kumasi.

February 1, 1983–Son-in-law (name withheld) arrived at Mampong from Agege, on Nigeria's expulsion orders on Monday, 31st January,1983. Presented to his wife 1 hand sewing machine, 1 half piece of cover cloth and pieces of material for his two children.

July 17, 1983–Birthday Party celebration was performed in honour of my grand-daughter –Hannah Darkowah, by my senior daughter, Freda on the 17th of July 1983.

November 18,1983–Marriage performance:-Mr. Isaac Agyaaning of Agogo did come to perform the marriage rite of his new found wife Miss Freda Agyenkwa Appiah on this date. He was accompanied by Elder Ntiamoah of Agogo Pentecost Church; with him were Deacon Mensah also of Agogo and Brother Anane of Catholic Church who deputized for Mr. Isaac Agyaaning's mother. The amount expended on the marriage was to the Father's side-One thousand, eight hundred & 8 cedis; to the Mother's side, One thousand and fifteen cedis, totaling-three thousand, and thirty-five cedis (the numbers do not add up but I guess the difference cover other payments such as monies given to brothers-in-law (*akonta gye sikan*)-<u>emphasis mine</u>). *Brother E.K. Gyasi deputized for the church, by the District Pastor F.T. Obuobi.*

November 20,1983- The wedding between Isaac Agyaaning and Freda A. Appiah was performed today by Pastor F.T. Obuobi, the Church of Pentecost-Mampong Ashanti.

December 14,1983-FREDA, my daughter and her new found husband took leave of us on their way to Abidjan, where the husband lives. MAY THE LORD BLESS THEM with CHILDREN, AMEN!

Births:

My father documented on births in the family as follows:

(1) *December 17,1983- Miriam…gave birth to a baby girl today at 10 o'clock in the night.*

(2) *May 7, 1984-Nyamekye delivered a female child on Monday 7th May 1984 at Asaam;*

(3) *May 21, 1984- Nyarko delivered on Monday the 21st May 1984 a male child;*

(4) *May 25,1984- Takyiwah…delivered on Friday the 25th of May 1984, a male child. Kingsley Appiah-Sokye, who was named after me by my son and his wife. Takyiwa's baby boy was dedicated to God Almighty through his son Jesus Christ on 20th June 1984;*

(5) *June 10,1984-Freda, my daughter who is at present in Abidjan with her husband Isaac had brought forth a baby boy, who became a still born on the 3rd May 1984.*

(6) *June 12, 1984-My female cat delivered 3(three) kittens. This is the fourth time.*

June 29, 1984-Freda took leave of us to her new station to resume duty in the Hospital near the Ghana- Ivory Coast border. She took with her...,Kyerewah.

December 1,1984-Mirriam went to Sefwi-Asafo Hospital to visit her senior sister, FREDA and baby Kyerewah, for a flight and returned on 4ᵗʰ December 1984.

On his part and from Liberia in West Africa, my elder Brother Samuel added:

> *"I am still alive through the sure mercies and power of Our Ever-Living God... Many people lost their lives both great and small. Several nationalities including Ghanaians, Nigerians, Sierra Leonians, and Guineans died in great numbers by gun-shots, beheadings, as well as, pestilences, etc...The one who knew me before I was born, delivered me from death. I am still alive"* (August 20, 1991).

EXTENDED FAMILY

On his extended family, my father offered:

December 12, 1982-After six years in America, my niece Grace...landed on Ghana soil from America on 13ᵗʰ December 1982, Accra and arrived at Mampong on the 15ᵗʰ of December 1982. My son-in-law, Grace' husband at America, presented me a Jewell date watch No.360 through his wife, my niece on the 18ᵗʰ of December 1982, Saturday.

August 10, 1983-...(Brother) left here on the 9ᵗʰ of August 1983 to Accra, on his way to Austria via Germany on the 10ᵗʰ instant.

December 27,1983- Received gifts of two jackets, three trousers, two shirts, and four flying ties from my nephew, Daniel (not real name, my Sister's son, who resides at America on Xmas tide on 27ᵗʰ December 1983.

Sister Ama (name withheld) presented to me,1 large towel and three cakes of LUX soap.

As of October 2016, the Lord had blessed my parents with 9 children, whose ages ranged from 50 to 70; there were 38 grand-children, and 42 great grand- children (Total 89). God has blessed my parents with children, grandchildren, and great grandchildren, and in-laws. May His Name Be Praised!

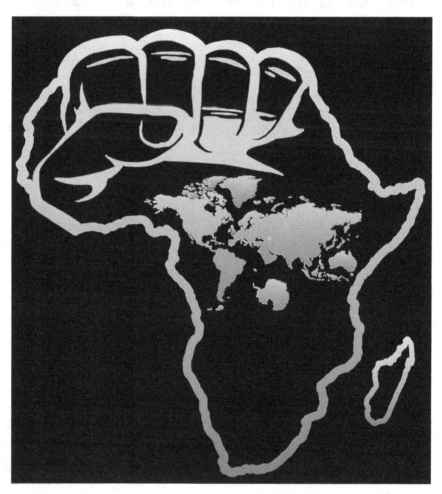

African Diaspora Power in Leadership-Unity, Pride, and Impact.

CHAPTER 3

※

LEARNING AS A LIFELONG JOURNEY

LEARNING IS A LIFE-LONG JOURNEY. While learning can be both formal and informal, my learning experience begun with the informal format; where my father became my first teacher by teaching me how to read and write. Specifically, I remember learning the five-times on the multiplication table first to permit me to determine the time at any given period. I learned that the five times was critical in the ability to read the chronometric (watch) time correctly. Furthermore, after the ability to recite the first Aramaic numerals from *1 to 10* and later from *11 to 20*. These numbers were written on the floor for me to attempt to copy correctly over time. The approach was used to learn the alphabets from *A to Z*.

Experimentation and theorizing on forms of life writing from the field of history has grown substantially in recent decades, as historians understand how autobiographical narrative may contribute to understanding both the past and our processes of accessing it (Aurell & Davis, 2019). In this way, I begun by reading and identifying objects to build foundational vocabulary; because Aurell and Davis sees them as related but defines the later as a hybrid genre; and as a result, conceives autobiography as a vivid kind of history, although an unconventional one (2019). Nyansah Hayfron (2018) asserted that:

> *Height is the greatest enemy of stability. The higher an object, the higher the center of gravity; and the less stable it is. I believe you want to stand to the end. Again, I say, be grounded very well and you will make it. I pray for you that you make it (p.203).*

By implication, any determination to attain any flight in life must have a corresponding willingness to maintain a level of stability because heights are subject to the forces of *gravity* on one hand, and *buoyancy* on the other. While gravity introduces uncertainties and volatility into life equations, buoyancy provide stability for success. For that reason, Stedman theoretically distinguishes history from autobiography (Aurell & Davis, 2019).

MAMPONG AS A CENTER OF LEARNING

The Mampong township in the Ashanti region has rich educational history in Ghana, just like Cape Coast in the Central region of Ghana. All institutions across the educational spectrum could be found in the town back then and continues this relevance to this day. At the public *elementary school level*, the schools include the following: Saint Monica's Primary or Infant Junior (I.J.), the Roman Catholic, the Presbyterian, the Methodist, the Ahmadiyya, the Anglican, the Seventh-Day Adventist (SDA), and the Local Authority. Later on, the Apostolic schools, and other private schools, including Senyah, Unity, Progressive, and *Appiah-Sokye* were added. At the *secondary or High School level*, the notable schools were: Amaniampong, Sekyereman and Saint Monica's; as well as, Serwaa Amaniampong Vocational (SAVIS), Akosah Business and Commercial School. The *training college-level* institutions encompassed: Saint Monica's, Mampong Technical Teachers Institute (MTTI), and Saint Andrew's. Later on, the status of the Saint Andrew's Training College was changed to a *full-fledge* College or School of Agriculture under the University College of Education (UCEW) umbrella. A lot of Ghanaians have received education in one form or the other from the different institutions in Mampong and I am no exception.

THE GENESIS

My informal education started at Mampong in the Ashanti region of Ghana before 1970, when I was sent to a *day nursery* operated by Reverend Kissiedu (a minister of the Evangelical Church of Ghana). Initially, the school was in a rented *mission house* of the church (owned by the late Madam Abena Kwabena or Maame Sofo) and near our house. We had a teacher and an attendant. Later, as the number of pupils increased, the school was moved to a store-front (owned by the late Opanin Kofi Dwomoh) located opposite the *Tadiem* Park. Real learning took place for me at this location because of the foundation provided by my father was grounded. At the beginning of the 1970 school year, my cousin (Yaw, not real name) and I were sent to the Seventh-Day Adventist (SDA) Primary School for admission processes because of proximity to our house. Back in the days, one of the means by which maturity for admission into the primary school was determined was by stretching forth one's hand across the head to touch one's ear lobe. I missed the opportunity because I could not pass the *selection test*. I came home disappointed and about to return to the day nursery I was attending.

SAINT MONICA'S PRIMARY AND ANGLICAN MIDDLE

My father secured admission for me at the Saint Monica's Primary School (also called Infant Junior or I.J. at the time). The implication of this was that I was to be separated from my other siblings (staying with our mother) to join my father and my elder Sister Freda at the Mampong Maternity Hospital, where my father was working. The Mampong Maternity Hospital was located about two miles away from our home in the Mampong township. While I was to begin Saint Monica's Primary School, my sister was attending the Saint Monica's Middle School. My sister and I stayed with our father during the weekdays and we spent the weekend with the rest of the family at Mampong township. The exigencies of my father's work as the electrician of the hospital required him to be housed at the hospital compound because of emergencies. In those days, the Mampong township used stand-alone plants to generate electric power and the hospital had its own plants manned by my father.

On the first day of school, on my way to school I felt feverish so my father's nephew (Kofi, not his real name), who was in the upper primary of the same school asked me to go back home to receive treatment. Arguably, the second day of school became my first day of school and I have fond memories of this experience. I found myself in the class or grade two classroom and the class teacher called me and asked me of my class and I told her I was coming to class two. Not convinced, she asked me to accompany her to the Headteacher's office to get clarification of my class. In the office of the headteacher, we met other teachers and after they interviewed and subjected me to oral tests, they determined that I was a class two material.

Upon reflection, I am grateful to my father and my teacher at the Evangelical Day Nursery for the preparatory work towards my formal education. Every experience in life counts towards the ultimate goal or purpose of man on earth. Some of the teachers whose names come to mind include the following: Master Mensah and Mrs. Brown (head teacher and headmistress respectively; and my teachers were: Miss Comfort Osei (Class 2), Mr. Naana Frimpong (Class 3), Mr. Acheampong (Class 4), Mr. Dick (Class 5), and Mrs. Segbafia (Class 6). In the Anglican Middle School, Mr. Kenneth Addo (Form 1), and Miss Florence Akosah (Form 2). I adjudge Mr. Kenneth Addoh as my best teacher in the elementary school, who has made a lasting impact on my life. I continue to use several of the English expressions and the literary stories he taught me in the 1970s now. Master Owusu was the headmaster and taught form 3 and Mr. Obeng taught form 4 but the two did not teach me.

In those days, Year books were not maintained by schools in Ghana so I do not have one to refer to; and for that reason, the names of some of my classmates in the elementary school are provided in the table below. Table 1 shows the list of some of my classmates from my recollection:

Table 1: *Elementary School (Saint Monica's Primary and Anglican Middle (1970-1977)*			
S/No	**Names**	**S/No**	**Names**
1	Samuel K. Anokye	2	Yaw Yeboah
3	Richard Acheampong	4	Veronica Agyakomah
5	Peter Owusu	6	Akua Konadu
7	Baffoe (Lit)	8	Mercy Mends
9	Elizabeth Addai	10	Hagar Owusu
11	Osei Yaw	12	Bernice Adomako
13	Kofi Yeboah	14	Kwabena Yeboah
15	Atta Kwame	16	Ophelia Addai
17	William Kwabla Klu	18	Agyei-Badu Akosua
19	Emmanuel Darko	20	Yaw Koduah
21	Francis Boateng	22	Rose Anane
23	Constance Nyantakyiwa	24	Mirriam Baiden Amissah
25	Eshun	26	Afia Konadu
27	Doris Ampratwum	28	Rosina Manu
29	William Boateng	30	Adwoa Dwomoh
31	Kwadwo Antwi	32	Kofi Abunyewah
33	John Nketiah	34	Stephen Kofi Atta
35	Adu-Gyamfi	36	Kwadwo Agyei
37	Anthony Sarpong	38	Faustina Achiaa
39	Opoku Mensah	40	Adwoa Serwaa
41	Akosua Tabiwah...and many more		
Source: *Created from memory*			

The Saint Monica's Primary was a mixed school, comprising of all male day (non-residential) pupils and both boarding (residential) and day(non-residential) female pupils. Several of the boarding pupils came from Kumasi, Accra, Koforidua, and other parts of Ghana. All the male and female pupils from Mampong and its surroundings were day pupils. Interestingly, I have not met majority (90 percent) of my elementary school classmates. I have met a few in other secondary schools and some in Mampong, when I visited. There are a lot of childhood memories to be shared anytime we meet. I want to share the following stories: (I) **River Monica**- One afternoon, while we were in the school farm working, we saw water gushing out from a particular location so we all started creating gutters to allow for the flow of the water. Our thought process was that a new river source had been located. Early the following morning when we came to school, the water was still flowing so we began to discuss among ourselves the appropriate name to give to this *new river*. The first suggestion was to use the name of the pupil who discovered the source, others suggested we name the river after the headmistress; and finally, the suggestion was to name the river after Saint Monica (the mother of Saint Augustine), whom the school was named after. Little did we know that the flow of the water was as a result of a burst pipe line serving the township and Saint Monica's Secondary and Training College, as well as, the Mampong District Hospital.

(II) **Multiplication recital and retaliation**- One of my teachers (name withheld) sent me after the morning school session to collect his lunch from his wife. I had done so for him a couple of times. On this fateful day, I was carrying the food and the wife had given me money to be given to him to buy something. After leaving the house and having walked for about hundred meters. I decided to put the money in my pocket and in the process lost balance and the basket containing the food fell. The *palm nut soup* was salvaged but the flat plates in which the *fufu* was got broken. I returned to the teacher's wife to report what had happened. She managed to do the necessary damage control and gave me food to be sent to the husband and requested that I tell the husband before he comes home.

When I got to school, I told the teacher what has happened, and he told me never to worry. At shorter interval throughout the afternoon session, the teacher called and asked me of some of the specifics relating to the incident, especially, the broken plate. I realized that I had caused the teacher much pain or trouble even though, he had indicated to me not to worry. Not quite long, in one of the routine multiplication table recitals, he asked me one X * Y, before I could open my mouth to give an answer for *better* or *-for-worst*, he hit my head with his pointer. I deduced that the teacher was using this to atone for the broken plate. I recommend to older people not to inflict pain on younger ones because those things are never forgotten as I remember what the teacher did to me vividly now.

THE EXODUS

Some aspects of my experience in the elementary schools have been shared in the preceding section of this chapter of the book and in this section, the concentration is going to be on the attendance to Secondary or High School outside of Mampong-Ashanti of Ghana. In 1976, my father decided to enter into arable farming for the purpose of attending to the specific needs of the younger children. One day while in the farm at *Hintado*, my father asked one of my brother's what he wanted to be done for him out of the proceeds of the farm at harvest and he requested for a driving license to enable him drive. When I was asked of what I wanted to be done for me from the proceeds of the farm harvest, I asked to be supported to continue my education in the secondary school. My father promised to do according to our requests.

PENTECOST SECONDARY SCHOOL

In 1977, I received an admission offer from the Pentecost Secondary School (P.E.S.S.) in *New Suame*-Kumasi in the Ashanti region of Ghana. At the time, the Church of Pentecost had withdrawn the late Pastor L.A. Nyarkoh (the Headmaster) from the school into the mainstream ministry and handed over to Mr. Frimpong (believed to be a cousin of Lt. General F.W.K. Akuffo-Onetime Head of State of Ghana). The Pentecost Secondary School (P.E.S.S.) is located in the New Suame in Kumasi. The main school building housed the main administrative offices, the dining hall, the girls' dormitory, and classrooms for forms 2 to 5. The boys' dormitory was a converted hotel and rented for the purpose.

The classes for form 1 were held in a wooden structure near the Lorry Station in New Suame at the time. Typically, the day started from the dormitory to the main administrative building for an assembly, followed by breakfast; then, to the classroom for academic instructions. When classes were closed in the afternoon, all boarding students converge on the main administrative block for lunch. After lunch, students dispersed to the dormitory for respite. The afternoons were devoted to homework and other class assignments and students reconvened in the main building for dinner or supper. After supper, the *prep* session (preparation for the next day) followed. Students retire to the dormitory after prep to sleep. The daily routine followed this triangular fashion. The system required self-discipline because the school activities were not confined to one location but rather students attended various activities at different location within the New Suame enclave.

Some of the tutors whose names come to mind are: Mr. Daniel Danson Danquah Damptey, Junior (4Ds), Mr. Bansah (French), Mr. Kyeremateng (Business-related courses), Mr. Ntim (Mathematics); as well as, other part-time tutors from other institutions in Kumasi. The names of some of my classmates are as detailed in table 2 below:

S/No	Names	S/No	Names
	Table 2: *Secondary School–Pentecost Secondary School (1977-1978)*		
1	Emmanuel Owusu-Ansah	2	Emmanuel Appau-Asante
3	Samuel Addai	4	Robert Pakis
5	Bernard Kuffour	6	Afia Obenewaa
7	Albert Kofi Amoako	8	Samuel Appiah
9	Samuel Larte-Lartey	10	Anastasia Zanu
11	Philip Engbi	12	Emmanuel Engbi
13	Kennedy Banafoh	14	Patience Aboagye
15	Samuel Engbi	16	Bernice Owu
17	Augustine Danso		
	...and many more		
Source: *Created from memory*			

I have not seen most of my classmates totaling about 50; except Albert Kofi Amoako (I met in my next school), Emmanuel Owusu-Ansah (I met in PIWC-Kumasi years back), and Augustine Danso (who visited a friend in my next school). As might be expected, the school fees of private schools were very high as compared to the government-assisted secondary schools. I quite remember the school was charging fees of two hundred and seventy-five cedis (¢275), but after one year when I moved to the government-assisted secondary school the fees were eighty cedis (¢80). I had to pay the private school fees on instalment-basis (payment plan). These numbers appear to be low in today's terms but in those days, it was considered very expensive and parents also complained about it. This will give you a sense of the reason why I left for a Government-assisted secondary school.

Upon reflection, I want to believe that my one year stay at the Pentecost Secondary School, which is the least known information about my life also helped me to adjust faster to the secondary school life. I remember one senior used to laugh at me for bringing books from home instead of provision; however, another senior rebuked him and reassured me that was good. The temptation presented to students was that one could easily lose focus because the school was right in town. Perhaps, this has influenced my preference to have my children attend colleges outside of cities.

JUABEN SECONDARY SCHOOL

My transfer from the Pentecost Secondary School to the Juaben Secondary School was facilitated by the late Mr. T. M. Donkoh, a distant uncle and a contractor of foodstuffs to second cycle schools in Ashanti region in Ghana. Two schools were suggested to me-Aduman Secondary School and Juaben Secondary School. My family settled on the Juaben Secondary School. I accompanied Mr. T. M. Donkoh to meet the headmaster of the Juaben Secondary School in his office to finalize my transfer into the school. The headmaster of Juaben Secondary School (Mr. Daniel Atakorah, deceased) explained that there was no vacancy in form 2 but he could admit me into form 1. While I made my case on the basis of my academic performance, he aligns my age with his decision. Uncle T. M. Donkoh encourage me to accept the offer to be in form 1 because the government-assisted secondary schools were better than private schools; and as a result, promised to convince my parents on our return. I agreed and we returned with the admission letter and prospectus, as well as, a schedule of school fees.

In terms of preparation, I had most of the items needed in the prospectus because of my one-year schooling at the Pentecost Secondary School. I had a trunk, a chop box, a student's mattress, an aluminum bucket, a couple of underwear, handkerchiefs, footwear (pairs of shoes, sandals, and canvas or gym shoes). My clothing needs were provided by my auntie, as follows-2 bedsheets, 2 khaki shorts, 2 khaki trousers (pants), 2 blue shirts, 2 white shirts, and 2 *wadre* trousers (pants).

The re-opening date for school was *September 28, 1978*. I left home with my luggage (English) and baggage (American) *enroute* to school. I joined a passenger vehicle from Mampong Ashanti to Effiduasi-Ashanti, but it was difficult in getting a direct vehicle to Juaben-Ashanti. After waiting for a long time at the Effiduasi lorry station, I approached the conductor of a bus owned by the "Kumasi Cornerstone Football Club" plying between Effiduasi and Kumasi in the Ashanti region of Ghana. The Ashanti town of Juaben was located along the bus route. When the bus was almost full, the conductor invited me to board the bus after loading my luggage into the compartment. Alas, the journey from Effiduasi to Juaben started and the conductor started collecting the fares and when he got to my turn, he asked me to hold on until we get to the school gate.

When I alighted from the bus and off-loaded my items and asked him how much I am to pay. He said: "*Small boy, you resemble my nephew. Keep your money and remember to learn very hard*" I thanked him for his kind gesture because I had a total of ¢20 as pocket money for the term. This kind gesture of the conductor of the bus lingered with me for a long time in my life to the extent that I started getting to learn of who this man was. The information I gathered was that he is called *Agya Appiah* (an executive of the Cornerstone Football Club) in Kumasi. Until I meet him *in-person* to show my gratefulness to him, I am using this book to place on record of his kind gesture to a poor and small school boy who did not have much then; Agya Appiah, May God bless you.

My five-year stay at the Juaben Secondary School from 1978 to 1983 has left lasting impressions on my mind and has impacted on my perspectives and experiences; because the period is part of my formative periods. It would be impossible to recollect everything but I would endeavor to touch on few things that present lessons to us all. *First,* the entire period was *eventful and memorable*. The late Mr. Daniel Atakorah was the headmaster of the Juaben Secondary School for the entire period I was a student. However, the assistant headmaster's office was occupied by different people at different times such as: Mr. T. B. Gaisie (who later became the headmaster of Nkawie Secondary School, now deceased); Mr. P.B. Acheampong (who taught me French), and Mr. Opoku Mensah (my Physical Education teacher). The Senior House Mistress was Ms. Mercy Kademgbah (who taught me Home Science) but the office of Senior housemaster was occupied at different times by Messrs- Brefoh (Art), Afrifa (History), and Sarpong (History and Twi).

Second, the *names of my teachers* are but not limited to the following: Messrs-Danso (Modern Mathematics), M. T. M. Dokpoh (Mathematics), Dan Coleman Deletsu (French), Afrifah (History), Yeboah (Bible Knowledge), Ameyaw (General Science); Mrs. Comfort Acheampong (Agricultural Science), Ms. Naomi Nkrumah (Home Science and Literature), Ms. Vida Asante (English Language), and Mr. Baah (Biology). Additionally, Messrs-Odoum (Geography), Mr. Nketiah (Geography), Thomas Acheampong (Accounting, Commerce, and Economics); Serebour (French), Donkoh (French), Shaibbu (Mathematics), Antwi (Music), Kwasi Amakye Boateng (French, now Dr. Amakye Boateng of KNUST, Kumasi); Ms. Dwumfour (Home Science), Mr. Brefoh (Art), Rexford Anokye (History- later became the District Chief Executive of Afigya Sekyere District Assembly-Agona), Agya Poku (Geography), Mr. Justice Yidana (English Language), and many more.

Third, *some of the products of the school* other than my classmates include: Honorable Joseph Osei-Owusu (First Deputy Speaker of the Parliament of Ghana), Honorable K. T. Hammond (MP for Fomena in Ashanti region), Mr. Osei Simperemo (Auditor-Minerals Commission and GETFund), Akwante (Esq) of Ghana Immigration Service, Samuel Yaw Berko (Businessman in Kumasi), Lt. Colonel Thomas Acheampong, Dr. Kwasi Amakye Boateng (Department of Political

Science-KNUST, Kumasi), Just to mention a few. *Four,* table 3 shows the list of *some of my classmates* out of a class of about 120:

| \multicolumn{4}{l}{Table 3: *Secondary (High) School-Juaben Secondary School (1978-1983)*} | | | |

S/No	Names	S/No	Names
1	Eric Amoah	2	Edward Adubofoour
3	Samuel Boafo Asiedu	4	Stephen Owusu-Ansah
5	Eric Atta Frimpong	6	Opuni-Mensah Stephen
7	Omane Hayford	8	Osei-Lah Frederick
9	Samuel Agyapong	10	Dauda Sulley Lugey
11	Samuel Owusu Bobbie	12	Oworae Eric
13	Dwomoh Acheampong	14	Michael Ocquaye
15	Kwabena Asante	16	Joseph Appiah
17	Mary Nketia	18	Vida Atuahene
19	Comfort Adubea	20	Juliana Fordjour
21	Angela O. Abban	22	Olivia Fordjour
23	Comfort Fordjour	24	Charles Agyemang Gyamfi
25	Ameyaw Gyamfi	26	Patrick Owusu Ansah
27	Olivia Frimpong	28	Felicia Kru-Kaning
29	Agartha Ekuban	30	Kwaku Agyemang Duah
31	Angela Fynn	32	Oheneba Badu-Poku
33	Alexander Agyei	34	Edward Adusei
35	Edward Ansah	36	Peter Kwaku Kankam
37	Stephen Acheampong	38	Agyei Dankwah
39	Gladys Ampofoh	40	Frimpong Dankwah
41	Cecilia Ampadu	42	Vasti Cole
43	Adu Gyamfi Kwame	44	Stephen Acheampong
45	Charles Boanor	46	Samuel Ankapong
47	Felicia Duah Boateng	48	Charles Bamfo
49	Cyril Nimako	50	Kwame Owusu
51	Samuel Nuamah	52	Adjei Richard
53	Cecilia Asante	54	Hubert Abebbrese Boateng
55	Boakye Mensah	56	Patrick Owusu-Ansah
57	Doris Acheampong	58	Arthur Gustavus

59	Krobea Asante	60	Mary Sarpong
61	Lydia Sarpong	62	Kofi Brenyah
63	Theresa Yamoah	64	Obeng Akrofi Samuel
65	Sampson Osei-Amoako	66	Emma Sarpong
67	Rose Anane	68	Mary Adade
69	Mabel Opoku-Marboah	70	Thomas Boadu
71	Rosemary Omane	72	Rosemond Ofori
73	Felicia Mensah	74	Paul Tieku
75	Samuel Kwabena Yankyerah	76	Florence Agyei Odame
...and many more			
Source: *Created from memory*			

The interaction of classmates has continued because I met some of them at the University of Ghana and in other spheres of life, including Sulley Lugey of Ghana Post Company Limited, Joseph Appiah (Ghana Commercial Bank Limited), Stephen Owusu Ansah (Esq.-deceased), Boafo Asiedu Samuel, Obeng-Akrofi Samuel, Kwabena Asante (Esq.) of Krobea Asante Chambers in Kumasi, Osei-Lah Frederick (formerly of Bank for Housing and Construction Limited, Kumasi; Columbus, Ohio), Paul Tieku (SG-SSB Bank Limited), Peter Kwaku Kankam (CPA, New Jersey), Okyere Boanor (Bank for Housing and Construction Limited, Tudu, Accra) and many more.

My appreciation goes to the following people: (i) *Mr. Richard Opoku Boamah*, the senior I was assigned to serve in form 1. I am thankful for offering me protection against any maltreatments, a form 1 student was subjected to in schools back then; (ii) *Mrs. Mercy Kademgbah*, our senior house mistress for pieces of advice and providing me food from time to time; (iii) *Master Seth Owusu*, my junior who was assigned to me as my server in form 4 and his willingness to continue to serve me in form 5. Thanks for visiting me after school and grateful for our meeting at the Asafo Market Stall. (iv) *Mr. Nketiah* (Geography teacher) *and Opoku Mensah* (Physical Education teacher and later Assistant Headmaster), the teachers I served in forms 2 and 1 respectively. Specifically, Mr.

Opoku Mensah provided me home away from home. He gave me access to his house at all times, while he travelled out of town. I spent most of the weekend in his house, where I washed clothing, iron clothing, and all his food from the school kitchen was available to me. Again, he provided me with the needed counseling. I am forever grateful. (v) *Mr. Daniel Atakorah* (headmaster), I am indebted to him for going the extra mile to provide my class with additional tuition in French, Oral French, English language, and Oral English; as well as, pieces of advice to all students during our assembly sessions on Mondays, Wednesdays, and Fridays. At the time, we did not take his sayings seriously but with time I have come to acknowledge the depth of his impact upon my life.

Five, experiences to be shared-(I) **Motivation** -the late Mr. Daniel Atakorah (Headmaster) used to tell us the following: *"Time and tides waits for no man" "Make this place more beautiful than you finds it" "We shall pass this place but once, so if there is anything I must do, let me do it now; for we shall not pass this place again" "The height that great men reached and kept was not attained by sudden flights but they while their companions slept were toiling in the night"* (Henry Ward, American Congregationalist Clergyman). On his part, the late Mr. Timothy Benjamin Gaisie (Assistant headmaster) also told us on the eve of his departure to assume the position of headmaster in another school: *"We come we do what we can and when we no longer can, we go."*

(II) **The Spontaneous Leadership Role of Martin**- Master Martin (not real name) is singled out for mention because of the unique and spontaneous leadership role he played on our behalf. Martin joined our class in form 1 from a technical school form 4 to learn English (as he told us) and he was older than most of the average classmates. At the time, apart from few who were *smallish*, most of the form 5 students were *thick and tall*. In fact, that was a different *breed* of students. I never saw anything like that thereafter in my opinion. Consequently, as form 1 students, most of us looked up Martin for leadership and protection from some of the troublesome seniors, because he could stand up to some *bullying* seniors. Interestingly, if you *beat* him in any class test you must answer for that. Peradventure, he associated age with knowledge. I recollect vividly, during our *homo's* night (a variety show night of entertainment by freshmen), Martin was tasked to blow out an electric bulb light and, in the process, coincidentally, the school experienced a total *blackout.* So *dumsour* (load shedding) is not a new phenomenon.

Sadly, one day somebody stood on the varander or corridor of the first floor (second floor in America) of the Boys dormitory to urinate (pee) and the seniors called an assembly of all form 1 students because they averred that a form one boy might have done that. No proof -Can you imagine that? All form 1 students were subjected to a routine punishment of kneeling down in front of the dormitory. In the process, Martin stood up to a bullying senior and that attracted many seniors and fearing for the worst, he run from campus and that was his last day in school. We missed Martin dearly.I met him once after school at Kwadaso, a suburb in Kumasi and he hosted me briefly in his uncle's house.

(III) **Divine Provision**- The final year of my secondary or high school was characterized by the *1983 severe draught* (famine), with its concomitant bush fires across the length and breadth of Ghana. The impact of this national phenomenon is fresh in the memory of all who experienced this in their lifetime. Just as this generation will forever remember COVID-19 pandemic. To give a sense of the gravity of this national crisis, people queued for raw *kenkey* to do the boiling themselves. Others also substituted leaves of plants such as *ogyama* for *plantain* and *cocoyam* in the preparation of *fufu*. Likewise, some peeled cassava and cut them into very small piece to dry immediately so that cassava flour can be made for *Kokonte* preparation.

Against this backdrop, the school authorities requested the final year class to come to school ahead of the formal re-opening of the school to prepare us for our final examinations-General Certificate of Education (GCE) ordinary level conducted by the West African Examinations Council (WAEC). The daily and typical menu for this period was *rice, rice, and rice;* meaning that our breakfast rice porridge, and the lunch was cooked oily rice with *kacco* (preserved fish or meat), and the dinner was rice and stew or *omutuo* (rice balls). Yellow corn was prevalent at the time. To be honest, we were never full after eating from the dining hall.

One day a group of five, decided to go to the Juaben township to find cooked food to buy and eat. After combing through the town to find food to buy, all our attempts proved futile and so we began to ask some of the residents for leads to any place we could find food to buy. Fortunately, our lead pointed us to a house where a lady had started selling cooked rice and stew in the preceding day. When we entered the house, the rice was on fire. At last, there was hope for us so we decided to wait.

While waiting and to our surprise, the old lady in the house invited us and set up a table and treated us to fufu and light soup, with the explanation that she had grandchildren in other parts of the country and it was possible that just as we are looking for food to buy, they might also be looking for food to eat. For that reason, she finds it obligatory to feed us and also requested that we come every evening to eat.

(IV) **Divine Selection**-There are experiences to be shared, as follows: *first, 1978/79* **Mount Mary College Educational Tour,** In form 1 at Juaben Secondary School, I was selected by the French teacher (Mr. Dan Coleman Deletsu) of the school as the only male among three female classmates, who were the best French students to join forms 4 and 5 French students for a *three-day* study tour of the Mount Mary College (an institution that prepared French teachers for second cycle schools). The journey started from Juaben-Ashanti at 6:00am through Ofori Panin Secondary School (OPASS), where we had our lunch in their dining hall; thereafter, we traveled through, Larte-Akwapim until we came to Somanya (all in the Eastern region). The activities lined up for the trip included a language laboratory experience, film show in French, and an excursion to the Akosombo dam (Ghana's primary hydro-electric power generation site). *Second,*

Selection for Interview, One day somewhere in the 1980s while I was in the dormitory, the assistant headmaster sent for me and asked me to go and call another student (who was one year ahead of me) and come with him to see him. When we came together, he told us that the following day the school truck will take us to the Ghana Education Service (GES) Regional Office in Kumasi for an interview. Our breakfast and lunch were arranged to facilitate this appointment. At the Regional Education Office, we met two students from each school in selected secondary schools in the Ashanti region of Ghana. During the interview, I was asked some questions about my family background and also the specific country I wanted to visit. I mentioned Canada and at a point the panel asked me whether I was given details of the interview; for which I responded-No.

All interviewees were asked to wait for the outcome of the interview and two people were selected to represent the Ashanti region in the national interview in Accra at a future date. We did not make it; however, I take solace in the fact I was divinely selected for this opportunity, except that we did not get all the information and we did not also ask the assistant headmaster for more details. Perhaps, in those days young people were not allowed to ask too much questions from older people.

Third, **Debate in Form 1,** As one of our entertainment activities on a Saturday in 1978/79, I entered the debate floor to engage other seniors on the topic: "*This house believes that women are naturally superior to men*" I argued in support for men. *Four,* **Class Captain,** in form 3, I was appointed by the class as the Class captain for the Form 3A and also Form 4 (Business). *Five,* **Boys School Prefect,** when I got to form 4 and the need arose for leadership to take over from graduating seniors. The teaching staff administered a survey on the general student population to solicit responses about possible candidates for student administration. Surprisingly, my name emerged as the preferred candidate for the Boys Senior prefect for the school for the 1982-83 academic year. Three students were presented for each office for the entire students to vote for the preferred candidate. One of my classmates (Agyei Alex) and fellow French student joined me to do some campaigning and finally, I was elected as the Boys School Prefect. I enjoyed a fruitful and peaceful reign and I was duly respected by my fellow classmates and school population.

Upon reflection, a lot of life skills have been acquired during this phase of my developments. *One, Talkative,* I was a talkative in class and also during the *Prep sessions.* The Class captains used to write the names of talkative and in most cases double punishment (DP) was written in parenthesis against my name, indicating that I continued to talk after my name was initially written. In most cases, the list was destroyed and a new one was started. Talking has served me well in life as a *teacher, presenter, speaker,* and *preachers* in later years. *Two, Sense of Humor,* the development of my whimsical sense of humor started in form 1, when one senior requested me to give daily humorous stories before bedtimes. For this reason, I had to solicit stories from my classmates during the day to permit me provide this senior with the requested number each night. At times, if I am able to give a very hilarious stories, I am discharged earlier than normal. This skill has helped me in the delivery of difficult material to any audience.

Three, Early Rise, in the secondary school, a typical day started with a rising bell at 5:00 am to allow student to complete their daily chores of sweeping of plots on the compound or sweeping classrooms or dormitories (depending on the assignment for the class). Followed by the fetching of water to take one's bath; then, fetching water for the senior you serve. The next thing is to run to the classroom ahead of time to start the day. Unfortunate for me, I used to doze off during the "preparation (PREP) period" One day, I was asleep during the PREP time and the headmaster was going round to monitor things for himself. He got to form 1A and found me put my head on the writing desk and he ask a classmate to wake the gentlemen up. I heard the voice of the headmaster and I told the classmates to leave me alone because I was *praying*. That was a lie, I feared he was going to punish me. My headmaster advised that I do the prayers before PREP.

As I progressed in the school, I discovered that sleeping early and waking up early was the best time for learning and preparation for the day. Consequently, I have come to be used to waking up at 3:00 am each day and going to bed between 7:00pm and 9:00pm. This time has served me well since time immemorial because it makes me productive. I get a lot done by the start of each work day. My suggestion is to learn what works best for you and being consistent over time. *Lastly, Systems and Processes*, the systems theory states that: "the whole is greater than the sum of its parts" (Aristotle-Retrieved from www.arxiv.org -accessed on 01/06/2021). Life is stepped or based on processes and systems to be respected. I want to counsel young people to accept processes rather than desiring to circumvent the existing structures. I am a believer in prosperity of the person but existing systems ought to be respected. You would recall that I explained that I skipped class 1 and started school at class 2, however, I had to start form 1 in Juaben Secondary School not because of performance but because of availability of vacancy and my age. A lot of people who rush into politics discover their inadequacies in power and at times struggle to make up for the deficiencies. In life, preparation should be taken seriously because that brings you to the right place at the right time. I will discuss preparation in Chapter 26 of this book. So, stay tuned.

THE PROGRESSION

Unlike today's global trends of having High (Secondary) School graduates immediately preceding to the universities or colleges for undergraduate studies, that was not the case during my time. In those days, students spent 10 years (6 years of primary and 4 years of middle school). Students could shorten this period before graduating with the *Middle School Leaving Certificate* (MSLC) or the *Hall* to get to the secondary school through two ways- *Common entrance* (universal) or *Late entrance* (school specific) *examinations*. Additionally, there was a two-year intensive preparation for the undergraduate work known as the *Sixth-form*. The admission to the *sixth-form* was through a rigorous selection process using passes at the General Certificate of Education (GCE) *Ordinary(O)* level in: English Language, Modern Mathematics or Additional Mathematics, a Science subject; plus 5 best subjects to meet the cut-off point for the particular schools. Arguably, the cut-off point was very competitive for the *grade A* schools because of performance. In those days, some of the *grade A* schools in Ghana encompassed-Achimota School, Aburi Girls Secondary School, Saint Rose's Secondary School, Presbyterian Boys Secondary School, Prempeh College, Opoku Ware Secondary School, Saint Peter's Secondary School, Bishop Herman Secondary School, Wesley Girls Secondary School, Navrongo Secondary School, and many more.

THE BIRTH OF THE AWAITING GROUP

Around this period and after our final G.C.E. 'O' Level Examinations, a few of us regularly met *informally* to share information regarding the release of results by the West African Examination Council (WAEC), comprising: (1) Emmanuel Agyapong Appiah, (2) Cornelius Osei-Fosu, (3) Kwame Appau Attakorah, (4) Kenneth Kwame Wiafe,

(5) Darko Asamoah Baffour, (6) Nana Kwakye Marfo, (7) George Appiah-Sokye, and (8) Charity Marfoh. By way of analysis, Attakorah and Wiafe were Science students, Cornelius was Arts student; and the Business students were Emmanuel, Darko, and George. Charity was one year behind us. The meetings continued before, during, and after the release of our results. Invariably, Atakorah went to Institute of Management Studies (IMS) in Kumasi, Kenneth and Darko went to Konongo-Odumasi Secondary School, Emmanuel went to Tweneboah Koduah Secondary School (all in the Ashanti); Cornelius went to Wenchi Secondary School in the Brong-Ahafo region, and George went to Saint Peter's Secondary School in the Eastern region of Ghana.

With time, *the Awaiting Group* (awaiting results) has grown to become a permanent social interaction group until today. The group used to meet on *annual-basis* and on *rotational basis* in homes of members and during those times parents were invited to advise group members generally about life. Elections were conducted to select the chairperson of the group for one year. The initial togetherness has persisted until today. Currently, Reverend Cornelius Osei Fosu is the Senior Pastor of the Elim Pentecostal Church in the United Kingdom, Dr. Emmanuel A. Appiah is with the Federal Government, Messrs.-Kenneth K. Wiafe and Nana Kwakye Marfo are Businessmen in Virginia, Kwame Appau Attakorah is in the California, U.S.A.; Darko Asamoah Baffour is an Accountant in Ghana; and Ms. Charity Marfo is a Professional teacher in Ghana. The families of members are yet to be integrated into the group as of the time of writing this book.

TESTIMONIAL OF A DIFFERENCE

The journey from the Juaben Secondary School (GCE 'O' Level) to the Saint Peter's Secondary (GCE 'A' Level) begun with a testimonial with a difference from my headmaster, the late Mr. Daniel Atakorah.

After the release of the final GCE 'O' level results by the West African Examinations Council (a sub-regional examinations body), I traveled to my High School to complete end-of-school clearance from the bursar's office, the bookshop, and the library; as well as, obtaining original copies of the WAEC Results Slip from the school. I went through the clearance process and came to the office of the headmaster and he asked me of my first choice for *sixth-form* school and I told him I chose the Saint Peter's Secondary School at Nkwatia-Kwahu in the Eastern region of Ghana.

The headmaster called the school secretary in my presence and requested him to bring my personal file and gave him a draft of a testimonial to be prepared and added to my results slip for onward transmission the Saint Peter's Secondary School. The headmaster handed my results slip and sealed testimonial to me; and he said: "George, you are the third product from this school to be going to that school. Please remember that your behavior and character at the school can affect the extent to which future students from this school can be admitted into that school. So be guided accordingly"

I travelled from Mampong-Ashanti to Nkwatia-Kwahu one early morning with the *Accra-bound* State Transport Corporation (STC) bus, alighting at Nkawkaw in the Eastern region and continued to the Kwahu Ridge (Adwanama Mountains-the land of Bauxite deposits). The Kwahu ridge has a cluster of towns such as-Obomeng, Mpraeso, Atibie, Nkwatiah, Abetifi (the highest settlement in Ghana), Obo, Abene, Twendroase, Bepon, Hwehwee, Asakraka, Afram plains, and so on. There were a lot of Schools on the Kwahu ridge, including: Mpraeso Secondary School (MPASS), Nkwatia Secondary School (NKWASEC), Kwahu Ridge Secondary School (KRISS), Saint Peter's Secondary School (PERSCO), and Abetifi Presbyterian Secondary School (APSEC).

SAINT PETER'S SECONDARY SCHOOL

I met the Assistant headmaster (Mr. Augustus Nettey) on arrival in-front of his office and he asked for my aggregates in English, Mathematics, Science, and the best number of subjects and determined that I met the requirement. He went on to open and read the testimonial given by my headmaster and told me that my headmaster has given me a very good testimonial and so he would ensure to pick my form during the selection process. He gave me the date for the schools' selection process and an estimated date for me to come back and check on the status of my admission. Back in the days, there were no effective means of communication as we do today. The reporting date was re-scheduled from September 1983 to January 1984, implying that the *two-year* course has been reduced to one-and-half years of instruction and final examinations. Typically, the *sixth-form* or *pre-university* course should have lasted for three years, when you come to think of the volume or quantum of materials to be covered at the Advanced level studies. Father Alloysius Hugouth (German, taught Mathematics at times) was the headmaster and assisted by Mr. Augustus Nettey (Ghanaian, taught History). Father Lariosah was the Chaplain (taught lower levels) and the Senior housemaster was Father Nomoh (Ghanaian, taught Biology and General paper). Father Nomoh later became the headmaster of Pope Jones Secondary School in Koforidua and later the Head of SVD in West Africa. I once picked up a piece of old newspaper on the floor and to me surprise, it was the obituary of Father Nomoh. He was truly a father and he will be sorely missed.

The challenge was to complete this arduous task within one and half years; against the backdrop of shortage of tutors for some subjects such as Accounting. I offered the following subjects at the Advanced Level-Geography, Economics, Accounting, and General Paper.

The General Paper was not taught at Saint Peter's Secondary, but the African Traditional Religion (ATR) components was handled by *Father Nomoh* (Senior House Master). We had two tutors for Geography. One for Geomorphology and North America; and another for Tropical Africa and Climatology; and the Paper 3 (Surveying, Map Work, and Statistics) was shared between the two. All-in-all, Mr. Asante Amankwah showed a strong dedication to duty and left no stone unturned to complete the exhaustive syllabus. Likewise, Messrs. Debrah Sarpong and Sono came to teach us Economics.

The problem area was *Accounting*. We did not have a teacher for the first year, except that one of the alumni of the school (Senior Sampson Omari, the last time I met him, he was working with the Ghana Commercial Bank Limited), who came to stay on campus because the universities in Ghana had been closed down and he did not want to be a burden on his mother. So, he came over to provide us with tuition on some accounting topics in Paper 2 such as: containers accounting, branch accounting, royalties accounting, consignment accounting, and many more. As far as Paper 1 (theory) was concerned, we shared topics among ourselves for preparation and deployment for the benefit of the entire class. Likewise, we copied and studied the lecture notes from the New Juaben Secondary School in Koforidua in the Eastern region of Ghana.

Around this same time, the French students had three teachers for all aspects of the language. I decided to substitute French for accounting so I went to meet one of the teachers (Mr. Fuseni) about my intention so I can formerly effect the change. As a matter of fact, he was willing to admit me into the class, however, he told me he had adjusted the timetable to accommodate one of my mates (now CPA in Virginia), who was pursuing Mathematics with the Science students. When I met the classmate, it turned out to be that the agreed upon times coincided with my Geography classes. However, Geography was my favorite subject back then. I went back to the French teacher to update him on the development and it was then he asked me why I wanted to change the subject. I told him the reason was as a result of lack of teachers and he took that as a teaching moment to suggest that no condition is permanent and I should hang in there and learn from all possible means. I retained Accounting as a subject. Interestingly, in the second year, while the French students lost all the three teachers, Accounting students had two teachers for the two Papers.

Table 4 shows the list of some of my classmates [Arts, Business, Science I (Mathematics)and Science II (Biology)]:

Table 4: *Sixth-form-Saint Peter's Secondary School (1983-1985)*			
S/No	Names	S/No	Names
1	Robert S. Blay	2	Adwedaa Ebenezer
3	Mark Asante	4	Michael Appiah
5	Evans Boakye	6	Charles Allottey
7	Charles Osei	8	Seth Dankyi Boateng
9	Arko Nana Fred	10	Owusu Ofori
11	Desewu Joachim	12	Ameta Boateng Ephraim
13	Ofosuhene Agyekum	14	James Darkwah
15	Samuel Asiedu	16	Nimako Boateng
17	Gerald Omari	18	Gyasi Nimakoh
19	Larweh Yola	20	Opoku Boateng
21	Mark Frimpong	22	Essumang Joseph
23	Asomaning Wiafe	24	George Antwi
25	Anthony Ofori-Atta	26	Owusu Boateng
27	Edward Antwi	28	Mark Frimpong
29	Anthony Ofosu	30	Francis Baidoo
31	Osei Mensah	32	Stephen Antwi-Asimeng
34	Adu Peprah	35	Charles Owusu Boamah
36	Charles Godo	37	Justice Boahen
38	William Sarbah	39	Atta Agyepong
40	Alfred Agyenin	41	Daniel Dwamena

42	Yaw Ankomah Boafo	43	Seth Tauler
44	Gatsi	45	Gyabaa
...and many more.			
Source: *Created from memory*			

The total number of classmates was sixty (60), comprising 40 Science students and 20 Arts and Business Students. I am proud to announce that majority (98 percent) made it to the universities in Ghana and beyond; and I can report that we have about 10 medical doctors, 10 pharmacists, and 20 engineers (civil, electrical, mechanical, etc.); as well as, about 10 accountants (including chartered and certified) and finance experts, an attorney or lawyer, some businessmen, and other notable professions.

Few experiences will be shared here: (I) **School farm**-The school operated a farm at a village called *Ntomemu* on the *Bepon-Kayera* road, with a view to providing foodstuff to feed the students. A roster was prepared for students to go and work at the school farm on monthly and rotational basis by the Senior Agricultural Science Tutor and prefect, who is now a professor of Agriculture at the University of Ghana (Dr. Seth Denkyi Boateng) to pair some form five cohorts with certain sixth form (lower six or first year) cohorts.

During the farm days, students going to the farm were served with two standard plates of food each throughout the day. While some students harvested foodstuffs from nearby farms and cooked in the very homes of the farmers; a few students picked foodstuffs from passing vehicle carriers and the drivers reported the conduct of those students to the Agricultural Science Master, who investigated and administered punishment to the culprits.

(II) **Dawn singing practice**-Saint Peter's Secondary School was a catholic institution and so the need to learn songs engaged the attention of the administration of the school. Music was not part of the curriculum of the sixth-form course but the school administration required students

45

to attend singing practice, which was scheduled by the Music tutor for the dawn of some days. The students did not turn up for the dawn singing practice because we view it as unnecessary and complete waste of time. So, the tutor reported the class to the headmaster, who punished the entire class to go to the school farm to cart firewood for the kitchen of the school. Thereafter, we started attending the class and one of the songs we learned was:

1 There's a land that is fairer than day,
And by faith we can see it afar;
For the Father waits over the way
To prepare us a dwelling place there.

Refrain:
In the sweet by and by,
We shall meet on that beautiful shore;
In the sweet by and by,
We shall meet on that beautiful shore.

2 We shall sing on that beautiful shore
The melodious songs of the blest,
And our spirits shall sorrow no more,
Not a sigh for the blessing of rest. Refrain

3 To our bountiful Father above,
We will offer the tribute of praise
For the glorious gift or His love,
And the blessings that hallow our days. Refrain

(Source: digitalsongandhymns.com; hymnary.org -accessed on 04/01/2020).

Anytime, I hear or sing this song I remember the punishment

that was metered out to us for non-attendance to the song practice. Nevertheless, the song brings hope to the mankind. (III) **Descending and Ascending the Kwahu Mountain**- The road from Nkawkaw to the Kwahu ridge is very steep. While there was no passing; meaning that all ascents to the ridge utilized the Nkawkaw-Obomeng road (IN) and descents made use of the Atibie-Nkawkaw road (OUT). As students, whenever, school vacated and we were in buses toward Nkawkaw, we changed our songs from secular to Christian songs, when descending the ridge.

(IV) **Shortage of Water**-The period of my sixth-form education started at the time when the country had emerged from a severe draught in 1983, as recounted above. The school had a water pumping machine to pump water to the reservoirs on campus but because the water table had dropped to its lowest level, water could not be pumped and all the wells and water reservoirs were empty. Students had to walk to the Nkwatia township to a course of a stream, where wells had been dug to harvest water from the water table under the river bed. Consequently, I developed skin rashes all over my body, which left indelible marks on my skin for a long time.

(V) **Cold weather and cloudy skies**-The location of the school allowed for students to benefit from the cold weather, low population, remote location from the town, and intermittent downpour; created enabling environment for teaching and learning. (VI) **Trip to Obo-Kwahu**- During one vacation, few of our classmates (Stephen Antwi Asimeng, Evans Boakye, and myself decided to visit to Obo-Kwahu. Much had been heard about the beautiful layout of the town. We encountered a lady in a passenger vehicle who decided to take us through the tour of the twin towns of Obo and Twendroase in Kwahuland. In the course the of our conversation, the lady got to know that I am a member of the Church of Pentecost and she immediately started addressing me as "Brother Appiah" because she was also a member but called the other by their names. So, my friends started calling me "Brother Appiah"

(VII) **Food Depot**-The arrangement most of the schools in the Eastern region of Ghana had was to create a fund to support the supply of foodstuffs to schools on regular basis and this was accomplished through the food depot system. Under this system, every student paid a one-time payment of ¢500,000 towards a long-term emergency food supply strategy. Graduating students will have their deposits refunded and newly-admitted students will pay into the fund. Such was the arrangement until, we were about to complete school, when we asked the school to arrange to get us the refund of our moneys, the headmaster argued that he can only do that the following year when new students have been admitted and deposits collected.

We found this explanation at variance with the terms of agreement, so we matched to the *Fathers House* (the residents of all the Roman Catholic Fathers on the Kwahu Ridge). The school chaplain (Father Lariosa) came out to engage with the students and requested us to converge at the Lecture Theatre near the Fathers House. At the meeting, Father Lariosa listened to both sides (headmaster and students) and pleaded with the headmaster to attempt and go to Koforidua to request for the refund for the students. Fortunately, the money was refunded and payment begun in earnest. "Ask and you will be given"

(VIII) **Divine Provision**-*One*, the bursar of the Nkwatia Secondary School (Mr. Osei) provided my friend (Evans Boakye) and I with *accommodations, food, and maintenance* during our final vacation to allow us the opportunity to remain in town to prepare for our final G.C.E. Advanced level examinations. *Two, Compulsory Question Accounting Paper 1*-In the process of preparing for my final examinations, I was reading an accounting textbook authored by Vickery and I came across a question. I attempted to solve the question but there were two paragraphs or segments I could not solve so I showed it to my - Evans

Boakye but the two of us could not solve the problem beyond where I reached. We put it aside and continued with our preparation.

On the day of our Accounting Paper 1 examinations, when the questions were distributed to us, to our surprise, the question was the exact question we could not solve completely. The only difference was the change of name of the business to a Nigerian name. I looked at my friend and he looked at me but we could solve up to where we got to during the prior period. Nevertheless, we took solace in the fact that we had chanced on the question before as compared to perhaps most of our classmates who might be seeing the question for the first time.

Upon reflection, the life skills I have acquired during this period of my development revolves around the following: (a) *Group Learning*, At Saint Peter' s Secondary School, there were a lot of facilities such as classroom to allow for group learning. There was a separate lecture room for the Geography department. Apart from the School library, there were Art and Science libraries. As a result, small groups of sixth-form students chose a particular location for studies outside of classroom instructions and the sixth-form Arts library became the learning place for the group comprising: Evans Boakye, James Darkwah, George Appiah-Sokye, Daniel Dwamena, and Stephen Antwi Asimeng.

My candid suggestion is that students should continue to support one another to trade weaknesses for strengths; and as a result, to complete and not to compete as suggested by Apostle Sampson Ofori Yiadom. Likewise, the practice of hiding useful academic materials from classmates should be rejected because it is counter-productive. Knowledge can be useless until it is shared.

(b) *Learning for Long Hours*, the learning culture at the Saint Peter's Secondary made all the difference because, students accounted for and computed the number of sleeping hours as compared to the number of learning hours. As a result, if you sleep for more than six hours you have incurred losses. The school authorities moderated the learning hours by insisting on lights-off at 9:00 pm for forms 1-4; 10:00 pm for form 5 and Lower 6; and 11:00 pm for Upper-6 students. Consequently, any student who studied beyond these times is given an internal suspension.

The authorities did not want to give students external suspensions for studying because parents will be proud of their students for learning. Moreover, if any of the watchmen (Security) should report a student for flouting this school rule, appropriate punishment will be meted out to the student. For this reason, we gave the watchman provisions, soap, tins of *milo* and milk, and so on. If the watchman continues to remind you that you have been going beyond the time, then, we considered that as request for fresh supply. So, we all contributed to provide so we can have extra time to learn. That was bribery. Group learning for my graduate and professional education; as well as, learning for long hour has been a good practice for me over the years. I remember a student who transferred from a school in Kumasi bragging that he was ahead of his class because all the topics being treated has been covered in his previous school; only to place at the bottom of the class at the end of the year examinations.

(c) *Acquisition of Textbooks*, the policy of St. Peter's Secondary School was that textbooks were rented to students of forms 1-5; however, the sixth-form students were required to buy their textbooks outright from the School Book Shop. I did not have money to buy a lot of textbooks from the school but some of the Alumni came to buy textbooks from the School bookshelf for university studies. I sold some of the text books I owned but did not need at the Legon Bookshop on a *sale -on-return* basis in order to buy those I needed at the university. I have developed the habit of buying books over time from this practice. (d) *Repeating Students*, Saint Peter's used to repeat students who did not meet the set standard. While this practice was very difficult for the affected students, I look back and see those students in very respectable positions and professions now. My suggestion is that failure is a temporary setback and it is not targeted against your person but against your output. Just re-organize for success.

(e) *Parental Involvement in Education of Children,* Times have changed, the role of the parent was to provide fees and support to facilitate the learning process and teachers were trusted with the custody of students. In my experience, none of my parents ever visited me in school throughout my second cycle education. To us, it was normal, students rather came home with exeats and during vacations. I quite remember, my Sister Freda visited me at the Pentecost Secondary School, my Brother Willie also visited at the Juaben Secondary School, and my brother-in-law (Johnson Koduah) visited me at the St. Peter's Secondary School. Students communicated with parents through telegram and letters through the post at the time.

I left home early at age 13 to attend secondary school but today, in the United States of America, most students leave home to attend College (University) at a later date. This partly explains the development of decision-taking capacity in us. Another issue is that parents continued to have a say through monitoring of the performance of the students. School bills and annual academic reports were sent to parents directly and that acted as a check on the students.

In the U.S.A., once a student attains the age of 18, a parent will not be given access to information affecting the academic life of the student unless the students give the colleges the authorization so to do. For this reason, some students have been academically suspended without the knowledge of parents, who have been tricked to believe that students are undertaking internship and other excuses.

(f) *Location of Schools,* the three schools I attended for my secondary cycle education present different locational advantages and challenges. *First,* The Pentecost Secondary School is located in the New Suame township with no borders because all school activities took place in the town. There were lots of distractions and this can breed indiscipline.

Second, the Juaben Secondary School is located at the outskirts of the Juaben township and by a major road. Even though, the school compound was fenced, the proximity to the road permitted students to get out of town without permission. *Third,* not only is the St. Peter's Secondary School located on the Kwahu ridge in Nkwatia-Kwahu, the location is far away from the town and the compound is fenced. The Saint Peter's Secondary is a well-resourced second cycle institution in Ghana. Partly due to the investment made the Catholic church's SVD of Germany. Unlike other similar schools in Ghana at the time, the school had a fleet of vehicles such as a double-cabin pick up, *three-ton* and *seven-ton* trucks; as well as, Gas (filing) station, a cold store for the kitchen, a bookstore, a stadium with a pavilion, accommodation for teachers, a lecture theatre and small-sized classes, a well-resourced science laboratory, libraries (main and sixth form science and arts libraries), and a chapel. The problems included water supply and lack of teachers for the sixth-form classes at the time partly due to the location. Sports preparations were done in the night after study hours. In my opinion, the location of a school can facilitate teaching and learning without much distraction from the environment.

CHAPTER 4

ACADEMIC JOURNEY

EDUCATION IS NOT AN END in itself but rather a means to an end; yet, the decision to opt for education has been a game-changer for me. There are as many views on education as there are people in the world; yet, education can best be described than be defined. To give you a sense of the plurality of the description of education, a few of the views will be presented here. Nelson Mandela stated that: *"education is the most powerful weapon which you can use to change the world"* Likewise, *"education is the ability to listen to almost anything without losing your temper or your self-confidence"* (Robert Frost). Similarly, *"the object of education is to prepare the young to educate themselves throughout their lives"* (Robert M. Hutchins). Nevertheless, *"education is what remains after one has forgotten what one learned in school"* (Albert Einstein). From autobiographical standpoint, "hunting for the truth is not an adequate approach to analyzing and discussing autobiographies; because autobiographical writing varies in both genre and content, we are apt to perceive it as belonging to the borderland between reality and fiction; *i.e.,* somewhere between what 'really happened' and the author's subjective, reflective ideas about what happened (Hanssen, 2019, p.318).

The implication of the above can be summarized as follows: That education is powerful to change the world (Mandela), can develop the listening abilities (Frost), prepare young people for life (Hutchins), and what is internalize is education (Einstein). At the time of my undergraduate education, Ghana had three universities, which were all public, namely, the University of Ghana (UG), Legon in the Greater Accra region; the University of Science and Technology (UST), Kumasi in the Ashanti region; and the University of Cape Coast (UCC) in the

Central region of Ghana. The system at the time was for prospective students to apply to the individual university for specific programs after the sixth-form (G.C.E. Advanced level). By way of comparison, in the UST, admissions were department-based and that prospective students applied to programs from departments. So, it was possible for a student to get admission into one or more departments at the same time, while others will not have admissions until after a deadline for acceptance of programs. Prospective students to the UCC were admitted into compulsory diploma (associate) programs in education; plus, an academic program-thereby permitting students to graduate with a bachelor's and associate (diploma) degrees. As a result, the products of the UCC were best trained as teachers; even though, not all products ended up being teachers.

In the UG, admissions were centralized with departmental involvement and the process allowed for students to select three disciplines or courses and in the event that an applicant did not make it to the desired choices, the university went ahead to admit prospective students to alternative programs based on considerations such as availability, national need and an opportunity for exploration. The system made it possible for students to make changes of one or two courses while on campus by following a procedure involving one head of department accepting and another releasing a student to and from a course, with the approval of the dean of the faculty. This system existed but the procedure was designed to make it difficult for students to make changes. Nevertheless, few students were able to make changes to the original assigned courses.

The only university I applied to was the University of Ghana and for the Bachelor of Science (BSc.) in Administration program. My first, second, and third choice were the same course. The approach was risky but I was willing to take a 'gamble'. Fortunately, for me, I was admitted into the First University Examinations (FUE), the equivalent of current Level 200 or Sophomore (read the explanation below). My undergraduate (FUE) admission reference was AA.11 of October 22, 1986.

I wish to explain that the duration of the undergraduate studies in Ghana at the time was three (3) years and keep in mind that the two-year sixth-form transition (GCE Advanced level) was a pre-university or college preparatory program. Later on, when the educational system was overhauled to reduce the length of the education system to align with other countries, the Junior High and Senior High School equivalent were introduced. Products of the Senior High Schools entered the universities at Level 100(Freshmen) and applicants with the GCE Advanced level entered at Level 200 (Sophomore). By extension, while the Senior High School products spent four year in College or the university; applicants with the Advanced level of the GCE spent three years (FUE, Part 1, and Part 2).

UNDERGRADUATE (OCTOBER 1986 TO OCTOBER 1989)

I began my undergraduate studies in October 1986 at the School of Administration (University of Ghana). The University of Ghana was headed by Professor Akilagpa Sawyerr as the Vice Chancellor, with the late Professor George Benneh as the Pro-Vice Chancellor. The School of Administration (popularly called- *the School*) was a prestigious School, but was an equivalent of a Faculty in the university's larger scheme of things. There were differences in names of designations, title, or positions such as the following (a) The School was headed by a director as compared to a dean of a faculty. At the time I entered the school, Professor B.C.F. Lokko was the director and later on Professor S. N. Woode became the Acting director. The Heads of department in *the School* were referred to as *Coordinators* and there were four departments-Accounting, Health Service Administration, Management, and Public Administration.

The names of my lecturers are as follows: **first,** *BSc. Administration FUE*-Catherine Phillips (Principles of Management), S. K. Tsahey (Accounting I-Fundamentals), Kwamena Ahwoi (Commercial Law), S. N. Woode (Introduction to Public Administration in Ghana), Augustine Gockel (Economy of Ghana), Kwabiah Boateng (Elements of Economics). Others included S. S. Boye (Introduction to Mathematics-a preparatory course), and Kwame Osei Safoh (Introduction to Computers-GW Basic); as well as Dr. Awedobah (Culture and Development) and Adoquaye (Ga Language) of the Department of African Studies.

Second, *BSc. Administration Part 1*-Mr. Banuakoh (Human Behavior in Organizations), Takyi-Asiedu (Quantitative Methods and Statistics), Newman Kusi and M.A.K Gyasi (Managerial Economics), Dr. J.E.A. Mills (Company Law), M.A.K. Gyasi (Accounting II-Financial Accounting). **Lastly,** *BSc. Administration Part 2*- Dalan Quarde (Marketing), J.S. Arku (Accounting IV-Cost and Management Accounting), Dr. Boon (Business Policy); as well as, Accounting III-Auditing (M.K.A. Gyasi) and Taxation (S. K. Tsahey), and Business Finance (M.A.K Gyasi). I remain grateful to all the lecturers of the University of Ghana for imparting precious knowledge unto me and assisting in my development both conceptually and analytically.

Out of a total of 108 students in my 1989 year group, majority (about 90%) are male and about 10 percent are female. Unfortunately, as of April 9, 2020, we have lost three-(1) David Nii Ayi Hammond (died after graduation but before Congregation or Commencement); (2) Isaac Adu Mensah (Accountant/Banker); and more recently, my good friend (3) Lawrence Yirenkyi- Boafo (former Managing Director of the Trust Bank and Deputy Director-General of the Securities and Exchange Commission). My heart goes out to the families of all these gentlemen. I remember each of them on different things because each is unique in his own right. They would be sorely missed. The names of my classmates are listed in table 5 below:

S/No	Name	Base Country/City	
	Table 5: *Undergraduate Class of 1989-University of Ghana School of Administration*		
1	Adams, Jessie Ewurefua	USA	
2	Addo-Kufour Kwame (Kaddoks)	Johannesburg	
3	Adjei, Divine Kwame		
4	Adjei, Emmanuel		
5	Adjei, William Edmund Okang	Ghana	
6	Adomako, Michael		
7	Adotey, Benjamin Adotei (Abenhu)	Ghana	
8	Adu, Richard		
9	Adu-Mensah, Isaac (Cosaro)	Ghana	Deceased
10	Adu-Poku, Gabriel		
11	Adu-Sarkodie, Tweneboana		
12	Adutwum-Ameyaw, Kofi	Australia	
13	Agbanyoh, John Kwaku		
14	Agbemabiase, Mabel Denya		
15	Agbo, Emile William Kofi	Ghana	
16	Agyapong, Joseph		
17	Agyapong, Sono Richard		
18	Agyeman, Charles Gyamfi (Lakeside)	UK	
19	Agyeman, Yaa Peprah	Ghana	
20	Akuoku, Ankrah	Ghana	
21	Akwetey, Samuel Nuerteye		
22	Alomcnu, Aaron Kwesi		
23	Amankwah, Boateng Peter		
24	Amankwah, Kwadwo Takyi		
25	Amekudzi, Daniel Kwabia	Ghana	
26	Amoabeng, Matthew		

27	Amoo-Gottfried, Nana Afua	UK	
28	Ampofo, Anthony Kobina		
29	Ansah, Kingsford		
30	Antwi, Adu Abebrese		
31	Appiah, Daniel Osei Kofi (Chepillah/Failure)	Ghana	
32	Appiah, Michael (Zorro)	Ghana	
33	Appiah-Sokye, George	USA	
34	Ashirifi, Boadu, Francis		
35	Ashitey, Valerie Barbara Naa Shirley		
36	Asiedu, Samuel	Canada	
37	Assasie, Rosemary	USA	
38	Awuku, Gladys		
39	Baah, Isaac:		
40	Baah, Joseph Wellington		
41	Baidoo, Francis	Canada	
42	Baimbill-Johnson, Samuel	Ghana	
43	Bame, Adwoa Pokua		
44	Bartels, Ebenezer Fitzgerald Ebo		
45	Bediako, Clement Okyere		
46	Bempong, Frank Asirifi		
47	Benneh, Kwadwo (Awuzu)	Ghana	
48	Boakye-Mensah, John Kingsley (It appears)		
49	Boamah, Owusu Charles	Ghana	
50	Boateng, Nicholas		
51	Boateng, Opoku-Gyamfi	Ghana	
52	Brew, Samuel Kwaku		
53	Butler, Juliana Aba Dansoa	Ghana	
54	Chinery. Patrick Cleland N. A.		
55	Cobbinah, Christian		
56	Coker, William Zacheus		
57	Cornah, Francis'		

58	Darko, Gilbert Agyepong		
59	Dovlo, Mawuli Kwabia		
60	Dzomeku, Selorm	Ghana	
61	Esseku, Mavis Elaine A.		
62	Gatsey, Charles-Hope Yao		
63	Gray-Deh, Francis Yao		
64	Hammond, David Nii Ayi Anthony'(Ohio)		Deceased
65	Heloo, Dela		
66	Hervie, Eugene Tetteh	Ghana	
67	Iddrisu, Salamatu	USA	
68	Kaleo-Bioh, Vitus Gundona	Ghana	
69	Kholi, Jacob Kwame		
70	Klufio, Morag Adzekai		
71	Kodjiku, Rebecca Mamle-Dole		
72	Konadu, Amoako Paul		
73	Koomson, Moses Gordon	Ghana	
74	Kumoji, Korkor Cynthia		
75	Larbi, Enoch(Lord Puma)	Canada	
76	Manu, Alfred Sarpong		
77	Manu, Amankwah John		
78	Marfo, Amanianpong		
79	Mensah, Abramoah George(Peter Self)	Ghana	
80	Dwamena, Gabriel Kwadwo		
81	Mohammed, Rumila Mudasiru		
82	Norgbedzie, Daniel Kwaku		
83	Ofosu, Foster Nicholas	Finland	
84	Ohene-Obeng, Twum		
85	Okwabi, Eugenia Dorothy		
86	Opon, Stephen (Ajaspa)	Ghana	
87	Oppong, Francesca Brenda		
88	Osei, Bonsu Bosompem	USA	

89	Osei-Akoto, Andrew	Ghana	
90	Osibo, William Kwasi		
91	Owusu-Ansah, Stephen	USA	
92	Padi-Tetteh, Edmund		
93	Pongo, Godwin Kojo		
94	Quarshie, Samuel Anum		
95	Quaye, Daniel(Skinny)	Ghana	
96	Siaw, Richard Kwarteng	USA	
97	Tease, Pater Paul		
98	Tenkorang, Seth Kwame (Ecoute)	UK	
99	Tetteh, Daniel Ogbarmey	Ghana	
100	Tevie, Justin		
101	Tsawe, Peterkin Tetteh-Anoryoe		
102	Twum Ohene Obeng (Onana)	Ghana	
103	Wiafe, Akenteng Adwoa Serwaa	USA	
104	Wilson, John Kwesi		
105	Yankey, Mansfield Ackah		
106	Yeboah, Samuel Seth		
107	Yeboah, Christopher Tsumashie. .		
108	Yirenkyi-Boafo, Lawrence	Ghana	Deceased

Source: *Updated from a list compiled by Seth Tenkorang (Ecoute) on July 3, 2018*

I am proud of what my classmates have achieved together over the years. Each has contributed in no small way in human development and advancement. Indeed, my classmates have made the world in general and Ghana in particular proud. I salute my classmates for their achievements and accomplishments.

Sharing Experiences at the University of Ghana- *One, Trimester* 'Bubra': The academic calendar was based on trimester-First term (Michaelmas), the Second term (Lent), and the Third term (Trinity). The university education was scheduled as a *brick and mortar* approach. Students received instruction throughout the year and the final examinations were administered at the end of the year. All the examinations were *pencil* and *paper* format. Typically, seven discussion questions were asked but students were required to answer four questions; as a result, when one reads the first three questions and you have no idea about those question; then, the remaining four questions became compulsory for you to attempt. In those days there were *casualties* because students who waited until the end of the year before attempting to study ended up in the hospital or rushed to the hospital. For this reason, a stand-by ambulance was positioned near the examination centers to take care of *casualties*. All our examinations were administered from Monday to Friday (one working week), meaning there was a paper to be taken each day once the examinations get started.

The advantage of the trimester system was that slow learning students were able to master the course content over the year; and the structure afforded the students the opportunity to do more research to support classroom instructions. Professors or lecturers provided students with the course outline showing the topics and supporting references for students to explore. The negative payoff is that of the difficulty to retaining one year's work for final examination at the end of the year.

Two, **Students' Unrests**-The entire three years of my undergraduate education at the University of Ghana at the time was characterized by students' unrests and agitations because successive government have been trying to introduce the payment of school fees in the universities. The criteria for the selection of students' leadership included militancy because students voted for candidates who could take the bull by the horns, leaving no stone unturned to maintain the status quo. The payment of school fees at the time would have meant that university education is the preserve of the rich and consequently, most of us would not have had that privilege.

The universities in Ghana were closed to protect lives and property almost every year; thereby, disrupting the academic calendar. The university rules permitted the boycotting of lectures by the student body as a way of making a protest for a maximum of three days but beyond that the school is closed down. I remember on one such occasion, the student body had boycotted lectures for the first day and on the second day, I traveled with my friend- Atakorah to Lome in Togo.

We returned the same day but around mid-night and not sure to get transport back to campus, we decided to alight and spend the night at the Kotoka International Airport because of 24/7 activities of the airport. On reaching the Airport entrance, a taxi pulled up and we negotiated for our trip to the Legon campus. At *Okponglo* near the Legon campus, some policemen stopped our taxi and after inspecting the vehicle, they asked us whether we are returning students and we replied in the affirmative. The police asked the driver to 'carry on' or to continue the trip. Just as we were about to enter the main university entrance, the security men at post explained that the university had been closed by the Minister of Education) and so the taxi could not go beyond the gate. We got down and allowed to taxi driver to depart.

The security told us that there are armed police and military personnel on guard and so it would not be safe for us to enter the campus. In the circumstance, we decided to get back to the roadside to get taxi to Madina (a suburb in Accra). None of the passing vehicles moving towards the Madina direction stopped because it was very late. We sat at the Bus Stop (Terminus) for some time and later gave up on getting a taxi and went ahead to sleep on the bench at the *bus stop*. Getting to dawn, people who were walking along the roadside on getting close to the bus stop and seeing images of persons sleeping on the bench crossed the road to the opposite side for security and safety reasons. Well, I do not want to speculate what they took us for.

Three, **Spectacular Memories**- My three-year stay at the University of Ghana for my undergraduate education presented a lot of memories. I share a few, as follows: (a) The bungalow of Mr. Kwame Osei Safoh (a lecturer at the School of Administration and from my home town) became my home on campus. I left most of my belongings at his garage during vacations to reduce the cost of transporting them to and from school. (b) I put on record the support I enjoyed from my classmate-Group Captain Aloysius Awusima. He showed much care towards me. Even though, he was much older than me, he supported me in varied ways such as the provision of transportation and lunch in some afternoons. He welcomed me to his residence at the Burma Camp in Accra. I thank you, Sir.

(c) The class 1989 was taken to the British Council by Ms. Catherine Phillips (Lecturer for Principles of Management) to watch the educative movie: *"The organized manager"* That was refreshing! (d) There were limited number of library books relative to the number of students who needed to read them. Against the backdrop of the inability of most students to afford the buying of textbooks at the time. So, serious students have to visit different libraries, including the Balme Library (Main University), libraries of the halls of residence, departments, faculty; as well as, those in town such as the British Council Library and organizational libraries. At times, books had to be hidden in different location inconsistent with the library catalogue to be able to gain access to it. Students were willing to read but the most essential books were limited in supply and we did not have money to buy at the time.

(e) I presented a paper on the *"Johari Window"* to the 1989 class as part of the Principles of Management course outcomes. The Framework was introduced by Joseph Luft and Harrington Ingham in the 1950. The framework had four quadrants as follows: (i) *Façade-* things that are known only to one's self (secret), (ii) *Arena-*things that are known to all, (iii) *Unknown-*things that are known to no one, and (iv) *Blind Spot-*things are known to others. This concept is based on feedback and disclosure. The *Johari Window* can be applied to create and build self-awareness, as well as, relationships within a group. Consequently, asking for and accepting feedback from others can make you a better person.

More so, there are times when one must go beyond the *comfort zone* to test the limits. Accepting uncommon challenges can bring fulfillment in life. At times, feelings and thoughts should be shared with others to enable them rise to the occasion. Likewise, it is not uncommon to reveal your skillsets and capabilities to assist you reach your desired goals in life. The purpose of this book is partly in response to the *Johari Window*, I learned and presented to my class in 1986. This has been very helpful in my personal development.

(f) I was in the Legon Hall Annex B (Room 308) in the first year and Room 206 in the second and third years. The Annex B of the Legon Hall of residence was popularly called-*Jatokrom*. We welcomed visitors especially ladies into the building with drumming using silver plates and tins. The visitors I received regularly includes my brother-Willie and the then Pastor and Mrs. Emmanuel Owusu Bediakoh, among others. (g) I thank Mr. Kofi Amardie Sarpong for donating some of his textbooks and lecture notes to me prior to embarking to the United States of America after graduation. I appreciate Mr. Kwame Twum Antwi of Canada; J.C. Akosah, and Mr. William Obeng of the United Kingdom.

GRADUATE SCHOOL (SEPTEMBER 1999-MAY 2001)

The journey to the Graduate School did not come to me on a silver platter. I joined the workforce after my undergraduate studies for ten years before going back to school. During this time, the idea of pursuing further studies engaged my attention. I applied and obtained admission to Switzerland to read International Relations but I could not find the sponsorship towards the financial burden associated with studying abroad at the time. I started sitting for my professional examinations at the time (This will be discussed in subsequent chapters). I was admitted into the Master of Business Administration degree (MBA-Accounting Concentration or Option) program at the University of Ghana School of Administration in 1999, after two unsuccessful attempts. At the time of my Graduate education in Ghana, Professor Ivan Addae Mensah was the Vice Chancellor of the University of Ghana and Professor S.K. Nkrumah was the Director of the School of Administration. In my candid opinion, I consider Professor Nkrumah as a transformational leader during his tenure.

Unlike my undergraduate program that was *trimester-based*, the academic calendar of the universities in Ghana had undergone modification to accept academic programs that utilized the *semester-basis*. The semester was defined as 13 weeks of instruction, 2 weeks of revision, and 1weeks of end of semester examinations. There was a mid-semester examination (weight of 30%) and end of semester examination (weight of 70%).

The names of my lecturers were: Tetteh Quashie (OBM-Organizational Behavior and Management), Akua Ejisu (Management Science), Alfred Barimah (Economics), S. S. Boye (MIS-Management Information System), Professor John B.K. Aheto (Accounting Theory I, Accounting Theory II, Financial Reporting I, Financial Reporting II, and Investment Management); Dr. Ansah Offei (Advanced Business Policy and Strategy), James Otieku (Advanced Taxation), Research Methods (Dr. Boame/Akua Ejisu), Dr. J.M. Onumah (Advanced Governmental Accounting), Dr. Yankey (Corporate Finance), M.A.K. Gyasi (Advanced Auditing), Dr Kofi Osei (International Financial Management),and my long essay was supervised by Ransome Kuipoh.

The MBA (Accounting 1999-2001) class was composed of the following: Thomas Ameyaw (Class captain), Benjamin Amoah, Dr. Amidu Mohammed-CA, Ntoah -Boadi Samuel, Awuttey Seth Selorm-CA, Morrison Alfred Bassaw, Abaka Kobina Evans (deceased), Jacob Benson Aidoo-CA, Akakpo Victor Kodjo-Attah-CA, MCIT;

Siffah Yaw Agyei, Larri Kofi Yumandam, Dzandu John Kwesi, Donkor Enoch, Benjamin Amoah, Bleboo Patrick-ACCA, Barneah Collins, and Opoku Nana K. Table 6 shows MBA-Accounting class 2001:

S/No	Name	Base Country/City	Remarks
Table 6: *Graduate School Class of 2001-University of Ghana School of Administration*			
1	Alex Cofie	Ghana	Former head of Finance-UCEW-Kumasi
2	David Ofantser	Ghana	Formerly of VATS
3	Henry Acquah, CA	Ghana	Ghana Revenue Authority
4	Sulemana Zakari, CA	Ghana	World Bank
5	Assan Yakub, CA	Deceased	CAGD
6	Thomas Ameyaw	Ghana	
7	George Appiah-Sokye (CA, CPA, CICA, FCIT)	USA	
8	Benjamin Amoah	Ghana	
9	Amidu Mohammed, CA	Ghana	University of Ghana Business School
10	Samuel Ntoah Boadi	Ghana	Sunyani Polytechnic
11	Seth Selorm-Awutey, CA	Ghana	Bank of Ghana
12	Morrison Alfred Bassaw	Ghana	UCEW-Kumasi
13	Evans Kobina Abakah	Deceased	UCC
14	Jacob Benson Aidoo, CA	Ghana	Securities and Exchange Commission
15	Victor Kodjo-Attah Akakpoh, CA, MCIT	Ghana	Bank of Ghana

16	Siffah Yaw Agyei	Ghana	Ghana Audit Service
17	Larri Kofi Yumandam	Ghana	Ghana Trade Fair
18	John Kwesi Dzandu	Ghana	
19	Enoch Donkor	Ghana	Bank of Ghana
20	Patrick Bleboo, ACCA	Ghana	Ecobank Ghana
21	Collins Barneah	Ghana	
22	Nana K. Opoku	Ghana	
Source: *Updated from MBA Accounting Option Year Book-2001*			

The names of my study partners cannot be left out: Alex Cofie, (former Head of finance (University College of Education, Winneba-Kumasi campus), David Ofantse (formerly of Ghana Revenue Authority-GRA), Henry Acquah-CA (GRA), Sheiley Seidu Jiagge (Volta River Authority), Dede (Ghana Air Force). I appreciate the comraderies of Sulemana Zakari-CA (World Bank Office-Ghana) and the late Assan Yakub-CA (Controller and Accountant- General Department), they have been a source of inspiration to me in my educational experience.

Experiences and lessons- first, *Divine selection*, As I mentioned above, I was admitted to the School of Administration of the University of Ghana for my Masters of Business Administration (MBA) program with Accounting concentration at my third attempted application. I missed the selection for the accounting concentration. During that period, I was having conversation with a neighbor of mine (name withheld) and he told me he had applied for the MBA (Management Information System-MIS concentration) and was sure of admission because he knew people who will help him through. I did not tell him that I had applied. Just around that time the university was closed. After the hope of going back to school was gone, I received a letter in the mail and when I opened and read the contents-guess what it was my letter of admission to the Graduate School. I proceeded to the Office of the Dean of Graduate Studies to register because the dead line was very close.

Second, **Diving provision**, My application for residential accommodation was dated August 21, 2000. There was a day in my second year in the graduate school when I had neither money nor food to eat. I locked myself in my room not knowing where any help can from. I laid prostrate on the floor of the hostel room and waiting on God for his will to be done. Just as I had fallen asleep getting to noon. I heard a gentle knock at my door. Initially, I thought I was dreaming. When I opened the door, it was my good friend-Alex Cofie. When he entered the room, he dropped an envelope on my study table and told me that he had a feeling that I do not have money.

I expressed my appreciation to him still not knowing what the envelope contained. He went on to inform me that he has been given some accounting project in one of newly established universities to build the accounting books, with a view to preparing financial statements and first Budget statement for the University Council. He asked if I would be available for the project and I did not hesitate to indicate my willingness to be part of the project. When he left and I opened the envelope, it contained an amount of ¢100,000.00 and invariably the amount I received from the accounting project was ¢1,600,000, enough to cover my budget for a whole semester. I thank God for the life of Mr. Alex Cofie.

Third, **Parental sacrifice**, there is another story I want to share about my good friend-Alex Cofie. We were preparing for parts of the Institute of Chartered Accountants, Ghana (ICAG) examinations while on campus. The time came for us to register. So, I called at his hostel for us to go the ICAG House to register for the examinations. Then, he told me that he has received a message from the daughter in Archbishop Porters Secondary School-Takoradi in the Western region of Ghana concerning her final examinations fees.

According to him, he has sent the money for the registration for the ICAG examinations to the daughter to register for her examinations instead. He did just that to enable the daughter register for hers instead of his. I remember several years thereafter, when I visited him in Kumasi, the daughter came home from work-then, having graduated from the KNUST with a Master's degree and working as intern Architect in a professional firm. I asked her to thank the daddy and she obliged and I told her of the father's sacrifice towards her education. I had gone on to *charter* as an accountant, but the father had not. What a sacrifice for fathers to emulate.

GRADUATE SCHOOL (SEPTEMBER 2011 TO OCTOBER 2016)

A decade after my Graduate studies at the Master's level, I have long been interested in pursuing law so doctoral education was not my priority. I remember the Institute of Professional Studies (Ghana) had a relationship with the University of Illorin in Nigeria and that association allowed for lecturers to pursue doctoral studies at that prestigious institution. In Summer of 2011, while in the United States of America, I visited my childhood *body* (now Dr. Emmanuel A. Appiah) and he encouraged me to sign-up for the doctoral studies. Among the *Awaiting Group* members, I discussed in prior chapters, the two of us had most things in common, including our academic and professional trajectory. At the time, he had started his program and he was on the seventh course of the classwork. I applied and was admitted into the Northcentral University of Arizona for my doctoral studies with a concentration on Advanced Accounting, after going through the necessary admission processes. I was admitted in September 2011 but I started the program in January 2012.

The President of the University was George A. Burnette. The Provost was David Harpool (JD, PhD), and the Dean of the School of Business and Technology Management was Dr. Peter Bemski. The university maintained a 100 percent doctoral faculty. The structure of my degree plan ensured that I passed all my: (I) coursework of the program comprising General doctoral courses, accounting specialization courses, research courses; (II) passed the Comprehensive Examinations (popularly called COMP); and then (III) to the dissertation phases-encompassing (a) the Concept paper phase, (b) the Proposal stage, (c) the Field work phase after IRB processes and approval, (d) the Dissertation manuscript stage, and (e) the Defense stage. Each of these milestones presented both a challenge and accomplishment in the milestones.

The names of my professors are as follows: Dr. Terri Tallon (Foundations of Doctoral Study in Business), Dr. David Moody (Ethics in Business), Dr. Chery Moore (SKS-7000-Doctoral Comprehensive Strategic Knowledge Studies), Dr. Mary Shaw (Statistics), Dr. Linda Leatherbury (Advanced Managerial Accounting and Advanced Auditing Methods and Practice); Dr. Iyer Kris (Advanced Forensic Accounting Theory and Practice), Dr. Steven Munkeby (Business Research Methodology), Dr. Alfred Chad Greenfield (Advanced Tax Strategies and Advanced Accounting Theory and Policy), Dr. Nathaniel Litton (Research Design), Dr. George Kalidonis (Quantitative Research Design), Dr. Eremin Demitry (Planning Dissertation Research in Business).

The professors for my Comprehensive Examinations were: Dr. Christopher Sharp and Dr. Craig Bythewood. The Dissertation Committee was composed of: Sharon Kimmel (PhD, Chair), Mary Chmielewski (PhD-Subject-Matter Expert-SME), and Robin Throne (PhD-Methodologist-MCM). During the dissertation process, Dr. Sharon Kimmel replaced Dr. Asher Beckwitt; however, the other two Committee members remained from start to finish.

The Northcentral University held our Graduation on *Saturday, July 8, 2017* in Phoenix, Arizona at the J.W. Marriot Phoenix Desert Ridge

Resort and Spa, where Hooding and the Commencement Ceremony took place. The 2017 Commencement Speaker was Bakari Seller, JD (CNN Political Analyst, Lawyer with Strom Law firm, Activist, and former State Representative); the Dissertation of the year was won by Renee J. Squier (PhD in Business Administration with concentration in Organizational Leadership, CAPT, US Navy); and the 2017 Alumni of the year was Jennie De Gagne (PhD) in Education (Education Technology Management, 2009). It was a memorable occasion that marked the achievement of academic accomplishments. Some pictures have been provided in Chapter 22.

Summary of lessons and experiences- *Life Capacity development,* the doctoral journey can be very exciting but also daunting. A lot of people make it to the (ABD) and not beyond. The attainment of ABD is rewarding but not an end in itself but a means to an end. The dissertation trajectory can be challenging because candidates do not have control of the composition of the Dissertation Committee. *First,* I would advocate for people in the candidate's field of study to supervise the work but the institutions argued that the work of the Dissertation chairs is research-focused. At times, jargon in some field such as accounting can present misunderstanding between the candidates and say the Chair. *Next,* there is convergence on the abilities that can be developed along the way such as: (i) humility, (ii) affability or teachability, (iii) perseverance, (iv) patience from frustrations, (v) purpose-driven mentality because of distractions, (vi) education is a means to an end and not an end in itself.

In the process, cheer leaders such as family and friends are critical part of the support needed for success. *Next,* the key skills to be acquired through the dissertation process such as writing skills, presentation skills, synthesis of literature, paraphrasing of scholarly materials, self-study and research, annotation of articles, and critical thinking. I developed the skills of *synthesis, paraphrasing,* and *avoidance of direct quotes* in response to the initial problem I had with my Comprehensive Examinations.

Lastly, the dissertation process is broken down into specific milestones based on inherent characteristics, challenges, lessons, and reflections-The specific milestones, encompass-(1) Concept paper, (2) Dissertation Proposal, (3) Institutional Review Board (IRB) and Fieldwork, (4) Dissertation manuscript, (5) Dissertation defense and completion.

SUMMARY AND CONCLUSION

Upon reflection I wish to observe as follows:

- *I have been interacting frequently with my classmates more as I moved up the education ladder. Consequently, I have engaged and interacted more with my classmates at the sixth-form level than those in the secondary school level and the same is the case for my undergraduate and graduate levels.*

- *All teachers have made positive contributions to my development but some have left indelible marks or imprints on my mind. For that reason, not all teachers are remembered by students. If you are a teacher, aim at impacting your students positively at all times. This is priceless! Therefore, teachers should not hurt young ones because such events are never forgotten.*

- *Teachers should not destroy any of their students because as you descend the ladder, they are the very people you will meet on their way up. For that reason, mentors should seek ways to affect lives for a lasting impact.*

- *In approaching this project, some names were easily recollected whereas other names were difficult to remember. I find that positively impacting names are difficult to forget.*

CHAPTER 5

ACADEMIC SUCCESS IS INFECTIOUS

Hanssen (2019) stated that researcher-initiated autobiography can offer illuminating insights into how we as humans and nonhumans are associated in networks (p.311). Statistically, undergraduate degree holders make up 6.7 percent of the global population (www. independence.edu -accessed on 01/26/2021). An estimated 9 percent of the USA population have Master's degree and less than 2 percent of the Global population has a doctoral degree. These statistics seem startling, yet that is the plain truth and the implication is that a lot of people are educated up to the High School level partly due to the fact that in most countries, High School education tends to be free. In most cases, the financial burden for university education can be heavy on the student and the family and in some cases, students incur huge students' loans if that option exist.

I want people to consider education as an investment in oneself because it cannot be taken away from you (Nelson Mandela) and cannot also be bequeath to others. While I can bequeath my moveable and immovable property to my children and grandchildren; my education remains a personal asset that cannot be given out after death. At best my educational certificates can only be displayed on the walls of my personal library for decoration purposes because it is personal to me and for that matter a personal asset. Yes, I recommend education to all. Nevertheless, I contend that education is a means to an end and not an end in itself, implying that what matters most is what you do with the education such as impacting and improving lives of others.

The evaluation of my academic journey will be discussed from the undergraduate education to doctoral level. Academic education places emphasis on the *Whys?* As compared to the *hows?* The focus of academic education is to develop critical thinking, or problem-solving abilities as well as, teamwork, communication, and scholarly writing such as the use of active voice and the skill of synthesis, paraphrasing, and annotation of bibliographies. The most challenging level of my educational experience has been at the Sixth-form and the Master's degree level despite that each milestone presented a different focus on my educational experiences and perspectives. The question of whether the academic educational experience should be a lifelong experience as in my particular case or should be accomplished upfront is an individual preference. I have gone back to school at a decade internal and I have acquired qualifications at five-year interval. A lawyer friend of mine had commented that: *"George, you have not rested at all"*

My family circumstance did not permit me to jump to Graduate School immediately as was the case of a few of my classmates. In the case of some of them, they were not the first in their families to achieve university education and so had support for the continuation of their education almost immediately.

Upon reflection, I find that those who went to Graduate School and also pursued their professional education immediately after college became ahead of the rest of the classmates who went straight to join the workforce. I have consistently advised young people to aspire to get at least a Master's degree and a professional qualification to stay ahead of the competition and I wish to re-iterate this suggestion here. Yes, it might be difficult to enter the workforce with a higher qualification, with the exception of the academia; however, a person can always accept a job below his or her qualification and with time progress or move out with some experience after qualification. This strategy can be rewarding because at times the temptation is that once a person enters the workforce, it becomes increasingly difficult to go back because of family circumstances. I have gone through such situations along the line.

Age should not be a determinant in the decision to further education. Specifically, I was 22 years when I entered the University of Ghana and completed at age 25; I entered the Graduate School at age 35 and graduated at age 37 for my Master's degree. I was 47 years when I was admitted into my doctoral program and I graduated at age 52 years. I want to emphasize that it can be done even at an advanced age. I can remember that the oldest person in my doctoral graduating class was 78 years in 2016.

In my undergraduate class, there were older students from the *matured student* category. In my Graduate school in Ghana, there were students who were returning to school after 20 years of graduation. The aged-old suggestion for people to spend the first thirty years learning, another thirty years working, and the last thirty years in retirement makes a lot of sense. In my experience, I have combined both learning and working and the sacrifices have been huge. It has taken much determination and perseverance to be successful over the long haul. Family life and responsibilities can weigh heavily on working students irrespective of the format.

Familiarity with and consciousness of internal norms and relationship in other cultures help readers to be comfortable with culture (Dadashova, 2018); as a result, there is a wide educational knowledge gap between the G.C.E. Ordinary level and the G.C.E. Advanced level and the situation is the same for the knowledge gap between the undergraduate and master's level. At the Master's degree level, you come to appreciate that you did not learn much at the undergraduate level; in spite of the investment of efforts and hour learning at that level. This is also the case, at the doctoral level, where most of the work is done by the students with guidance from faculty. Nevertheless, doctoral degrees are terminal qualifications and candidates are developed for problem-solving, research, and development. Consequently, a lot more knowledge is needed to bridge the gap between the level of academic accomplishments.

Deployment novelty- I wish to share two teaching-learning-outcome (TLO) approaches I experienced at the Graduate School during my MBA studies: (i) Dr. Yankey (my professor for Corporate finance) allocated topics on the course outline to students based on perspectives of specific authors to be presented in class. After different students have presented on the same topic from different authorities on the reference lists of the course outline, Dr. Yankey will respond to questions from students; then, he will go ahead and summarize the key points of the topic, and in the process bringing out what had been left out and emphasizing on critical learning outcomes.

(ii) A case study was administered by Dr. Yankey for our Corporate Finance final examinations. The case study covered the entire course content and the call of the question was- *Answer the question*. To attempt this case study, all the topics treated in class had to be listed and each applied to aspects of the case study material. I remember more than half of the time allotted (3 hours) for the examination was used in reading the entire 7-paged case study to appreciate the facts and figures before proceeding to address the call of the question. We called this experience- *Gyese wo bre*-meaning the qualification does not come on silver platter.

Knowledge sharing- To advance the course of learning in the world, I have given open access to my dissertation on the topic: *Exploratory Multiple-Case Study of Illinois External Auditors' Perception on Fraud Education in Undergraduate Accounting Programs*, 2016, 349 (Northcentral University, DBA dissertation, ProQuest, 10181182). ISBN: 9781369298314. Doctoral degrees allow for access to Global Academic Database such as ProQuest, Wiley, Science Direct, SAGES, Google Search; as well as, a network of classmates who grow together. Additionally, my long essay is available in the Library of the School of Administration (University of Ghana, Legon. The topic is: *The*

Determinants of Taxpayer Level of Compliance: An Investigative Study of the Internal Revenue Service, 2001, (MBA dissertation).

Academic Accounting Education- I quite remember my decision to pursue accounting education was a difficult one for me. I am thankful to Dr. Emmanuel A. Appiah for his input that partly influenced my decision in this direction. At the sixth-form level, the two of us wanted to have common subjects for mutual support purposes; and for that reason, the subject-*accounting*-became the subject we both pursued. This afforded us the opportunity to compare notes and to solve problems together. Likewise, I am grateful to Emelia Hansen (a product of Westley Girls High School). She was one year ahead of me in the School of Administration and an Accounting major. Emelia's sister was the Principal of the Saint Monica's Training College at Mampong Ashanti in Ghana. One day, we met on an Omnibus Service Authority (OSA) bus from Kumasi to Mampong and we had a conversation on my selection of a college major. Truth be told, I was contemplating going for the Management Option (concentration) when school re-opens because I was more qualitative. Indeed, my interaction with Emelia that day and on the bus settled my argument.

I will discuss how I view accountancy as a call in another chapter of this book (see Chapter 17). I appreciate the contributions of both Emalia and Emmanuel in this regard. A brief background of Accounting education in Ghana; based on accounting scholarship (Anyane-Ntow,1992; Ghartey, 1992), is provided below:

a) The beginning of university business education in Ghana dates back to 1952 when the Kumasi College of Technology prepared students for external professional bodies (p.40).

b) In 1960, a decision was made by the government that the Commerce Department of the Kumasi College of Technology (KCT) be moved to Accra to form the nucleus of a new independent educational institution to train accounting and management personnel for industry, commerce and the public service-The College of Administration or the School of Administration (p.39-40).

c) On the recommendation of the International Commission on University Education in Ghana, the ACCA course and the secretaryship and Administration courses were replaced by a BSc. (Administration) course in 1962 and became integral part of University of Ghana as School of Administration.

1. Most of the top students in the graduating accounting class were offered scholarship overseas for post-graduate studies-Most never returned.

2. The remaining 25 percent of the other graduates that remained in Ghana have not attempted the Institute's professional examinations, for the following reasons:

- *No training facilities for preparation for examination;*
- *Students believe it is too great a sacrifice to undergo the internship program in Ghana.*
- *The demand for BSc accounting graduates is high and the remuneration is also high;*
- *Over-concentration of activities in Accra makes it difficult for graduates outside of Accra to prepare for the examinations;*
- *By the Chartered Accountants Act,1963, Act 170, the Institute of Chartered Accountants, Ghana was established (p.43).*

T.A. Hammond writing in 2002 on: *A white-collar profession-African American Certified Public Accountants since 1921* explained the state of accounting education in the United States of America. Additionally, the career was dominated by whites and that accounting was deemed a white-collar profession. He sums up as follows:

In the early 1990s, in over 600 four-year accounting programs in the country, there were only 75 African

American professors with Ph.D's in accounting, half of whom were clustered at a few HBCUs. It is therefore not surprising that 40 percent of the African American doctoral students in accounting had never met an African American with a Ph.D in accounting (Hammond, 2020, p.142).

Financing University Education in Ghana-From the foregoing, financing of university education became topical and one of the prominent ideas was cost-sharing. The government introduced Ghana Commercial Bank (GCB) loan of ¢5,000 for a year. This was in addition to what the students termed as *bunglar,* an arrangement where the government provided the cost of breakfast and any one meal-lunch or dinner. A *stipend* of ¢314 was paid fortnightly to students to provide for the cost of feeding. However, students were at liberty to: (i) buy coupons at the cafeteria of the residential halls, or (ii) provide their own meals, or (iii) buy from food vendors across the campus.

These schemes were not sustainable and subsequently discontinued. As might be expected, the Social Security and National Insurance Trust (SSNIT) Students Loan Scheme was introduced. Under this scheme, the trust provided fixed sums of money per student per year. The SSNIT loan scheme was not based on needs assessment because there was no such way of determining need of students. During my time as an undergraduate student, three different ways of financing university education were explored as part of the cost-sharing theory.

Inaugural lectures-The inaugural lecture was part of the dissemination of research output of academic faculty. From time to time, inaugural lectures are held on topical areas such that opportunities are presented for the gathering of students, faculty, policy makers, staff, and the general public to engage in processing vital research insights. In the process knowledge is acquired through the processing of the shared information. I suggest that if possible, participation in such programs can be very profitable. ***Management Day Celebrations***-The management day celebration at the School of Administration is a special day that enabled the academia to exchange ideas with the practitioners once a year. The cross-pollination of ideas has been established to be very rewarding and effective. Each year, the attention of academia is focused on one industry. Topics of interests are chosen and activities are held to engage academia and practitioners on common societal agenda. I recommend academic programs of such nature to students on campuses.

Re-Sit of MIS, the policy for the Graduate School was to accept grades from *A* to *B* as *pass* grades; and grades *C* and *D* deemed as *fail* grades. I had *grade C* in Management Information System (MIS) in the Graduate School. Interestingly, all my study mates made a minimum of grade B+ in the same course and I had to re-sit for this course. I wish to let the younger generation know that life is not always rosy because there can be temporary setback and the most important thing to remember is that failure is a mindset. When I went back to prepare, I passed. The old poem states- *"If at first you do not succeed, try again…"* **Honor Societies,** I belong to two honor societies namely, Delta Mu Delta and the Golden Key International Honour Society.

There are *cost-benefits* of academic education and I argue that the benefits outweigh the cost. Lucila Duarte in November 2016, identified the following as the significance of education: *One*, (i) development of amazing organizational skills, (ii) getting a higher paying jobs through opened up opportunities, (iii) making new lifetime friends, (iv) avoiding mistakes made by people who have gone before us, (v) learning time managements skills to be able to get things done on time, (vi) teaching how to handle responsibilities, (vii) appreciating world and current events, (viii) giving the required tools to think for yourself and to be able to back your arguments up, (ix) exposing individuals to peers through diversity in experience and points of view, (x) linking bad actions with associated discipline, (xi) developing social skills for interaction, and (xii) helping people to realize potential to fulfill purpose of life.

Two, the importance of education revolves around the following: higher paying jobs, handling responsibilities, thinking abilities, experience in diversity, potential realization, and making new lifetime friends (Duarte, November 2016); *three,* other justification cover, understanding global events and trends, opening up opportunities, proactively avoiding mistakes of others, acquiring time management, social, and organizational skills, and associating discipline with unaccepted behavior and actions (Duarte, November 2016).

The challenges of academic education encompass the following: (a) *higher cost of university* education (both undergraduate and graduate), leading to higher student debt arising out of students' loans or sacrifices of retirement funding of parents for children's education; (b) *investment of time*-I have spent my entire life learning. To give an idea, I have invested over 30 years of my life studying: 3 years at the undergraduate level, 2 years at the graduate (Master's level), and about 5 years at the doctoral level; totaling 10 years of academic education alone. As I will discuss in the next chapter, in-between these programs, I have studied for my professional education and also studied before my university education. (c) Striking the right balance between *family life and education*-Some have focused on one to the detriment of the other.

(d) *Unrealistic societal expectation-* The expectation of society is not fair to products of universities. In some families, once a person completes the university, it is expected of the person to solve all financial problems of the family. Yes, I agree that families do make financial investments in the education of members. I can confirm a case where one of the students in my department benefited from the sale of family property (land) to pay for the first-year fees. I would imagine that if this family is not understanding, they would demand pay back whether his income is able to support the family or not. I dare say from fraud detection and prevention standpoint that such people come under intense pressure and when opportunities present themselves, they are likely to do the unthinkable and to proceed to rationalize their actions. This is what the fraud triangle framework is about.

Quite apart from this, there is also the societal pressure for university products to know everything irrespective of the person's area of specialization. One of my professors told our MBA class of a story that happened in his hometown. An elderly man received a letter (mail) in German and sent for a student in the university in the village to come, and explain the content to him. This gentleman explained to the Oldman that the letter was in the German language and he did not understand that language. The Oldman expressed his utmost disappointment in the university student. The oldman argued that if the university student could not read and explain to him; then, who else can. I contend that both the oldman and the university students had a case.

While appealing to society to be fair to university graduates; university products should also bear the expectations of society in mind towards their development.

I provide the following suggestions: (I) University graduates should be humble because they do not know it all; (II) the products of the universities should be honest with themselves and should not pretend to know everything; (III) the graduates should be understanding that family resources might have been sacrificed to bring their purposes to fruition and as much as possible should be able to help where they are able; (IV) graduates of universities should not compare themselves to their mates.

I have come to appreciate that, in the long-run success is possible. While some start early and fall along the line, others suffer initially, and yet others grow gradually over time. (V) University products should also know that learning is a life time enterprise so there is nothing like "I have finished school" Life is a learning process and there is something to learn from every situation and circumstance. It pays to listen to news of current happenings in the world, read novels and magazines, and enhance your vocabulary by games such as *Scrabbles, Egypt to Canaan,* and many more. Lastly, (VI) university product should give back to society in different forms through any of the following: serving voluntarily on committees, boards, and offices; offering national service, internships, and volunteers; as well as, mentors and role-models for students in the lower levels of education.

CHAPTER 6

PROFESSIONAL TRAJECTORY

THE PROFESSIONAL TRAJECTORY APPEARS TO be rewarding and the path has become popular in recent times; yet the path has been unchartered by many. The majority of candidates who start the professional examinations across the globe tend to discontinue along the line. Consequently, only a minority is able to complete the professional examinations from start to finish. The reasons for this state of affairs will be discussed in this and the next chapters. A professional certification (United States of America) or qualification (Ghana) connotes authentication, or authorization; acquired through a process that assures official attestation to a level of achievement to confirm some desired characteristics. This process is enhanced by rigorous preparation and examinations organized through outside evaluation, peer review process, and assessment. The discussion of my professional education will be presented under one of four themes, as follows: (1) *foundation of professional education*; (2) *intermediate professional education*; (3) *advanced professional education I*; and (4) *advanced professional education II*.

FOUNDATION OF PROFESSIONAL EDUCATION

Every important life pursuit begins with the first and initial steps and my story regarding my professional path is not different. In 1983, I enrolled in the **Trans-World Tutorial College** (the United Kingdom) in two courses: One, *Book-Keeping and Accounts I*, with a distinction on July 18, 1983; and two, *Economics* in which I finished with a credit on July 22, 1983. These courses were deployed through correspondence fashion; where study materials were sent to the students to study within a period followed by the administration of examination in paper and pencil format.

The examination responses were sent to the Institute in the United Kingdom for grading. The tuition fees for the courses were paid in Great Britain Pounds (GB£) through the Banking System. Typically, I do not have to show any of my qualifications below the undergraduate level in my resume or curriculum vitae; the contribution of these courses toward my ultimate certifications cannot be over-emphasized. I thank Senior Antwi Agyei (Secondary or High School) for exposing me to these courses. Indeed, I have benefited from what preparations and writing of examinations has to offer in my personal development.

INTERMEDIATE PROFESSIONAL EDUCATION

My intermediate professional education will be discussed to encompass the following: (1) The Chartered Institute of Taxation, Ghana; (2) The Institute of Internal Controls (USA), and (3) Courses organized by the Ghana Stock Exchange. These certifications are tailored toward specific sectors of the economy or aspects of academic and professional disciplines.

CHARTERED INSTITUTE OF TAXATION, GHANA

The Chartered Institute of Taxation Ghana (CITG) was incorporated on August 10, 2016 under the Chartered Institute of Taxation Act (2016), Act 916-To promote the study of taxation and regulate the practice of Taxation in Ghana (Retrieved from http://www.taxghana.org -accessed on 04/19/2020). At the time I registered with the main taxation body in Ghana, the Chartered Institute of Taxation, Ghana (CITG) was known and called the Ghana Institute of Taxation (GIT). Over time, the change of name has been associated with modifications to the course content and structure. Consequently, the GIT or CITG has been operating as a professional body since 1978 under the Companies Code (1963), Act 179 on May 2, 1980 (Retrieved from http://www.taxghana.org -accessed on 04/19/2020).

The membership of the taxation body was by examinations and experience, acquired to assist in tax compliance, taxation, advisory services, and many more (Retrieved from http://www.taxghana.org -accessed on 04/19/2020). The current structure of the program is made up of three parts as follows: (a) **professional level**-involving strategy and governance, indirect taxation, public sector economics, accounting and finance, revenue and business law, and income taxation (Retrieved from http://www.taxghana.org- accessed on 04/19/2020).

(b) **Final Part I**- encompassing international taxation; Oil, gas, and mineral taxation; and tax audit and investigation (Retrieved from http://www.taxghana.org -accessed on 04/19/2020); and (c) **Final Part II**- covering strategic tax planning, advanced taxation practice, and taxation practice administration and ethics (Retrieved from http://www.taxghana.org -accessed on 04/19/2020).

Unlike the current structure provided above, the old structure provided for the subjects to be grouped under two main parts. I was exempted from Part 1. I prepared for the examinations on my own and sat for all papers in the Part 2 and I was referred in Paper 2. I could not make it through the two attempts provided. Consequently, I had to rewrite the entire Part 2 papers again. We called the first attempt *foul* (as in soccer or football) and the second attempt *penalty* (as in soccer or football). I prepared for a retake of all the Part 2 papers and this time, I passed all the papers in 1995. I was admitted into membership of the taxation professional body in Ghana in the same year. Consequently, I became a Chartered Tax Practitioner (MGIT) in 1995 and later a member of the Ghana Institute of Taxation (MGIT) in July 1995.

Here, I want to thank Mr. Emmanuel Kwame Nyamordey, the

Regional Head of The Internal Revenue Service in Central region of Ghana for providing me additional learning support. I approached him for solutions to taxation problems because of his rich experience in tax administration and also his teaching experience from teaching taxation in the Business School of the University of Cape Coast. On August 18, 2011, the Council of the Institute of Taxation Ghana bestowed on me an award of Fellowship. As a result, I became a Fellow of the Chartered Institute of Taxation.

I am forever grateful to the institute for recognizing my little contribution in teaching taxation and fiscal policy at all levels (professional, undergraduate, and graduate); as well as, serving on some *adhoc* sub-committees of the Institute. On the occasion of the award of fellowship by the Chartered Institute of Taxation, Ghana to me, one of my distinguished professors wrote:

"Hi George,

The only product a teacher has is his students. As the students' progress and shine, the teachers have delivered and are proud of their products. We display them as trophies and awards. We are proud of them as they accomplish

You are one such products of mine in whom I am well pleased. Move on and do not look back. Accomplish as much as you can and should develop and build up yourself. You have the environment to do so. God be with you and keep you focused. Keep in touch" (Personal Communication, Wednesday, August 31, 2011 at 1:02am).

At a point in time, When I gave my business card to this professor, he remarked: *"George-You are accumulating the credentials"*

GHANA STOCK EXCHANGE

The Ghana Stock Exchange (GSE) was registered in July 1989 and commenced trading in 1990, *inter alia* with the aim of providing the framework and facilities to the general public for the purchase and sale of shares (stocks in USA), bonds, and other securities (Retrieved from http://www.gse.com.gh -accessed on 04/19/2020). The GSE course is focused on developing financial professional personnel for the Securities industries to encompass the Ghana Stock Exchange (GSE) for securities trading, the Securities and Exchange Commission (SEC) for securities regulation, the Banks, the Licensed Dealing Members (LDMs) as Brokerage firms for the Ghana Stock Exchange, the Authorized Dealing Officers (ADOs, certified representatives of the LDMs) on the GSE; as well as, financial journalists, and the general public.

The Securities industry course was held in GSE in Accra (Ghana) and the specific courses were: (i) Basic securities, (ii) Advanced securities, (iii) Securities selling and investment advice, and (iv) Securities trading. I attended the Securities Industry Course, Accra – Ghana and passed in all the four (4) courses in February 1998. The instructors included: Ekow Awunoor (Investment lawyer-deceased), Prince Kofi Amoabeng (Founder of UT Bank), Dr. Adu Anane Antwi (Former Director-General of the Ghana Securities and Exchange Commission and my undergraduate classmate), Yoofi Grant (The current Head of the Ghana Investment Promotion Council), and Mike Ashong (Formerly of Ecobank Stockbrokers Limited).

The passes in the Securities industry course were necessary requirement for becoming an ADO; but the sufficient condition was to work with an LDM. I did not seek sponsorship towards becoming an ADO in Ghana because I did not work for any LDM. Nevertheless, the knowledge from the course has opened the eyes of my understanding towards investments in the Ghana's financial markets.

INSTITUTE OF INTERNAL CONTROLS

The Institute of Internal Controls (IIC) exists to promote an effective internal controls environment and to support internal controls excellence (Retrieved from http://www.theiic.org -accessed on 04/19/2020). Established in 2003, the IIC is the product of a group of auditing professionals coming together to form a professional body because of the concern over the failure of the auditing profession and oversight bodies to uncover and prevent high profile financial fraud cases that have occurred over the years (Retrieved from http://www.theiic.org -accessed on 04/19/2020). The membership is through a rigorous qualification process towards two certifications- (I) Certified Controls Specialists (CCS); and (II) Certified Internal Controls Auditor (CICA), backed by education, professional development, and collegiality among industry practitioners (Retrieved from http://www.theiic.org -accessed on 04/19/2020).

The philosophy of the institute is based on the recognition of the need to change the profession to address all areas of internal controls, revolving around the following-(i) management controls, (ii) financial controls, (iii) operational controls, (iv) IT controls, (v) physical controls, and (vi) risk management (Retrieved from http://www.theiic.org -accessed on 04/19/2020). It was against these principles and values that I applied for membership in 2009 and the CICA designation of the Institute of Internal Controls. The Nominations Committee of the Institute approved my application for membership and certification under the Grandfathering provision based on my prior accomplishments in education and practical experience. The Office of the Chairman approved the Committee's recommendation and authorized me to use the *CICA* designation forthwith, dated July 31, 2009 and signed by the Chairman (Dr. Frank W. Nasuti, PhD, CPA, CICA, CFE).

Seminars and Workshop-As part of my professional development,

I have participated in tax conferences and workshops such as those held on September 13-14, 2005 in Accra by the Chartered Institute of Taxation, Ghana and another one organized by the Ghana Internal Revenue Service in in Accra in 1996 themed-*The complementary role of the accountant, the taxpayer, and the tax administration*: *The Tax Administration View Position*. The topics covered the following: Towards an effective tax administration, Successful handling of tax investigation, Double Taxation Agreements (Treaties, DTAs), Making tax compliance work, Ensuring the compliance Burden – the taxpayer point of view; as well as Tax Tribunal in the 21st Century.

Similarly, I participated in 2011 in the Annual Tax Conference, organized by the Chartered Institute of Taxation (Ghana) on August 24-26 at the Alisa Hotel on: Shaping strategies for tax revenue enhancement in a global economic downturn, Sustaining the business enterprise in the wake of the Global meltdown, transfer pricing rules, the relevance of Double Taxation Agreements (DTAs) and Exchange of Information Agreements (EIA) for the Multinational Enterprise, and Business strategy development challenges.

ADVANCED PROFESSIONAL EDUCATION (ICAG)

Institute of Chartered Accountants Ghana (ICAG) was incorporated on April 19, 1963 as the main accountancy body by presidential assent and has been at the forefront providing accountancy training at both professional and technician levels (Retrieved from http://www.icagh. com -accessed on 04/19/2020). As of 1992, there were 50 accounting firms in Ghana, comprising 46 Ghanaian-owned and 4 foreign-owned; in another analysis, 43 of the firms have main offices in Accra, 4 in Kumasi, 1 in Koforidua, and 2 in Takoradi (Ghartey,1992). Comparatively, out of 318 registered firms, 309 firms fully paid their license fees. Listed firms on the Quality Assurance Monitoring (QAM)

Directory stands at 359 at the end of 2018 (ICAG Annual Report & Financial Statements, 2018, p.15). The ICAG listed 342 firms, comprising of 157(46%) with D Category and 185(54%) with Category A to C (Retrieved from www.icagh.com -accessed on 02/27/2020).

Per the ICAG Annual Report & Financial Statements (2018), the number of students registering for the CA Professional programme, encompassed: 3371(2015), 3746(2016), 3400 (2017), and 3473 (2018, p.21). Membership grew by 562 (new members who were admitted into membership in April and November 2018), bringing the members in good standing to 4,892 (ICAG Annual Report & Financial Statements, 2018, p.8). Likewise, the ICAG in collaboration with the University of Ghana Business School (UGBS) appointed Professor Michael Ofosu Mensah as the occupant of the UGBS/ICAG Chair of Accountancy for 2018/2019. The professional chair was established to create the opportunity in the field of accountancy to benefit both academia and industry. Professor Ofosu Mensah is a professor of Accounting, occupant of the Leadership Chair in Business Education, and Dean Emeritus at Kania School of Management, University of Scranton Pennsylvania, USA (ICAG Annual Report & Financial Statements, 2018, p.8).

I enrolled to sit for the ICAG examinations after my undergraduate education as soon as I started working with the Ghana Internal Revenue Service. I was given exemption for Part 1 of the examinations based on my undergraduate qualification with a concentration in accounting. I sat for the Part 2 examinations in both Accra and Takoradi and received Grade *F* with associated remark of *"Bad Fail"* I wrote the examinations with a colleague at the Cape Coast office of the Ghana Internal Revenue Service. We lodged at the Ghana National Association of Teachers (GNAT) Hostel in Takoradi. At one of my examination sittings, Mr. Okai Tetteh hosted me in his residence at Sekondi in the Western region. Mr. Tetteh was a year ahead of me in the School of Administration in the University of Ghana and he was then the

Regional manager for Mobil Ghana Limited (Central and Western regions of Ghana).

Later on, I met Mr. Kofi Ofori, who was working in the Internal Auditing Department of the Ghana Internal Revenue Service. Kofi Ofori asked me whether I have started writing the professional examinations and I answered in the affirmative and told him of the *bad fail* remarks I had received. Then, he inquired into the study material I was using in my preparation and I mentioned them. Kofi explained that my study material was the reason why I failed. He was sitting for the Association of Chartered Certified Accountants (ACCA) at the time of our interaction. As a result, he advised me as follows: (1) to focus on the use of accounting manuals prepared by the various accountancy bodies such as ACCA, Chartered Institute of Management Accountants (CIMA), Institute of Chartered Accountants (ICAG-England & Wales); and (2) to concentrate on the best approach of answering professional examinations question. At the time, I did not know that the approach in answering examination questions was different for both academic and professional institutions.

Upon reflection, I want to thank Kofi Ofori for the insight and I later determined the pieces of advice were on point and also helpful in my professional education. I was a member of a study group that met as part of our preparation for the ICAG examinations. I began with one of my MBA mates and we passed the Part 2 together; but I passed the Part 3 so I had to move on to join another study group for the Part 4 examinations preparation. The professional discussion group comprised of the following: (1) Sulemana Zakari, (2) the late Assan Yakub, (3) Okofo Darteh, (4) Osmanu Ayobah, (5) Alhassan, (6) Asumaila Issaka, (7) Adams, (8) Bartholomew, (9) Taufik. Interestingly, we all 'chartered' but at different times.

The ICAG restructured the course from four parts and condensed into them into three levels, as follows: **Level 1**- (i) Accounting foundations,

(ii) business management, (iii) economics, and (iv) business law; **Level 2**-(v) financial accounting practice, (vi) management accounting, (vii) company and partnership law, (viii) taxation, (ix) management information systems and business systems, (x) audit and internal reviews, (xi) strategic management; **Level 3**-(xii) corporate reporting strategy, (xiii) assurance and audit practice, (xiv) financial management strategy, and (xiv) advanced tax planning and fiscal policy. I completed the ICAG examinations and became a Chartered Accountants (CA, Ghana) in November 2006 and admitted into membership of the Institute 2008.

I am thankful to Mr. Paul Osei Kwabena (BSc. Administration, CA) the Managing Partner of Osei Kwabena and Associates (Chartered Accountants) for his encouragement.

Seminars and Workshops- My professional developments had revolved around participation and facilitation of seminars and workshops to encompass the following: *first*, I participated in the conference on Oil and Gas organized by the Institute of Chartered Accountants (Ghana) at the Erata Hotel in Accra from October 26 -28, 2010 on: (a) History of oil exploration, (b) petroleum exploration in Ghana, (c) financing oil and gas projects and risk management, (d) taxation of oil and gas business in Ghana, (e) decommissioning and remediation, (f) social performance, (g) legal and fiscal regimes of Ghana's upstream oil and gas industry. *Second*, in October 2005, I facilitated in a seminar on finance for non-finance managers by SMME Consult Limited for the Ghana Post Company Limited on: Income Statement, Case Study for group discussion, Cost analysis, Forecasting using Break-Even Analysis, and Reconciliation.

ADVANCED PROFESSIONAL EDUCATION (AICPA)

American Institute of Certified Public Accountants (AICPA) is the global and largest member association of accounting professionals and dating back to 1887 and composed of over 418,000 members in 143 countries-in (i) business, (ii) industry, (iii) public practice, (iv) government, (v) education; as well as, (vi) student affiliates and international associates (Retrieved from http:// www.aicpa.org -accessed on 04/19/2020). My association with the American Institute of Certified Public Accountants commenced on August 8, 2005, when I applied in Ghana for membership as a student of the AICPA in the U.S.A. I received my Student Welcome Kit and Congratulatory letter that highlighted special benefits-covering: (I) access to the Journal of Accountancy, the AICPA News Update, and the CPA Letter; (II) AICPA Competency Assessment Tool, and (III) the AICPA resource Online. However, I did not start writing the AICPA examinations until a later date because of the residency requirement for my State Board of Accountancy.

I came across a book authored by T.A. Hammond (2002) on *A white-collar profession-African American Certified Public Accountants since 1921*, which examined the CPA profession in the past. The paragraphs that resonated with me is:

> *African American who managed to become CPAs prior to the 1960s had exceptional characteristics. All of them personified talent, persistence, and resilience. These pioneers were remarkably accomplished students with outstanding educational backgrounds, exceeding those of many of their white counterparts. Some moved hundreds of miles to achieve their educational goals, to obtain employment with an African American, or simply to find a state that allowed African Americans to take the CPA examinations. Some spent years seeking employment in the field. A few of the earliest CPAs came from the most elite African American families in the nation. A handful appeared to be white. All these*

> *characteristics reduced the difficulties they faced; nevertheless,*
> *intense challenges remained* (Hammond, 2002, p.5).

After reading this piece, I came to appreciate that the personal characteristics required to pass the CPA examinations is to become accomplished students and to have outstanding educational background.

Specifically, the pioneers- African American who became CPA were: (1) resilient, (2) personified talent, and (3) persistent. For that reason, all these characteristics were responsible for the reduction of the difficulties they faced in their professional trajectory. Against this background, I applied to the Illinois Board of Examiners (ILBOA) to sit for the CPA examinations. I submitted my credentials, including original copies of certificates of degrees from the University of Ghana, certificate of membership and official examination history from The Institute of Chartered Accountants of Ghana, and G.C.E. Advanced level certificate; as well as, a request for the evaluation of credentials for the purpose. Even though, the ICAG designation and membership could have provided me with additional 30 credit hours, my graduate school education was sufficient to provide me with the required 120 credit hours. I was a resident of the State of Illinois. Additionally, the following courses had been taken: (a) Audit, (b) tax, (c) financial accounting, and (d) managerial accounting.

The structure of the CPA examination was quite different from the structure of the ICAG examinations discussed above. While the ICAG's examination was structured along three or four levels with different subjects and the progression is by passing the current level; the CPA examination was structured into four Parts-(1) Regulation (REG)- comprising all law and taxation courses; (2) Business Environment and Concepts (BEC)-all courses other than financial accounting, auditing, laws, taxation such as economics, financial management, and many more; (3) Financial Accounting and reporting (FAR)-covering all financial accounting courses; and (4) Auditing (AUD)- comprising all auditing courses.

The major challenge for me as a student was the deep variation in auditing and accounting standards and the wide disparity between the taxation in Ghana and the taxation in the USA, developed over about 200 years. Also read my book on *Taxation of Ghana: A fiscal policy tool for development* from 1943 to 2018. While Ghana's accounting standards leaned towards the Ghana National Accounting Standards Board (GNASB) and later to the International Financial Accounting Reporting Standards (IFRS), the USA's was based on Generally Accepted Accounting Principles (GAAP). In response to the problem, I enrolled in the Becker CPA Review and I attended review class on Saturdays from 8:00am to 5:00pm at the Oakbrook Terrace. I used any available time in the library. Within a period of three years and after a mixture of passes and failures, I passed all the Uniform CPA Examination on August 26, 2010 in AUD, BEC, FAR, and REG; administered by the National Association of State Boards (NASBA). The ILBOA's letter of October 12, 2010 communicated the Board Approval of my Illinois CPA certification based on Certification by Examinations.

I thank Elder Richard Osei (Nyameadom) for giving me his study material when thieves broke the glass into my car and made away with my bag containing Becker CPA Review Manual on Financial Accounting and Reporting. I guess the thief thought the bag contained a laptop. Additionally, Elder Richard Osei and I attended a Christmas Convention, and a Word of knowledge came to the effect that "there is a person in the Sanctuary who is writing professional examinations and contemplating discontinuing the path, but the Lord is asking the person to go back to write the examinations because the Lord is assuring success" The bit about the persons contemplating discontinuing the path was the aspect that did not resonate with me.

When the service was over, Richard came to me and said- "the message that came is for you" I was very impressed because I was wondering why somebody will surrender such a divine intervention to a brother. That was thoughtful of him. Likewise, I thank Elder Albert A. Buabeng (now Dr. Buabeng) for having conversations with me regarding the CPA process of certification. I am grateful to Deacon Bright Asante Appiah (currently Assistant Professor of Lehigh University), whom I attended some of Becker CPA Review Sessions with. He completed his Graduate School in America and was familiar with some of the concepts and at times pointed out key points to me. I must note that the above named persons had the CPA designation around the same time.

Seminars and Workshops- The State of Illinois required all CPAs to get a certificate of completion of Professional Ethics- The AICPA Comprehensive Course for 8 CPE credits. I have participated and facilitated in seminars and workshops in the USA to be involved with some of the following: **One**, I participated in a Shelby accounting software training for Not-for profit organizations, organized by The Church of Pentecost U.S.A, Inc in 2008 and facilitated by Shelby trainers. **Two**, on December 8, 2017- I facilitated in the Annual Audit Conference of the Church of Pentecost U.S.A., Inc in Wayne, New Jersey on: audit evidence and significant internal auditing findings, stewardship and the fraud triangle, overview of the internal auditing function, systems of internal controls, and reporting. **Three**, on March 30, 2019- I facilitated in 2019 Chicago Regional Financial Seminar in Cincinnati, Ohio on: significant internal auditing findings, systems of internal controls, and steps in managing the internal auditing process. The participants for this seminar were those charged with financial stewardship in the Mid-west of the Church of Pentecost U.S.A.,Inc.

CHAPTER 7

PROFESSIONAL ACUMEN IS SOCIETAL-FOCUSED

PROFESSIONALISM IS A HALLMARK OF excellence through the certification process. Professional education has emphasized more on the *hows?* As opposed to the *whys?* and compared to the *hows?* The synthesis of my professional trajectory has been discussed in the preceding chapter to encompass, the following: certification in accounting (Ghana and USA), taxation, and internal controls. Iuliu-Marius (2019) asserted that self-development is related with school and education (p.219). The benefits of having a professional certification can be refreshing because of the status, symbolism and the hallmark of authenticity in the areas of specialty; as a result, professionalism is highly-rated in practice, or in industry. Additionally, the continuous professional education (CPE) ensure that the professional stays updated and ahead of changes in the environment. Consequently, a minimum number of credits are required for a period of time.

The regulatory framework, including laws and standards are evolving every day; yet the professional cannot rely solely on the laws and standards of yesterday to solve today's problems. Suggesting that the practitioner has to respond to the changes in the environment in a timely fashion. Another challenge emerging is the role of technology in the accounting profession.

Currently most of the accounting and auditing functions can be performed by technology and the appropriate response is for the practitioner to develop technology adeptness or focus on the advisory aspects of the professional spectrum. I have responded to emerging issues by making up for any skill gaps.

The attempts I have made in the past to bridge the skill gap encompassed, the following: *One*, when the internet became available in Ghana, I visited Internet Centers in Osu Oxford street in Accra to spend at least an hour to familiarize myself with the browsing of the internet, using emails, and researching from the internet. *Two*, I arranged for two weeks between my Graduate School and going back to the world of work to learn the basic computer applications- *Word* and *Excel*. Learning of computer and other applications have become an entire life experience from work, church, and profession. Likewise, the accounting profession has provided avenues for networking, which assures peer review processes, society meetings, annual general meetings (AGM), Year Group interactions, and many more.

The job security and assurances provided by professional certification is very in sighting. Professionals can lose their jobs especially by demonstrating professionalism, but can also establish their own firms. The impact of the professional certifications is to be felt by society at large. Otherwise, it is of less value. Professionals are required to solve problems with less or no direction. Consequently, the ability to know where to find the requisite material for problem-solving is inherent in the certification process. My career objective over a period of time has revolved around: (I) blending both academic and professional qualification; and (II) the addition of a global dimension, as follows:

> *A self-motivated person with extensive technical experience in accounting, auditing, finance, management, and taxation and fiscal policies acquired through positions that best utilized my knowledge and provided opportunity for growth. Having acquired a very strong analytical and/or conceptual background through academic and professional pursuit as well as extensive exposure, now seeking a career in accounting, finance and/or management. Ultimately want*

to be an astute consultant in finance, accounting, auditing, taxation, and management across the globe.

The two perspectives are explained in the Sections below:

BLENDING PROFESSIONAL AND ACADEMIC EDUCATION

There is equivalency in depth of knowledge between a bachelor's degree and a professional certification such as CPA or CA (Ghana). However, employers prefer to rate the professional certification above the undergraduate degree in practice. While undergraduate degrees became a coveted qualification in Ghana in the past; with time, emphasis was placed on professional qualifications. In the process, a lot of people opted for either: (i) a bachelor's degree, or (ii) a professional qualification. With time, the supply of holders of undergraduate degree surpassed the supply of professional certifications, relative to the demand for them.

Partly because of the higher failure rate at the professional education level aimed at restricting entry into the profession to maintain earnings. It became apparent that people with either qualifications, never made it to the managerial level; albeit, with very long years of service. Nevertheless, people who combined at least a bachelor's degree with a certification became managers with time with ease. The implication was that it was not enough to possess either qualifications but a combination of professionalism and scholarship stood the test of time.

I dare argue for a blend of both academic (at least a master's degree) and professional education to make for a robust knowledge base and relevance.

Accounting scholarship (Bowling, June 2019; Center of Audit Quality, June 2019; Chun & Cho, May 2019, p.229; Drew, June 2019; Gepp, Linnenluecke, O'Neill, & Smith, June 2018, pp.102-115; Journal of Accountancy, June 2018, pp.21-30; Nkansah, Bailey,

April 2018, pp. A7A14-A16) has identified the following accounting and auditing trends: (1) technology covering (i) artificial intelligence (AI), (ii) data analytics tools, (iii) blockchain, (iv) increased automation procedures, (v) robotic process automation (RPA), (vi) cyber and data security, (vii) web-based integrated systems, (viii) audit management systems, and (ix) interactive forecasting models. (2) talent development, (3) continuous auditing, (4) environmental and social accounting; as well as, (5) utilization of big data techniques to be combined with traditional auditing techniques, and (6) expert judgment; (7) continuous risk assessment, (8) changes in legislation and standards, (9) corporate social responsibility (CSR), and (10) social sustainability debates and research. Most of these concepts have been discussed in my book-Fraud Prevention and Detection Puzzle: Skills, Strategies, Competences, and Programs.

GLOBAL PERSPECTIVE OF EDUCATION

The world has become a global village, allowing for a lot to be achieved with time and space, irrespective of location. As a result, holistic accounting education has evolved over time. The accounting profession has assumed a worldwide dimension and so there is the need to smoothen the rough edges in principles, practices, and policies. Per Accounting literature (Anyane-Ntow, 1992; Awayiga, Onumah, & Tsamenyi, 2010; Ghartey, 1992), the evolution of the Institute of Chartered Accountants, Ghana (ICAG) is summed up below:

1. Accounting scholarship (Anyane-Ntow, 1992; Awayiga, Onumah, & Tsamenyi, 2010; Ghartey, 1992) has provided the following insights into accounting education in Ghana:

2. The Republic of Ghana lies almost in the center of the countries along the Gulf of Guinea, covering a land area of 92,100 square miles or 239,460 square kilometers (Anyane-Ntow, 1992).

3. A substantial sector of the economic activity in Ghana is agricultural; broadly defined to include livestock, fisheries, and forestry and account for more that 40 percent of the gross national product (GNP-Anyane-Ntow, 1992).

4. It provides employment for 60 percent of the labor force and accounts for 70 percent of export earnings. Cocoa is by far the most important crop in the country but most of the other agricultural products are distributed by small scale private farmers who, after harvesting, transport them to local agricultural markets (Anyane-Ntow, 1992).

5. Distribution is one of the most important aspects of the Ghanaian economy (Anyane-Ntow, 1992).

6. The 1911 Census report showed three groups, as follows: (a) **professional and clerical,** while 79 percent is composed of clerical, the professional class was made up of 21 percent totaling 87, including surveyors (6), doctors (3), lawyers (27), ministers (26), photographers (24), and nurse (1); (b) **commercial and industrial;** and (c) **manual and unskilled**.

7. By 1948, the composition of professional and clerical class had changed but there was no African accountant; but there were 29 British accountants and one (1) German accountant for a total of 30.

8. There was no African professionally-qualified accountant in the Gold Coast until 1950s; even though, there is evidence that the significance of accounting and auditing was duly acknowledge by the Gold Coast Africans.

9. The King of Ashanti made it mandatory for his subjects or traders to keep proper accounts of all activities; and the King's Treasury served as the Central bank (Ghartey, 1992, p.39).

10. Accounting education has come under criticism over the past decade for failing to meet the demands of the changing business environment; accounting and information technology skills are relevant to prepare accounting graduates for career as professional accountants; however, analytical and critical thinking was rated as the most important professional skill by both the employers and the graduates (Awayiga, Onumah, & Tsamenyi, 2010).

11. The single most important challenge facing the accounting profession and the education of accountants in Ghana today is to adapt the educational process to respond to the unique environmental needs of the Ghanaian economy (Anyane-Ntow, 1992).

12. Per scholars (Anyane-Ntow, 1992; Ghartey, 1992, p.46), the number of students passing the CA Examinations is as follows: **One**, a total of 1,357 students passed the *Intermediate examination* from 1966 to 1985 and the breakdown is as follows: 13 (1966-1970), 133 (1971-1975), 388 (1976-1980), and 823 (1981-1985). **Two**, the number for students passing the *Final Part 1* is 359; broken down as follows: 17(1966-1970), 39(1971-1975); 163 (1976-1980); and 140 (1981-1985). **Three**, *Final Part 2* recorded 45 under the old version (1966-1980) and 172 for the new syllabus (1981-1985); **Four**, 51 students passed the *Final Part 3* (1976-1985); and **lastly**, the total number of students passing the *CA examinations* from 1966-1985 is summed up as follows: 35 (1966-1970), 185 (1971-1975), 637 (1976-1980), 1,127 (1981-1985).

13. The accounting and reporting practices are significantly influenced by political, legal, institutional, and economical factors and the regulatory environment is neither effective nor efficient due to the weak monitoring and enforcement of compliance (Assenso-Okofo, Ali, & Ahmed, December 2011).

14. Urgent measures need to be undertaken to reform and build the capacities of institutions charged with the responsibility of regulating and monitoring Ghanaian accounting and reporting practices to ensure best practices and build investors' confidence; as well as, advancing the course of standard setters, regulators, accounting practitioners, and policymakers to improve the corporate reporting and accounting practices (Assenso-Okofo, Ali, & Ahmed, December 2011).

CHALLENGES OF PROFESSIONAL EDUCATION

I identify the following challenges with professional education: (a) **The cost component**-Professional certification can also be expensive, apart from the cost of preparing and sitting for the rigorous examinations such as cost of textbooks and study manuals. Likewise, the profession requires the payment of annual subscriptions and the acquisition of continuous professional education (CPE) credits to maintain membership of the professional bodies. Yet, the networking from professional colleagues from societies, lectures, presidential luncheons, annual general meetings (AGMs) provide means for interactions and sharing of experiences; as well as, updating of knowledge arising out of changes to auditing and accounting standards, tax laws and fiscal policies, and many more.

(b) **Higher failure rates**-The failure rate for professional examinations can be very high. While the professional bodies blame students for poor preparation towards the examinations in most of their chief examiner's reports, the students contend that the failure rate is intentional to limit entry of people into the profession.

My candid view is that both positions are right, and all parties are to be fair to the other. By way of illustration, the pass rate of the ACCA hovered around 60 percent and that of the ICAG was pegged at 25 percent from studies conducted by Professor Ato Ghartey and others. I was privilege to be the ACCA course head at a point in time and discovered that the ACCA made available enough study material to assist students towards preparation for examinations. Ghartey (1992) postulated: *"The entire 20-years production of qualified accountants represents less that 50 percent of one year's estimated requirement of qualified accountants. To state that the results are discouraging would amount to an under-statement"* (p.47). The principal reasons include the following:

- *Absence and/or inadequacy of training and educational facilities for candidates;*
- *Lack of education and adequate preparation on the part of applicants. This view is corroborated by the Institute, as follows: "The pass rate was impeded by the non-availability of reading materials for students. This trend experienced a turnaround in the 80's and has seen a major boost since accounting manuals for the four levels were introduced in November 2008 (Retrieved from http://www.icagh. com –accessed on 04/19/2020)";*
- *The nature of the examinations-foreign material used by students to prepare-inadequate;*
- *A monopolistic intention on the part of the examiners to minimize competition within themselves* (p.47).

The ACCA established a National Office to provide service to students in Ghana and organized series of workshops for trainers and students alike.

(c) **Absence of classmates**- A major characteristic of professional accounting education is the non-existence of classmates. Unlike academic education where students enroll with a view to learning along with other learners, the case of professional education can be done or pursued on a solo basis. It is possible for some students to meet for tuition or as a discussion groups but graduation list can be made up of people you have never seen before. Instead of calling people classmates, they could be called professional colleagues. The question is: Is a classmate the same as a professional colleague?

(d) **Study materials**- The decision by the ICAG to develop study manuals is the best thing that has happened in the institute for the benefit of students. My colleagues and I had to resort to study manuals developed for other professional studies to adopt to our particular situation and circumstances. Keep in mind that Ghana had a different tax and fiscal regime, different companies code, and accounting standards, as compared to the United Kingdom from where most of the accounting professional bodies were based.

(e) **Disconnect between Universities and Professional bodies**-In the past, there was an apparent rivalry between the universities and the professional accounting body to the detriment of Ghana. There is an adage which goes: "When two elephants fight the grass suffers" The two stakeholders should view each other a partner in the development of accountancy in particular and the country in general. There should be a complementary role of those in academia such as: (i) the preparation of study material, (ii) the conduct of accounting research, (iii) the championing of due processes of accounting and auditing standards, (iv) providing tuition for accounting students.

The accounting practitioners can focus on accounting practice and the solution to problems. I remember the case of one professor with a concentration in accounting who applied to sit for the professional examinations and was given exemption at level one just as bachelor's degree holders. By implication, the professional body determined the prior academic qualification of the professor is equivalent to level one. This position was rejected by the professor. Later on, it turned out that the same professor was setting questions for the professional body.

(f) **Certification Vs. Membership**- The two terms are not the same. The professional trajectory leads to passing a professional examination towards certification but that is not enough, some requirements are to be met in order to become a member of a professional body. In theory, it is possible to be certified by the State Board of Accountancy but not a member of the professional body such as the AICPA, American Accounting Association (AAA), and many more.

(g) **Entry requirement**-The minimum requirement for entry to write the professional examination in Ghana is the High School and that of the State of Illinois in USA is the equivalent of a master's degree in accounting. Other master's degree holders have to pass in addition some accounting subjects at say the Community College before qualifying to sit for the examinations. Historically, students with a High School diploma have successfully passed the professional examinations while some degree holders have failed the same examinations. The argument is that of establishing equivalency between two professional bodies across the globe. When I was at the University of Ghana, legal education was a combination of academic (bachelor of law) and professional (LLB) education but with time this has changed. The legal profession in Ghana has moved to establish a master's degree as the entry requirement.

RECOMMENDATION

I proffer the following suggestion for professional accounting bodies, as follows: *In the first place*, **Continuous collaboration**- There should be continuous collaboration between accounting academics and profession. Nkansah and Bailey analyzed 75 article in April 2018 covering the period from 1981 to 2016 and finds a lower survey response rate of 15 percent as compared to 60 percent in the 1970s and 1980s. Consequently, accounting researchers include auditors in all processes such as inclusion in survey construction, formulation of the research questions, promoting interest in topics of interest, and data collection.

Additionally, auditors should hold accounting researcher accountable by questioning research findings that are incongruous with accounting practice; by offering perspectives into the applicability of the study findings; as well as, offering suggestions for follow-up research. The authors of the research study contended that a good association between practitioners and researchers can improve non-response rate in accounting research (Nkansah, Bailey, April 2018, pp. A7A14-A16).

In the second place, **the role of accounting is certain-** Accounting scholarship (Anyane-Ntow, 1992; Ghartey, 1992) have offered the following suggestions:

i. To achieve development, resources should be safeguard, properly allocated and accounted for, and utilized efficiently: (a) requires designs, implementation, and maintenance of effective and efficient accounting systems; (b) requires research to adapt and establish accounting standards to cope with the subtleties of the Ghanaian local environment.

ii. Accounting provides financial and other information essential to efficient conduct and evaluation of activities-investors, creditors, government; agencies, tax authorities, and general public; in budgeting, cost controls, profit planning, internal reporting and controls, and making constructive suggestions on financial, tax, and other policy and operating matters.

iii. Accountants have a distinctive role in examining financial statements submitted to stakeholders; and in expressing opinion on the fairness of such statements.

In the third place, **expanded societal role-** The statutory role of accounting has stood the test of the time. It is about time the impact of the accountancy profession is expanded into other areas of national importance. I recommend that the accounting profession be involved in the National Elections in Ghana and other countries, including the *collation* and *certification of results* until electronic format becomes reality in the future. There is an existing auditing standard to allows for this performance of this role. This can be performed as a national responsibility. A good example was set by the KPMG in Ghana, which helped the Supreme Court of Ghana to validate some evidence before the Apex Court in the landmark Election Petition in 2013. In the 2020 Election Petition of Ghana, the issue of Collation of results came to the fore. Again, several of the concepts have been treated in my book- Fraud Prevention and Detection Puzzle: Skills, Strategies, Competences, and Programs.

In the fourth place, **Segregation of duties-**The professional accounting body should separate the provision of tuition to students and the examination role. The professional accounting body should not organize classes for students because there can be some degree of bias towards students attending the classes at the accounting body's school to make it attractive. That role should be given to organizations outside of the accountancy body. There can be collaboration but the accounting bodies should not be in the process of offering tuition. The practice of having the same professional body provide tuition, administer examinations, and issue certification is unacceptable to me.

In recent times, the legal profession in Ghana has come under some criticism regarding administration of entrance examinations. Some organizations contract out testing and examinations to bodies such as the West African Examinations Council. In the USA, the CPA Review classes are organized by external bodies such as Becker/Conviser, Wiley, Gleim, etc. *In the fifth place,* **Flexibility in exams scheduling-** In Ghana, the professional accounting bodies organized professional examinations twice in a year. So, once you miss two times a whole year is passed. I suggest that the examination administration should gravitate towards technology to permit flexibility in examinations scheduling.

In the sixth place, **Graduated subscription regime**-In Ghana, the subscription payment tends to be across board. This regime assumes that all subscriptions are paid by employers and this might not be the case for all. The payment of subscriptions to professional bodies is a lifelong annual duty. I suggest that the annual subscriptions be graduated for levels such as CEO, CFO, partners, educators; as well as passive, and retired members.

In the last place, **Motivation to students**-The professional accounting bodies should not demoralize students who will become members in future. The argument is that all students who start the examinations and remain consistent and hardworking invariably pass the final examinations. Against this background, the use of *Bad Fail* remarks that existed on our results slips should be reconsidered. Similarly, the setting of very long questions that the examiners cannot answer within the time allotted for the examinations should be revisited. Some of the questions required more than the allotted time to solve under normal conditions let alone under examinations conditions.

CONCLUSION

It is common experience to care about notional entities and suggest that this comes about by way of 'trans fictional disavowal' of selfhood. As a result, reading position of autobiographical writing is based on 'affective metalepsis to propose that a new modality of the 'paradox of fiction' which can offer a satisfactory reading position of autobiographical or a re-evaluation of 'selfhood' (Lovat, 2019). I reiterate the observations made by Accounting scholars and practitioners (Aboagye, June 2018;

Aheto, February 2020; Onumah, n.d.; Simson, Onumah, & Oppong-Nkrumah, November 2016), as follows:

a) Leaders should not only think about their personal interests but to first build good reputation for themselves as a key corporate governance practice (Retrieved from http://www.classfmonline.com -accessed on 02/27/2020).

b) Leaders of today have lost their competencies, including courage, vision, and long-term focus; because risk management has not been taken seriously to deal with risk head on as they arise. Consequently, a leader must be able to positively inspire others and always be ready to lead (Aheto, February 2020).

c) There is a decline in the number of accounting majors and variables encompass: job opportunity, job security, broad exposure to business, high future earnings, business people they know, parents, teachers, grades, and mathematical background have greatly influence students' choice of an accounting major (Aboagye, June 2018).

d) Creativity levels of accounting major are low; and the dominant personality traits possessed by the accounting majors are social according to the Holland theory. The most important referents for male and females are business people they know and parents respectively (Aboagye, June 2018).

e) Future studies may examine the phenomena to postgraduate levels studies, and to explore how internal factors such as the age, size, financial wealth, and autonomy; as well as, the ranking of university may influence the integration of ethics education into accounting programmes (Simson, Onumah, & Oppong-Nkrumah, November 2016).

f) The variables in order of preference such as positive attitude, communication skills, strong work ethics, good interpersonal skills, analytical and problem-solving skills, flexibility and adaptability management, and organizational skills, and strong IT skills are some of the key skills employers expect accounting graduates to have in order for them to be deemed ready for the banking industry (Onumah, n.d.).

On his part, Professor Ato Ghartey has thrown the challenge to the accounting profession in Ghana, as follows:

> *"If Ghanaian accounting profession wishes to sustain its claims as being comparable to other major professions; then, the minimal pre-entry formal education requirement must be revised to conform with those of comparable professions. This implies that the Ghanaian Institute should aim at making a university degree the minimum pre-entry qualification to the profession. It also indicates the need for the revision of curriculum and syllabus at the professional level, and incorporating formal requirement on continuing professional education"* (Ghartey, 1992, p.54).

There is the need to learn from the past to guide the future. In the above chapters, I have shed lights on my personal experiences; as well as, drawn extensively on accounting scholarship to illuminate insight to help the younger population draw life lessons to direct their own life paths and choices.

CHAPTER 8

❧

EVERY EXPERIENCE IS RELEVANT

LIFE WRITINGS ARE COGNITIVE AND social activities being both author and reader oriented because they serve as participatory methodology aimed at consciousness raising, strengthening of empathy and increasing intercultural understanding of sensitive issues (Dadashova, 2018). In Chapter 2, parental ethos and values were discussed. While my father was an *electrician* in the main, he was also a farmer and transport owner at some point in time; my mother also was a *fish monger*, but took to farming; plantain, kenkey, tomatoes selling at other times in her life.

In chapters 4 and 6, my academic and professional trajectories were addressed. The training received from these areas have helped in shaping my professional and work experiences. I am of the view that every experience is relevant in life. As a result, in this chapter, I am going to recount some of my experiences. I am *not* going to repeat the contents of my resume or curriculum vitae here; rather, I am going to provide the stories behind the information on the section *on about the author* below (after the epilogue).

The general knowledge is that *experience is the best teacher*, suggesting that experiences can best present teaching and learning moments and opportunities for desired outcomes. Interestingly, the knowledge acquired in the classroom are a combination of the works of others, including theories, formulae, thesis, principles, and many more. The collections are known as a *body of knowledge*. For that reason, it makes sense to give credit where it is due in the interest of integrity and honesty by pointing to the knowledge frontier you seek to extend. As a result, the types of experiences become critical because negative and positive experiences are good teachers. While the negative experiences can teach preventive or deterrence lessons; the positive experiences can help to deliver curative and detection lessons. Negative experiences are not bad in themselves but the lack of appropriate responses to deal with repetitions on those experiences is the problem.

Frank Outlaw (n.d.) has opined-*It's all about character:*

> *Watch your thoughts; they become words.*
> *Watch your words; they become actions.*
> *Watch your actions; they become habits.*
> *Watch your habits; they become character.*
> *Watch your character; it becomes your destiny.*

The need for proper development of character is important because actions and character have a bearing on our success in the workplace. Some people get opportunities through their knowledge and experience but the absence of good character has brought them down in one way or the other. Frank Outlaw (n.d.) has traced the source of good and bad character from the mind (thoughts); implying that what comes out of the mouth of a person is a bye-product of what has already been conceived in the head ahead of time. Therefore, actions are initiated based on the words from the thinking of man. For that reason, continuous actions lead to positive or negative habits. For example, I have consistently slept early by 9:00pm and woken up by 3:00am for over three decades and these actions have become part of my habits over time. The difference between habits and character is over all outcomes.

Some of the character traits to be cultivated should encompass the following: *One,* our everyday moments should help provide practical strategies in self-care so that such important reminders and techniques will enable us get rooted in the present because of the sanctity of life. *Two,* we need to demonstrate leadership by example and also learn to cultivate resilience based on desired expectations. Bearing in mind that everyone is unique and so be mindful to mitigate the effects of bad character. *Last,* investment in education has proved to be sustainable because no one can take it away from you. Educational certificates and credentials cannot be bequeathed to children but the knowledge I share here will outlive me. This Chapter will be discussed along the lines of: (1) Classics, (2) Problem-solving, (3) Value-addition, (4) Professional, (5) Global, (6) Peoples skills, and (7) Other experiences. Readers may refresh their memories regarding some of these areas of interest in my other professional books.

MERRY-GO-ROUND

I have been involved in different areas over the years but I have to state that the accounting specialization has been the pivot upon which the wheels of most of my experiences have rotated. As a result, the complexities of accounting as a discipline revolves around many knowledge frontiers or boundaries. The definition of accounting should be stretched to mean an embodiment of the core accounting areas, including: taxation and fiscal policy, auditing and assurance, cost and management accounting, forensic accounting, governmental accounting; as well as, other business environment and concepts areas such as statistics, economics, management science, business ethics, organizational behavior and management, and business policy. Other related areas are finance courses covering business finance, corporate finance, investment management, international financial management, personal finance, and investment analysis. Typically, accountants go through most of these subjects in their training, no matter how they are designed and categorized. Readers may refresh their memories regarding some of these areas of interest in my other professional books.

ACCOUNTING

In the proceeding chapters, I have outlined my journey into accountancy field and that has exposed me to accounting practice. At the time I received a word of knowledge from my bosom friend and cousin- Emmanuel on God's call for me into accountancy, I took the message with a pinch of salt. The period was characterized by a spate of embezzlements by bursars of our Secondary Schools and Training Colleges in Ghana.

Against the background that I am more qualitatively endowed than quantitatively. With time, I have come to accept accountancy as a calling and so I seek ways to add value to any situation that I am presented with. President Robert Mugabe has said that: "*if you do not fulfil your purpose in life, others will employ you to fulfil theirs*" Consequently, it is imperative that one's purpose in life is identified early so that precious life will not be wasted. Dear reader, my question to you is: *Have you identified your purpose in life?* If you have not identified your purpose in life; then, it is not too late to ask yourself: *Why am I here?*

I began accountancy with my relationship with the Trans-World Tutorial College, involving economic, book-keeping and accounts. Likewise, the Secondary schools I attended emphasized business courses including accounting, economics, commerce, business methods, and office practice. I did not take typing in the High School because my school did not offer the course. At the sixth-form level, I offered accounting, economics, geography, and general paper. I offered accounting as a common subject between Emmanuel and I so we can compare notes and solve problems together. I once upon a time applied to Institute of Professional Studies (IPS) for the Institute of Chartered Accountants of Ghana (ICAG) program but I did not get sponsorship from my employers (Ghana Internal Revenue Service) so

I had to abandon the plan in favor of private preparation in sitting for the professional examinations.

On three occasions I applied to University of Ghana Business School (UGBS) for the MBA (Accounting Concentration) program. I have gone further to complete an: (a) Undergraduate program with the help of my family (extended family); (b) Master's degree with support from family and friends, as well as self-financing; (c) Doctoral program with assistance from student loans and family; (d) Professional certifications with the help of family and self-support; (e) the Ghana Stock Exchange (GSE) course I attended was sponsored by my employer (IRS); as well as, participation in (f) workshops, seminars, conferences, and training sponsored by different employers, the Ghana Co-operative Credit Unions Association (CUA) Limited, the Church of Pentecost, and many more.

After my undergraduate studies, I interviewed for the following organizations: the Public Services Commission for entry into the Ghana Civil Service, the Electricity Company of Ghana (ECG), the Volta River Authority (VRA), the Ghana Commercial Bank (GCB) Limited, and the Internal Revenue Service (IRS). I was offered a job at the Internal Revenue Service; first, spent three months in Accra for orientation and then to Cape Coast for over 5 years. Back to Accra, my transfer to the Legon District Office was changed to the Kinbu District Office because the accountant I was to replace had requested for additional days to attend to some pressing personal issues. The Kinbu Office was later remodeled into the Large Taxpayers Office (LTO) in response to the recommendation of the Bretton-Woods institutions. The LTO concept allowed for specialized tax assessments and collection to be concentrated in one unit to account for over 60 percent of taxes at a lower cost; while the rest of the tax offices cover lots of grounds.

By way of synthesis, the accounting career has taken me through several organizations, including-Albert Academy Limited, Pomadze

Poultry Enterprises Limited (POMAPEL), CTI-Tech Limited, the Church of Pentecost (COP) U.S.A., Inc, Osei Kwabena and Associates (OK&A-Chartered Accountant), Internal Revenue Service (IRS, Ghana), Premier Resource Management Limited, Institute of Professional Studies (IPS, Ghana), and the Youth Connection Charter School (YCCS).

At the Albert Academy, the owner was Mr. Albert Nsiah (deceased). The few names I remember are- Ms. Augustina Amponsah Mensah, Mrs. Brantie, Mr. Benard Ahwireng, Mr. Agbey, and headmasters and tutors. I taught business related subjects for a little while between my second-year national service and my full-time employment. As I explained elsewhere, accounting is involved in four phases, as follows: (i) transactions finding, (ii) transactions recording, (iii) transactions analyses, and (iv) transactions reporting. While transactions finding and recording are book-keeping functions of the profession; the transaction analysis and reporting components are the accounting functions of the profession. I have applied accounting theory and practice in the following areas: events organization, fund raising, business process outsourcing, effective tax assessment, tax auditing, and optimal collection; auditing of occupational groups and entities such as hotels, and transport operators; as well as, writing and implementation of accounting manuals.

CLASSICS

My parents explored a number of vocations and occupations at different points in times; and as I indicated above, I found myself involved in a number of activities as a way of helping my parents and also generating income for myself. I will highlight briefly eight of them in this section of the book, as follows: tomatoes selling, fish selling, kenkey selling, shoe polishing, maize selling; as well as, farming (both arable and poultry), and preparation of beverage for sale. **Arable farming**-I am told my paternal grandmother was very industrious and had a lot of farmlands. When I was in the Secondary School, I asked my father for a portion of land for farming. I planted maize and harvested a few maxi-bags of maize in 1980. I remember I bought some items for school, including the buying of my first accounting book, authored by Frank Wood (Volume 1) from the proceeds of the farm produce. I remember one of my elder sisters and another woman in the local church bought a maxi-bag of maize each on credit but never paid up. Based on the farming success story, I contracted a loan from my mother to expand my farm targeting about 12 to 15 maxi-bag of maize. The season co-incided with the 1983 draught and I harvested only about three or four American tins of maize. That was a great disappointment. I have not gone back to farming after this experience and I have rather focused on education.

Beverage-The beverage preparation for sale was a one-off project in response to a National Convention of the Ghana Apostolic Church held in Mampong-Ashanti, Ghana. The convention grounds were near the location of my father's kiosk in the current Mampong-Ashanti Lorry Station. The place used to be called *Bodey* but now it is the *Main Lorry Station* for Mampong Ashanti. While my sister Miriam fried *kelewele* (fried chopped ripped plantain) for sale, I prepared beverage for the convention participants who came for tea, Milo, coffee, and cocoa after and during the convention. I prepared the beverage in the mornings and the evenings.

At the end of the convention, I made a profit of ¢30, which I used to open a Post Office Savings Bank accounts. Initially, the Mampong Post Office was reluctant to open the account for me because they were not sure of how I made the money. I sought reference from my uncle (Seth Addai), whose official quarters was just opposite the Post Office and also known to the Post Office staff. The savings account was opened for me and a saving account passbook was issued to me. I developed the savings culture by depositing small sums of money I get from time to time into this account. The account offered me the opportunity of withdrawing a set limit at any post office in Ghana. Amounts above the limited threshold could only be withdrawn in the Kumasi General Post Office or any branch of the National Savings and Credit Bank (Later become the SG-SSB). Consequently, the account was useful to me when I was in the High School. I deposited my school maintenance monies into the account and made withdrawals when the need arose.

Fish Selling-You would recall that my mother was a fish seller and so I helped her in the fish business by carrying the inventory or stock-in-trade to the market before going to school. Later on, my mother acquired a truck for conveying her stock in trade to and from the market. Occasionally, we went through the neighborhood selling fish such as herrings on wooden trays. As will be expected, my mother provided me an opportunity to make profit from fish selling. By this, she bought a basket or two of herrings for me during the main season and assigned me the cost to be covered, such that every extra amount constituted profit for me. Out the profits some shirts and other items were bought for me. This was win-win for all of us.

Kenkey Selling- My involvement in kenkey selling will be discussed in a *two-fold* fashion as follows: **first,** some native Gas used to rent a room in our house and they prepared kenkey for sale with fried fish and hot pepper (sauce). Initially, it was Auntie Adisa (not real name), who started the business. I helped her by carrying the pepper, *shitto* (a kind of hot source), and fried fish on a metal tray and she carried the boiled kenkey. We passed through the Mampong township to the Saint Monica's Secondary and Training College. I remember Auntie Adisa did not like selling along the route until she gets to the destination. With the passage of time, I accompanied the truck pushers carrying the pans of kenkey and in the middle of the journey she will pass us in a taxi (cab) and direct us to the part of Saint Monica's compound where to meet her. I did not charge for the *service*, however, I got kenkey and fish to eat anytime I wanted. Along the line, she was joined by the sister and children. I was no longer involved in the kenkey business of Auntie Adisa.

Second, long after Auntie Adisa and family were gone, my parents harvested a lot of maxi-bags of maize from one of our farms. A decision was made to prepare kenkey for sale from the farm produce. The kenkey selling component of the strategy fell on my sister (Freda) and myself. While my sister sold the kenkey in the Mampong market, I sold the kenkey in the Zongoland and ended up at the Mampong Maternity Hospital. I have come to know the entire process of preparing *Ga*-kenkey.

Maize Selling- This was also a one-off activity to allow for me to sell some of our farm produce on the Yeji market. The town of Yeji is in the Brong-Ahafo region of Ghana and located on the Volta river in Ghana. The participants of the market lived around the fishing communities of the Volta river. I saw at first sight, the *barter system* in action. Traders exchanged items like clothes, Kerosene, and many more for assortment of fishes. I sold the maize in tins used for measurement called either *American* tin or *Olunka or Muru*. Each maxi-bag of maize contained 40 tins. It was more profitable to sell in tins than to sell in maxi-bags. The trading caused me to stay overnight but I had to sleep on a jute bag in the open market. Typically, several traders slept in the market but some were quite prepared so they brought some clothes to stretch on the bare floor and another to cover themselves. By the following morning there was evidence of mosquito bites all over my face.

Shoe (Shine) Polishing-I joined our pastor's son called Oteng (name withheld) in this enterprise. The business was carried out on Saturdays. I carried the Shoe Shine Box (SSB) and also announced from time to time-*Yes, Shine Yes*. Usually, we started from one place such as the Saint Andrews Training College or the Amaniampong Secondary School (one end of the continuum) and ended at another end of the spectrum (Saint Monica's Secondary and the Training College). In-between these schools, we polished shoes, sandals, and traditional sandals. My involvement was limited to roles given me by Oteng. After a hard day's work, I will be treated by Oteng at the Ebony Restaurant at the center of the town. I quite remember Oteng requested fork and spoon (*ma me fookoo ne atere*). Any time I got home; I was not interested in eating because I was full. One day, my mother asked me, and I told her Oteng takes me to the restaurant. Little did I know that our mothers were comparing notes because Oteng was also not sending any money home. We spent the money at the restaurant every Saturday. Later, when his father was transferred to the Eastern region, I took up the Shoeshine business for a while before ending it.

Tomato Selling-My mother dealt in tomatoes during the lean season for fish business. Again, my mother's cousin and her friend, and bosom friend were all dealers in tomatoes; except that they dealt on a large scale in boxes from Ejura to Kumasi and other parts of Ghana. My mother requested for a box or two for me to sell in the Mampong-Ashanti market utilizing a big wooden tray (apampah). Surprisingly, my major customer was the daughter of the woman who operated the Ebony Restaurant I used to visit with Oteng. Some of my classmates also patronized the tomato I sold. I remember one of my middle school classmates used to buy a lot from me.

PROBLEM-SOLVING

In the preceding section, I talked about my classical experience and in this section, the discussion will be focused on problem-solving experience. The problem-solving experience will be presented to include my experience in consulting and investigation.

CONSULTING

I continue to look for opportunities in consulting area because my interest in consultancy is borne out of the blend on knowledge and experience in this market place. My professional services revolve around the following areas-(1) Professional audit, (2) Taxation, (3) Accounting services, (4) Internal audit outsourcing, (5) Finance, accounting, and tax training services; (6) Business support; as well as, (7) Others, including: (i) Customer care strategy, (ii) Business planning, (iii) Budgeting and vouchering, (iv) Resource audit, (v) Internal control projects, (vi) Special financial audit, (vii) Preparation of manuals-operational and financial, (viii) Review of internal controls, (ix) Financial management training, (x) Valuation of assets and audit of fixed assets register, (xi) Managing delinquent loans, and so on.

In this area of competence, professionalism is duly blended with scholarship to deliver expert solutions to practical and theoretical problems. By this arrangements, every education and practical experience tends to be critical; using the system theory anchored on-"The whole is greater than the sum of its parts". My association with the SMME Consult in Ghana has been a springboard of success. For me, consultancy is a problem-solving undertaking based on desired outcomes. I worked with my good friend to prepare the books of accounts, culminating into the preparation of the first Financial statements and Budget statements for the Council of a Faith-based university in Ghana. The first accounts of the university were created from the source documents covering redeemed pledges and foundations from membership of the orthodox church across Ghana. The writing of business plans, a course component I taught to graduate students in finance; as well as, the writing of business policy and manuals will continue to engage my attention.

INVESTIGATION

I continue to look of practical opportunities in financial and forensic investigation. I have undertaken three major investigations for the Church of Pentecost in the United States of America, as follows: (I) One for the Office of the Chairman the Church of Pentecost, (II) another for the Office of the National head of the Church of Pentecost U.S.A, Inc.; and (III) for the Office of the Regional head-Chicago region. The above assignments were executed as part of my inclusion in the National and Regional Audit Committees of the Church. Typically, investigations begin from the initial prediction from the terms of reference or instrument of engagement. The methodology is involved with utilizing research tools, auditing methods, evidence gathering protocols to emerging themes to arrive at a conclusion for each specific allegation. The evidence gathered should support the conclusion, which could be any of these: (a) substantiated, or (b) unsubstantiated, or (c) insufficient evidence or indeterminate.

PROFESSIONAL

In the preceding section, I discussed my problem-solving experience. In this section, my concentration will be professional exposure. The professional experience will be explained to encompass taxation and fiscal policy, auditing and assurance, and forensic accounting.

TAXATION AND FISCAL POLICY

My experience in taxation has been varied. I trace my taxation and fiscal policy exposure to my employment with the Ghana Internal Revenue Service (IRS) in 1991. I spent three months at the Internal Revenue Service Headquarters as part of my orientation exercise and the following are some of the people I associated with: Messrs- Bruce Tusah and Edward Bannerman (all Chief Inspector of Taxes-Accounts); In Room 320 we had the following-Messrs-Christian, Wornyo (Togbi Botuvor), Joseph Ablor Adjei, Yaw Appaa, Sammy Grupone, Adade, Owusu Sekyere, and Kojo Peter Pieterson. In the Budget Unit, we had Messrs-Justice Kpentey (deceased), Banahene, and Miss Grace Bampoe. Others in the accounting departments included: Comfort and Brian Addo (Petty cashiers), Mrs. Rita Asabere (affectionately called Mrs. Paa Akwasi), Mr. Billings (Check Writer), Okpoti (deceased) and Berkoh (Salaries Unit), Mrs. Tina Appiah, and Mrs. Winnifred Adu Brobbey, and Mrs. Veronica Abankroh. In the Revenue Unit, we had Messrs-Yaw Adu, Boateng, Opare, and many more.

Prior to that point, I had studied taxation as part of the courses leading the award of my bachelor's degree with a concentration in accounting in 1989. At the Large Taxpayers Office (LTO), I worked with the following persons in the Accounts Unit: Messrs-E. S. Ansah, Agbanyoh, and Lawson; as well as, Mrs. Dzifa Ayivoh, Mrs. Ruby Armah, Miss Margaret Adjetey (Chief Cashier), Mrs. Monica Osei, Miss Elizabeth Jiagge, Miss Cynthia Okertchire, Miss Pamala Obuobi, Miss Bernice Abban Tagoe, and Miss Silvia Ewool. In Cape Coast, my accounting staff comprised the following: Messrs Moffatt Haizel, Peter Abaka Davis, Francis Gaddah (Cape Coast and Mankessim), Frederick Latzoo, Miss Mary Dankwah-Smith, Miss Hope Lartey (Mankessim Sub-Office), and Miss Mercy Amparbeng (Mrs. Lamptey). Beyond the accounting department, other staff I worked with in the Cape Coast office were-Mr. Emmanuel K. Nyamordey and Joseph K. Esssandoh (all Assistant Commissioners); Messrs- Acquah, Patrick Deamesi, and Yaw Afram (Wofa Yaw), all Chief Inspector of Taxes), Messrs-Atandah, E.A. Sackey, Atta Amonoo, Yahya Mohammed, Kenneth Okine, John Mensah (deceased), Clement Azu, George Quainoo, Isaac Nyarkoh, Acquaah, Joseph Amparbeng (Regional Accountant), Ato

Yankson, Harrison Baidoo, Nartey (deceased); Messrs-Ekow Tanfo, Asare, John Essel (all drivers); Messrs- Ali Grunshie, Kojo Forson, and Aghana Etieme. Others include: Miss Rebecca Acquah, Miss Charlotte Twintoh, Faustina, Agnes Aidoo (deceased), and Lilian.

While working with the IRS, I pursued a professional certification in taxation with the Ghana Institute of Taxation (now Chartered Institute of Taxation). In Ghana, I taught taxation courses at the Ghana Institute of Professional Studies (now University of Professional Studies, Accra-UPSA), as follows: (1) Taxation I and Taxation II to accounting majors at the undergraduate level; (2) Advanced taxation and fiscal policies to accounting and auditing students at the School of Research and Graduate Studies (SORAGS); (3) Taxation and Advanced taxation and tax planning to professional ICAG students.

The specific projects I was involved in encompassed the following: (a) payroll audits, (b) tax education, Occupational Groups audits covering The Ghana Private Road Transport Union (GPRTU) of Trades Union Congress (TUC), Co-operative distillers, and hotels. Under the auspices of Commonwealth Association of Tax Administrators (CATA), I was in the group in the Central region of the IRS that hosted the tourism component of the CATA conference held in Ghana while I was in Cape Coast. The delegation was treated to a tour of the Elmina Castle, Kakum National Park for ecotourism, and Hans Cottage Botel for crocodiles in a pond. I attended regional meetings at different times in Agona Swedru, Assin Fosu, Dunkwa-On-Offin (all in the Central region of Ghana). I hosted tax auditors, tax examiners, internal, and external auditors (Ghana Audit Service). I also liaised with staff of the Bank of Ghana such as Messrs-Millison Narh, Atta Poku, and cashiers; as well as, staff of the Ghana Commercial Bank in both Cape coast and Accra (Ghana).

My daily involvement with taxpayers centered on endorsement of checks for payment. I resigned from the Internal Revenue Service per my letter LTC 8244 of September 1, 2001, with effect from October 1, 2001 and the Commissioner accepted my resignation per his letter C.8244 of October 8, 2001. In the United States of America, I have taught Federal taxation of the individual at the graduate level. I have attended several workshops, seminars, and conferences on taxation; and also authored a few articles for professional magazines or journals in Ghana. Beyond that, my Master's research work was on taxation. I have written a research-based book on the development of taxation in Ghana, covering 75 years, as of 2018. My interest in taxation and fiscal policy is linked to research, policies and strategies.

AUDITING AND ASSURANCES

I have learned auditing and assurances in all my accounting programs at both academic and professional levels and so auditing is ingrained in me so to speak. I worked with Osei Kwabena and Associates (firm of Chartered Accountants). Mr. Paul Osei Kwabena was the Managing Partner, Mr. Aning was the associate partner. The other accounting and auditing staff were-Messrs- Michael Genego, Sackitey, Ernest Appau, Asamoah, Bilson, Hagan, James, and Niboh. Others were-Mrs. Mary Boafo (Front Office) and Caroline (Back Office), Esi, Salomey, Bridget, Mariam (Intern from Guinea). I also served on the Supervisory Committee (Internal Audit) of the Ghana Co-operative Credit Unions Association (CUA) Limited for six years; incrementally, as member, secretary, and chairman. Each of these offices offered different perspectives within the context of financial co-operatives.

I have been involved with the SMME Consult, auditing some National Health Insurance Scheme (NHIS) in Ghana and other entities. In the Unites States of America, I have been teaching Advanced Auditing at the Graduate level since 2015 on a consistent basis. I have also served as a member of the National Audit Committee of the Church of Pentecost U.S.A., Inc from 2015 to date. I have also been serving as a member of the Chicago Regional Audit Committee from 2013 and as chairman from 2018 to date.

Today, the concept of auditing has become an important component of financial stewardship and accountability in the church. The greatest challenge is in regards to bank reconciliation statements preparation and review, budgeting and budgetary controls, supervision of staff, and capacity to handle disagreements. While fieldwork is crucial, yet the art of report writing has become very demanding on professional auditors. By default, most accountants are quantitative and so writing skills tends to be hugely important.

I argue for auditors to seek collaboration with other professionals such as lawyers, valuers, IT specialists, and engineers in specialized engagements to be solid. Technology has become an emerging trend in auditing now so all prospective auditors and accountants should develop competencies in this area; plus, the advisory functions which cannot be easily done by machines.

FORENSIC ACCOUNTING

Forensic accounting is the application of auditing methodologies to financial accounting data for the use of the Courts. Forensic accountants should be well versed in accounting and auditing theories and practice to be successful. Nevertheless, suggestions and inputs from the legal profession will make the output more robust. My doctoral research covered fraud detection and accounting education. Beyond that, I have written a book **on *fraud prevention and detection puzzle: skills, strategies, competences, and programs** b*ased on variables provided by my 12 research participants' responses to key research questions. I seek more opportunities in this area to apply the concepts I have learned to test.

VALUE-ADDITION

My value-added experiences will be treated in this section. You would recall that in the preceding section, my focus was on my professional experiences. The value-additional experiences will revolve around the following-mentorship, teaching, writing and research, and service to humanity.

MENTORSHIP

I find mentorship rewarding because of the direct touch on peoples' lives. Some of the people I have mentored are not personally known to me. I have mentored a lot of people in my capacity as Sunday school teacher in the church. Additionally, while in the university or college, some of the then High School students in my local church informed me that I have become their mentors. I assisted one of them in looking for a school. I visited some of them in the boarding house during visitors' hours, eating *gari soakings* (mixture of cuscus, sugar, milk, and water) with them. Notably, two are apostle of the Church of Pentecost. To God be the glory!

Surprisingly, I did not know that several of the students I thought at the undergraduate, professional, and graduate levels viewed me as their mentor. I got to know after teaching them and the feedback I received from some of them. Others reached out to me via Social media-LinkedIn. For the sake of self-disclosure, I am not a fun of Social Media. As a head of department, I helped a lot of my students navigate their withdrawal process from school for not meeting the minimum Grade Point Average (GPA). In this section, I present a few of the messages I have received from people: **One,**

Hi, I would like advice from Accounting, Audit and finance experts. I have strong interest in those fields and I aim to become professional accountant.

I now have BCOM. Thinking of furthering with either ICA or ACCA Please help me with your expert advice to choose between ICA and ACCA (Mentee B, Personal Communication, June 6,2018).

Two, this email excepts is a response I sent to one of the students I taught and also supervised their Group Project at the undergraduate level:

> *Hello Student 1: I hope this email finds you doing great this morning. I will be delighted to provide you with the reference you need for the master's program. Kindly send me copies of the following:(a) resume or CV, (b) transcripts of academic record, and a personal statement...* (Student 1, Personal Communication).

I responded to his request for a reference for his Master's program. I want to report that Student 1 has successfully informed me of his completion of his Master's program. I have confidence in Student 1 that he can survive a rigorous doctoral work. Student 1: *Thank you Dr. Please I have finished with the MSC Accounting and Finance and I graduated last year November. I am very grateful for your assistance. May God richly bless you Dr.* **Three,** I am humbled by the gesture of Mentee A for considering me as a mentor. He stated as follows: *Hello Sir, I just viewed your profile.... Wawooo you are a learned Man...God bless u more... Will take u as my mentor. Thank you. My regards* (Mentee A, Personal Communication, March 30, 2017).

I continue to seek opportunities in making peoples' lives better than myself. In this I find fulfillment and accomplishment of purpose.

WRITING AND RESEARCH

While writing came to me naturally, research was learned with intentionality. I contend that writing goes *hand–in–hand* with research.

My writing skills have been developed over the years throughout my academic and professional journeys; especially, the transition from British English Language to the American English or Language Art. While some of the variations are quite obvious, others are not; professional writing tends to be very close. For example, the British English uses-*learnt* but the American equivalent is *learned*. In America, we say the phone is *busy*, but the phone is *engaged* is the alternative for British English.

The obvious one is the omission of the letter 'U' from the following words-neighbor, favor, savior, and so on. As someone, who had spent considerable learning years in Africa, the American accent becomes another interesting issue; but the good news is that there is no accent issue regarding written English. Again, the concept of accent is also relative; and for that reason, those who speak English not based on the British are also considered as having accent. Another difference is the phrase- "I like for you to..." Likewise, there are variations in terminologies such as a pair of trousers (pants), boot of car (trunk), Camphor (mouth bubbles), cross-country vehicle (SUV), and many more.

My research acumen has come as a result of my doctoral studies and prior research components of both academic and professional studies. My competencies in research has been developed to permit me to analyze any research document to sift the important information from the scholarly databases. I find research very interesting and in sighting. I will call on policy makers to spend some quality time to appreciate the most current knowledge from research. Additionally, the results of research should not be left to gather dust because some practical ways of addressing problems are available in research findings. Likewise, organizations should sponsor research into aspects of their operations to confront what is unknown. The key is to read critically research outputs with a view to finding the gaps in literature proposed for future research. Moreover, research conducted in one area can be replicated in another area to test the findings and to also expand the population and sample size to confirm or disconfirm the generalization associated with the study.

My interest in research and writing has been focused on writing textbooks and also supporting a few through the dissertation process on topics of interest. Unlike peer-reviewed journal materials which has a lot of reviewers because of promotion-related consideration; the problem I have come across in the writing of books is getting other people in the area to review for quality assurance (a kind of peer review). To me life is not about promotion through fair and foul means but staying on purpose of life.

I want to repeat my call to ministers in general and those in the Church of Pentecost in the United States of America in particular, to write at least a book in the course of active ministry. The proceeds from book publication can support their personal retirement plans. The book can be based on a sermon topic or specific experience in ministry. I remember having conversation with one of our retired ministers about the consideration of writing a book and I went ahead to suggest an area to him because I knew him personally and what he brings to the table on the topic; but he told me he was tired. At times, when I listen to expositions by some of the retired ministers and come to think of those who have been lost through death in the past. I wonder the wealth of knowledge that has not been passed on to the younger generation. I know in recent time several ministers are writing and I applaud them for that. The contents of their books will out-live them and their ministry will go beyond the geographical delimitation of their oversight.

TEACHING

Per Professor Aheto, the best testimonial of the teacher is his or her students. I still remember teachers who have made significant impact in my life. Such memories live on for a long time. I received the gift of teaching as a grace gift from God. As I said elsewhere, a young lady in my local church had identified this gift which I did not recognize at the time. Prior to this encounter, I had explained the encounter I had at the PENSA conference in Aburi. You may refresh your memory on the chapter on faith, foundation, and focus. I started teaching the Children ministry (Sunday School) of my local churches (Mampong-Ashanti, Madina West, and SSNIT Flat assemblies).

I actually went into teaching in response to major change in my personal circumstances. I have taught an estimated 1,000 students in Ghana comprising of 50 professional students [Institute of Chartered Accountants Ghana (ICAG), Chartered Institute of Management Accountants (CIMA), Association of Chartered Certified Accountants (ACCA), Institute of Chartered Secretaries and Administrators (ICSA)], 150 graduate students (accounting and auditing), and 800 undergraduate students (mostly junior (Level 300) and senior (Level 400) classes in accounting and an elective class to other business students). As of August 31, 2020, the number of students I have taught in the USA is about 250, mainly graduate students in the following courses: Advanced Auditing, Capital budgeting and financing, and Federal taxation of individual.

Some of the names of the individuals I worked with while in the employment of the Ghana Institute of Professional Studies (now University of Professional Studies, Accra) are provided in table 7 below:

Table 7: *Some of the Staff of Ghana Institute of Professional Studies*			
1	Fr. J.J.M. Martey (Director/Rector)	2	W. B Dapaah(Registrar)
3	Professor Joshua Alabi (Rector/VC)	4	Dr. Seidu Mustapha (Registrar)
5	Sylvester Mensah	6	Professor Anthony Ahiawordji
7	E. J. Attipoe (Esq)	8	Joseph K. Antwi (Director of Finance)

9	Gerald Dapaah-Gyamfi	10	Stephen T. Akrobor
11	Elijah Mensa (Librarian)	12	Justice Ampiah (Assistant Director)
13	George Quartey	14	Daniel Bukari
15	Oko Abednego Feehi Martey	16	Charles Barnoh
17	Frederick Doe	18	Mawuli Fegloh
19	Kwaku Mensah Mawutor	20	Ezra Alabi-Borqyaye
21	Nicholas Adjei	22	Florence Dei Bediakoh
23	Albert Puni	24	Stephen Acheampong
25	Bediako	26	Amoh Bediakoh
27	Agyen Asamoah Agyapong(deceased)	28	Joseph Harrison (Adjunct)
29	Rufus Mensah	30	Vincent Sapaku (Adjunct)
31	T.K. Kankam	32	Kwadwo Obeng
33	Mrs. Ward Brew	34	Jennifer Hammond Eshun
35	Dr. Kwame Aveh	36	Edward Bannerman Wood
37	Edward Odjidjah	38	Samuel Larbi
39	Philomena Dadzie	40	Theodore Tetteh (B4B4)
41	Ampem Darko Aniapam	42	Veronica Chaway
43	Reverend Mrs. Dr. Goski Alabi	44	L.O. Sakyiamah
45	John Bosco Danyang	46	Celestine Nudanuh
47	Samuel Batchison Offei	48	Solomon D. Akrong
49	Peace Mawoyo	50	Vivian Amoakoh
51	Mary Naana Essiaw	52	Ayernoh
53	Brian Senyoh Akrong	54	Asare
55	Mrs. Helen Akorful	56	Koranteng
57	Godwine Adagewine(Esq)	58	Agbenyoh
59	James Ami-Nahr	60	Afedzie
61	Richard Quasigah	62	James Fosu
63	Elvis Afriyie Ankrah	64	Atuam (Internal Auditor)
65	Harunah Iddrissu (Esq)	66	Patience Abindaw
67	Raymond Dziwornu	68	
	...and many more		

Source: *Created from memory as of December 31, 2011*

NOTE/ *Some of the people listed above have completed their terminal degrees and there has been changes to the designation of a few.*

UPSA-Update

A review of the 2019 Annual Report of the University of Professional Studies, Accra (UPSA) shows that some faculty and staff have gone ahead to acquire terminal degrees, including the following:

- Dr. Stephen Teye Akrobor
- Dr. Mrs. Philomena Dadzie
- Dr. John Kwaku Mensah Mawutor
- Dr. Raymond Dziwornu
- Dr. Mrs. Helen K. Arkoful
- Dr. Kwadwo Obeng
- Dr. Mrs. Mary Naana Essiaw
- Professor Charles Barnor
- Dr. Ampem Darko Aniapam
- Dr. Mrs. Vivian Amoako
- Dr. Edward Bannerman Woode
- Dr. Fredrick Doe
- Dr. Anthony Sumnaya Kumassey
- Dr. John Bosco Damnyag
- Dr. Harriet Lamptey
- Dr. Edwin Ayernor
- Dr. Ibrahim Mohammed
- Dr. Gerald Dapaa Gyamfi
- Dr. Aku Shika Andoh
- Dr. George Agbemebiase
- Professor Albert Puni
- Dr. Redeemer A. Y. Krah

(Source: *2019 Annual Report, 2020*, Public Affairs Directorate, University of Professional Studies, Accra, pages 399)

I have attended several workshops, seminars, and conferences to develop me as a better teacher. Keep in mind that I entered the teaching profession with academic and professional qualification and experience in accounting. I did not have any knowledge in education but I have studied a lot *on-the-job*. I was intentionally taught how to prepare course outline, the skills of setting questions for all levels, development of a marking scheme, and practical sessions on grading.

I share some generational impact messages with readers, as follows: *In the first place*, Student 2 elaborated:

Dear Sir,

My name is Student 2, your former student in the Accounting class of 2011. Although not necessary, but let me add that I was the student you...Please sir I know many of your present and past students might have told you this before and on several occasion, but I believe you can't be tired of hearing the same thing over and over again. The truth is that, sir you are an outstanding lecturer. I am never surprise whenever we meet as a year badge whiles on campus and now out of campus and your name emerges unanimously during our discussions as the most admirable and best lecturer, we met during our four-year studies in ...

This conclusion it will interest you to know Sir was made after considering your unique features as a lecturer. Some of this include: your level of commitment, punctuality, discipline, your ability to understand the non-verbal communication signals of your students to give them some short brake whenever necessary, your lecturing methodology which always make it easier for almost all your students to understand you, and above all how you always go beyond the books to appeal to our conscience to be useful citizens to bring the needed change to our society. As a Christian, I saw you running a complete ministry in your lecturing.

Sir, I might not be able to communicate clearly what I want to say but the truth is that you have affected most of us beyond the lecture notes. Your life style was something some of us have also leant from. I saw in you one who know what he is doing and love doing it. One who could not be distracted by corporate politics and always ready to do what he is paid to do. Sir if I may be right, I saw in you one who first love the job before the money.

I don't know what your previous and current students, as well as the management of the ...say about your performance, I can confidently say that you have made an indelible impact in the life of most of us in the 2011 Bsc. Accounting class.

Sir let me proudly say that in whatever field I may find myself, I will crave to surpass you in all the good I saw in you whiles on campus. You have affected my life positively with your work style beyond what I can describe. Whenever I remember you and your work, I get a better demonstration of this scripture (Mathew 5:16).

The good Lord bless you sir that you will continue to be a blessing to the many more generations who will be meeting you in the years to come.

Yours faithfully,
Your former student

(Student 2, Personal Communication, 02/24/2012, 12:13pm).

In the second place, Maxwell's (not real name) message blew my mind, as follows:

"George,

Your kindness brings tears to my eyes and warms my heart. I want to share something with you: I am pursuing my degree to better myself and I am not doing it for a big salary, prestige, status, or even recognition. Knowing I am doing my very best with the minimal resources I have keeps me focused and disciplined. It is easy? No. Nothing good comes easy, and I have my mother and grandparents to thank for that. My wife has been so supportive of my efforts and remains my biggest cheerleader. I want to portray an attitude of the highest professionalism, objectivity, and morality, while being flexible at the same time. I have already been told by many that I am not a young man anymore and the working world is becoming a younger person's realm. I have learned at this point that people's opinions are not facts, and I will continue working toward being the best professional and person I can be. That is something which no job title, salary, or status level can put a price tag on" (Maxwell, Personal Communication, 2019).

In the third place, Mable (not real name) offered the following:

"Professor Appiah-Sokye,

I missed this email that you had sent in December. I apologize for not replying at the time, but I wanted to say thank you for recognizing my effort. I will be taking the … course next semester and graduating with my MS with a concentration in Forensic Accounting. It has been challenging at times juggling work, family life, and school, but the knowledge I have gained has been worth the sacrifice. I have an incredibly *supportive family, who has picked me up when I wasn't sure if I wanted to continue school. <u>I have also had many wonderful professors along the way, so thank you for being one of them</u>"!!* (Mabel, Personal Communication, 2020).

In the fourth place, Student 3 elaborated as follows:

"Mr. Appiah-Sokye was my lecturer in Taxation I and Taxation II when I was an undergraduate in…. His extensive knowledge of tax laws and practice made him an excellent resource for students. His engaging style of lecturing simplified complicated topics and left me with a good grasp of tax practice. He is certainly an asset to any faculty" (Student 3, Personal Communication, May 26, 2016).

In the fifth place, Student 4 stated as follows:

"Dear Mr. Sokye,

I am student 4, a former student of yours at…with index number… I want to thank you so much for your advice, motivation and inspirational words you gave us some 5-7 years ago, in fact to the Glory of God and the words you gave us has brought me this far. I'm now a Chartered Accountant and a member of ICA-Ghana. You were an inspiration to us especially me, your method of teaching, your respect for humanity among others. I get more inspired any time I read your profile at LinkedIn.

I pray the Good Lord grants you joy in whatever you do.

I have no other means to show my appreciation than using this email you included in your Public Sector Accounting handout.

Please I will be glad to hear more advice from you Sir. I really need them.

I pray this mail gets to you.

Thank you sir.

You are my greatest mentor!!" (Student 4, Personal Communication, 04/30/2015).

I want to tell a few stories of interest in my teaching career. One fascinating thing is that students tell their teachers- "I got *A grade* in your paper" but in least desirable grades- "Sir, you gave me *F* grade" Suggesting that better grades are by their efforts but fewer undesirable grades are assigned by the teachers. If I can give *grade F* why not *grade A*? My advice to the younger generation is that such attitudes are part of the unconscious denial of failure; thereby, making the setting of the right tone of success very difficult. If you have failed, admit that and put in strategies for success.

I am going to recount a few things: *first*, **Brilliant but needy student-** Maxwell (not real name) approaches me as the head of department concerning his inability to register for the year because he did not just have the resources to pay the fees. Apparently, the family had sold a property to enable him to pay for his fees in the first year. In the second year, there was no hope in getting the needed funds for registration. I did not have the kind of money to pay for him and the help I could provide him was limited to enforcing the school policy of registration upon payment of 60 percent of the fees before registration.

I directed him to one of the telephony companies that sponsored some students in my department. Unfortunately, that did not work and around the same time, I remembered from knowledge from one of the courses, I was teaching that Members of the Parliament (MPs) of Ghana (Legislature) were allowed to use portions of their MP's Common Fund (Budgetary allocation for Local Governance) in supporting brilliant but needed students in their constituency. Fortunately, the MP of his area, through the District assembly sponsored his education subject to maintaining the right GPA.

Second, **Perseverance pays-** David (not real name) applied for admission for the BSc Accounting program but did not meet the first selection list posted on the board. He came to meet me in my office and I explain to him that once his name was not on the notice board; it meant that he did not meet the selection criteria. I left the office and when I was going out for my lunch break with the dean at the time, we saw that he was following us so we asked him not to follow us. When we returned from the break, he was still waiting in front of the office so I asked of his name. When I got into my office, I pulled a copy of the summary sheet from the admissions office and discovered that he did not have one of the requirements. I called him into my office and confronted him with the missing requirement and he insisted he had that so I asked him to get me a copy of the document, which he did the following day. I noted that the copy of the document in the application package could have gotten missing in the process. At the next academic board meeting, I made a case for him and he was admitted into the program.

Third, **Charity begins at home-** I have had a few students try to influence me in one way or the other. The first one, attempted to register his colleague (a professional student) in the ACCA Course Unit, who had overstayed his vacation in the United Kingdom. This student pulled ¢10,000 (now GH¢1) from his pocket to offer me; and when I asked him what it was for and he said he was giving me for lunch. I rebuked him. The other teachers in the room asked me to report him to the school authorities but I counseled him and let him go. Today, this gentleman is a chartered accountant in Ghana. The second one, was in regard to a lady in the same professional program whom I caught with a falsified result slips intended for registration. When I queried her, she told me the truth that led me to uncover a scheme regarding falsification of result slips for course registration.

Another elderly student booked an appointment to see me and when I met him in the Staff Common Room, I saw uneasiness on his part and when I asked what I could do for him, he handed a white envelope and I asked him what it was for, he said he was just giving me some few *Cedis* to buy petrol (gas). I thanked him for his thoughtfulness and asked him to use the money to support his education because he was a student. I told him that if he finishes school and in future, he wants to give me any gift, I will be willing to consider that. Later on, I got to know that he had failed my paper in the previous year and had to write the current year's paper and the re-sit paper.

Lastly, Teaching opportunity for ICSA students-I remember being assigned a course- Advanced Corporate Financial Management to teach for the ICSA professional program. I had only 1 registered student, who had attempted this course and failed. At the same time, the secretary to the Director of the school was also writing the final part of the ICSA examinations and so when she saw my name on the School's notice board as the assigned teacher for the subject, she approached me with a view to joining the class. I allowed her to join the class and at the end of the period when they took the final examination in the subject, Mr. Asiedu Forson got-*Distinction* and Ms. Hammond had-*Credit.* As might be expected, news got to ICSA students in town that there is a teacher in the Ghana Institute of Professional Students whose students have passed this ICSA paper.

I started getting part time teaching appointment on one-on-one basis. Each session took 2 hours a day for 5 times a week for a total period of 2 months. I helped to prepare some professional ICSA professionals such as: one in CEPS and another in SG-SSB, and a Roman Catholic brother, who came all the way from the Northern Ghana to receive instructions. It is refreshing that I have made little impact in the lives of these professional.

SERVICE TO HUMANITY

In Chapter 20, I will discuss my involvement in the Credit Union concept from the primary society level to the National level in Ghana and so I will not provide a detailed presentation in this section of the book. I served concurrently as the Chairman, Board of Directors of Ghana Internal Revenue Service (IRS) Co-operative Credit Union in Cape Coast and the Greater Accra. I served as the district secretary of the National Service Personnel Association in 1985. My bosom friend (Atakorah) continues to call me secretary to date.

I was called to the office of an elder of The Church of Pentecost both in Ghana and U.S.A. since January 1994. I have recounted some of my experiences in the chapter on faith, foundation and focus. By way of a summary, I have served the church in different capacities-Regional Executive Member, Local Secretary, Presiding Elder (PIWC-Chicago); Elder for Special Duties, Member, District Finance Committee; Member, Regional and National audit committees, Secretary, Retirement Trends Research Committee, Assistant District PENTYEM Leader, Chairman and secretary, Church building foundation stone laying and dedication committees; Secretary, local marriage committee; Assistant District Financial Secretary, Children's ministry teacher, Chairman, Welfare Committees, Bible study teacher; Dean of School of Ministry; Facilitator for workshops, seminars, and conferences, etc.

While working with the Ghana Institute of Professional Studies (GIPS), I have served on several Boards and committees because educational and religious organizations tend to be run on the Committee system based on the collective wisdom of many. I was privilege to serve on the following statutory, as well as, *ad hoc* committees and boards of the University of Professional Studies, Accra (formerly the Ghana Institute of Professional Studies) as follows: **One,** Member, Convocation; Member, Academic Board; Member, Academic Planning Committee; Member, Admissions Committee; Member, and Time Table Committee.

Two, Member, Accounting Faculty Board; Member, Senior Members Disciplinary Committee; Member, Sub-committees on Research and Conference; as well as, Member, Oversight Committee of Business Development Centre. **Lastly,** Chairman, Provident Fund Drafting Committee; Member, Committee on IPSTA joining UTAG; Chairman, Student Hostel Outsourcing Committee; Member, IPS-NAPTEX Course Project on Accounting and Finance; and Exemption from Professional Bodies, etc.

In recognition of my contribution to the development of taxation and fiscal policy in Ghana, I was awarded with a fellowship by the Chartered Institute of Taxation Ghana in August 2011. I received the Credit Union Sterling Management Award by the Internal Revenue Service Credit Union-Cape Coast. A Certificate of Recognition was given to me by the Ghana Co-operative Credit Unions Association (CUA) Limited for my contributions to the Supervisory Committee. In 2014, I received a Leadership Appreciation for Special Skills and Outstanding Leadership Award by the Church of Pentecost U.S.A., Inc-Chicago district.

I continue to look for opportunities to be of service to humanity because giving back to society or humanity is a good inner trait. Society has made tremendous investment in me and I cannot help but to share my knowledge and services for the greater good of mankind.

REGISTRAR OF PENTECOST BIBLICAL SEMINARY

A privilege to serve as the Registrar of the Pentecost Biblical Seminary (PBS), Wayne, New Jersey emerged in July 2020 as part of the efforts needed to develop structures and systems to seek accreditation for the Seminary. Two different levels of accreditation were required, as follows: *One*, accreditation from the State of New Jersey to operate a seminary and *two*, accreditation from the Association of Biblical Higher Education (ABHE). So far, my role has covered the following: proposing designs of Boards and Committees; crafting job descriptions, proposing financial model to support organizational strategy; and initiating the development of policies for the seminary.

PEOPLES

The need for people's skill in this contemporary world has assumed an alarming proportion. Employers are better of engaging workers who have the competence to deal with the human being. Over a long period, machines and technology have replaced most of the technical aspects of the job. However, the complexities of handling the human factor has become paramount.

In the preceding section, I discussed my value-added experiences but in this section of the book, my conversation will be on people's skills. The people's skills to be discussed will cover management and leadership experiences.

MANAGEMENT

Management will be discussed to encompass administration in both hospital and church settings. Theoretically, management is composed of planning, directing, or organizing, decision-making, and controlling. A detailed discussion of these concepts is beyond the scope of this book.

Administration-I have been associated with administration when I worked with the Mampong District Hospital in the Ashanti region of Ghana for my first year of National Service; as well as, my role in finance and administration in the Internal Revenue Service in Cape Coast of the Central region of Ghana. The opportunities offered by this role encompassed the following: report writing, medical reporting, drafting official letters, correspondence, minutes taking for departmental meetings, minuting on documents in files for action, and dispatching and receipts of official letters.

Unlike today where most business correspondence are accomplished through IT systems; in the past, most business correspondence were done through written letters. An interesting issue was in regards to the position of *Higher Executive Officer* (HEO), which I thought was a very high position but I later got to know that it was not as high as I thought. Some human resources functions were included in the administrative roles. I have commented on the finance and accounting roles above. At the Mampong District Hospital, Dr. Asamoah was the Medical Superintendent; Mr. Mathias Apen (Hospital Secretary), Mr. Peter Mensah (Hospital Secretary-Houseman); as well as Messrs.- Owusu, Oppong Mohamed, and other Administration staff. Sister Rose (Matron), Messrs-Agbenyeto (Mechanical Superintendent), Oppong Dankwah (Radiography), Abekoh (Records), Owusu (Biostatistics), Osei (deceased, Welfare); Kwarteng, Seth Addai and Kumah (all of Accounts department).

Church Administration- My involvement in church administration has been related to the Church of Pentecost U.S.A., Inc. in Ghana and the United States of America. I have served as Regional accounts officer in the Chicago region. While Apostle Albert Amoah was the National head of the Church of Pentecost U.S.A., Inc.; Pastors John Kudolf Ansah (Finance and Administration Manager), Ebenezer Dei (National Accountant), Frank Asirifi (Assistant National Accountant); Pastors- Maxwell Kofi Kusi (deceased-Regional head), Mbanyane S. Mhango (Regional secretary), and Elder Albert A. Buabeng (Regional deacon). The Ministers in the Chicago region included-Pastors Mike

Agyemang Amoako (Chicago district), Joseph Frimpong Antwi (Columbus district), Prince Nana Kobi (Cincinnati district), Mbanyane Mhango (Indiana district), and David Brown Ntiamoah (Minnesota district). This was the original Chicago region of the Church of Pentecost U.S.A., Inc. I have also served as presiding elder, elder for special duties, linkage with committees and boards. My experiential learning through faith, foundation, and focus has been expatiated in another chapter of this book. I have been involved in membership database management systems at the local level. Likewise, the church accounting information systems such as *Shelby* and *Quick Books* software; and financial managements systems.

LEADERSHIP TRAINING

I participated and facilitated in seminars, workshops, and training in the church. Other areas of engagement have been in attendance to local, district, regional, and national presbytery meetings. This is part of the governance systems of the Church of Pentecost across the globe. Similarly, appreciation of meeting protocols and decision-making processes. Moreover, I have become a repertoire of church history because of the experiential dimension of church history. I argue that IT platforms should be deployed in the church, including: online and newsletter.

GLOBAL

The world has become a global village within my lifetime. A lot of technological advancements have taken place for the better. Some experiences were alien to Ghana (Africa) when I was growing up but today the story is different. In the above section, I outlined some of my people's experiences but my attempt in this section is to discuss my global experiences for the benefit of all. I will present my global experiences to encompass: property management, fiscal compliance, and Business Process Outsourcing (BPO).

FISCAL COMPLIANCE

The thrust of *fiscal compliance* is the application of regulatory framework to accounting information using auditing techniques to assure compliance with contracts and programs. In the process, policy is amplified through budgeting, and budgetary controls or variance analysis; emphasizing budgets, actuals, year-to-date numbers, and many more. The compliance component is focused on laws, policies, procedures, contracts, and programs. Additionally, the *vouchering* system is associated with fiscal compliance in the Unites States of America as compared to the *returns* system in Ghana.

Auditing of vouchers is also involved with fiscal compliance, culminating into the issue of audit review or finding sheet to document and report deficiencies and deletions. While accounting theory is the same across businesses, accounting practice varies; and as a consequence, opportunity is provided to appreciate the different practices in different organizations across varied campus partners, funds, campus affiliates, and head office. I have been privileged to utilize accounting software such as *FundEz* and Enterprise Resource Planning (ERP). The table 8 below shows the names of the YCCS family:

Table 8: *The Staff of the Youth Connection Charter School*			
1	Sheila Venson (Executive Director)	2	Larry Vaughn (Assistant Director)
3	Gersome Carrera	4	Linda Goodwin
5	Kimberley Hopson	6	Cynthia Levi
7	William Moore	8	Kenneth Morsby
9	Denise Puckett	10	Edwana Rodgers
11	Carmen Cruz Trujillo Mendez	12	Yolanda Thomas

13	Traci Brown	14	Myrel Cooke
15	Lorrain Cruz	16	Erick Malone Kofi
17	Phillip Peterson	18	Lashandra Smith Rayfield
19	Albert A. Buabeng (Controller)	20	Donetta Baxter(Assistant Controller)
21	Carlos Moore	22	Marie Ortiz
23	Yolanda Williams	24	David Hansberry
25	Anthony Rodriguez	26	Jeneen Whitenhill
27	Donna Sante Cote	28	Allen Covert
29	Rosario Donahue	30	Cynthia Hern
31	Lee London	32	Adam Turry
33	Angela Ballard	34	Martha Franco
35	Sandy Sanchez	36	Kathie Davis
37	Qulanda McClendon Lacy	38	Lilian Mata
39	Doris Whittman	40	Earlene Giles
41	Kendall Martin	42	Edward Morrow
43	Richard Brough	44	Alex Cruz
45	Jessica Mata	46	Cliff Rallins
	PRINCIPALS OF AFFILIATED SCHIOOLS		
47	Irma Plaxico	48	Dionne Kirksey
49	Earl King	50	Lorrain Cruz
	...and many more		
Source: *Created from Staff Directory*			

Some people had left the employment of YCCS over the period, and they include- Earlene Giles, Raul Giles, Mary Hope Mueller (Comptroller), Mushuska Matthews, Jonte Banks, Quinn, Cynthia Zimmerman, and so on.

At YCCS, I am responsible for fiscal compliance reviews regarding the following contracts of funding sources: SBB/Non-SBB, or Per Capita Tuition Charge (PCTC), or Tuition fund; SGSA or Supplemental Aid (SA); and Facility Supplements. The fiscal persons I interacted with from our campus partners, included the following: Teresa Galvan (Aspira), Lina Joya (Association House), Debra Williams (Austin), P.

Kumar (William Youth Services-Chatham Academy and Campos),
Wanitha Pope (Association of Scholastic Achievement-ASA), CCA
(Emerald Bett, Fany Reyes, and Jan Simpson), Robin Walker (CYDI),
Oscar Argueta (Circle Foundations/ Innovations), Tara Brown (City
Colleges- Olive Harvey and Truman), Jun Suh (Jane Addams), Sharon
Dillion (Sullivan House), Lisa Burnett (Greater West Town), Michael
Dow and Cassandra Watkins (Latino Youth).

Likewise, I acted as fiscal person for the YCCS affiliated campuses
for the Alternative Schools Network (ASN) programs- YES and YS3
(McKinley Lakeside Leadership Academy-MLLA), YS3 and TXX
(Youth Connection Leadership Academy-YCLA), and YS3 for Youth
Progressive Leadership Academy-YPLA). The ASN is headed by Jack
Wuest and other staff includes: Matrice Manuel, Kevin, Veronica
Suarez, and Ken Hoffman; but the fiscal persons were Doreen Plummer
(YS3) and Oscar De Luna and Ramiro Arroro (YES and TXX). The
mentors of these programs include: Joseph Williams and Mosley
Dominique (YS3-MLLA), Danita Allen (YS3-YCLA), Carlos Payne
(YES-MLLA), Eboni Bingham (TXX-YCLA), Teague Maranda
(YS3- YPLA).

PROPERTY MANAGEMENT

I have been privileged to be involved in property management in
Ghana back in the 2000s when I worked for the Premier Resource
Management Limited in Ghana. I had a Managing director who was
well versed in property management in the USA, involving preparation
of tenancy agreements based on square footage; and collection of rental
payments; utility payments, inspection of units, etc.

The source of income for the firm was a percentage of fees collected.
The Premier Resource Management Limited had a few workers,

including-Mr. Alex Asiedu (Managing Director), Messrs-Taah, Joshua Hlordjie; Miss Sylvia Ayittey, and Sybil Larmie (all at the Front Desk).

The accounting functions were concentrated on accounts receivables and payables, relationship with bankers and governmental entities; as well as, revenue recognition, and maintenance aspects of the properties using *make or buy* considerations. The property portfolios under management covered those of companies, individuals such as residential and warehouses. I do not know of any certification programs on property management in Ghana, except the general knowledge from finance, accounting, law and taxation, among others. Contrarily, the USA has certification for property management for practitioners. I can recount a case of one person getting stuck in the lift (elevator) overnight under disturbing circumstance.

BUSINESS PROCESS OUTSOURCING (BPO)

While working with a property management company in Ghana, an associate company was formed to undertake business process outsourcing (BPO) covering: (I) Medical Transcription, (II) Call Center, and (III) Data Processing. In the CTI-Tech Limited, some of the people I came into contact with were-Mr. Alex Asiedu and Dr. Opoku Edusei (CEOs), Mr. Sammy Crabbe (Operations Director), Mrs. Suzie Sam (HRM), Ishmail Mustapha (Facilities Manager); as well as some medical doctors and pharmacists.

This project did not see the light of day, except for the initial training of medical transcriptionists by Medical doctors and pharmacists. The training was concentrated on typing competencies, medical and pharmaceutical terminologies; as well as, medical transcription concepts that allowed for medical doctors in the USA to send information via V-SAT to Ghana for transcription. The transcribed information is sent back to Pharmacies in USA for patients in the USA to pick up medication from the pharmacies within a turnaround time of few minutes. My association was limited to the initial phase of the project.

OTHER EXPERIENCES

In the interest of space, I will aggregate all other experiences under this -*Other experiences*-section of this chapter. Specifically, I will touch on *inter alia* poultry farming, conference and workshop facilitation.

POULTRY FARMING

I offered my second-year national service with a Quasi-Governmental company involved in poultry enterprises-production of *day-old chicks* (DOC), using *grand-parent* stock imported and subjected through the **brooding** (preparing the grand-parent breed), **breeding** (making parents out of grand-parents breed), and hatchery (production of DOCs from parent breed) phases. The Feed Mill was the forward linkage component, integrated to provide poultry feed for the poultry farm. Provisions were made to safeguard emergencies arising out of the poultry farm because the birds could die overnight if precautions were not taken. For this reason, the residence of the production manager was on the farm to attend to emergencies.

The names I remember include the following: Dr. B. L. Nutor (Managing director), Messrs-Adjakojoe (Esq- Personnel Manager), Mrs. Asare (Marketing), Mr. Addai Mensah (Purchasing), Mr. Adom (Head of Finance). Others include: Messrs-Asamoah and Kojo Baiden, as well as, one lady. I came on board with Mrs. Florence Yeboah as a co-National service personnel. I have been involved in the implementation of accounting manual prepared by an accounting firm within the context of a re-organization.

The challenge I encountered here was in regards to the role played as the head office accountant and the role of finance manager occupied by two national service personnel as prescribed by the accounting firm as part of the implementation of the manual. There were few accounting staff who felt offended by the engagement of national service personnel to be placed above them. Some were not co-operative initially but with time through good inter-personal relationship, the apparent tension was reduced (if not eliminated completely).

CONFERENCE AND WORKSHOP FACILITATION

In the foregoing sections, I have given a sense of my involvement with conferences, workshops and seminars as either a participant or a facilitator. These avenues have provided continued professional education (CPE); as well as, a teacher, a professional, an academic, and a layman in some respects. I facilitated as a consultant with the SMME Consult in training postmasters and assistant postmasters in Ghana in both the Southern and Northern sectors of Ghana. I remember facilitating in a seminar on the importance of education for some High School students in the Bolingbrook area in Illinois. I am glad to see most of them complete college or university now. I have also facilitated as a member of the national and regional audit committees on topics of interest in auditing in the church. This is refreshing! I continue to look for opportunities as a facilitator for conferences, workshops, and seminars.

WATER BILL ARREARS COLLECTION COMMITTEE

The Water Bill Arrears Committee (WBAC) was constituted at a meeting of the residents of the Social Security and National Insurance Trust (SSNIT) flats in Elmina in the Central region of Ghana. This was in response to an urgent need for solving problems surrounding water bill arrears payment in the SSNIT flats. The entire community was provided with one main meter through which water getting into the overhead tank was recorded for the six residential blocks. Consequently, the apportionment of the bill among residents was met with fierce resistance based on fairness.

The committee was composed of the following members: Messrs.-(1) Alex Willie Enu (Estates Manager/Chairman), (2) P. K. Essandoh (Assistant Regional Secretary, GNAT-Member), (3) Thomas Amoh (Headteacher-Methodist School-Member), (4) Mrs. Hannah Dogbey (Birth and Death Registrar-Member), and my good self as Secretary. The Committee worked to get separate meters installed for each of the 6 blocks to ensure a fairer assessment of water bills and also collected the bills on behalf of the residents and paid same to the water supplying entity-Ghana Water and Sewerage Corporation (GWSC). Our reports were WBAC/2/93 of November 2, 1993 and March 17, 1994. A community service at work.

ORGANIZING

I was part of the team that organized the *Introduction to Britain Program* in 1988. The leader was Nana Efua Amoo-Godfred (Nanette). Participants were drawn from the three universities in Ghana at the time. The 40 participants encompassed, the following:(1) **University of Ghana**-Atta-Ullah Issa, George Appiah-Sokye (organizer), Seth Kwame Tenkorang, William Obeng, Francesca Brenda Oppong, Josephine Ama Coleman, Eric Kwaku Boadu, Evans Boakye, Rosemary Osei-Ababio, Genevieve Josephine Annan, Kwabena Agyei-Boahene, James Clifford Akosah, Emmanuel Anokye, Kwadwo Gabriel Dwamena, Kwaku Manteaw Kankam-Boadu, Leonard Kwabia Gbekie, Kweku Ricketts-Hagan, and Michael Appiah. (2) **University of Cape Coast**-Frank Ohene Okraku, Albert Kodwo Aiduenu (organizer),

Leticia Quansah, and Janet Eva Arhin. (3) **University of Science and Technology**-Henrietta Fiawoo, Joseph Benjamin Essilfie, Victor Emmanuel Wood, Richard Cofie, David Mowbery Adu, Osei Kuffour Owusu (organizer), Regina Esumamba Essilfie, Kwasi Nuamah Kutin, Samuel Gyan, Amaning Kwarteng Afrifa, George Yaw Obeng, and Maxwell Appiah (Extracted from Introduction to Britain Documents, May 20, 1988).

LESSONS LEARNED- I will share a few general experiences, as follows:

Every Experience Is Relevant- The topic of this chapter is on purpose because there is great latitude of life experiences. I can confidently say that my whole life has been experiential and so this chapter cannot adequately cover all my life experiences. My experience revolves around cultural, physical, failure, family, sickness and pain; as well as, spirituality, and self-fulfillment.

In this chapter, the experiences I share are in regards to work and other voluntary activities. For other experiences, the reader is encouraged to read the following chapters of this book, as follows: *One*, involvement in credit unionism (Chapter 20), life revealed as bittersweet (Chapter 11), stewardship of grace (Chapter 12), service to humanity (Chapter 19), and my life told in pictures (Chapter 22). *Two*, some challenges in life (Chapter 23), and some lessons learned (Chapter 28). Lastly, mentorship and leveraging technology for teaching (Chapters 15 and 14 respectively); as well as, lessons presented from living in Ashongman in the Greater Accra region of Ghana (Chapter 21).

Events along learning trajectory-I have shared some of experiences in other parts of the book and I want to emphasize a few here, as follows: (i) I had grade *C* in Management Information System (MIS) at the Masters level and had to re-sit that paper; (ii) I had to re-write my comprehensive examinations for want of better synthesis and paraphrasing at the doctoral level; (iii) I wrote Ghana Institute of

Taxation (GIT) final examination (Paper 2) twice but failed. I forfeited all the final level credits (penalty); however, I passed all the final part at my next attempt; and lastly (iv) the Institute of Chartered Accountants of Ghana (ICAG) examinations writing was characterized by a mixture of passes and failures. The most important lesson is that I survived the failure and went on to pass all examinations.

Discipled to disciple others- The discipleship course material I received from the *Every Home Crusade,* and passing of the examination leading to an award of a Diploma is refreshing to me. I thank Reverend F.D. Manyah of Tema (Ghana) for this opportunity. ***Living in good health-***Per 3 John 2- I thank God that I have lived in perpetual good health. I have been admitted once to the Komfo Anokye Teaching Hospital (KATH) in Kumasi for one month as a child, hospitalized for one weekend at the Legon Hospital during my freshman days as student; and also detained once for observation at Cape Coast University Hospital in the Central region of Ghana in 1994. Quite apart of these events, I have followed routine medical check-ups at my doctors' offices – have had routine check-up at the Eye Clinic. I am on routine medication for High Blood Pressure and Cholesterol. My colonoscopy procedure was conducted at 50. I have successfully undergone a surgery in October 2020. I praise God for good health!

Traveling mercies- I thank God for saving my life in an accident on my way to secondary school. The accident occurred on the Effiduasi-Juaben Road in 1979-80. My life was preserved by God. The taxi (cab) driver retorted *"This is my first time".* Likewise, I celebrate God for the grace and mercy in air travels. I travel a lot on different assignments but I will recount two events: (a) Once upon a time, I was on a British Airways flight from London to Accra. In the course of the cruising in air, the airplane plunged down all of a sudden but regained the altitude; (b) in another trip in Southwest flight from Chicago Midway to Columbus, Ohio, the airplane plunged down unexpectedly but the flight continued to the destination. To God be the glory!

Disappointments- I have had a few disappointments regarding two or three on my subordinates who have been dismissed for financial impropriety after the time of my stewardship. The prayer of accountants should be: *"And lead us not into temptation but deliver us from evil"* (Matthew 6:13). I do not intend to comment on the specific acts of complicity.

Service is not slavery-I have come to understand that service in any form should not be misconstrued as slavery; and as a result, there is dignity in labor. Additionally, supervisors should be viewed as God-ordained because God appoints supervisors. Likewise, young people should come to the point where they can serve under people they consider as behind them in stature. While this can be a test of humility, the lesson that the world is not fair should be learned early in working life. I remember two tutors I had who felt they were seniors to the Assistant headmaster of a High School and so were not prepared to take instruction from him. Invariably, the students were the losers. Years ago, I witnessed the Speaker of Ghana's Parliament (Justice D.F. Annan) take the brief case of one Presidential staffer (Mr. Nathan Quao).

Later, I learned that Mr. Nathan Quao had taught the then Ghanaian Speaker of Parliament in High School. Wow! I have served under a lot of people who considered themselves as privilege to have me under them, the result has been that those people have also treated me with utmost respect and allowed me to function at my best. I call on young adults to shun any aura of arrogance and avoid the feeling of self-importance to allow God to lift them up for His own glory. The Bible stipulates that "if one wants to be great, one must learn to be the servant of them all" Consequently, we should not struggle to lead but lead when called upon.

CONCLUSION

Life experiences are the best lessons that can lead to better learning outcomes. As a result, difficult times ingrain in us the virtues of hard work, dedication, positive practices, and commitment. There is the need to manage the extra time because most dreams take longer than we initially thought to materialize. For this reason, surrounding yourself with people who can offer positive environmental support is key because the choices and decisions we make; backed by the determination and hard work will provide the urgently needed success. I have established that *accounting* is a call for me. Consequently, accounting as a discipline is rooted in principles and standards called *generally-accepted accounting principles* (GAAP) in the USA. Additionally, there are underlying processes, procedures, and accountability in the discipline and implicit in the stewardship role are the authority, responsibility and accountability functions.

CHAPTER 9

LOSSES ARE COUNTED IN NUMBERS

SMITH AND WATSON (2010) CLAIM that, as we read autobiographies, they often seem to be 'speaking' to us; we 'hear' the author's voice distinctive in its emphasis and tone, its rhythms and syntax, its lexicon and affect" (Cited in Hanssen, 2019, p.313). In the course of my life, I have suffered loss of lives but I will be talking about a few in this book in general and in this chapter in particular. Looking back, I can state that I did not come to meet any of my paternal grandparents; however, I met my maternal grandmother for a brief period before she died in 1972. Nevertheless, I met most uncles and 20 maternal aunties from the extended African family; but over the long period of time, almost all of them have passed; leaving the next generation of family made up of cousins, brothers, and sisters and their off springs. In the Asante tradition, the term 'cousin' is unknown so the concept of aunties, uncles, brothers, sisters, nieces, nephews have expanded application than the definition in other parts of Ghana and the world.

A simple mathematics shows that there can either be a profit or a loss because the expression: Selling price- Cost price = Profit or Loss, or at best a break-even point. For that reason, the concept of profit is an *either/or* situation. However, the accounting income statement is also called-The profit *and* loss account. While the outcome is the same as the mathematical concept; the accounting concept contemplates that implicit in the same statement can be aspects of transactions that can produce profits such as profit from normal activities and losses arising out of *say* disposal of non-current assets or investments.

My heart was very heavy for several years because of a singular loss.

The lesson here is that losses can be counted in numbers-whether in attributes or accounting numbers. Additionally, the accounting concept of prudence or conservatism requires that losses be anticipated rather than profits. In this chapter, I will count a few of my personal losses in human terms with emphasis on numbers (figures).

TIME-BASED LOSSES IN NUMBERS

The concept of death is known to all but the impact of death differs considerably based on relationships and influence. At times when issues are being discussed in the public domain regarding issues of national interest such as gun violence and death of people under an epidemic or a pandemic; the position taken by some policy makers point to the lack of appreciation or experiences from the phenomena or debacle. The experience from the loss of loved ones can be a life-changer for most people. Some do not come back to normalcy. I have seen a mother who never regained her physical appearance after the loss of a son in the primary school. I have seen a woman who could not get organized again after the passing of the husband and the list goes on.

In this chapter, the point to be made is that losses can be both time and number-based.

LOSS OF DAD

I lost my father *at 22 and at the time I was about to begin* my undergraduate program in 1986. As discussed in Chapter 2, my father was born on September 23, 1922 and interestingly died on September 23,1986. Consequently, he was 64 years when he joined the silent majority. On February 23, 1986, my father called my Sister Freda (a nurse) and I into his bedroom and showed us evidence of the development of hernia in his groin. Per his account, the situation was affecting his appetite and he could not enjoy oily foods. I was working as a national service personnel at the Mampong District Hospital and so I presented the case to the medical superintendent the following day and he requested me to invite him for examination and determined that he needed a surgery. He was admitted, operated upon, and later discharged. While at the hospital, he shared the side ward with an agriculturist from the Cote d' Ivoire who came to visit relatives and later had to come to the hospital for a surgery. The man could not speak the English language, so my Brother Willie and I became French interpreters for him at the hospital at the time. Thank God my French was sharp at the time but unfortunately, I have lost the language prowess now due to the prolong period of not using it. Thanksgiving in the church was on Sunday, April 6,1986.

In August 1986, while in Accra to check on my admission to the University of Ghana, I was informed of the hospitalization of my father. He was diagnosed of having a mild stroke and for that reason, he could neither move his legs nor raise his hands freely. Additionally, he could not talk but when I arrived at the ward of the hospital and started sharing jokes, he burst into laughter for the first time in a few days of hospitalization. He was discharged and reported regularly to the hospital for review. On September 23, 1986 he died and was buried a few days later at the Mampong cemetery. To those hurting due to the loss of a father, Psalm 68:5-6 is instructive, as follows: "*⁵ A father to the fatherless, a defender of widows, is God in his holy dwelling. ⁶ God sets the lonely in families, he leads out the prisoners with singing; but the rebellious live in a sun-scorched land* (NIV).

The death of my father inflicted indelible pain on me because, my father was fond of education and my number one cheer leader and so passing just at the time I was about to enter college (university) for my undergraduate program was devastating to say the least. Additionally, combining pain from the loss at this crucial time in my development, coupled with the long litigation we had to endure was difficult for us. I have reflected on the documented daily journal entries of my father regarding information about my post- Secondary(High) School and Pre-University (college) financing, as follows:

- *George Echie Appiah-Sokye, my sixth born completed his secondary education on the 6th of June 1983 at JUABEN Secondary School, Ashanti.*

- *September 15,1983-George Echie Appiah-Sokye, left here to Accra to visit his brother, ...and to chase his GCE Results.*

- *December 8,1983-Paid one thousand cedis (¢1,000.00) for George's Admission fee towards sixth-form school at Nkwatia-Kwahu as part-payment.*

- *December 31,1983-Received a loan of five thousand cedis (¢5,000.00) for my son George's school expenses to be paid through the sale of maize.*

- *March 12, 1984-Remitted ¢900.00 (nine hundred cedis) as school fees and ¢300.00 (three hundred cedis) as lorry fare and other expenses, in all making ¢1,200.00 (one thousand two hundred cedis) through Master Addo Kofi to George my son who is attending Sixth form at Nkwatia-Kwahu.*

- *January 7, 1985-George Echie Appiah-Sokye left home for Nkwatia-Kwahu to continue his education (Upper 6). Gave him one thousand cedis (¢1,000.00) to pay his school fees of ¢325 and use the rest.*

- *March 14, 1985-Sent Mirriam's husband to deliver foodstuffs and money to George, at Nkwatiah St. Peter's Secondary School Upper 6- two thousand cedis (¢2,000.00), Gari, Soyam (grinded maize), Milo, and sugar, and shitto (hot sauce).*

Nevertheless, in the midst of the pain, an opportunity for leadership was provided for me because of the absence in Ghana of my elder brothers. One lesson I have learned in life over the years is that implicit in every problem is an opportunity to be explored.

LOSS OF SPOUSE

At *36 and in the middle* of my Graduate (Master's) program, my spouse passed in the year 2000. Born on October 11, 1964 and died on August 5, 2000. She gave up the ghost at age 35 as of year 2000. Per the Holy Scriptures, in 1 Peter 5:10:

"And the God of all grace, who called you to his eternal glory in Christ, after you have suffered a little while, will himself restore you and make you strong, firm and steadfast" (NIV).Read also Psalm 46 and Psalm 146. We were expecting a baby girl in the year 2000 but this positive anticipation turned out to be rather sorrowful for me. My tribute read in part: *"Afia, we first met in Cape Coast whilst you were on holidays. You went on excursion in Accra and continued to Cape Coast to visit your auntie and family. This interaction finally ended up in marriage which was celebrated in Kumasi on the 2nd January, 1993. You joined me on the 4th January,1993 at the SSNIT flat (Daddies Block (Block 5) First floor 7D. We began life as husband and wife from that date forth"* (Funeral Brochure, August 2000).

I have narrated in Chapter 21 on Ashongman-from a village to a town; and then, to a conurbation. My wife and I used to get home at the same time. If she gets to the village before 6:00pm, she was to proceed home; otherwise, she had to wait for me in the village before we both go home together.

LEGON HOSPITAL- One day, I got home early and just about to go to the village to check on her, she arrived with an uncle at about 7pm. The next day when I got to the Ashongman village at about 8:00 pm she was waiting but this time she could not walk due to a sharp pain in the pelvic girdle. I arranged for a cab (taxi) home and the next morning, I accompanied her to the University of Ghana (Legon)

Hospital and was admitted for two weeks. We were advised to limit movements to allow for the pelvic to close. The uncle with my consent sent her to his house in Madina because of the distance and there was no vehicle in the house by the time. The readers in the USA might be asking why not use 911. The answer is that we did not have such emergency response in Ghana back then.

In the process of time, my wife had initially been treated for malaria but had to proceed to labor with some effects of malaria. I went to the Labor ward to speak words of encouragement and had to excuse the Medical doctor and the nurses attending to her. At the time in Ghana, husbands were not allowed to be in the labor rooms because other women may also be undergoing labor so their privacy is of utmost concern. The Maternity Hospital Report number was 2000/148. Later on, the medical doctor came out and spoke with me in the presence of Mr. Alex Cofie (my friend) and said the mother was doing good but the baby was being resuscitated because she had tied the umbilical cord around her neck (breach). At 9:00pm thereabout, I was advised to go home and come the following morning because everything looked good. As might be expected, when I got home it was quite late but I prayed to thank God for the successful delivery and also committed the words I heard from the doctor into God's hands.

On my way to the hospital the following morning, I passed by the Electricity Company of Ghana (Legon) to inform my presiding elder (Elder David Mensah), who was working there at the time. I did not meet him and so I left a message for him. When I got to the hospital, I saw Ms. Addo-Quaye (a Nursing Sister and very professional at what she does), whom I have met at the Labor ward talking seriously to my wife; and there and then, I suspected that *something* might have happened. She took me to her office and briefed me on the passing of the baby and accompanied me to view the dead baby. I still have a pictorial impression of my daughter for a long time, especially, any time I was called upon to name a baby girl as an elder, her memory and mental picture lived on for some time.

To cut a long story short, with the help of Elder Mensah, my friend (David Ofantse), my wife's uncle and wife, we arranged for her burial at the Madina cemetery. I still remember and appreciate the role played by my Presiding elder in: (1) digging the grave on the land allotted to us for the purpose, and (2) performing a brief but impressive committal service at the cemetery. Elder Mensah performed the service from his heart without any Minister's Manual. Wow! I thank God for the gift of our Spiritual fathers.

We were moved from the Maternity wing of the hospital to the regular wards for about 2 weeks because the opened pelvic was not healed. Just at the time, the doctor was contemplating discharging my wife, the doctor discovered a swollen internal organ and needed to observe her further. After series of tests and X-rays in the 37 Military Hospital, I was told there was an opening in the pelvic. Consequently, the idea of discharge became out of the equation.

KORLE BU TEACHING HOSPITAL (KBTH)- The entire admission at the KBTH lasted for exactly 4 weeks. The Legon Hospital arranged for a referral to the KBTH and provided an ambulance, a nurse holding the paper work, and my good self-one early morning. The nurse sat in the front passenger seat by the driver and I sat close to the stretcher (bed) in the ambulance where Pat laid. As the serene of the ambulance begun to sound, I saw tears flowing down her cheeks. I became the consoler/encourager-in-chief throughout the journey. The driver opted for the Accra Central route through the beach road instead of the Kwame Nkrumah Circle-Abossey Okai road. We got to the Emergency Wing of the Medical Department at about 8:00am but had to be detained there up to 4:00pm before we secured a transfer to the Intensive Care Unit for the next 3 days. In the Emergency Unit, doctors with different specialties came to examine, read information on file, and interview relatives to rule out possibilities and to determine whether the sickness fell in their category.

At the Intensive Care Unit, in addition to nurses, there were medical doctors who permanently sat amid the patients in the unit. We made it to the Medical Ward at the end of the third day. Actually, when one is able to survive the Intensive Care Unit it was considered as a good sign to recovery. Additionally, prior to this experience, I have been told that the most serious medical cases were handled on the fourth floor of the Medical block. I cannot independently confirm this. We made it to a side ward of the second floor (USA) or first floor (Ghana). The side ward was good for privacy and other consideration but it became difficult to get the attention of nurses to respond to calls. For that reason, my wife was transferred to a bigger ward housing about 6 patients with a nurses' station.

The Medical team was headed by a Professor and Dr. Dadson (not real name) was the medical doctor assigned to us. Initially, when the medical team did their usual rounds together and exchanged ideas, Pat was able to pick nuggets of truths from their conversations. She will tell me about the whole discussion. I feared the medical information could adversely affect her recovery so I told the doctors to reserve their comments at the bedside so I can always come for my briefing after the rounds in the Doctor's office. I received daily updates from the medical doctors. In those days, technology was not as advanced in the Ghanaian medical system as it is now. Many a time, we were asked to disregard the medications that have been bought on prescriptions after series of medical tests, X-rays, and CT scans. Some tests were to be conducted by medical professors such as pathologists but such tests took a very long time to get results because such people had very busy schedules.

THE LAST DAYS OF PAT- On the August 4, 2000, we (Mum Comfort, uncle and wife, and myself) were at the hospital bedside until 9:00pm. She finished eating and received her bath in bed and for this particular night she looked very beautiful and extremely cheerful. She asked us to go home. On our way back home, we agreed that I was going to do some laundry in the morning so I could come to the hospital in the afternoon to relieve Mum Comfort and uncle, who agreed to get to the hospital in the morning. When we finally dispersed, it was late, and I was also tired, so I decided to spend the night at my friend's (The late Larbi's) house. The wife of my friend got me something to eat in the night. In the morning, I asked to go home to do some laundry. After everything was set, I was about to leave the house and I happen to pick a book- ***"Where there is no doctor"*** with the following citation: *Werner, D. (2013). Where there is no doctor-a village heath care handbook. Revised edition.p.330-assisted by Thumum, C., & Maxwell, J.*

I opened the book and it took me to the page with the caption- ***"Accepting Death"*** I was about to close the book because it was not worth reading. At this point, I heard 'something' telling me: *"You are an elder –read what the book offers to be guided in ministry"* I obliged and finish reading that portion of the book and I put it on my bed. I have reproduced the information below:

Background: This is the message given to me on August 5, 2000 at 8:00 am. I first shared it publicly after 15 years; because coping with a loss as an elder of the church is challenging. The loss of a dear one can shake the very core or foundations of your Christian faith; yet elders are supposed to be the custodian of the faith. This leads to a lot of unanswered questions and uncertainties.

Excerpts of the book:

1. *Old people are often more ready to accept their own approaching death than are those who love them. Persons who have lived fully are not usually afraid to die. Death is, after all, the natural end of life.*
2. *We often make the mistake of trying to keep a dying person alive as long as possible, no matter what the cost. Sometimes this adds*

to the suffering and strain for both the person and his family. There are many occasions when the kindest thing to do is not to hunt for 'better medicine' or a 'better doctor' but to be close to and supporting of the person who is dying. Let him know that you are glad for all the time, the joy and the sorrow you have shared, and that you, too, are able to accept his death. In the last hours, love and acceptance will do far more good than medicines.

3. *Old or chronically ill persons would often prefer to be at home, in familiar surroundings with those they love, than to be in a hospital. At times this may mean that the person will die earlier. But this is not necessarily bad. We must be sensitive to the person's feelings and needs, and to our own. Sometimes a person who is dying suffers more knowing that the cost of keeping him barely alive causes his family to go into debt or children to go hungry. He may ask simply to be allowed to die and—and there are times when this may be the wise decision.*

4. *Yet some people fear death. Even if they are suffering, the known world may be hard to leave behind. Every culture has a system of beliefs about death and ideas about life after death. These ideas, beliefs, and traditions may offer some comfort in facing death.*

5. *Death may come upon a person suddenly and unexpectedly or may be long-awaited. How to help someone we love accept and prepare for his approaching death is not an easy matter. Often the most we can do is offer support, kindness, and understanding.*

6. *The death of a younger person or child is never easy. Both kindness and honesty are important. A child—or anyone—who is dying often knows it, partly by what her own body tells her and partly by the fear or despair she sees in those who love her. Whether young or old, if a person who is dying asks for the truth, tell her, but tell her gently, and leave some room for hope. Weep if you must, but let her know that even as you love her, and because you love her,*

you have the strength to let her leave you. This will give her the strength and courage to accept leaving you. To let her know these things you need not say them. You need to feel and show them.

7. *We must all die. Perhaps the most important job of the healer is to help people accept death when it can or should no longer be avoided, and to help ease the suffering of those who still live* (p.330).

To continue from where I left off, I picked my bag containing the stuff, I will wear to church the following day, if I am not able to come home in the night. I set off from the house enroute to the KBTH at about 9:00am. After walking for about 200 meters from the house, I lifted up my eyes and saw uncle and Mum Comfort. I suspected something might have gone wrong because of our prior arrangements. At that point, uncle requested that we return home but just around the same time, Mum Comfort could no longer hold her tears and she burst into tears. When we got home, uncle informed me officially of the passing of my wife. To say it was devastation and difficult is an understatement. Our Certificate of Marriage bore the number ABMC 21 and Marriage Licensed Number was AN 371737 of January 2, 1993. The Certified Copy of Entry in Register of Death had Entry Number 3511 of August 28, 2000; as well as, the Burial Permit number of C 44767 of August 23, 2000; the Medical Certificate of Cause of Death (Section 18, Act 301, Form V) was dated August 10, 2000; coupled with Request for Postmortem dated August 7, 2000 and the Autopsy Report PM number 2528/2000.

DEAR READER, I want to admonish you never to tell a bereaved person- "It is nothing" (*Enye hwee*). *Who told you that?* I contend that "it is something" (*Eye Biribi*). Christians should not further inflict pains on people mourning the loss of loved ones. Yes, we mourn differently; nevertheless, the Holy Scriptures postulates, as follows: "Blessed are those who mourn, for they shall be comforted (Matthew 5:4). For there to be comfort, there must have been mourning.

Later on, in 2008 at the Church of Pentecost Prayer Conference in Canada, Apostle Sampson Ofori Yiadom delivered a message on *"the Personality of the Holy Spirit"* and explained that: *"and something told me"*-Is the workings of the Holy Spirit. By way of application, I can now say that it was God (The Holy Spirit) who announced the death of my wife to me ahead of time. I learned that the medical doctors pronounced her dead at *2:00 am on Saturday, August 5, 2000*.

Uncle and Mum did not want to leave me alone in the house at Ashongman so I asked that I go to my friend's house at Agbogba (North Legon). When I called my friend on phone, he was in Accra Central transacting some business and told me to remain at the very location I was standing because he was coming to me.

The Larbi's decided to keep me in their house until further notice and so his house became my family house and I stayed with them until burial on August 19, 2000 at the Madina cemetery. When the University of Ghana re-opened, I took up a residential accommodation on campus because my loved ones were of the view that it was going to be difficult for me to be in the very house, I have been staying with Pat alone at the time; as well as; coping with school work.

LESSONS LEARNED

I share the lessons below:

MONEY CANNOT SAVE HUMAN LIFE- I thank God for the moral and financial support I received from family, friends, church family, and the IRS family. Indeed, people gave in support of this cause. I never lacked money at the time and the church prayed. I spent a whopping ¢5 million in year 2000 price levels at KBTH alone for the one month. I had over ¢800,000 in my bag at the end of the day. **APPRECIATION OF THE VANITY OF HUMAN LIFE-** Whilst in KBTH, I experienced death at first sight. Meaning, I saw several dead bodies being thrown into cargo van for the Last Office (morgue). I saw the death of the patient to our *left* (an old lady) whose husband (old man) sat by her bed always except the day she passed. The adult children had to meet their father at the gate to send him home. I met this family the day we arrived at the Emergency wing and traveled to the ward around the same time. Likewise, I saw the death of the patient to our right (a nurse), who sung Presbyterian hymns aloud for others to join until she gave up the ghost.

During one of my encounters with the Medical team, I met an elderly woman whom I got to know was the wife of a professor of the Medical School whose prognosis had been determined to be uncertain. The medical doctors were preparing her psychologically for his evitable death. They elaborated that as students of the dying professor, they have done everything humanly possible to *save* his life but unfortunately, he was not going to make it. Prior to this experience, when I was on admission at the University (Legon) Hospital in 1986 for three days. That was my second hospitalization. The first one was at the Komfo Anokye Teaching Hospital (KATH) in Kumasi- Ghana, where I spent a month as a child. At the Legon Hospital, I was admitted from the Students Clinic on campus and sent to the Main hospital for the weekend.

An elderly man was brought to the ward on Friday night and throughout the night, the man engaged by saying that he did not understand why he is going through such pain. He recounted how he has been faithful to God and serving as a catechist in a village church (names withheld). He questioned, why he should be going through all these. After the engagement, there was a definitive silence and by the morning, he had given up the ghost. At times when I see people lifting their shoulders as if the world is for them, I feel sorry for such people. I dare say that I have been humbled by these events and stories and any time I remember any of these stories; I consider myself as nothing but the product of the manifold grace of God. I owe everything to God. I am nobody and I am nothing before the Lord.

THE NATURE OF THE LOSS- The loss of a spouse is a very difficult one. I compare it to a boxer who had been hit a deadly blow and found dazed. Life had to be restarted all over again. I was 36 years of age at the time. I did not want to marry again, It took the likes of Apostle E. K. Apea, Prophet J. O. Amaniampong, the late Apostle Dr. Emmanuel Owusu Bediako, and Apostle J. A. Mensah, to convince me to change my position. Some countered my argument citing my age. **WORDS OF ENCOURAGEMENT**- The Biblical message that was able to hold the center was: *"David encouraged himself in his God* (I Samuel 30:8). My good friend (Bekoe Boampong) also using the account of Job in the Bible offered that: *"Perhaps the Lord is bragging about you"* He opined that *"For all you know, God is bragging about you"* I have come to understand that *"Relationship with God is critical during crisis(I Corinthians 1:9).* My long-time friend (Evans Boakye) also told me: *"Appiah, I know you can stand but I am not sure if I could have"*

THE SUPPORT OF THE PEOPLE- My local church put together a Funeral Committee comprising of the following: Elders-David Mensah (Presiding/Chairman), William Owusu Yamoah, Lawrence B. Larbi; and Deaconesses-Gifty Owusu Yamoah and Gladys Agyemang. Funds for the funeral were raised as follows:

Table 9: *Financial contributions towards the funeral*			
S/No	**Names**	**Amounts(Cedis)**	**Remarks**
1	Lawrence Larbi	2,000,000	21/08/2000
2	George Appiah-Sokye	1,000,000	
3	Charles Owusu Boamah	1,000,000	
4	Evans Boakye	1,000,000	
5	Steve Antwi-Asimeng	500,000	

6	Isaac & Christie Nyarkoh	500,000	
7	Willie Appiah Appenteng	1,230,000	
8	Auntie Comfort & Children	1,000,000	
9	The Asafo-Adjei Family-Agomanya	500,000	
10	Ibrahim Wiredu & Comfort family	2,000,000	
11	Comfort Twum	210,000	Canadian $50
12	Daniel Dwamena	500,000	
	TOTAL AVAILABLE FUNDS	¢11,400,000	

Total funeral Expenses amounted ¢8,179,600 and Total Donation of ¢7,345,000, resulting in a deficit of ¢834,600; the families agreed to apportion as follows: Family ¢278,200 (one-third), Husband ¢278,200 (one-third), and Father's family ¢278,200 (one-third). The settlement was completed on August 21, 2000. Estimate for the grave was as follows: 80 pieces of 4" sandcrete blocks ¢112,000, 6 bags of cement totaling ¢150,000, 2 length iron rods for ¢30,000, binding wire costing ¢5,000, water ¢10,000; as well as digging ¢0 (done by some deacons and members of the local church). I am grateful to the following for their kind acts of generosity: (i) Mr. Kenneth Oppong-Kyekyeku (cousin) for providing sandcrete blocks and Mr. Kyei Mensah (cousin) for bags of cement for the graveyard construction works.

The tomb stone was constructed between August 1, 2001 and August 24, 2001 at a cost of ¢1,500,000.00 by Fred Amarlai Armah of Amarlai Ventures. The tomb stone was unveiled during the one-year celebration at the Madina Cemetery in Accra-Ghana.

I thank God for the support he sent my way. The support of all women is appreciated. I thank all women both old and young for the support they gave me. Some related as possible replacements or suitors, others as possible mothers-in-law, others as sisters. I quite remember one of my friend's wife thanking me for the honor done women for remarrying after 5 years and not sooner.

I appreciate all that the *Larbi's* have done for me and my family. I am eternally grateful to them. I ask God to directly bless them for my sake. I thank my brothers (Kyei Mensah and Oppong Kyekyeku) for providing iron rods, cement, and sandcrete blocks for the grave of Pat. Additionally, my brothers Willie (Belgium) and Alexander (France) for their financial support. I have already mentioned Elder David Kwabena Mensah (my presiding elder) and then Pastor E.K. Apea and Obaa Yaa (his wife) for their encouragement. I thank the church public-Mampong, SSNIT Flats, Madina West and Madina Central assemblies. Madina West was phenomenal. They took ownership of the entire funeral to the extent that my relatives had nothing to do. We appreciate them.

Several well-meaning people supported me and the family during the period of our loss and their varied contributions is acknowledged. Without them it would have been difficult if not impossible to meet all the demands of organizing a typical African funeral. I will attempt to mention the names we were able to capture at the time. **One**, the following *friends of George Appiah-Sokye* as coordinated by Ms. Aisha Tiwaa Gyasi showed special love: Messrs-Kwame Owusu, Oppong Damoah, Afoakwah, Walter Brown, Yaw Appiah Kubi, Emmanuel Sackey; Mrs. Aisha Ashun, Mrs. Janet Riley, Sister Mabel Arthur, Ms. Margaret Pimpong, Ms. Patience O. Nyantakyi, Mr. Frank Ansah Otu, Mrs. Djabatey, Mr. Eddie Akpakli, Nii Kwabla Ayite, Mr. Daniel Nuer, Mr. Bobby Brown, Mrs. Lucinda Teiko, Mr. Eddie Doh-Nani, Mr. Emmanuel Awuah, Mr. Rudolph Amega-Etego (Esq), Mr. Yaw Ntow, Ms. Joyce Mensah, and Mr. S.T. Tetteh.

Two, the list continues, as follows: my Atwampumah family, Mr. Joseph Amparbeng, Mr. Bernard Ossom, Osu Home School, Teacher Ernest, I.R.S.-LTO Drivers, Mr. Joseph Appeah (PENTAX), IRS Credit Union Welfare Society, IRS Credit Union Board of Directors, IRS Finance Officers Welfare; Friends from Madina West Assembly (Vida, Jane, Mary, Beatrice, Faustie, Mrs. Ansong), and Agya Yaw (Ashongman). **Three**, Reverend (Mrs.) and Mr. Yirenkyi, Nana Yaa

(Naomi), Kwaku Adu's nephew, Kwame Attakorah (Adizo), IRS-LTO staff; Mr. and Mrs.-Oti-Akenteng (Coach, Winneba), Baah Achamfour, Baidoo Harrison, Antwi and family, Nat Ayivoh, and Edward Koomson. **Four,** the following IRS Management staff deserve special mention: Messrs-G.K. Katamani, Humphrey Otoo, Emmanuel Nyamordey, J.B. Awuku, Rodney Kusorgbor, Yeboah Boateng, Kwame Appenteng, and Andrew Korankye.

Five, the trainee cashiers' category, included: Helena (Achimota district), Stella (Agboblorshie district), Lydia Ankra, and Regina Cofie. Others included: Cynthia Okertchire, Mr. Parry Aboagye, and Yvonne Martey. **Six,** Madina District Women's Movement, IRS Credit Union-Makola district, Mr. Duodu (Tax Examinations), Mr. Ebenezer Aryee and Mrs. Sethlina Donkoh (Supervisory Committee, CUA). **Seven,** I thank (i) Mr. and Mrs. Ossom Boafo and (ii) Madina West Assembly Six Sisters (Vida and others) for providing assorted drinks; (iii) the Internal Revenue Service placed a vehicle at my disposal, (iv) Elder and Mrs. Dwomoh Amaniampong (My big brother) provided food; and (v) I received foodstuff from Mampong Ashanti from family.

The donors for the August 19-20, 2000 are listed for recognition, as follows: **Eight,** Abusuapanin Kwaku Nsiah (Asona Atwampumah Abusuapanin), Mr. and Mrs. Nolasco, The Church of Pentecost-Madina West, Osei Tutu, Kwasi Saka Dankyi, Mr. Adams, Akosua Nyantakyi, Nana Afia, Monica Sekyere, Maame Nyamekye, Reverend and Mrs. E. K. Ofori, All Sisters from Begoro, Joyce Adjei, Maame Anyamsem, Kofi Dwomoh, Kaefer Allen Gyimah; **Nine,** Maame Naa, mother and family; Kwasi Addae Owusu, Elmina District, Bantuma Assembly, Elmina Number 1 Assembly, SSNIT flats assembly, Brother and Sister Kayne, Sister Elizabeth Arthur, Elmina Number 2 assembly, Kofi Ofori, Lawyer Lamptey, Philip Acquah, Fred Latzoo, Sister Rebecca Acquah, Augustina Pakyi, Elizabeth Ayertey, Dina Prah, Lydia Amponsah, Mr. and Mrs. Nyame, Mrs. Darkwah, Dora Tabi, Comfort

Adubea, Faustina Aframea, Mr. Eghan (SSNIT flats); Sister Josephine, Mr. Segoe, and Hilda (all of Dr. R.P. Baffour JSS), George Ayinan, Seth Obuobi, Gladys Asuming, Hanna Osei, Margaret Mensah, Vivian Kobi, Kpeshie Sub-Metro Teachers Welfare Association, the Headmaster and staff of South La Estates 2 JSS-Accra, Accra Metro Professional Teachers Association Welfare, Mrs. Antwi and children.

Ten, Reverend & Mrs.-Oppong Asare Duah, Appiah-Kubi, and Johnson Agyemang Badu; Professor and Mrs. Safo (Pro-Vice Chancellor, UST-Kumasi), Dr. and Mrs. Ofori (Atua Government Hospital), Dr. and Mrs. Amanda Darkay. *Elders*-Koomson Biney, John Elliamo, Kwame Essuman, Napoleon Anang, Tetteh, Dr. Annan, Paul Beddim, Tony Owusu, Offin, Boadi, JWK Asare, Adomako Bonsu, Baffoe, Asamoah Manu, E.O. Kissi, Asuta, Adjetey Solomon Esq., and Ben Yeboah. *Elder and Mrs.*-Frimpong, Asare, Yankson, Boateng, Asamoah, Tetteh, Owusu Yamoah, Yakah, Konadu, Amoako, Appiah Mensah, Amponsah-Asante, Osei Kwaku, Ofori Fodjour, Asante, Adu (Estates), Appiah Danquah, and Eric Ofori Adarkwah. **Eleven**, *Deaconesses*-Rebecca Eshun, Angelina Awotwe, and Comfort Adu; **twelve**, Mr. and Mrs.-Jacob Asare, Yeboah Duah, Albert Nsiah, Brakoh, Obeng Nsiah, Mensah, Larweh, Gabriel Sosu, Braku, Acquaye, Akuffo, Acheampong, Antwi, Amoah Oduro, Amofah, Akaa (SSNIT Flats), Peter, and Mensah.

Thirteen, Charity Opoku, Mrs. Owusu Ansah, Mrs. Vincentia Manu, Mr. Kofi Marfo, Jemima Okwei (GBC News Room), IRS Head Office Accounts Department, Suhum Bethel House, Samuel Darko, Brother Atta (Zongo), Lucy, and Mercy. **Fourteen**, Gawuga, Auntie Grace, GOKA Pharmacy, UST Community, Sister Selina, Mr. Sly (IRS), School mates, Rebecca's parents, Maame Amaniampong and children, Sister-in-law, Agnes Attakorah, S.H Appiah and family, Accra Metro Professional, Mamle Data Circuit, Staff of Osu Home JSS, Osu Home JSS PTA, Kpeshie Sub-Metro Welfare, Mary Osabutey,

Esther Ayeh, and Mr. Mark Kwofie. **Fifteen,** Jospong Printing Press Limited, Larweh Narh, Sister Azumi, IRS-LTO Staff Welfare, IRS Other Districts, the Appiah Twum family, Maame Nyamekye and family, and Mr. Charles Sackey, COP Mampong District.

Sixteen, D.K. Amponsah (Estates), Gifty Axorsi, Quansah and family, Nana Anim Bediakoh, Ebenezer Temple, Jackson Anoahpufle, Sister Sarah Adipah, IRS Welfare-Cape Coast, Comfort Kumi, Enock Sey, Felicia Adomah, Olivia Asare, Lawer family, P.K. Deamesi; and **lastly,** COP-Madina District, Sister Mary Dankwah-Smith, George (IRS-Assin Fosu), A.T. Koduah, Mr. Amishadai Ashley, Teye Quao, Bertha (Ebenezer), and IRS-LTO Accra.

DIVINE PROVISION-I have talked about the financial support I received from family and friends during this period. In this segment, I will touch on four. (1) My friend (Mr. Larbi) raised an amount of ¢2 million towards the funeral; (2) My brothers-in-law in UK and Canada also gave a helping hand during the funeral. I want to recount one testimony. Before the loss, one of my brothers-in-law in Canada came for visit in Ghana and wanted to marry a lady, who was working in a building adjacent to my office block at the Ministries in Accra (Ghana). He introduced the lady to Pat and I. When he went back to Canada, he decided to send some money to the sister but addressed the envelope to me using the address of the adjacent building. I was not working there and the letter was returned back to him. When he got the letter back and corrected the address and mailed the letter back to Ghana, the timing co-incided with the period of much spending at the KBTH.

More so, (3) just before the funeral, some of my friends and classmates came together to raise ¢500,000 each and one of them contributed ¢1 million for a total of ¢8 million. This money was handed to my friend (Mr. Larbi). After the funeral, I went round all these friends and classmates to thank them and to refund the money to them. Surprisingly, none of them collected the money back. I thought the money was a loan but they deemed it as their contribution to support me in this time of loss. I thank God for their lives. May God continue to bless them all. Lastly, I continued to receive financial blessings long after the final funeral rites and those assistance have gone a long way in my bouncing back to life.

MATTERS ARISING- I want to say that when a loved one is lost through death. As human beings, there isn't much we can do because we cannot reverse the process. I went through this experience without any prior knowledge of how best to handle things but God never left me nor forsook me. He was ever present help and I literary got married to *Christ* and that too moderated my sexual passion. Nevertheless, I have a painful recollection of events that happened before, during, and after the loss of my better half; yet, I feel I have the responsibility to share to the minutest detail to serve as lessons to others.

I do not pray that any young person should go through what I have endured; but, should it happen to any person. May the contents of these pages minister to the heart of the person. In all things, remember the *5GPs- (i) God's purpose, (ii) God's presence, (iii) God's protection, (iv) God's promises, and (v) God's provisions.* Similarly, Apostle J. A. Mensah (my former Area head) has asked me never to compare the two women (the past and present).

Another suggestion is to get completely healed before re-entering into marriage. I know people heal differently and there is no Biblical injunction preventing people from re-marrying any time; but I propose *Rule 3-5* to ensure proper adjustment. *This is my opinion.* I have seen people rush into re-marriage supposedly to forget about the past loss and respond to heightened sexual demands only to find themselves in serious problems arising out of improper healing.

I remember one of our deaconesses informed me of her desire to pray to God for forgetfulness.

As might be expected I did not consent to such a prayer. I told her

I was in the middle of my Master's program and so an answer to such a prayer will be serious to me. I do not know why people think you can just erase such an indelible *mark* from your memory completely. Yes, you can make conscious efforts to try to forget so you can move on with life but the truth be told, the memory lingers into perpetuity. I can say it is rather the pain of the loss that subsides over time.

THE ENEMY COMES IN LIKE A FLOOD- The Bible states that the enemy comes in like a flood but the Spirit of God lifts up a standard against the schemes. I have narrated how an anticipated good news turned into *a flood of negative happening* such as the death of a daughter at birth and at the time of preparation for my final examinations of my first year in Graduate school. I am thankful to my friend (Mr. Alex Cofie), who was very patient and frank with me during our preparation for our first paper. To the glory of God. My grade in that paper was an *A*. The series of events culminated into the death of my spouse. As believers, we continue to place our trust in God. Yes, I was troubled and buffeted all over but I was not destroyed. To God Be the Glory. Dear reader, put your trust in God because he stands between us and the enemy so that we will not be consumed.

EPITAPH: The tombstone reads:

**THIS TOMB IS LAID TO THE EVER-
BLESSED MEMORY OF THE LATE
MRS. PATIENCE OLIVIA APPIAH-SOKYE
(ALIAS "PAT")
BORN ON: 11TH OCTOBER,1964
DIED ON: 5TH AUGUST 2000.
FONDLY REMEBERED BY THE HUSBAND,
CHILDREN, FRIENDS, THE CHURCH
AND THE ENTIRE FAMILY.
MAY YOUR SOUL REST IN PEACE.**

One-year celebration was observed on Sunday, August 26, 2001 at the Madina Cemetery. Unveiling of tomb took place at the Madina Cemetery at 7:00am. Some of the people who attended included the following: Elders- David Mensah, Agyemang Dugbatse, Owusu Yamoah; Mr. and Mrs. Stephen Antwi Asimeng, Mr. and Mrs. Evans Boakye, Mr. Ben Amoah (Caplow), Mr. David Ofantse, Mr. Jacob Aidoo, Mr. Kojo Peter Pieterson, Mrs. Mabel Bakatue, Mr. Attakorah Appau, Mr. Eric Appiah, Mrs. Baah, Mr. Samuel Appiah, Sister Akosua and many more. Others are-Madam Gladys, Veronica Asafo-Adjei, Mr. and Mrs. Solomon Asafo-Adjei, Madam Janet Asafo-Adjei's daughter.

MY FAITH IS BUILT ON NOTHING LESS

I have been encouraged by the song:

1 My hope is built on nothing less
than Jesus' blood and righteousness;
I dare not trust the sweetest frame,
but wholly lean on Jesus' name.

Refrain:
On Christ, the solid rock, I stand;
all other ground is sinking sand,
all other ground is sinking sand.

2 When darkness veils his lovely face,
I rest on his unchanging grace;
in ev'ry high and stormy gale,
my anchor holds within the veil. [Refrain]

3 His oath, his covenant, his blood
support me in the whelming flood;

when all around my soul gives way,

he then is all my hope and stay. *[Refrain]*

4 When he shall come with trumpet sound,

O may I then in him be found,

dressed in his righteousness alone,

faultless to stand before the throne. [Refrain]

Source: Trinity Psalter Hymnal #459

LOSS OF MUM

My mother died when I was *52 years and towards the end* of my
Graduate (doctoral) program in 2016. As narrated in Chapter 2, my
mother was born in 1925 and died on June 5, 2016 but buried on
October 15, 2016. This translates to 91 years but we estimate that
she lived-between 91 and 94 years because her date of birth was not
documented at the time. For that reason, each of the estimates of her
age was based on different assumptions. Typically, my mother was not
a fun of hospital visitation because she had not visited the hospital for
over 40 years as far as my memory serves with right. Any time one
suggested sending her to the hospital she will insist that she will die if
sent and that she succeeded in refraining us from attempting to send her
against her will. When she is sick, she was fond of calling the names of
her children to announce her possible departure.

At her old age and on this fateful day, my Sister Miriam found her
motionless and speechless and consulted with a few relatives and sent
her to the hospital. She was diagnosed of having a higher blood pressure
and never gain consciousness; but passed overnight on that fateful day
and buried on October 15, 2016 in her Grave house in Asaam (her Holy
Village) near Mampong-Ashanti. Deuteronomy 10:18 states: *"He defends*
the cause of the fatherless and the widow, and loves the alien, giving him food

and clothing" (NIV); and for that reason, *"I will not leave you as orphans; I will come to you"* (John 14:18, NIV).

During my interaction with her in 2015 during my visit, 4 themes emerged from our conversation, as follows: (a) her desire was to be translated into heaven without seeing death. (b) The 5 years proceeding her passing was characterized by longing to go home (engagement with the life hereafter). Likewise, (c) she was very gratefulness to God for the life of her children. Understandably, she never lost any of her 9 children; as well as, (d) forgiveness of the treatment meted out to her and the children by my father's house. Consequently, I can say that she had peace with God and with men.

CONCLUSION

Over the span of 30 years, I lost 3 very close relations. The nature of our relationship with parents speaks volumes of the extent of our own linkage with other people; partly because of the values and attributes that are ingrained in the process. While my father died in 1986 when I was 22 years, my mother passed in 2016 when I was 52 years. In the middle of the continuum in year 2000, my wife was called to glory when I was just 36 years of age. Consequently, my spouse died 14 years after my father's and 16 years before my mother. By implication, my mother was with me throughout the 2 losses. Nevertheless, the Scriptures stipulate: *"Great peace have they that love the Law and nothing shall offend them"* (Psalm 119:165). While the death of my father happened at the beginning of my undergraduate studies, the passing of my mother occurred at the end of my doctoral program before my dissertation manuscript and defense stages; however, the departure of my spouse took place in the middle of graduate school (master's program).

Dear reader, ponder over the timing and implications of these events. Another development is that with time, I have come to appreciate the role of culture in times of death of a loved one and the appropriate responses. Unlike the USA, where dying people are surrounded by family and also funerals tend to be a purely private family affair; the story in Ghana (Africa) is different. The African focus is on the society. Consequently, I call the African funerals- "walk-in" celebrations because people can attend funerals due to their relationship with members of the extended families. I invite anthropologists to examine this area.

My prayer for those hurting is as follows: (i) that the Lord will grant you the enablement to go through this painful journey; (ii) that you will emerge stronger from this devastation and period of loss; (iii) that the Lord will be attentive to your prayers; (iv) that the Lord will grant you favor before men and God; and (v) that the Lord will provide all your needs according to His riches in glory from this day forth.

CHAPTER 10

◈

A TRUE FRIEND

ONCE UPON A TIME, I met a man who was the managing director of a company by name-*"Yen Panin Asa"*, meaning *"Our forebears have departed"* When I posed the question: *Why did you choose this name?* He explains that growing up there were a lot of people in the family but with the passage of time, all the forebears have died. In my life I have witnessed the passing of a lot of loved ones such as friends, family, and acquaintances. Just as I recounted the *loss of three loved* ones in the proceeding chapter; *a bosom friend* also passed in 2020. In the circumstance, I cannot help but to devote this chapter to his memory, especially, in regards to the legacies he left behind. This special friend of mine is **Lawrence Kwamina Baidoo Larbi,** born on *November 25,1958* and died on *July 2, 2020*; translating to 61years. He left behind a wife and four children, as well as, two grand-children.

The burial service took place at the *Transitions Funeral Home,* off the Haatso-Atomic Road, Accra and the interment took place at the *LA Cemetery,* Accra (All in Ghana). The Burial Service at the Transitions Funeral Home was held under the auspices of the Church of Pentecost-Madina Area, under the Chairmanship of *Apostle M. S. Appiah* (Area Head). Some of ministers who graced the occasion, included the following: Prophet David Kankam Bedetor (Member, Executive Council); Apostles-J. A. Mensah (rtd.), Ahalivor (rtd.); Pastors-Nicholas Darkoh (former Finance and Administration Director), George Asante, Enock Odame (Chaplain), Patrick Berimansu (Area Secretary), Samuel Awugya, and many more.

Also quoting from Revelation 14:13-14, *Prophet David Kankam* focused his exhortation to mourners on three points: (1) dying in Christ as a blessing, (2) resting in Christ from troubled world, and (3) deeds following the dead. Prophet Kankam also eulogized the late Elder Larbi as a good man and a counselor. A brother of the late Elder Lawrence Larbi thanked God, the church, his Group Executive Chairman, and invited guest for their support, presence, and presents. Many ministers and elders from far and near also graced the occasion.

In this chapter, the information shared in the Funeral Brochure (July 2020) will be covered, as follows: (i) biography, (ii) tribute from the wife, followed by (iii) tribute from the children, (iv) tributes from daughter-in-law and grandchildren, (v) the Church of Pentecost, (vi) the Group Executive Chairman, (vii) A business associate; as well as, (viii) former place of work-the Group 1 (Company 2 and Company 3). The eulogy I gave during the funeral is also presented.

LIFE STORY

The life story as encapsulated by close relatives has been expatiated by the biography written by the family and the tributes by the wife, children, grandchildren, and daughter-in-law. Keep in mind that different people bring varied perspectives on the same subject. *The family provided the biography, as follows: The righteous man perishes and no one lays it to heart, devout men are taken away, while no one understands. For the righteous man is taken away from calamity; he enters into peace; they rest in their beds who walk in their uprightness* (Isaiah 57:1-2).

Family background-The late Lawrence Larbi was born on **25th November, 1958** at Kwahu Tease in the Afram Plains in the Eastern Region of Ghana to Opanin John Kofi Larbi and Madam Salome Ama Kyeiwah of *Boso* in the Asuogyaman District of the Eastern Region, both of blessed memory.

Education and upbringing-Lawrence started his elementary education at the Tease Roman Catholic Primary School in 1967 and when the family relocated to Boso in 1969, continued at the Boso

Presbyterian Primary School. He attended the Anum Presbyterian Middle Boys School, where he sat for and obtained his Middle School Leaving Certificate (MSLC) in 1977. He then joined his siblings in Accra to attend Royal Academy of Accountancy at Accra Newtown and completed with flying colors in 1980 with various certificates.

Working life -In April 1981, he started work with AA Printing Press(not real name) but resigned to join the MM Company Limited(not real name), which necessitated his movement from Teshie-Nungua Estates to Madina in 1993. Again, he left to accept appointment with MC Company(not real name) but when company's contract was ended; he joined the Group 1 in 1999, where he continued to work until his retirement in January 2019.

Marriage life-Lawrence married the love of his heart and the Lord blessed them with four (4) children as indicated above. **Christian life**-The Scriptures state in Ecclesiastes 12:1 that *"remember your creator in the days of your youth, before the days of trouble come and the years approach when you will say, I find no pleasure in them"*(NIV). This passage resonates with Lawrence because he was baptized in 1971 while at Boso in the Church of Pentecost and has been an ardent follower of Jesus Christ till his death. The qualities identified by the family include the following: God-fearing, generous, hardworking, and dependable.

Generational impact-Lawrence was a pillar in the family and will be remembered in many areas where he brightened because he was a great gift to the church and family. **Reflection**-On Thursday, July 2, 2020 he passed on after a short illness. He was taken ill and was receiving medical treatment at the hospital in Accra. When the health continued to deteriorate, he was referred to another hospital but was pronounced dead on arrival. We will forever carry you in our precious hearts. As we celebrate the life of Elder Lawrence Larbi, may his memory be a blessing. *Farewell–Lawrence. Nantie Yie–Kwamina Baidoo.*

Damerifa Due-Elder Larbi. Lawrence deele. Kwamina dayie. Lawrence, rest in perfect peace.

TRIBUTE FROM THE WIFE

"Then I heard a voice from heaven saying to me," Write: Blessed are the dead who die in the Lord from now on. Yes, says the Spirit, that they may rest from their labors, and their works follow them" (Revelation 14:13-14)

My husband was such a wonderful man. I'm not sure I can really express just how much I will miss him. He was an amazing husband, wonderful father to our children, the best grandpa to our grandchildren, my best friend and big brother. He was and still remains the love of my life and was the best gift God gave me. It has been 35 years since we've been together and I look back over those years with so much happiness. His ability to make everyone feel comfortable, secured and loved was his greatest strength. His sense of humor was exceptional.

Lawrence was a proud father who would boast about our kids and show them off to all other parents. As the children grew into teenagers, I saw how he always advised them anytime they went wayward. He was always there to pick up the pieces and sort things out. Lawrence was such a gentleman, well-mannered and polite. His jovial manners and good nature attracted people to him everywhere he went and no one can forget his raucous and contagious smiles. He was a hardworking and generous man. His commitment was not only to the family but to the community as well.

KB (as I affectionately called him), I thought of you today, I think of you in silence. I often speak your name but all I have is memories. You will smile at me each morning when I wake up from bed and ask me the simple but caring question *"How are you doing"*. You cared for me as though you were my *mother*. With tearful eyes I observed your suffering, I saw you slowly fade away but I could not make you stay. Right in my arms a golden heart stopped beating, my heart is broken but God has proved to me that He alone takes the best.

My heart misses a beat anytime you called me-baby, baby, baby, when you came back from work or town. Who will be the first person I'll talk to when I wake up in the morning, I feel so empty and heart-broken. I will miss the devotional time we shared as a family with you being the leader. I will miss the inspirational messages you shared with me. I will do my best to continue the family devotion with the kids because I know that is what you would have me do.

You have the sweetest place in my heart, my energy source, my prayer warrior, my *Lord* on earth, you simply were the best. I know you are looking down at me from heaven saying *"Rosey – make the best of life. We have work to do up here too"*... Good Bye My Dear and Sweet Husband.

THE CHILDREN OF MY FRIEND elaborated in a letter to a father, as follows:

Dear Daddy:

This is a letter from your children. We are grateful to God for giving you to us as our father. We want to reiterate that if we are given the opportunity to choose another father in eternity, we will certainly choose you again because you are the only father we have known.

At every stage in our lives you have come down to our level to advise us and also inculcated in us that knowledge is power. In fact, there were times you interacted with us as though we were colleagues. You will say "Hi Man" and we'll respond 'yeah man". You found pleasure in having all of us around for fellowship and dinning together. Additionally, you shared your life experiences and plans for the future with us to serve as a navigator in life. You have taught us that life isn't a *sprint* (a short race)– but a *marathon* (into the long haul).

Oh our dear father, we want to recap your uniqueness, as follows:

One, you have proved to be selfless and humble, a principled father, always full of smiles, prayerful father, giving your children a priority in everything, strong to the very end, our best friend, and someone always ready to help us. **Two,** you fiercely loved the family, stood tall and sure, helped us mature because your strength and love for us has remained a part of your legacy.

Three, you taught us to always love one another and to always trust the Lord with all our hearts and not to lean on our own understanding but to acknowledge the Lord in all our ways; and for that reason, you made us happy. Likewise, we have learned that if at any point in the race we want to stop, we should not let our fortitude lapse because "no struggle no freedom." We will arise and keep on moving; even without the man we saw as our king. Nevertheless, the hole in our hearts will always be there.

Daddy, losing you at this time seem unfair to us because the pain in our hearts is difficult to deal with but we are trusting God to help us heal. You have left us but we haven't left you because you will forever be in our hearts and minds. We love you! We will miss you but we know that you are in heaven and smiling down on us.

We remember the day before your demise, you called all of us and prayed for us; mentioning each one by name and blessing us. Perhaps, you knew you were about to leave for heaven. We know you are in a better place. You served as our pillar, anchor, and everything. Your impact will be passed on to others. You told us to read *Psalm 27: 10* before you departed to your maker and the import of the text suggested that- *if my mother and father forsake me the Lord will never forsake me...* To God be the Glory!

The daughter-in-law and grandchildren provided their input as follows:

TRIBUTE BY GRANDCHILDREN

'Grandpa are you my friend" Yes
Has grandpa gone to be with the Lord?
That's why I have not seen him in a long time.
I will hear his voice no more
Grandpa I know you are in heaven
I see you when the sunsets, you are that shining star
Grandpa, I miss you already.

I told God to keep you safe for me because one day I will come to you in heaven and we will play together again.

TRIBUTE BY DAUGHTER-IN-LAW

Meeting my father-in-law for the first time seemed like we had known each other for years. The favor I obtained in his sight never faded till his last breath. I have my own special memories of my father-in-law. For me he was a gentle, caring and kind father. He was thoughtful and honest, a man with strong principles. Meeting him turned my whole life around.

He told me he was my personal lawyer and friend. I benefited from his many words of wisdom. He was my advisor and mentor. He shared motivational books with me from his library and as though it was not enough, he bought me some personal ones too. He gifted me lots of things, booked countless flights for me as I travelled to and fro within the country, always calling to check on me and sending me Christian and encouraging messages on WhatsApp, and a couple of times we ate together from one plate, he enjoyed these simple pleasures.

I could see the joy that lit up his face anytime I called him ASEW(father-in-law). He pampered me like I was his own daughter, he loved me to the core. I once asked him why he showed me so much love and all he said was "I want you to be happy". I saw his teary eyes when he told my mum and uncle that he loved me from the depth of his heart. My father-in-law was a best friend, he encouraged me to never give up. Anytime I had the chance to chat with him, he shared the Word of God with me. Any close person to me knows the relationship I had with my father-in-law, a gift from above is what he was.

Your memory is a treasure to me and hence it will never depart from my heart. Days will pass and turn into years but I will forever remember you with silent tears. Everything I am today is all because of you. Dada I'm still keeping the gift you gave me on that Valentine's Day. Dada, I am eternally thankful for everything. I am not perturbed because I know you are safe above.

THE GROUP EXECUTIVE CHAIRMAN, elaborated:

"Then I heard a voice from heaven say, 'Write this: Blessed are the dead who die in the Lord from now on.' 'Yes', says the Spirit, 'they will rest from their labour, for their deeds will follow them.'" Amen! **Revelation 14:13**

I am shocked to be standing here to read a tribute in honour of my brother, friend, and colleague- Elder Lawrence Larbi. The relationship between us began when we were both young, but I looked up to him as a senior brother.

In 1999, Mr. Larbi accepted my offer to join Company 1 to help with the restructuring of the fairly new company into a well-established business. By dint of dedication, loyalty, perseverance and godliness, he moved through the ranks to head Company 4, and Company 3, both within the Group 1. Here again, he led conscientiously until his retirement in 2019. He continued to serve the group even in retirement.

Mr. Larbi was passionate about his work and this commitment was evident in the various roles he played throughout his life. He was strong-willed and never took lightly anything concerning the core business. Indeed, whenever duty called, he readily availed himself.

His leadership qualities were admired by many who came into

contact with him. He made complex projects easier to execute, he drove changes and managed challenges with ease. He was an example to both young and old, with a high level of service to the group for which we are deeply grateful.

He was also a brother in the Lord, as we fellowshipped at the same church and as young officers, had the opportunity to be on a couple of programmes which helped us to meet some of the top hierarchy of the Pentecost Church. At work, he always ensured that every employee attended morning devotion. He simply lived his faith in Christ Jesus to the best of his ability.

As you lie before us this day, I say a big thanks to you for imparting in us your positive attitude to work. Your enthusiasm and commitment to duty were par excellence. Thank you for being the livewire of the workplace. Indeed, "If we live, we live for the Lord; and if we die, we die for the Lord. So, whether we live or die, we belong to the Lord."
Romans 14:8

Rest in perfect peace, Friend and a Brother. **Da yie!**

The tributes reproduced below, came from the Madina District of the Church of Pentecost, as follows: TRIBUTE BY THE CHURCH OF PENTECOST

For all the saints who from their labours rest,
Who Thee by faith before the world confessed,
Thy name, O Jesus, be forever blest.
Alleluia! Alleluia!
(William Walsham How, 1823-97; MHB 832)

Once in a while the Lord blesses his people with a unique soul. For such a soul, upon his transition, a tribute, such as this, written on a few pages, does not do justice to the calibre of person he was nor the quality of work he did. Elder Lawrence Baidoo Larbi, whose life on earth we are celebrating today is one such persons. Elder Lawrence Larbi got converted to Christianity early in life, in 1971 when he was baptized into the Church of Pentecost at Anum Boso in the Asuogyaman District of Ghana. Elder L.B. Larbi was extremely dedicated to worshiping his Lord. Over the past forty-nine years of worshipping with or serving in the Church of Pentecost, he remained a committed member of the church, devotedly fellowshipping till his passing.

After being with the Church in Boso for a few years, he joined the Teshie-Nungua Assembly of the church and later transferred to the now Ebenezer Assembly in Madina during the late eighties to the early nineties. In 1996/97, upon the separation of the then Madina West Assembly into two, he and others were posted to the new assembly. Consequently, he become one of the pioneering officers of the new Madina West Assembly, which has now grown into a *full-fledged* district called *Koonaa District*. Whilst there, he served as the Financial Secretary to the Local church.

In the early 2000s, during the tenure of Apostle Emmanuel Kwame Apea (rtd.), who was then the Madina District Pastor, he was ordained as an elder. Shortly after being ordained, Elder Larbi was once again transferred, this time to the Madina Central Assembly, where he served till his passing. Whilst with the Madina Central Assembly he served meritoriously, for eight years, as the Patron of the *Mmaa Kuo* (Women's Ministry) of the Central Assembly. It was during the same period that he was elected to serve on the Madina District Executive Committee as a Member, a role he played for ten years straight. Almost immediately in 2016, he was elected to serve as a member of the Madina Area Executive Committee. He dutifully served for three years in that capacity.

Elder Larbi came into the Local, the District as well as the Area as a gift of God to the church, for the ability to counsel and administer was mightily evident in his service to the church and his Lord. As is espoused in Romans 12, the ministry of counselling, exhorting, encouraging, and generally speaking leading people with care and compassion has been his forte. In addition to the above, he was seriously involved in serving the Lord in the Missions Department at the Area Level as well as Environmental Care and Protection as the Assistant Area *AyaGreen* Committee Leader. The Lord greatly blessed his church through the endowments of Elder Larbi.

Over these forty-nine years, Elder Larbi has served with phenomenal modesty. He never saw himself as one who is important. He only saw himself as a small cog in the Lord's machine. As a Christian, Elder Larbi lived his life in a manner that suggested that he was an ardent follower of Paul's advice as in Rom 8:3-8. His manner of service is in consonance with Rom 12: 3, Ephesians 6:6-7 and Colossians 3:22–24, just serving his Lord and master not to please any man. He was a down to earth Christian who did not think more highly of himself than he should, merely a tool in the Lord's hands.

At meetings when opinions have assumed divergence with members exhibiting passionate convictions he always sought and brought the path that will remedy the knotty situation and at the same time soothe the emotions of others who may have gotten passionate about their conflicting convictions. He spoke his mind always without fear or favour, yet he was able to do so without offending anyone. He has that rare ability to speak the bare truth without offence. And he spoke his truth quietly, knowing that the truth will surely convict even when spoken softly just because it has its own power.

Many are the ministers with whom he worked. The duration of his service as a member of one executive committee or the other attests to his capability and the quality of his wisdom and counsel. By his demeanour and countenance, he showed how much one can look like our Lord. He was gentle and exhibited a measured temperament. As a person, Elder Larbi is an example of one in whom the fullness of the fruit of the Holy Ghost is palpably manifest; by virtue of this, he has adorned his hidden man of the heart with that imperishable beauty of a gentle and quiet spirit which, in God's sight, is very precious. What some achieve with *sternness* and *toughness* he achieved by *affection* and *genuine care*. Elder Larbi was the one who will readily encourage and correct genuinely. He was an *enthusiastic* and *cheerful giver*; it is no wonder that he was greatly loved and admired by all members. His *humility* is as phenomenal as his *faithfulness* is monumental.

Elder Larbi by his life and testimony gave us a true example of deep-seated faith not shaken by the flow of tides and times. His faith and convictions were not showy. He simply was true to his call and salvation irrespective of surrounding conditions. It is by his life and testimony that we get a better understanding of what John Bunyan wrote:

> *Who would true Valour see; Let him come hither;*
> *One here will Constant be, Come Wind, come Weather;*
> *There's no Discouragement, Shall make him once relent*
> *His first avow'd Intent, To be a Pilgrim*

Even though we are sad about his transition; we are glad that he died in the Lord. As the MHB 832 vs. 6 puts it, to this faithful warrior, *"The golden evening brightens in the west; Soon, soon to faithful warriors cometh rest; Sweet is the calm of paradise the blest. Alleluia Alleluia"*.

We know our Lord will tell him, "Elder Larbi Well Done", *Mo Akwa Pa Nokware Fo. Wo ɔbɔ de.*

Ayɛkoo. We hope to see and join him in singing to the glory of our God and King in the Heaven to come. Till then, may he enjoy the rest that he so much deserves. Till then, we bid our Brother, our Mentor, our Elder Adieu. Elder Lawrence Baidoo Larbi, Farewell, Amen!

TWO COMPANIES (Company 2 and Company 3) within Group 1, stated as follows:

COMPANY 2

"They will see his face, and his name will be on their foreheads. There will be no more night. They will not need the light of a lamp or the light of the sun, for the Lord God will give them light. And they will reign for ever and ever. Amen! Revelation 22: 4-5

"TRIBUTE TO A DEAR BOSS"

We are profoundly saddened by the death of Mr. Lawrence Larbi, our dear Boss, who was one of the pioneers and very instrumental in the early days of the establishment of Company 1 from which Company 2 was born. Mr. Larbi joined the company in 1999, having left the MC Company with the intention of bringing his rich experience onboard to support the vision of the fairly new Company 1 and to restructure it into a world-class business.

He was promoted to Deputy Managing Director's role barely two years of assuming duty as Commercial Manager. During his tenure of office, he rolled up his sleeves and got into the trenches to lay a good foundation for Company 1. He was always ready to provide pieces of advice both along professional and religious lines. He always had a Bible under his desk with which he advised us on our personal lives. He did these with his tremendous sense of humour and intelligence. Mr. Larbi was also a very emotionally intelligent boss.

In 2003, when Company 2 was incorporated out of Company 1, that growth trend led to the establishment of another subsidiary in 2005-Company 5. Through his hard work and ingenuity, the company made progress and spawned many subsidiaries: including- Company 4 in 2005, Company A in 2006 and the Group 1 in 2010. *Mr. Larbi, we will forever remember you for your astute leadership.*

He had an obvious genuine interest in all aspects of the work, especially its spiritual growth and supported in placing God first with morning devotions, quarterly prayer sessions and playing a key role in the Annual Thanksgiving Programmes. His ardent love for God also became evident when he led praise and worship sessions during Annual Thanksgiving Services. This moved all and sundry to respond passionately in like manner.

He knew how organizations and their leaders should work in order to be effective and impactful so he displayed workplace discipline and ensured that each employee's role was perfectly played or be sanctioned. He was a determined, collaborative, goal-oriented, caring person who loved life and all that it offered. Mr. Lawrence Larbi, a caring and beloved family man, an unforgettable manager, and a friend, will be missed by many, but never to be forgotten by those of us who were fortunate to work with him! *Mr. Larbi, da yie! Damirifa Due!!*

On its part, **Company 3,** provided a tribute as follows:

COMPANY 3

"A good name is better than fine perfume, and the day of death better than the day of birth." Ecclesiastes 7:1

It is with great difficulty, deep sorrow and, a lot of heaviness that we are struggling to write the word "Tribute" to our father, Manager and Colleague, Mr. Lawrence Baidoo Larbi, our former General Manager, who today lies before us!

Mr. Larbi as we affectionately called him joined the then Company 1 as a Commercial Manager in 1999. Through hard work, commitment and dedication to work, he rose swiftly through the ranks to become Deputy Managing Director, and finally, Assistant Chief Executive Officer by 2008.

With the establishment of Company 4, he was made the head of that entity. His notable achievements in that role were that he started the first building at a famous Convention Centre in Ghana, and built the first three structures on the premises. He also started and completed an eight-storey structure at a faith-based University College; he was instrumental in the construction of an Institute and a Terminal.

Mr. Larbi took his exploits to Company 3, his last place of work prior to his retirement just a year and half ago, after successfully serving the construction wing of Group 1.

If we could sum Mr. Lawrence Larbi up in one word, it would be *'Graceful'*. He was incredibly thoughtful, helpful, unstinting in the amount of time and advice he was prepared to give. He gave us unfailingly good and thoughtful advice and was knowledgeable in a wide range of subjects and always cared to know how each staff was fairing.

Mr. Larbi was Godfearing, a counsellor and a warehouse of good things, and we considered him a pillar of immense expertise and practical knowledge. He effortlessly mixed these traits with a good sense of humour.

Mr. Lawrence Larbi was also a man of peace, humility, compassion and kindness. We felt comfortable around him because he came down to our level and vested a lot of confidence in us. We were always ready to go the extra mile when he called, especially in times of emergency in the workplace. He was always on the move and got things done even if it meant working during odd hours. How can we forget our very own *"Gye Kodi"* (take to go and spend) especially on Fridays just to put smiles on the faces of staff? Mr. Larbi would go the extra mile to assist you, just to make sure that you are comfortable. Fairness and punctuality were his trademarks.

After his retirement *one and a half years ago*, he continued to remain active and willing to help out as usual. But those days are gone, gone but not forgotten. It is really hard to accept your sudden demise, and we will never get accustomed to it.

Certainly, the precious memories of you will forever remain in our hearts. In everything, all we can say is, our heavenly father had better plan for calling you to rest...

A BUSINESS ASSOCIATE, eulogized my friend as a brother, friend, and business partner, as follows:

"Many are the afflictions of the righteous, But the Lord delivers him out of them all"

Psalm 34:19 [NKJV]

My brothers and sisters in Christ, to say **"what a statement"** will be an understatement! ...

I met Mr. Larbi more than two decades ago on my very first visit to the premises of Company 1 at the invitation of now Group Executive Chairman of Group 1.

From our very maiden encounter Mr. Larbi and I struck a bond, a brotherly bond that will continue even as he moves into eternity. It was only on July 15, 2020, that I got to know that Mr. Larbi and I were brothers! I received a copy of his funeral announcement from his son. I was awestruck by Mr. Larbi's clan – DWUMUANA CLAN of Boso, a subgroup of the ASONA CLAN, largest of the 8 Akan clans in Ghana. I am also a DWUMUANA from...

Mr. Larbi was a man who fit all the finest adjectives in our lexicon. Generous. Humble. Selfless. Collegial. Forgiving. Peaceful. Non-covetous. Name them! A one of a kind jewel. His life was a reflection of these virtues. And for all of these, may the God of Hosts have mercy upon him!

He brought to bear of his abundant virtues to his workplace and relationships. I know Group 1 and Company A will write copiously about his working life, but as one of the people who were privileged to have known and worked with Mr. Larbi for so long, it's important that I highlight his pioneering role in the conversion of Company 1 from a sole proprietorship to a limited liability company.

Mr. Larbi was selfless and firmly believed in collective prosperity. He also believed in the power and potency of prayer. I will share ...instances of demonstration of his love for fellow human beings. Sometime in 2003, I was in a deep crisis... I was going through what the Psalmist described in Psalm 34:19 as AFFLICTIONS...As I was pondering over what to do, when Mr. Larbi appeared in my house one Saturday dawn in the company of his late brother ... The duo prayed for and with me, for more than an hour. Mr. Larbi was very forthright and said to me "...I had a revelation to come to proclaim divine strength and restoration in your Life"! Lo and behold with less than 2 months of the spiritual encounter in my house I got an appointment...By the Grace of God within a relative short period, ...practice boomed...

Mr. Larbi would share anything, including his life where necessary... Mr. Larbi was hardworking and indefatigable. But he was also able to strike a perfect balance between work, church activities and family. He was a generous and kind-hearted soul. A gentleman quintessential. It was difficult to find his frailties...A good man is gone...

The eulogy I gave during the funeral service is reproduced below:

EULOGY BY DR. GEORGE APPIAH-SOKYE

I want to recognize all of you for honoring our invitation to the celebration of life of the late Elder Lawrence Kwamina Baidoo Larbi. He will be sorely missed. We are grateful for your thoughts and prayers, presence, and presents. May God richly bless you for coming. By way of introduction, I am Elder Dr. George Appiah-Sokye of McKeown Worship Center (MWC)-Pentecost International Worship Center (PIWC-Romeoville, Illinois) in the Chicago region; and formerly of the Madina Central Assembly of the Church of Pentecost. I am the *inseparable* friend and brother of our deceased brother in Christ. I am delivering this eulogy to the honor of my departed friend because of the travel limitations imposed by COVID-19, not permitting me to be physically present at this meeting. Our friendship has evolved over a period of 24 years, dating back to our meeting in the Madina West Assembly in the Madina Zongo. I can relate our association to that of the friendship between David and Jonathan in the Bible, culminating into the giving of David's eulogy as captured in II Samuel 1:19-27(NKJV), as follows:

"The beauty of Israel is slain on your high places! ᵂHow the mighty have fallen! 20 ˣTell it not in Gath, Proclaim it not in the streets of ʸAshkelon—Lest ᶻthe daughters of the Philistines rejoice, Lest the daughters of ᵃthe uncircumcised triumph. "O ᵇmountains of Gilboa, ᶜLet there be no dew nor rain upon you, Nor fields of offerings. For the shield of the mighty is ᵈcast away there! The shield of Saul, not ᵈanointed with oil. From the blood of the slain, From the fat of the mighty, ᵉThe bow of Jonathan did not turn back, And the sword of Saul did not return empty. "Saul and Jonathan were beloved and pleasant in their lives, And in their ᶠdeath they were not divided; They were swifter than eagles, They were ᵍstronger than lions. "O daughters of Israel, weep over Saul, Who clothed you in scarlet, with luxury; Who put ornaments of gold on your apparel. "How the mighty have fallen in the midst of the battle! Jonathan was slain in your high places. I am distressed for you, my brother Jonathan; You have been very pleasant to me; ʰYour love to me was wonderful, Surpassing the love of women (Emphasis mine). *How ⁱthe mighty have fallen, And the weapons of war perished!"*

The humble beginnings of the late Elder Larbi can be traced to November 25, 1958, when he was born in Kwahu Tease in the Afram Plains in the Eastern region of Ghana to Opanin Kofi Larbi and Madam Salome Kyeiwah (all of blessed memory). He recounts the difficulties the mother went through in raising his siblings, totaling 11, as follows: Moses Afunya Blankson (USA), Ebenezer Yirenkyi (Boso), Benjamin Nyarko (Nigeria), Mary Okyerebea (Boso), Ernest Ampene Larbi (Accra), Grace Adobea (Boso), Dr. Joseph Aduamoah Larbi (deceased), Felicia Lartebea (Accra), *Lawrence Baidoo Larbi* (Accra-In memoriam), Mercy Adobea (Boso), Margaret Boatemaa (USA.), and Janet Adofoa (Accra).

The late Elder Larbi decided to marry early to the love of his life. As a result, once he fell in love, he proceeded to marry and moved on with his life in the *1980s*. By the grace of God, the marriage is blessed with four children: three sons and a daughter.

The qualities of Elder Larbi are worth emulating and include but not limited to the following: generosity across board (church, friends, and family), hardworking, dedication to duty, focused, purpose-driven, and many more. The lessons from the Late Elder Larbi will be presented under *five* themes, as follows: **GRATEFUL HEART**- Elder Larbi shared a burden on his heart regarding his desire to buy a motor bike to support God's work at Kwahu-Tease. When the question was posed: *Why Kwahu-Tease?* He recounted his childhood experiences and offered that the motor bike acquisition was in response to his gratefulness to God as to how far he has come in life. The motor bike was duly delivered through the Madina Area Office of the Church (the gesture has been captured in the Chairman's State of the Church Address).

My bosom friend is appreciative of the love, support, care, and concern of his wife towards him throughout the over 30 years of marriage. Likewise, he is grateful to all his *siblings* but I would like to mention just a few: *first*, Brother Moses Afunya Blankson of the United States of America for supporting the family and their single mother. *Second*, Brother Benjamin Nyarko (Teacher) for providing a source of income to support his education. *Third*, Brother Ernest Ampene Larbi for housing him when he started life in Accra until he got married. *Lastly*, the late Dr. Joseph Aduamoah Larbi for collaborating with other brothers towards the construction of a residential building for the late mother before she passed; as well as, other sisters who volunteered to relocate to Boso to take good care of the mother.

The Group Executive Chairman cannot be spared mentioning. The relationship between the two started from the Teshie-Nungua church. Elder Larbi spent over two decades with the Group 1. May the Lord bless you richly. **GENEROUS TO THE CORE**-He has affected many positively with his kind acts of generosity and his sensitivity to the emotional needs of people who hurt from losses. He has made a mark in leading Special offering sessions in the church and this *grace gift* has endeared him to many. This is huge!

COMPASSION PAR EXCELLENCE-Indeed, Elder Larbi was the first to love me and my family; words are lacking to describe the state of our loss and devastation. He has been there for us for all these years. Elder and Mrs. Larbi have supported my family immensely from my losses to my recoveries. He has celebrated my academic and professional successes and identified with my pitfalls. Memories of our occasional trips to *Kwasi Nyarko*, a town near Nsawam on the *Adeiso* road and Dome (Saint John's) to buy foodstuffs in bulk; as well as, our trips to *Boso* and other towns to attend funerals of church members keep on replaying in my mind. He has been a reliable *cheer leader* in every sphere of life.

PERSEVERANCE AT ITS BEST- When we met, he had just moved on from the MM Company to the MC Company in Tarkwa. He used to spend the weekends in Accra until the contract came to an end. In every step of the way, he demonstrated assiduity and tenacity of purpose from Company 1 as a commercial manager; rising through the ranks to becoming the Chief Executive Officer at a point in time.

Likewise, his pioneering role in Country X's project of Company 1 is remembered. He is applauded for his selflessness and loyalty because there were suggestions from some quarters for him to break away from Company 1 to operate his own business. A suggestion he vehemently resisted. He is celebrated for rising to become the Group Projects Director.

Elder Larbi was the first local financial secretary of the Madina

West Assembly and later became a member of the district executive committee. With time, he won elections to serve as a Member of the Madina Area Executive Committee of the church and also served on the board of the Pentecost Preparatory School. An exemplification of leadership.

MAINTENANCE CULTURE ADHERENT- The late Elder Larbi is a strict adherent to maintenance culture, a quality that is not common in many societies. To this end, *repairs, maintenance, enhancements, additions,* and *replacements* have been done on regular basis on his property. A rare legacy to this generation.

As a matter of fact, and as always, he was going to pick me up at the Kotoka International Airport on *March 25, 2020* but for the COVID-19 lock-down in both USA and Ghana, which caused our meeting to be postponed *sine die*. During the period of our friendship, we have eaten together, worshipped together, discussed topical issues together, shopped together, and shared visions together. The opportunity of our *in-person* meeting has been missed for good.

Nevertheless, he remains in my sub-conscious mind and just as this *chapter* is ending; a new *chapter* has been created to allow for his life story to be shared in my *autobiography,* which will be published next year (if God permits). *The Lord giveth, the Lord taketh away. Blessed be the name of the Lord (Job 1:22).*

I thank God for bringing him into my life as a brother, friend, and his *first-born* son. The **loss** necessitated by his passing cannot be filled. I ask mourners to join the family to thank God for this precious life that is being celebrated here today. It can be categorically stated that he was a *self-made* person, who pursued professional development through *self-study.*

On *Thursday, July 2, 2020,* he died after a short illness. I am told. The Bible stipulates that "*it is appointed unto man to die once and thereafter judgment*" (Hebrews 9:27), so I am mindful that death is inevitable.

Nevertheless, having retired from active labor force, I expected him to have had a restful time because he had planned to go into farming on retirement.

Yes, we can contend that he has lived a short, yet very impactful life, touching many lives through motivation and financial support, including young people who have entered full-time ministry, a couple of elders, and other very influential *mentees* in the market place.

Brother, friend, and daddy-Rest in the Lord's bosom till we meet again. Fare thee well.

Nante yie. Enjoy your **favorite song** in your rest:

Yen Nyankopon ene wo
Yen were kyekyefo Nyame
Fa wo do nsa to yen so
Nyira yen dadaa nyinaa.
Translated as follows:
You are our Almighty God
A comforting God you are to us
As you place your loving alms on us
Continue to bless us as always

LESSONS LEARNED

The life story of the late Lawrence B. Larbi presents very good virtues that can be emulated because I have also been impacted in the process.

PERSONAL QUALITIES

The personal qualities **I** offered revolve around the following: *generosity, compassion, perseverance, adherence to maintenance culture; as* *well as, encouragement, mentorship, leadership, a good strategist, self-made, organization, self-learning,* and *planning.* From the foregoing tributes, several people provided similar and additional perspectives about my intimate friend's personal qualities, as follows: (a) the **extended family** in the biography identified: *God-fearing, generosity, hardworking,* and *dependability.* (b) On her part **the widow** provided *-hardworking, generosity, community-focus, sense of humor, well-mannered, polite, gentleman,* and *leadership.*

(c) **The children** saw in their father the following qualities *inter alia-selflessness, humility, principled, prayerfulness, supportiveness, putting children first.* (d) His long-time friend and boss, **His Group Chairman** observed-*leadership, dedication to duty, loyalty, perseverance, Godliness, strong-will, enthusiasm, commitment,* and *ability to confront challenges.* (e) **The Daughter-in-law** pointed to the following qualities-*gentleness, thoughtfulness, honesty, principled, kindness, caring,* and *gentleness.*

(f) A Business Associate identified the following qualities-*generous, humble, selfless, collegial, forgiving, peaceful, non-covetous, kind jewel, believer in collective prosperity, hardworking, indefatigable; as well as, balancing family, work, and church; and a gentleman quintessential.*

(g) **The Church of Pentecost**, in which my bosom friend was an Elder in Good Standing till his death, traced his 49-year Christian life and identified (I) **Specific grace gifts** as follows: *Counselling, leadership or administration, encouragement,* and *exhortation.* I want to add-*mercy and giving* to the grace gifts of my friend.

(II) **Personal qualities** gleaned from the life of my friend covered the following-*modesty, humility, enthusiasm, humility (down to earth), outspokenness, truth telling, faithfulness, measured temperamentally, affectionate,* and *caring.* **Company 1**, where my good friend spent the last two decades of his working life, serving in different subsidiaries of the group at different times from Company 1; then, to Company 2, Company 4, and Company 3. (g) **Company 2** disclosed that my friend possessed the following qualities- *emotional intelligence, humor, hard work, ingenuity, workplace discipline, determined, caring, collaborative, goal-oriented,* and *family man.* Additionally, (h) **Company 3** summed their perspective as Graceful, yet provided some insights, as follows: (i) graces- *humility, unstinting(or giving), kindness, counseling, peace*; as well as, the qualities below-*thoughtfulness, helpfulness, knowledgeable, God-fearing, caring, humor, punctuality, fairness, doer,* and *motivator.* Wow! A lot of food for thought. I am grateful for the above contributions. Table 10 below show a *snapshot* of personal qualities of the Late Lawrence K.B. Larbi:

Table 10: *Key Qualities of My Beloved Friend*		
Ability to Confront challenges	*Caring*	*Collaborative*
Collegiality	*Community-focus*	*Doer*
Commitment	*Determined*	*Fairness*
Dedication to duty	*Emotional intelligence*	*Family man*
Dependability	*Gentleman*	*Goal-oriented*
Enthusiasm	*Hardworking*	*God-Fearing*
Faithfulness	*Ingenuity*	*Helpfulness*
Forgiveness	*Kind jewel*	*Honesty*
Generosity	*Leadership*	*Indefatigableness*
Godliness	*Polite*	*Kindness*
Humility (Down to earth) Outspokenness	*Prayerfulness*	*Knowledge*
Loyalty	*Selflessness*	*Motivator*
Measured temperamentally Affection	*Sense of humor*	*Non-covetousness*
Modesty	*Supportiveness*	
Perseverance	*Truth telling*	*Principled*
	Well-mannered	
	Work place discipline	*Punctuality*
		Strong-will
		Thoughtfulness
Source: *Created from Biography, Eulogy, and Tributes from Family, Church, and Former Employers*		

A summary of qualities discussed in the various tributes have been *synthesized* and *analyzed* below: ***first,*** I find **convergence** on the following *12 qualities* because of their identification in the testimony of two or more sources-(1) *God-fearing, (2) caring, (3) enthusiastic, (4) Generous, (5) hard working, (6) humble, (7) leading, (8) gentle, (9) sense of humor, (10) principled, (11) thoughtful, (12) family man.* **Second,** I find **divergence** on *41 personal qualities* by different sources, as follows: *(13) able to confront challenges, (14) commitment, (15) dedicated, (16) dependable, (17) faithful, (18) Godly, (19) outspoken,* and *(20) loyal.*

More so, *(21) temperamentally-measured, (22) affectionate, (23) modest, (24) community-minded, (25) determined, emotionally-intelligent, (26) ingenuous, (27) polite, (28) prayerful, (29) selfless, and (30) supportive.* Likewise, *(31) preservers, (32) collaborative, (33) doer, (34) strong-willed, (35) truthful, (36) selfless, (37) supportive, (38) fair, (39) goal-oriented, and (40) helpful.* Similarly, *(41) honest, (42) kind, (43) knowledgeable, (44) motivator, (45) modest, (46) punctual, (47) disciplined, (48) well-mannered. Likewise, (49) collegial, (50) forgiving, (51) kind jewels, (52) non-covetous,* and *(53) indefatigable.*

Typically, people say very good things about the dead but I believe these 53 virtues cannot be discounted because the witness of two or more people converging on 12 of 53 personal qualities makes a strong case for the remaining 41. In his *unconventional approach* to eulogize his brother, friend, and business partner, *A Business Associate* stated that "it was difficult to find frailties" because my friend is "a man who fits all the finest adjectives in our lexicon" I am convinced he has paid his due to his maker and mankind; and for that reason, he has impacted many lives within this short, yet fulfilled life on earth. I thank God for his life. Amen.

LIFE LESSONS

My friend has told me that he has learned four important things from me-(a) savings, (b) maintenance of a personal library, and (c) investments; as well as, (d) supporting some members of extended family such as nephews and nieces to the extent possible and for that reason, asked me to order a laptop for a niece, who was a student at the University of Ghana. I have enjoyed his encouragement for me to further my education. I have observed his desire of eating together with loved ones. We have brain stormed on critical topics of interest and on a wide range of issues. One of the strategies I learned is how he supported his children by continuing to offer them free accommodation after graduation to enable them work for three years to five years to allow for them to focus resources on completing their personal houses to move-in.

CHALLENGES

There is no successful life without challenges. A few of the challenges that come to mind are as follows; (a) **Dealing with the spate of demolition of his residence**-The construction of his residence did not come on a silver platter. There were series of demolition when he started building his permanent residence and the situation could be compared to the story of Isaac in the Bible per Genesis 26:17-22. He was confronted with strive or opposition (Esek), contention or accusation (Sitna); before getting room (Rehoboth) to develop. Today, people see the magnificence of the edifice and not the initial problems encountered. The lesson is that success does not come on silver platter-"Nothing succeeds like success"

(b) **Overcoming temptations of the opposite sex before marriage and at Tarkwa**-Another challenge my friend was confronted with was the youthful temptation with sexual immorality from the Christian stand point. To overcome this temptation, he opted to marry early in life. Nevertheless, the greatest challenge was the period where he worked at Tarkwah (a mining town) in the Western region. Per his narratives, a few *street workers* were willing to offer their services free of charge without any financial commitment. As a result, as a way of overcoming this temptation, he moved to share the same room with a colleague during the weekdays and traveled back to Accra during the weekends throughout the whole period of the contract.

(c) **Unreasonable demands for financial support from people**-I experienced at first hand, how people from all areas, including the church made requests for financial help. While some had genuine needs to be considered, others took his generosity for granted. Some came to ask for money for a purpose under the pretext that they were going to repay but never paid up. In some cases, we later observed that they went round several people with the same reasons for the same purpose. I think these tendencies are not fair because it can deprive people with genuine needs from receiving the much-needed help.

(d) **Suggestions to part with Group 1**- There were suggestions from several business quarters for him to part ways with Group 1 to compete with them. Nevertheless, as *a business associate* explained, he believed in *collective prosperity*. For that reason, he was involved in the conversion of Company 1 from a sole proprietorship to a limited liability company. I can confirm that the preliminary discussions took place at the office of a business associate in the Asylum Down (a suburb in Accra, Ghana) and four people were in attendance, including myself. I bring this point up because in life there is the tendency for people to hurry into leaving to go on their own. In most cases, the motivation is money and the lack of trust. I have seen countless people in different spheres of life breaking away from institutions to go on their own. In most cases, the results tend to be disastrous.

I am not suggesting that everybody should remain in one place whether you like it or not, but what I am saying is that, in life preparation is critical and identifying your divine purpose is the most important thing. Again, collaboration is also a possibility. I have not done any scientific research on this matter but I have observed from accounting and auditing practice that in Ghana partnerships are not common but rather there are many private companies involving members of the family. I have no problem if the family members are qualified because they tend to be loyal. Yet, some do not even understand the role they are supposed to play in the company.

I contend that if people of like-mind can come together for a common purpose, the outcome can be fulfilling to benefit all. My bosom friend has demonstrated just that for all to consider.

ACCOMPLISHMENTS

I would not focus attention on physical but rather eternal accomplishments. My friend served as role model or mentor to some young men who stayed once upon a time in his house as tenants. These young men were incentivized to move into their own-properties on leaving his house. I know currently, he is applying the same principles to his children before his passing. Under this strategy, after graduation from college (university education) he provided the children with free accommodation for three to five years to allow them space to build their homes to move-in. Likewise, he took the building of a personal library serious and was fond of investing in the collection of books. The 53-qualities or virtues he has bequeathed to mankind should serve as the best accomplishment for this generation. My friend has touched many lives as exemplified in the personal qualities identified by different people and groups. See table 10 above providing the list of the 53 personal qualities. I thank God for his life.

REFLECTION

I give God the glory for providing me with such a true friend over all these years. I am eternally appreciative of this gift of God to me. I do not take this friendship for granted. I have stated elsewhere that he was the first to love me because when I met him in 1996, he had completed his residence and moved in. I had just been transferred from Cape Coast to Accra. Around the same time, we had been transferred to the Madina West assembly as part of the strategy to decongest the Ebenezer Temple of worshippers. The original church had grown beyond leads and bounds and the existing sanctuary could no longer contain worshippers. Meanwhile, the same assembly had a spacious church building under construction located in the Madina Zongo. So instead of running a shift system, the church agreed to divide the membership into two to allow for one group to worship in the other church building. The geographical boundary set for the delimitation of residence of members put us in the same category; and for that reason, we found ourselves in the same church.

I remember one day my friend told me that he was attracted to me by a simple but profound question, I posed to him: *What next?* This was during the time of his transition from MC Company, when the contract of the company in Ghana had come to a close and he was figuring out what to do with his life. He asserts that was a life changing question for him. He later decided to work with his long-time Christian brother, now the Group Executive Chairman. Later on, I had the honor of serving on the board of Company 1 in the early *2000s* responsible for Finance and Administration; with other members.

I wish to share the same lesson I learned based on the message I received from the Lord on August 5, 2000 on *"Accepting death"* based on a sub-topic of a book *"Where there is no doctor"* I have recounted the entire story in the preceding chapter and so I do not intend to repeat it here. I recommend the same message to my friend's wife, the children, and the entire family, and the church. I can categorically state that this same message has served me well in the losses I have enumerated above, albeit painful experience. I trust that you would emerge from this loss stronger. I have come to know most of his family members and friends. Actually, I have become a member of the family (both nuclear and extended). I remember his regular question: *Where exactly are you?* Similarly, he looked me in the eyes and told me things just as they are-He looks into my face and tell me the truth whether it is pleasant or not. I benefited from his candid views on issues. Indeed, he has been my confidant and a good comradery had been created among us.

CONCLUSION

I believe that my bosom friend is in a better place and resting in Abraham's bosom. I spent my mourning days with him and later on spent almost all my weekends together with him. I only retired to bed in the night at *Ashongman* (I have discussed Ashongman in another chapter of the book). In addition to what has been said above, his residence served as my "traditional family house" in Accra that hosted my daughter's engagement and my re-marriage in 2005; as well as serving me in the year 2000 when my first wife passed. In all these cases, he was pivotal in all arrangements and planning. I can recount that he was the first to make funds available towards the organization of my year 2000 funeral and he was deeply involved in the Funeral Planning and Co-ordinating Committee, composed of people from the church and families to handle all aspects of the funeral. I also witnessed him host marriage ceremonies of daughters of his brothers in his residence.

I want to corroborate the account given by a business associate in his eulogy regarding the business and personal crisis he went through. After the encounter he had with Mr. Lawrence Larbi and his late brother, he had a follow-up visit and this time, I went with him to the residence of this business associate on campus. On reaching the house, it was the wife who answered to the ringing of the doorbell. The story of the business associate is accurate. To the Group Executive Chairman, I want to say that more is your due than the wife, children, and the family can pay for your support in life and death. I am appreciative of all you did for my friend. May the Lord bless you richly. Through this interaction, my friend was exposed to a lot of influential people in the marketplace. Dear reader, *which of my late friend's qualities resonates with you?*

CHAPTER 11

LIFE IS BITTERSWEET

DADASHOVA (2018) POSITED THAT AUTOBIOGRAPHY is presented as a specific form of epiphany; but in a retrospective self-analysis the writer shapes a new look at the borders of personal power and the level of its dependence on others. In Chapter 9 of this book, I discussed losses that can be countered in numbers but just as I finished recounting my personal losses, a true friend of mine also passed on. In the circumstance, I had no other choice than to devoted Chapter 10 to his memory. In actual fact, he has been part of my life all along as can be gleaned from the narratives in other Chapters. I thank God for his life. In this Chapter, my focus is to address a few issues or matters that arise out of death. Apostle Sampson Ofori Yiadom, writing in his book-The meaning of life in 2019 asserted:

> In spite of Solomon's great wisdom and all the peace and provisions he enjoyed from the Lord during his reign he turned to a life of sin. And so, brought a lot of consequences on the very people he longed for wisdom to rule discreetly. Dear reader, you can't turn your back on the Lord and still expect Him to be accountable to you when calamity strikes. We are responsible for the choices we make. God promises to be a God to the country which will trust, fear, seek His will, and obey Him. Almost all the countries in the world have not met this basic requirement, and tend to seek their own ways; thereby, stepping on each other's toes and bringing about wars, sufferings, perils, and many evil consequences on ourselves (p.50).

Life and death are part of humanity and there is the need to spend some time to understand these concepts; however, the appreciation of this concepts are a matter of the worldview of the individual involved. Nevertheless, there is convergence on the fact that life is bittersweet.

COMMON PHASES OF LIFE

Life can be described as a journey through a rugged terrain, valleys, hills, and plains. Consequently, different people experience these phases at different times. While some find themselves in a valley at a point in time, others find themselves in other phases such as hill tops. Typically, it should be possible for people to begin their life journeys from the valley and end up on hill tops. Yet, others experience the opposite trajectory-Such is life.

This case is explained by the story of Joseph in the Bible who began his life on high hopes; yet found himself in a pit, where there was nothing to write home about and a place of obscurity and a state of nonentity. During this phase of life, one is rejected and isolated by all and nobody wants to be associated with you. The journey can be lonely. You do not have friends and relatives because nobody wants to be linked to a losing team.

In the plain terrain journey of life, everything appears to be working according to plan or destiny. No matter how short or long it can last. This phase is comparable to that experienced by Joseph in the house of the Egyptian influential Potiphar. A slave has been elevated to the status of steward with unfettered access to all privileges. A dream comes true. Many people experience periods in their lives where everything seem to be working for good in response to opportunities. I want to suggest that one takes advantage of the opportunities during time in life because in most cases such advantages do not linger for ever. I have seen many people who missed such opportunities in life and regretted forever.

Actually, I know one person who told me the opportunities he had in Israel and what he made out of the situation; however, he has not had any of such opportunities in the United States of America ever since. Another phase in life has to do with a rugged terrain, where the events of life appears to be normal but with occasional challenges that needs to be surmounted. In this vein, people see the suffering you are going through but do not go beyond sympathy to identify with the problems. This phase is analogous with the imprisonment of Joseph in Egypt. A stranger and a slave placed in jail has no advocate and he will soon be forgotten by all such as those he had rightly interpreted their dreams. When one gets to this area of life, all acquaintances are lost.

The desired phase of life is the place on hilltop. This is a phase of self-actualization, fulfillment, and accomplishment. At this phase, everybody wants to identify with you and remote relatives and friends make every effort to get closer and identify with you. There is the adage that the poor has no friend.

A friend of mine who lost the father in his infancy had to be supported by the single mother over years and was compelled to learn the mother's trade to be able to support the mother and himself. Later, he completed his undergraduate education and secured a job to support his family. One day while he was at work, he was paged to come to the front office because he had a visitor. When he got there he met an elderly woman who introduced herself as his auntie. Interestingly, she was able to answer some key questions so her relationship could not be questioned, but the question that arose for determination was: *Where has she been all these years?* I think it is not fair for the mother to be left alone to cater for the children just for the auntie to reap from where she has not sown. By way of application, Joseph becomes the second most important person in Egypt subject to only Pharaoh. A mountain top experience. If you attend a typical funeral and listen to the biographies and tributes, you would appreciate the phases of life the deceased might have gone through-Summed up as-Life is bittersweet!

THE JOURNEY THROUGH MOURNING

In the preceding Chapters, I have offered some insights into some of the appropriate responses to dealing with losses from my own personal experiences. In this section of the textbook, I am going to discuss the cycle of recovery from loss of loved ones. I am basing my admonitions on the information I gathered from various sources during my own personal experiences; as well as, the Scriptural text in *2 Samuel 1:19-27,* this eulogy was read by David in honor of his best friend Jonathan and father (Saul). All-in-all, different people mourn differently, but **5 stages** can be identified throughout the process from bereavement to recovery. The recovery is not total because life lost cannot be replaced. The Scriptural text-*Psalm 23:4* stipulates: *"Yea, though I walk through the valley of the shadow of death,* I will fear no evil: for thou art with me; thy rod and thy staff they comfort me". The loss of a dear one is characterized by a mixture of sadness, a feeling of emptiness, recounting of memories, and comparing to miseries. Consequently, life losses can be tragic and emotional experience. This position is confirmed by Mr. Omar (a character) in "Everybody Hates Chris" series. Mr. Omar will describe every death as "tragic" I will be dealing with the five stages or phases of dealing with losses below.

Stage 1-*Why Me?* The apparent difficulty in coming to terms with personal losses is real. A lot of memories engulf the person who has suffered the loss and at times these thoughts clouds the decision-making abilities of the persons involved. In several cases other close relatives and friends have to step into the situation to support the bereaved persons. The commonest question that is posed is: *Why me?* This question appears to suggest that death has not been fair to us. Yes, death is not fair to mankind even though life and death are associated with mankind. The portion of Scripture states: *"Thy glory, O Israel, is slain upon thy high places! How are the mighty fallen. Tell it not in Gath, publish it not in the streets of Ash'kelon; lest the daughters of the Philistines rejoice, lest the daughters of the uncircumcised exult* (2 Samuel 1:19-20). The stage is characterized by rationalizing very deep-seated memories and emotions. Take a look at the Chronicles of one of my losses:

May 16, 2000-Pat was accompanied home by uncle and offered us ¢100,000 in financial support.

May 17, 2000-Pat arrives at Ashongman with severe pain on one side of the pelvic girdle and could not walk. So, hired taxi(cab) from Ashongman home at ¢7000.00.

May 19, 2000-I was accompanied by Mr. Lawrence Larbi to the Legon Hospital, where Pat was admitted for Bed resting and Mr. Larbi gave me ¢100,000.00 check to assist me and also placed at my disposal a private car and his taxi to attend to the needs of Pat.

June 6, 2000-Sent Pat to Legon Hospital and was admitted for the same problem.

June 6, 2000-Exchanged Canadian $50 (¢135,000).

June 17, 2000-Uncle picks up Pat and Becky to their place At Madina Social Welfare.

June 24, 2000-Went to the house of uncle in the company of Mr. Alex Cofie but saw the condition of Pat was not good- labor signs and malaria. Accompanied to the hospital by uncle's wife, and her nurse friend. Admitted at 5:36pm.

Sunday, June 25, 2000-Mr. Larbi gave me ¢150,000 in respect of labor implication.

Pat gave birth to a baby girl at 8:00pm, with me was Mr. Alex Cofie. The Nursing sister permitted me to come to the Labor ward to assist my wife and see things for myself.

The medical doctor arrives to assist throughout delivery and discusses with me, as follows: (i) the condition of the mother was normal, but the child's neck was tied with the umbilical cord and the baby was being resuscitated. "The team is doing their best" Bid Pat farewell and good night at 9:00pm.

Monday, June 26, 2000-On arriving at the hospital, I was told that newly born baby died in the night after receiving intensive care.

Monday June 26, 2000- Buried our baby girl at Madina Cemetery with the help of Elder David Mensah, Paa Fio, David Ofantse, Justice Mingle (GBC), District Sanitary Officer, and a casual labourer.

June 30, 2000-Mr. Larbi gave me ¢100,000.00 for support.

July 4, 2000-The doctors examined Pat and suspected an enlargement of the liver and prescribes medication. Had discussion with medical doctor in the presence of Mr. Larbi. He explained that there is no crack in the bones rather there is an expansion of the cervix and bone. Recommended less movements for normalcy to be restored. The bigger issue was the possible enlargement of the liver which can lead to a failure; nevertheless, the new medication will would help to reduce the pulse and cause the liver to shrink.

July 5, 2000-Pat was referred from the Legon Hospital to the Korle Bu Teaching Hospital (KBTH) in an ambulance; and accompanied by Madam Comfort, Eunice Wiredu, and some staff of the University of Ghana (Legon) Hospital. The Nursing Sister I have mentioned elsewhere guaranteed the medical bills to permit us make it to the KBTH in good time.

July 8, 2000- Pat was transferred from the Emergency Unit (SME) to Ward 4(Side ward 2)

July 19, 2000-Received ¢100,000 from Mr. Evans Boakye on behalf of Bekoe Boampong (Agya) and wife on visitation and another donation was made to Pat by Evans and wife (Beatrice).

July 22, 2000-Alex Cofie called on us at the KBTH and brought us ¢120,000 from Study group members-Shirley, Dede, and Carolyn as support towards medical expenses.

Sunday, July 23, 2000-The following visited (i) Lawrence Larbi gave us ¢100,000; (ii) Madina West PEMEF (¢30,000); (iii) Madina Estates *and IPS assemblies (¢20,000), (iv) Sister Sara Adipah (¢10,000), (v) Sister Tawiah (SSNIT Flat 6A-¢10,000).*

July 26,2000-Antwi Asimeng visited and game me ¢100,000 for medical support.

Friday, July 28, 2000- Dr. Dadson told me that Pat is suspected to have cancer, but the type is not yet known. The team was waiting for the results of tests; but assured me that it could be managed, using rich diet and energy producing supplements. A repeat of earlier procedure will be done the following week.

Friday, August 4, 2000-Received ¢200,000 from Elder Joseph Siaw Agyepong (MD of Jospong Printing Press Limited). Went to Korle Bu in the morning and evening. Met Dr. Dadson at 7:00am with drugs(medication) for administration on Pat. Accompanied by Auntie Naa, the National Women's Movement Secretary came to the bed side and pray for Pat.

August 5, 2000-Pat passes away at 2:00am at the KBTH. The last day of Pat as a living soul.

Note: *I do not have space to mention all names and visitations but I have highlighted a few to make a point of the provision of God even in tribulation.* My question is: *Have you considered how finances were provided to meet the needs of the moment?* Indeed, God provides a way in our afflictions.

To continue from where we left off, at this stage, the bereaved has the audacity to question God, as follows: If God is an omniscient, omnipotent, and omnipresent; then, *Why did he permit such a bad thing to happen to good people?* A fair question but the import is that God is not what he claims to be. There are opportunities in our pain to explore. Per Isaiah 45:3, the Bible stipulates: *"I will give you the treasures of darkness and the hoards in secret places, that you may know that it is I, the LORD, the God of Israel, who call you by your name (*RSV*).* Additionally, pain has the tendency of causing us to gravitate towards the Lord; nevertheless, the Bible states: *"Now we see things imperfectly...just as God Knows me completely"*(I Corinthians 13:12); *"And we know that in all things God* *works for the good of those who love him, who have been called according to His purpose"* (Romans 8:28).

Stage 2- *Who Should Be Blamed?* The people of God should demonstrate love towards bereaved families and comforting them by praying for them, being present physically (if possible), and providing them financial support (presents). In the Scriptural text under consideration, David elaborated: *"Ye mountains of Gilbo'a, let there be no dew or rain upon you, nor upsurging of the deep! For there the shield of the mighty was defiled, the shield of Saul, not anointed with oil* (2 Samuel 19: 21). The second stage is characterized by complete resentment towards the departed for causing pain and bringing undue attention unto us. You wonder why David could heap curses on an *innocent* mountain simply because that was the location of the death of his bosom friend and father. A blame game is part of this stage.

People blame God for the loss; as well as other targets such as witches and wizards for inflicting pain on us. In some African societies, we asked: *Who killed the person?* Implying that every death is the outcome of orchestration of evil forces, who are responsible for negative things in society. In some western world, the analogous question is: *What killed the person?* Suggesting that there is a cause-and-effect dynamic in all life experiences. The pointing of accusing fingers can lead to unnecessary rifts and cracks in the already bleeding family. I counsel that: *"In your anger do not sin. Do not let the sun go down while you are still angry"*(Ephesians 4:26).

Stage 3-*What Went Wrong?* The next and related stage in the mourning process is the assessment of what possibly went wrong. The Scriptural text states: *"From the blood of the slain, from the fat of the mighty, the bow of Jonathan turned not back, and the sword of Saul returned not empty* (2 Samuel 19: 22). This phase is characterized by a dark and hopeless moments and contemplation of what was not done to save the situation. Some go to the extent of blaming themselves for not exercising much faith or not praying enough. Others also worry for not seeking medical attention on time. We are encouraged by Romans 8:35, which seeks answers to the question: *Who shall separate us from the love of God?* Fortunately, the writer of the Book of Romans goes ahead to offer some insights, as follows: (a) S*hall trouble or hardship? or (b) Shall persecution or famine? or (c) Shall nakedness or danger? Or (d) shall sword?* Our love for God should stand sure in good and bad times.

Stage 4-*What Can I Do?* The short to medium-term is characterized by getting worried about funding the funeral and burial cost, the long-term upkeep of children, and regular state of hopelessness. These are genuine concerns and for that reasons, loved ones should be ready to assist in any ways possible to alleviate anxieties associated with this phase. Friends and loved ones should demonstrate initiatives and creativity towards the family to the extent possible. In the Scriptural text under consideration, David elaborated: *"Saul and Jonathan, beloved and lovely! In life and in death they were not divided; they were swifter than eagles, they were stronger than lions. "Ye daughters of Israel, weep over Saul, who clothed you daintily in scarlet, who put ornaments of gold upon your apparel"* (2 Samuel 19:23-24).

The call of David for the daughters of Israel to weep over Saul for specific impact from the deceased is very instructive. In some African societies, people donate assorted items and seed money to foot bills associated with the funeral. In some western societies, insurance policies are activated to address the same concerns. Typically, people are moved by their relationship with the deceased and the family. The Bible clarifies that: *"I can do all things through Christ who strengthens me"* (Philippians 4:13). Let us be supportive of one another in hard times.

Stage 5-*How Do I Respond?* The final stage in the mourning process is characterized by the acceptance of loss. This is what the song writer explained: *"It is well with my soul"* In the Scriptural text under consideration: *"How are the mighty fallen in the midst of the battle!"*

Jonathan lies slain upon thy high places. I am distressed for you, my brother Jonathan; very pleasant have you been to me; your love to me was wonderful, passing the love of women. "How are the mighty fallen, and the weapons of war perished!"(2 Samuel 19: 25-17). In another development, I Samuel 3:18(b) offered: *"So Samuel told him everything and hid nothing from him. And he said, "It is the LORD; let him do what seems good to him"*(Emphasis mine). Likewise, God commissions Joshua in Joshua 1:1-3: *"After the death of Moses the servant of the LORD, the LORD said to Joshua the son of Nun, Moses' minister, ² "Moses my servant is dead; now therefore arise, go over this Jordan, you and all this people, into the land which I am giving to them, to the people of Israel. ³ Every place that the sole of your foot will tread upon I have given to you, as I promised to Moses"*

My suggestion is to find support by (a) drawing support from your faith, especially what you have internalized and accumulated over the period; (b) turning to a support group such as fellow elders, ministers, and matured Christians; (c) accepting support from family, friends, and the Church family; and (d) turning to God in prayer, worship, and praises. Similarly, follow the following nuggets of truth: (i) encourage yourself in the Lord, (ii) know that –"He is the Lord" (iii) direct your intimacy to the Lord, (iv) have regular conversation with God in prayer, and (v) in all things acknowledge Him.

MANAGING MATTERS ARISING OUT OF LOSS

I have seen people concentrating much efforts on weddings that take place in a day than concentrating attention on the lifelong marriage itself. Comparatively, more attention is focused on the funeral ceremony to the detriment of the matters arising out of the loss, which can have lasting effects of bereaved and loved ones. Many a time, there is no clear path for the bereaved families to follow to navigate the storms after the burial. Consequently, several bereaved families do not know where to start from in managing life thereafter. Yes, life must go on but how does a bereaved family member start the process. In this section, I am going to offer a few guidance to assist any family who will find the suggestions useful. I have dealt with loved ones who have died testate and others who have died intestate, so I will share some of the experiences to assist others. Most of the suggestions are applicable to Ghana in particular but I believe the lessons can be applied to other jurisdictions as well.

DYING TESTATE

A will is the statement of the desires of the testator, written while living but effective at death. The Book of Hebrews posited that: *"For where there is a testament, there must also of necessity be the death of the testator"* (Hebrews 9:16 NKJV). As a result, to die testate means the dead left behind a will or testament. A will should be written by a person of sound mind and the property stated in the will should be the self-acquired property of the testator. While there should be witnesses to the will, the witnesses do not need to know the contents of the document. Again, there are named trustees and executors of the will who are appointed by the testator to ensure that his or her wishes are carried out. **I have learned that wills prepared in other jurisdictions can be effective in Ghana per Ghana law.**

In one of the cases, the testator gave me a copy of the receipt from the High Court where the original and final will copy was deposited and disclosed two other places where copies could be obtained. So, the lead was followed to trace the lawyer who prepared the document and ultimately arranging to get all the family attend the reading of the contents by the Registrar of the High Court. In the second case, the testator informed me of the existence of the will and the name of the lawyers who prepared the document. The testator died eleven years after the preparation of the testament. The lawyer attended the funeral of the deceased. So, when he was contacted, interestingly, he did not remember the existence of the document. Fortunately, a copy of the document was retrieved from the records of the deceased and the details at the back confirmed the name of the lawyer.

It has been established that for a will to be effective, the testator should be dead and for the wishes of the testator to be valid, a Court process must commence through the application for a probate to authorize the actualization of the contents of the testament. The benefits of the preparation of wills include the offering of protection to loved ones such as spouses and children and also reduce any uncertainties regarding the estates of the deceased. In patrilinear system of inheritance, a will is good but may not be a great deal because property automatically transfers to children and spouses.

In matrilineal system of inheritance, the existence of a will is huge! Otherwise, the children and spouses may be at the mercy of the extended family members. A lot of people do not like talking about wills because it is linked to death and the fear is that once prospective beneficiaries get to know of the existence of a testament; they will move heaven and earth through fair and fowl means to bring about the ultimate death of the testator. I cannot confirm the accuracy of this concern but I have come to know that beneficiaries of life insurance policies can be suspects for unnatural deaths of policyholders.

Furthermore, it pays to share information on the existence of a will with trusted persons; otherwise, your bankers can act in that capacity.

DYING INTESTATE

I have encountered relatives and loved one who died intestate, or without a will. The situation is a bit complex as compared to those who died testate because most of the preliminary work of gathering pertinent information about assets and property is done by the testator at the point of the preparation of the document. The details of the property are captured with specificity except the omnibus clause, which states-"and any other property owned by the testator but not mentioned..." Contrarily, the gathering of information about the assets or property or estates is on the prospective beneficiaries in the case of those who die intestate. The case of the Social Security benefits does not present much challenge because the Pensions entity utilizes the beneficiary information provided by the dead, while alive to disburse the benefits. In the case of other assets or property, *a letter of administration* has to be obtained from the Courts to be able to distribute the assets or property.

The following steps will be helpful: (I) After the funeral, proceed to get copies of the death certificates (one is not enough) because usually the Pensions body will need a copy and the Court will also need a copy as evidence of death. (II) Gather information about property or assets such as all bank accounts and balances, marketable securities such as investment accounts and balances, moveable and immovable property such as automobiles and land and buildings, shares or stocks, and many more. (III) Upon the application brought before a Court of law, approval is given by the Courts for the administration of the estates of the deceased. My Letters of Administration is dated March 12, 2001. (IV) This is followed by the payment of estates duties or taxes on the value of the property. (V) The Letters of Administration will enable the beneficiaries of the estates to deal in them as permitted by law. The Power of Attorney granted to me by Eric Appiah (my brother-in- law) per affidavit dated April 9, 2001: "...*Granting of this power of attorney to Mr. George Appiah-Sokye is due to my inability to go about processing all relevant documents concerning the claiming of death benefits of the deceased Patience Olivia Appiah-Sokye which form part of the payment of her estates...*". I hope you will find the above information very useful.

CHAPTER 12

STEWARDSHIP OF GRACE

THERE IS NO RIGHT OR entitlement to a position or process. I have come to appreciate that *stewardship of grace* is ingrained in me, from my popular last name -Appiah-*Sokye* and the subject-matter of this book-"*Enough to be Shared*" and the fact that the name is a purpose-driven one. Once upon a time, one of the Apostles of the Church of Pentecost U.S.A., Inc. confirmed that I am a *steward of grace*- a rare combination of graciousness and stewardship. Stewardship is a concept which is rooted in the agency theory, establishing a relationship between a principal and agent. While the owner of the resource is deemed a master, the agent is viewed as a steward to whom much has been entrusted to provide desired outcomes. Former President Kufuor of Ghana has observed that "*it is not easy for old men to see their grandchildren rise and prosper the way this …is doing*" Consequently, there is the need to answer the question: *Do we have anything that we have not received?* This leads us to the stewardship framework.

Grace is a common phenomenon across the globe. Grace has been defined as *an unmerited favor* or *undeserved privilege*. While grace is called *adom* among the Akan; *amenuveve* is the term used by the Ewes in Ghana. "Whatever it is that God calls you to do, it is always beyond what we would, at first see or think (Swaggart, 2018)" "In reality, church is actually that which is preached and taught behind the pulpit. Everything else, one might say, is just an added on" (Swaggart, 2018). Grace is an affirmation and attribution to things that cannot be explained; and as a result, "there is nothing in the world more important than the Word of God" (Swaggart, 2018). Grace is a *cause -effect* phenomenon because you cannot give what you do have; suggesting that for you to be in a position to give something of value, you might have received it in one way or the other.

My life journeys have evolved from Mampong Ashanti in Ghana, where I had my primary and elementary education to my secondary education in Juaben-Ashanti; and thereafter, to Nkwatia-Kwahu for my *sixth-form* (pre-college) education. Throughout this period, I have enjoyed **divine provisions** such as a case in point during the 1983 draught, when some classmates and I were fed by an old lady in Juaben-Ashanti. While in the University of Ghana, God used my good friend-*Alex Cofie* to respond to my need for money at a point in time during my graduate education. I have narrated the story elsewhere in the book. Likewise, **divine selection** in an opportunity that caused me to be chosen in form 1(High School freshman) as part of the delegation to Mount Mary College in Somanya-Eastern region of Ghana, a college that trains French teachers for Ghana and had the *state-of-the-art* facilities for teaching and learning of the French language. Similarly, my participation in debates as a freshman and election as School Prefect in High or Secondary School; and ultimately making it to the graduate School are part of God's grand scheme and divine selection.

Aurell and Davis (2019) have explained that most of the autobiographical texts analyzed by contributors also have fictional aspects that complicates the process of analysis of history and tradition, and the practical past. I have enjoyed traveling mercies; involving traveling by land through the Mampong scarp, as well as, ascending and descending of the Kwahu ridge (Adwanama Mountains). The shortage of water experienced in the aftermath of the 1983 draught in Ghana, resulting in the use of water from wells dug out of the course of a stream in Nkwatia-Kwahu in Ghana while I was a sixth-former that resulted in rashes on my skin. Likewise, I have enjoyed investments in textbooks from my high school days.

I argue for involvement of parents, especially fathers in the education of children because it can make a huge impact. As my father counseled me against involvement in students' unrest, I pass the same advice to you all. There is the need to use all existing and available means to address grievances. Yes, I know that people in authority tend to respond swiftly to violence but that should not be the norm. I support articulation of views with facts and numbers and offered respectfully; because following laid down rules and grievance procedures provide *audit* trail. I dislike sycophancy and hypocrisy. Be honest with yourself and do not do the bidding of anybody.

My good friend-Alex Cofie has taught me that parents can sacrifice for children; as a result, it should not be all about parents, but the children should be at the center of all we do. I have been exposed to different deployment approaches as a student and as a teacher.

I have been *pruned* by the higher failure rates of accounting education in Ghana as I have recounted in preceding chapters of this textbook. Even though, there are no classmates during preparation for professional examinations; yet, the professional network provided through Societies and Year Groups can make up for the lost association during the preparatory stages. With time, the provision of study materials by the ICAG has improved through the publication of manuals. My membership of honour societies, including Delta Mu Delta and Golden Key Honour Society has been a hallmark of excellence. Again, striking a balance between education and family life has been rewarding even though challenging.

I have reiterated that every experience is key so young people should be open to plurality of job experiences. At times, a brief exposure can make all the difference. Grace has been categorized into three, as follows: (i) common grace, (ii) special grace, and (iii) great grace. A few Biblical references that converge on grace include the following: *Grace upon grace* (John 1:16), *He gives more grace* (James 4:6), and *Grace, grace unto it* (Zacharia 4:7).

COMMON GRACE

The term *common grace* can be misleading because it gives the impression that such graces are ordinary or less important but such categorization will be wrong. Common grace-is understood to be the routine and regular privileges enjoyed by mankind such as, rain that fall for the benefit of all, sun shine does not discriminate but available to all. I can state that I am a born-leader, who has been subjected to process to develop capacity for every area of life. I have been trained as a manager from Business Schools I have attended in Ghana and elsewhere. I know leaders can be born, trained, or spontaneously emerge from a group. In addition to my God-given abilities, capabilities, competencies, and endowments; I am fortunate to have been born from two distinctive families with different characteristics. While my **father's family** possess (a) *appealing physical appearance*, the males are handsome and females are beautiful; (b) *riches*, the average person commanded financial resources; and (c) *an appreciable level of education*; on **my mother's side**, the distinguishing characteristics encompass: (d) *leadership abilities*, (e) *biological fruitfulness*, and (f) *longevity*. I have claimed all the positivity of both families *in the name of Jesus*. At the same time, I have renounced any negativity, even in the name of Jesus.

Over the years, I have been exposed to the *trimester*, as follows: first term (Michaelmas), second term (Lent), and third term (Trinity); and later exposed to the *semester* in the graduate school. Nevertheless, I experienced *both* in my teaching career. Lifelong capacity development is possible. I have been connected positively to mature students as a young adult in college. The elderly (matured) population moderated the conduct of the young cohorts in Colleges leading to a balanced development. In their efforts to get acceptance from the young cohort who happened to be the majority on campuses; in the process, some matured students could also become notorious in the process.

I have been impacted by the *Johari Window* framework on **feedback** and **self-disclosure** in my principles of management course and *the unorganized manager;* a film, my undergraduate class watched at the British Council Hall in Accra. I have benefited from a few inaugural lectures on the university campuses and the May Day celebrations in the University of Ghana Business School. I have witnessed the whole spectrum on financing university education in Ghana over the years. I can identify the following basic skills and qualities: *first*, drive, initiative, leadership, information gathering, and ability to get along with others; *second*, research and ability to develop ideas, adopting to changing conditions and situations.

Third, effective communication across levels; combined with sophisticated skills for presentation, negotiation, and investigation; *Four*, critical thinking or problem-solving, and team-playing role competencies. I am a self-motivated person and independent-minded. Nevertheless, investment in time for seminars and workshops is fruitful. *Lastly*, in the area of technology, I have arisen to the occasion to be proficient in Microsoft Office-*Word, Excel, and PowerPoint*; as well as, internet usage for research, communication, and learning. The accounting applications (software) or accounting package cover-*FundEz, Shelby, NetSuite ORACLE, Quick Books, Bimbilla, E-merge, Topaz*, and so on. These skills had to be learned over time because technology advancement is quite recent.

SPECIAL GRACE

Special grace is the unique privilege that characterizes a state of affairs to meet expectations.

I have recounted my varied experiences from selling of fish, maize, tomatoes, and kenkey; to shoe shining; as well as, fiscal compliance, property management, business process outsourcing; problem-solving, involving leadership training, consultancy, forensic accounting; taxation, auditing and assurance; mentorship, writing, teaching, and administration. Other experiences have involved poultry and more recently the exploration of the role of Registrar to the Pentecost Biblical Seminary (PBS). There have been events along the learning trajectory, including disappointments and missteps; but through it all, I have come to appreciate that service is not slavery and money cannot save life; thereby, emphasizing the vanity of life as King Solomon articulated in the Book of Ecclesiastes (Yiadom, 2019).

A number of choices have to be made during my life process, including a combination of lifelong or ongoing approach to learning to help me stay abreast with the times; self-motivation in pursuit of knowledge for either professional, or personal reasons, or both; then, the issue of taking *full-*time job versus *full-time education.* During my time, taking a full-time job and full-time education were mutually-exclusive, but times have changed; and for that reason, new approaches in education have emerged. In the case of education, one can now evaluate options such as Weekend, Evening, Sandwich or Modular; as well as, Online platforms. Unlike the younger generation to whom this book is intended, I want to stress that the educational system in Ghana during my days used to be very long but times have changed. In those days, the typical structure of education was as follows: 10 years elementary school (6 years primary and 4 years of middle); 5 years of secondary or high school; 2 years of sixth form (pre-College); 3 years of university or college-**20 years**-Total.

The favor and grace of God is key from the foundations of my faith, which has propelled me to be focused on the bigger picture. There is the need for people to meet the emotional needs of bereaved families as part of the support systems to provide for words of encouragement. As the Holy Scripture stipulates, the enemy comes in the flood so life threatening events can occur in sequence. I have stated in Chapter 11 of this textbook that *life can be bittersweet.* I have been mentored by others (see also Chapter 15); So, I can mentor others in turn through career preparation and life choices. Additionally, leadership coaching is also a service to humanity.

I know it takes a simple idea to change the world and change one's life. I entered the University of Ghana at age 22 and completed at age 25. I went back for my Master degree at age 35 and finished at age 37. When I commenced my terminal degree, I was 48 years old and I completed at age 52. In-between these periods, I have pursued professional certifications and other endeavors. I have been a life-long learners and so, my *learning years* had overlapped some of my *working years* due to my personal circumstances-both controllable and uncontrollable; but I want my retiring years to be fulfilling and refreshing (if God gives me the opportunity because I do not have control over my life). As a result, I have developed the discipline of learning for long hours. Typically, beginning my day at 3:00 am and going to bed between 7:00 pm and 9:00 pm during weekdays; and sitting for long hours from 8:00 am to 8:00 pm with one or two breaks on Saturdays.

I have been a trail-blazer in my family and so I needed to chart my own course. As much as possible, I have encouraged the younger ones to pursue their education as early as possible in order to be focused on enhanced work and family life. My contemporaries who approached life that way had a head-start in life. I know the race is not for the swift per Biblical admonition but it is a good strategy to pursue. Another consideration to engage our attention should be: *Which should be pursued first-appointments or education?* The answer to this question is not very simple, in my candid opinion. I have seen people rush into politics in most cases for various reasons only to be given appointments they have not gone through process to handle and the consequence is anyone's guess. Some have used the opportunities offered by such appointments to bridge the knowledge and experience gap. Albeit, at the expense of the taxpayer.

In recent times, some prominent politicians in Ghana have been criticized for using taxpayers' money meant for the *brilliant but needy* in society to improve learning. As might be expected, some of those people tend to have divided attention in the performance of their job description. Compare this state of affairs to others who assumed office prepared from day one. Such people tend to be focused on their mandate and confident in their delivery. I am not arguing that either is right or wrong; but what I am saying is that set goals early in life and work towards them and be prepared when the opportunity is presented. I had a student in one of my professional classes in Ghana who was actively involved in the campaign of one political party. When the party won election, he was disappointed that the party did not give him any position. I would have wished that he focused on his studies to get the needed education before actively engaging in politics.

That is all. I have touched on the need for preparation in life in Chapter 26 of this book. So, I do not want to belabor the point here.

Writing on the topic: *Amazing Grace*, Swaggart (2018) quoted President Roosevelt as saying:

> *"It is not the critic who counts; not the man who points out how the strong man stumbles, or where the doer of deeds could have done them better. The credit belongs to the man who is actually in the arena, whose face is marred by dust and sweat and blood; who strives valiantly; who errs, who comes short again and again, because there is no effort without error and shortcoming; but who does actually strive to do the deeds; who knows great enthusiasms, the great devotions; who spends himself in a worthy cause; who at the best knows in the end the triumph of high achievement, and who at the worst, if he fails, at least fails while daring greatly, so that his place shall never be with those cold and timid souls who neither know victory nor defeat."*(Theodore

Roosevelt-Retrieved from https://www.goodreads.com/ quotes -accessed on 04/15/2020).

The critical success factors to be imbibed include the following: *One*, active participation, appreciative heart, communication, creation of linkages, creativity, decisiveness, execution of task for outcomes, implementation strategies, and initiative. *Two*, innovation, inspiration, interpersonal relationship, leadership, managerial capabilities, negotiation, and operational effectiveness and efficiency. *Three*, professional expertise, pushing strategies, relationships or network building; and *lastly*, shaping the world, spotting opportunities, and dealing with uncertainty.

GREAT GRACE

Great grace is an uncommon privilege that exceeds expectations. The question is: What is it that we have that was not received? I cannot give what I do not have in the first place-this is the *Nemo dat non quid habet*. To whom much is given, much is expected and so social responsibility is an appropriate response.

LESSONS OF LIFE

Life teaches us lessons and it is not everything that is taught in textbooks and schools. While lessons taught in schools have proven to be relevant and important; other lessons are learned through life experiences and so it is said that experience is the best teacher. I want to mention a few lessons below: **One**, as a child at age 6, I was invited to a birthday party organized by a nurse for her daughter at the Mampong Maternity Hospital, where my father worked. After we have eaten and refreshed; it was time for all children to take turns to sing one song but for no apparent reason, I could not remember any song to sing. After the event, the children on the hospital compound started teasing me for my inability to sing during the party. Perhaps, that explains why I do not fancy parties because I am not a fun of parties. As I learned more about our history, I want to understand if birthday celebrations are-*cultural* or *achievement* issue. I see birthday celebration more from a Western cultural dimension and not achievement-based as other celebrations tend to be. I have no objections if most birthdays are celebrated at the family level with the exception of celebrations associated with milestones. I am all for that.

Two, in the compound house I grew up in, there was a girl by name- Melissa (not real name), who will threaten to beat me at the least provocation. Her threats to beat me up was frequent until I went on admission at the Komfo Anokye Teaching Hospital (KATH) in Kumasi (Ghana). On my return from the hospital admission, one day I stood up to her and that was the end to her threats. I know that people capitalize on our vulnerabilities to take advantage of us. **Three,** a boy in our compound house called-John (not the real name) and I were wrongly accused of stealing a pair of shoes by a neighbor; and when we were subjected to search, all the searches proved futile. While I told the accuser to check from my hands if there is any pair of shoes; John told the person to come and search his mother's room if there is any pair of shoes. These responses in the *Twi* dialect spoken in Ghana resonated with the people in the house.

Four, I remember complaining about the behavior of one my sons and it was then that one of my presiding elders gave me a constructive feedback to the effect that my son's behavior was consistent with mine. In the African parlance, *"the crab does not begat a bird"* **Five,** I had been taught in school to stick to decisions for better outcomes and on this one occasion, as a took a position and not willing to modify my stand, one of my bosses reminded me that I am not a machine. In another development, the administrator of the institutions I worked for taught me that "It is only a fool who does not change his mind" These two lessons have taught me the need to make room for modifications if need be; even though, it pays to have opinion and positions on matters in life.

Six, I have learned from Apostle Professor Opoku Onyinah on the need to manage fame and pressure from success. Per his book "*the pressure of success*", successful people tend to come under intense pressure from all angles and so there is the need to be adequately prepared on the management of the pressure that comes with success. **Lastly**, there is a divine hand in the affairs of men. I remember responding to an altar call for writing in 1986/87 during an *all-night* with Ghana Fellowship of Evangelical Students (GHAFES). I also made a prayer request for a *quadruple* anointing of the Guest speaker (Emeka Nwapah-Esq.) at Pentecost Students and Associates (PENSA) Conference of 1987 in Aburi (Eastern region of Ghana) for teaching gift.

OBSERVATIONS OF LIFE

I am not very old but I have been around for some time and I can comment on a few nuggets of truths through life observations such as the following: (1) *disappointments in elected officials*-people with promise are voted into office by constituents; but all too soon come to discover that they cannot adequately and genuinely address all the needs of their constituents. For that reason, ignore all and the cycle continues. Therefore, it is important that constituents are treated with utmost respect because they can make and unmake political office holders. (2) *Reaping where one has not sown*- In life people tend to be lonely when *ascending* but as one gets to the peaks; then, all of a sudden, a lot of crowd is drawn, including people who want to identify with their success stories. I think this is unfair. A lot of people need support and help as they navigate through the terrain of life. If you are able please give a helping hand.

(3) *Misinterpretations*-I quite remember during my High School days, when we sat for our end of year examinations, our accounting and commerce tutor administered his examinations, he added a statement at the end of the examination questions *"May Your Road Be Rough"* Due to lack of appreciation of the statement, the class got offended because we thought the statement was a curse. When we got to the fifth form (final year) during one of our English comprehension lessons, we came across the very statement-*May Your Road Be Rough.* The passage went on to explain that the writer used the statement to spur him on to achieve greater heights. At this point, we realized that our teacher did not curse us but rather wished us well into accomplishments. The lesson here is that if you do not know or understand anything-ASK.

(4) *Supporting the supportable*-There is the need to teach people how to fish instead of providing them fish because such an approach is not sustainable. If people are empowered to stand on their own, it will go a long way to support many. For instance, instead of providing regular payments to support people into perpetuity, you may consider helping such persons to learn a trade, further education, or provide seed money for a venture. This approach can lessen future burdens. (5) *Sacrificial life of women*-I want to salute women for their kind acts of sacrifice that exceed expectations. I can confirm that on the whole, most women are willing to sacrifice time and work for the greater good of spouses during sicknesses and other events; yet, the men do not find the same level of time to support them during those times. To my fellow men, I wish to assert that life is not all about money.

(6) *Celebration of little things*-For ages, students have placed their trust, peace of mind, and security in grades to the detriment of knowledge acquisition. As a teacher, my focus has been to impart knowledge to the thought of my students but I have come to realize that most students

rather focus their energies on grades. Peradventure, the grades have immediate effects on the students' Grade Point Average (GPA). My question is: *Do we go to school to make grade or acquire knowledge?* Well, it can be argued that the grades come with knowledge but I have seen students with poor grades but very knowledgeable because the mode of assessment may not be fair to all. I remember in Ghana, those who entered the Secondary school with very good *Common Entrance* results could not appropriately respond to the demands of High School education. It did not take long for those who completed the *Middle School Leaving Certificate* (MSLC) to overtake them due to capacity-constraints.

Yes, aptitude tests such as SAT, ACT, GMAT, GRE, MCAT can be utilized to evaluate intelligence but beyond that I have seen people who have struggled even with splendid performance. Motivation *vs.* Mediocrity. There are students who come to College or Secondary school with very good results from their previous schools but what they fail to understand is that while being the best or among the best in those schools; they do not know the depth of knowledge possessed by their potential classmates from other schools.

I am told China has Mathematic Centers to support their students just as America has Libraries in the communities to assist students. So, when students from the two countries meet in a college setting, the tendency for the Chinese to excel in Science, Technology, Engineering, and Mathematics (STEM) is obvious. I contend that astuteness in Mathematics is a necessary if not sufficient condition to success in College; especially, as individuals advance in their chosen courses of study because several courses turn to be mathematical at higher levels of learning. Let us rediscover mathematics.

(7) *Experience at Nsusaden*-I boarded a train from Dunkwa-on-Offin to Sekondi-Takoradi in the Western region of Ghana. I had gone to visit my Sister Freda and I was returning to Cape Coast in the

Central region (Ghana). I sat on a window seat and a gentleman sat by me on the aisle seat. Throughout the trip, I was reading books and when the train got a town called *Nsusaden*, the gentleman sitting next to me got up and exclaimed *"So we are in Nsusaden?"* He reached out to the overhead luggage compartment for his bag but rather picked up my bag. I took hold of him and questioned why he was taking my bag and he said it was a mistake. He thought my attention was on the book I was reading. Much has changed since then because I have travelled by road and by air in most trips; but I have not travelled much using train after that event. Nevertheless, I do not ascribe the reason for traveling less by train to the *Nsusaden* experience.

(8) *Vehicular Incidents*-I have recounted some of my experiences involving vehicles in different parts of the book such as: my stolen car battery and fallen wheel knots (4 out of 5) at Ashongman-Accra (Ghana), a nail piecing one of my tires on my way to the O'Hare Airport to pick up my wife, broken shaft on my way to a conference at the La Palm Hotel in Accra and another broken shaft in another vehicle on my way from Mampong-Ashanti (Ghana), locked-in transmission knub, and many more. I thank God for His traveling mercies.

(9) *Introduction of Paulina*-The urgent need for me to move into residence after my first year in the graduate school has been explained in Chapter 9 of this book. As per my narratives, I suffered a great loss between the first and the second year of my graduate studies. I was a non-residential student in my first year staying with my wife in the Ashongman residence in Accra (Ghana) but due to the change in my personal situation and circumstance, I was counseled to move into residence. So, I applied to the Office of the Dean of Graduate Studies, who had oversight on the residential facilities for graduate students. I visited the Office of the Dean of Graduate Studies regularly especially in-between classes to follow-up on my application. I used to meet familiar faces including Lucy (not real name) of Legon Center

for International Affairs (LECIA) and Paulina (not real name) of the Department of Psychology.

On one occasion, I happened to enter then dean's office with Paulina and he approved my application and just at the time I was about to leave the office and he said: "*Gentleman, have you seen this lady, she is in the first year and you are in the second year. Consider marrying her after she completes her program*" Lucy and Paulina have become good friends of mine until now. Awesome introduction!

(10) *The awesome recommendation by a brother*-When I came back from Ghana to start my doctoral program. I was not working, and an employee was diagnosed of a terminal disease and there was the need for a temporary replacement to get the work done. Elder Albert A. Buabeng (now Dr. Buabeng) recommended me strongly to the then Comptroller. The Comptroller decided to take a chance on me by giving me the opportunity. I worked for a month initially; then, extended to two months and to three months. Later on, the human resource manager informed me that the short-term position has become long-term one. So, I agreed to continue to work as independent contractor. After working for six months, the position was determined to be vacant so I agreed to take up the full-time job so I can get other benefits such as health insurance, parking, and so on. I have continued to work for the organization because the overarching objective of giving second and best chance to at-risk students resonates with me because it involves the youth.

(11) *A teacher with a difference*-As I have indicated elsewhere, Mr. Kenneth Addo is one of the teachers I had in the Middle School who had made a lasting impression upon me. Teacher Addo has made inspiring and empowering footprints on me and I remember some of the English expressions he taught me back then in the mid-1970s. Examples of the expressions include: "*fragrance of the blossom fills the air*" and "*at this dark and hopeless moment, an inspiration burst upon me*" He

told us stories in some afternoons from the literature books. Similarly, I applaud the selflessness of Mr. Asante Amankwah (my Geography teacher in Saint Peter's Secondary School). This teacher's devotion to duty was unparalleled. He taught me *Geomorphology, North America, and Map work and surveying*. The early classes he organized at dawn in addition to the normal classes just to cover the demands of the elaborate Geography syllabus without charging any additional fees is hereby recognized.

(12) *One good turn deserves another*-once upon a time; I gave a full piece of cloth to a lady- cleaner who was responsible for cleaning my office in an institution in Ghana. To my surprise, one day as I got to my office this lady had arranged for a stand to be made for my office fridge. I am grateful to her for the gesture.

(13) *The young lady who impressed me with her seriousness*- I used to join my Graduate School study group discussion sessions during the weekends at the West African Secondary School (WASS) at Adenta in the Greater Accra region of Ghana. I used to meet a young lady in my local church (the Madina West assembly of the Church of Pentecost) anytime we went to this school to study. I took notice of her seriousness and not quite long, there was going to be a Youth Camp at the Pentecost University College at Sowutoum in Accra and when I asked her if she was attending, she told me that the grandmother with whom she was staying was not able to sponsor her for the camp meeting. In the circumstance, I sought permission from the grand-mother to sponsor her for the program and she agreed. On my wedding day, this young lady sent me a big wall hanging. I appreciate her gesture very much.

(14) *Reaching out to a person in need*-One fateful day in Ghana, I received a call from a lady by name Mercy (not real name), who was a family friend. She had a promising marriage with the husband and children. She wanted to meet me urgently so I decided to meet her halfway along the way to her house. She told me about the husband

who had left the house to stay with a mistress. She informed me that the husband goes to the school of the children to pay fees but did not support the home any longer; and for that reason, she had run into a financial problem and needed urgent assistance. I signed a check for her and she wanted to know the terms for the assistance, but I told her I was not expecting her to pay back.

I want to encourage married men to take their marital vows seriously and should also think about the effects of such actions on their children. There is a devastating blow to the family unit when the husband vacates his matrimonial home to stay with the mistress. I also want to advise the wives not to take their marriages for granted because there has been the tendency for several women to have taken their marriages for granted.

(15) *Selflessness in ministry*-In chapter 18, I have emphasized the selflessness of Pastor James McKeown, the founder of the Church of Pentecost for paying the price to get the Gospel out to the Gold Coast (now Ghana). This singular act of Pastor James and his wife- Sophia has paid off and blossomed to become a global religious network or church. Another person I have observed from a distance is Father Andrew Campbell for his selflessness in Ghana toward the poor and needy. He has been consistent, authentic, and passionate at what he does best. I applaud Father Campbell for his involvement with humanity.

APPROPRIATE RESPONSES

I have come to appreciate the following important lessons: **first,** it is *God's amazing grace* that leads to a balanced Christian living and a higher level of thinking that can change worldviews and mindset. While "God is my only source and supply" (GIMOSAS) at all times, it is true that "Only Jesus can do" (ONJECADO). **Second,** *chesting the ball* in soccer (football) before shooting at the goal or scoring is akin to one thinking before leaping based on: clarity of purpose, supported by consistency in commitment; translating into tangible benefits from comforting grace.

Third, *community involvement* has the potential of leading to greater recognition from compassion through service to earn trust. As a result, there is the need to consider the following critical courses of study-entrepreneurship, project management, law, and language competencies in Spanish, French, and Hausa. Additionally, the desired competencies should encompass, but not limited to the following: technology adeptness, teamwork, business communication, problem-solving or critical thinking (Appiah-Sokye, 2016).

Four, *liberties vs. restriction*-The exercise of rights goes with commensurate responsibilities. Consequently, liberties granted by the constitution on one hand should be compared to the restrictions placed by the COVID-19 protocols on the other. COVID-19 has taught this generation that if you do not respond to changes, you would be compelled to change into anew normal, whether you like it or not.

Five, *dreams matter a lot* in life; as a result, credibility is hugely important because dreams can be pursued, achieved, and maintained. **Six,** you *do not need to co-operate with evil and torture* due to either failed weaknesses in filling a void but good practices can be implemented over time for better results in turning our fortunes around. **Seven,** *enhanced awareness,* let goodness emanate from wickedness because in life great people do quote from great people.

In my 57 years of life (as of April 2021) and 36 years of work experience (as of 2021), I have been impacted by the early influences of parents, mentors, and teachers; as well as, courses bordering on management, including taxation and fiscal policy, financial management, auditing and assurance, internal auditing, and many more; that have made great impressions on me when I reflect on the past.

Eight, *expertise in passions* can lead to definition of personality such as special likes and dislikes, events and memories, and influences and achievements. History is instructive in guiding heads and hearts in turning problems around to bring about the desired change. **Nine**, the key attributes in life include–*honesty, authenticity, supportive character, trust,* and *moral clarity.* As a result, hopeful engagement in every fiber of our being can cause us to avoid petty mistakes; thereby, influencing logical victories of utmost importance that involves creativity and precision to bring about stories concerning our passions.

Ten, *insightful leadership*, suggests that people can be immortalized by events and stellar progress in the attainment of goals that can be written in the form of narrative to encompass early influences regarding *in-depth* self-appraisal. As a result, planning for the future, based on hope for legitimacy and cohesion can be used to identity critical voices, reflective perceptions, deep-rooted views, and wide-range of experiences. This is a plus and a must.

Eleven, *Joy will come in the morning* and just as God is the *alpha* and *omega* (the beginning and the end); He starts and accomplishes it. We can also rely on this assurance that what God starts, He is able to accomplish and this must serve as a motivation for what we set for ourselves to achieve. Nevertheless, man's failure is inconsistent with this position.

Twelve, *leadership through uncertain life paths* can helps us to learn from our mistakes and to internalize the fact that life is not a contest or race but lived experiences in every season of life to bring about both purpose and time. As a result, it is *love* that drives *faith* to keep *hope* alive; and as a result, faith produces love for hope to thrive. **Thirteen**, *the passion for quality*, activated through skill for development can be achieved through endless potential to give back to society. Peter Drucker has asserted that *"our mission in life is to make a positive difference not to prove how smart or right we are"*

Fourteen, *there is the need for speaking up for the defenseless* or *speechless* to bring about the much-needed change, which can be achieved through the spotlights of supporting commitment. Therefore, building about a purposeful and impactful outcome can provide practical solutions from the taking of ownership of concepts, views, and experiences to unearth a pure, radiant, and spotless personality. **Fifteen**, it was *unwavering perseverance*, an epitome of the pilgrim fathers, who exercised puritan virtues of hard work by leaving no stone unturned to bring about development and advancement in the United States of America.

Sixteen, the book of Ecclesiastes has provided mankind with 28 *seasons of life* and for that reason, if you have nothing to live for, you may lose hope from pain through purpose. Consequently, young people must repossess the required capacity, talent, and power to make the expected change from capacity mobilization. **Seventeen**, while contradiction, dilemmas, paradoxes are inevitable in life; *vulnerability* can get us broken with the foundation because we are in this life together. Nevertheless, we can always do better. In most cases, the career decisions to be made involve challenges that can be surmounted through rich experiences gained along the way that produces a fulfilling accomplishment. **Eighteen**, the negative tendencies in peoples' lives is the "thorn in the flesh" categorization referred to by the Apostle Paul. I present four stories for discussion in this segment of the text, as follows:

Getting the Best Out of People-I remember on my way to Mampong-Ashanti in Ghana to visit my mum, I decided to take public transport from the *Neoplan Station* in Accra. When I got to the bus terminal, I decided to buy some loaves of bread for the family back home. Then, I got closer to where the Kumasi buses were loading (passengers boarding) simultaneously. A number of bread sellers tried to get me attention and I went towards the direction of one of them. The other bread seller queried why I should be buying from a *witch* because my targeted bread seller was hairy. I told her that it the hair that attracted me to her.

Suddenly, I saw excitement on the face of this bread seller. After I paid for the bread, she requested to see me off to my bus. I asked her to suggest a bus for me and she pointed me to a bus. I demanded to know the reason for her suggestion, and she intimated that the driver of the other bus drinks and so would not want to recommend his bus to me. The case of the bread seller in the Neoplan station in Accra has taught me that it is possible to get the best out of people if you treat them as human beings. Even though, I wandered why such a driver would be allowed to drive a bus of that size, the guidance of the bread seller was on point.

Painful Outcome- One night after the usual preparation for the next day (popularly called *prep*) in the secondary(high) school, one of my classmates in another house in the dormitory punished a form one student (freshman), who happened to be a brother of one of my classmates. Another classmate in the same dormitory came to meet the form one student on his kneels (the typical punishment meted out during our time in secondary school). So, he asked the form one student to go and sleep because it was quite late. When the classmate who punished the student came back to meet the student on his bed, he asked him why he has gone to sleep without his knowledge. The form one student explained that it was the other classmate of mine who released him. The unwritten rule at the time was that it was only the one who punishes who releases and should any other person wanted to release the student under punishment, (s)he must get clearance from the person who punished the student. There were heated arguments between these two classmates of mine, which led to a scuffle.

In the process, the classmate who released the student bit the forehead of the classmate who punished the student and the other also bit his ear lobe, which fell to the ground. At this point, pandemonium broke out attracting other students to the scene. One of my classmates put the fallen ear lobe into his pocket and run outside the school compound to get the school driver. Another run to the headmaster's house out of the school gate. Yet, the third run to the residence of the assistant headmaster who lived on campus. When the assistant headmaster came to the scene and getting ready to send my two classmates to the hospital, he could not find the ear lobe and so he asked the students in the room where the bitten ear lobe was; it was then that the classmate who had run to look for the school driver, pulled the piece from his pocket.

This incident happened during the 1981 revolution in Ghana and there was an imposition of curfew in the night. I was told when the students and the assistant headmaster got the hospital, it was very late in the night and the doctors had gone home because of the curfew so only first aid was administered to the students and the hospital staff determined that the ear lobe had shrank so could not be restored. The following day the students were released to go home for further medical treatment. Fortunately, the doctors in Komfo Anokye Teaching Hospital (KATH) were able to piece together the remaining ear by molding an ear for the classmate whose ear was bitten off. The two classmates were never in good terms until they left school. There was parental involvement in the situation but the worse had already happened.

With the benefit of hindsight, I think the conflict that led to the biting of the ear of a colleague at Juaben Secondary School in Ashanti region of Ghana in 1981 could have been averted and the effect of that exchange had left an indelible mark on the restored ear of a colleague-forever.

Are Two Individuals the Same?-I had one senior in Saint Peter's Secondary School, who was also from Mampong-Ashanti in Ghana. He was one year ahead of me in school. Specifically, when he was in Upper 6, I was in Lower 6 (sixth form). We used to exchange visits but I realized that anytime I got to his house and exchange pleasantries with the elder sister she could not look me in the eye. She would be looking down as she talked with me. Interestingly, their father liked me very much and spent time having conversations with me.

One day, my senior's sister told me that *"Brother, any time I see you I remember my late brother. You two look alike"* It was then I remembered that when I reported to school the first time, I was told that senior had lost a brother so he had gone back home but I did not know him. After this disclosure by the sister, she could now talk with me without any problem. My supposed resemblance with my senior's brother that was divulged by the sister to me, made me to reflect on the question-*Are two individuals the same?*

Misunderstood Dad-While I was at the SSNIT flat assembly of the Church of Pentecost in Elmina in the Central region of Ghana. A lady whose father was staying in the flats used to come to church anytime she visited the father. She was a teacher by profession and stationed at a town called-Agona Swedru in the Central region of Ghana. One day she shared her marital plans with the leadership of the church and everyone was looking forward to the marriage ceremony. During one visit we realized her countenance had changed, suggesting a possible problem. When we tried to have a conversation with her, she broke into tears and disclosed that the daddy had accepted the man of her life but her problem was that the father had limited participation to her marriage ceremony to only 20 people; 10 for the family and 10 for the church. Her worry was that a lot of people would wish to attend her marriage ceremony and the 20-participant quota was not fair to her, but the father is not prepared to modify his stance.

We encourage her to see everything through the lenses of the father and that her father was not opposed to her marrying, but he is not a fun of large numbers for marriage. We assured her that the church will co-operate with the father to bring the marriage to fruition. Our pastor was willing to accommodate the wishes of the father and the marriage was celebrated as one of the best marriages I have ever witnessed. The lesson I have learned is that the success of a marriage is not linked to the size of the guests who attend the ceremony.

Lastly, I am particularly humbled by *President Jimmy Carter*'s role as a Bible Study teacher in his local church in United States of America. I find that humility very instructive and worthy of emulation. Likewise, I find commendable *Elder (Professor) Otoo Ellis'* role as a Sunday School Teacher in Pentecost International Worship Center (PIWC)-Asokwa-Kumasi in the Ashanti region of Ghana. I recommend this high level of humility to all young people in this generation because it pays to serve.

REFLECTIONS

Some life paths can be lonely, calling for unwavering determination based on timely encouragement because all problems can be surmounted over time to lead to accomplishments.

As a steward of grace, I have determined that failure is a mindset and that building up students and not destroying them is a **good sustainability strategy**. The need to leverage technology for teaching and learning has been confirmed in the era of COVD-19 because the infection rates of the virus made the use of technology the new-normal and the place of technology for the future is not in dispute. Education has been able to stand the test of the times, when all other major sports have been put on hold. Several workers could work remotely using technology but other workers whose work could not be done remotely painfully lost jobs.

The *40-70 rule* for decision making is critical and allowing informed decisions to be made. At times, people hasten to take decisions without any review of information. Good decision is made on basis of some level of information and the recommended quantum is a minimum of 40 percent and a maximum of 70 percent.

A number of students have made me proud. The *1-2-3-4* guidance prescribed by the Southern Illinois University, Edwardsville (SIUE) is very instructive to the youth. The number 1 means students can join at least one club or association on campus. The number 2...The number 3 suggests that students must maintain at least a grade point average (GPA) of 3.0 throughout the duration of the degree program. The number 4 implies that the student must endeavor to complete the undergraduate degree in four years.

Selflessness pays because despite the burden of regrets, dislikes, and acknowledgments; selfishness has proved to be destructive in the long run. As a result, the preparation of wills has proved to be a noble task and so is the preparation for funerals through insurance; by setting up funds for the purpose can be considered. I have been associated with the management of funerals of close relatives within the African cultural context and I have come to know the burden of raising funds for that purpose. I am cautiously optimistic that something can be done about this phenomenon.

Process and Capacity-I attended a combination of public and missions' schools. As I recounted earlier in the preceding chapters (Chapter 3), I started my education informally at a nursery run by the Evangelical Church of Ghana; then, to the Saint Monica's Primary School owned by the Anglican Church to the Anglican Middle School. Thence, to complete my Secondary school education or High School. The main High School I attended was owned by the Methodist Church and the sixth-form school was owned by the Catholic Church.

All the tertiary institutions I attended in Ghana were public schools. As a result, I bring an aspect of religious perspectives on public discourse. The calls for change in thinking and the level of engagement suggest that the welding of power should not lead to revenge, but rather a change in direction towards human race transformation and development.

Differences in terminologies- Within the local settings, the spider is used in Akan folklore in Southern Ghana and the rabbit is used in the Northern region of Ghana; nevertheless, the leading roles played by these characters remain the same. I have come to understand that there are differences in nomenclature the world over and one of the problems of globalization is differences in terminologies. Such that different countries have varied culture and lifestyles. By way of illustration, while Father Christmas is used in the United kingdom; the equivalent in the United States is the Santa Clause. Transmission of vehicles is called gear box in other jurisdictions.

Investment

I have dealt with investments in my other book on: *Taxation in Ghana: A fiscal policy tool for development*. It has been established that it is not too late to start investment at any time or age; and as a result, no amount is too small because *little drops of savings* lead to mighty funds in investments. Consistency is also critical. While paying God first is the Christian discipline called Tithing, paying yourself second is a good guide. Pay yourself before you begin to pay off your bills and the power of compounding will help the funds to grow over time. There are risks associated with investments but a calculated risk is unavoidable in life. Manage your life with the 80 percent of your income left. You can always either increase your income or reduce your cost. Diversification (not putting all of one's eggs in one baskets) based on *Markowitz's* portfolio building strategy is a good guide. Otherwise, the investment accounts can be entrusted to professionals to manage. A distinction should also be made between physical assets such as personal property like homes, and land; and financial assets such as stocks or shares, bonds, and many more. For example, a land that was sold for ¢2 million (equivalent of GH¢ 200) is now selling for GH¢100,000 over a period of 20 years.

Retirement and Social security

I have discussed social security scheme in Ghana in my book on: Taxation in Ghana: A fiscal policy tool for development. Ghana has a three-tier pension scheme, as follows: **One,** *First tier* is purely monthly pensions (annuity) payments managed by the Social Security and National Insurance Trust (SSNIT) to the pensioner's death or the actuarially-determined years of retirement. **Second,** *tier two* is managed by Fund Managers selected by the National Pensions Authority; and **three,** *tier three* is for personal investment.

Typically, the social security is capable of paying retirees above the poverty line because pension payments tend to be lesser than the last salary of employee before retirement. The reason is not far-fetched because the formula for calculating the pension or annuity amounts is based on the average salary of three best years, translating into a lower average salary and other variables of interest. The pension regime is two-fold: (I) defined benefit plan such as the social security scheme that is not based on contribution of the employee but on a pre-determined formula; and (II) defined contributor plan based on the contributions of employees and employers; plus, earnings and minus professional management fees. Examples include retirement plans such as: Individual Retirement Accounts (IRA), 403b, 401k, ROTH IRA, and many more.

As pointed out, retirement is not much talk about because incomes tend to drop but it is very important stage in life whether we prepare for it or not. It is a question of time. The major characteristics of retirement is that as income decreases, living expenses increases; establishing a negative relationship between income levels and living expenses. There is no retirement age in the United States of America per se, except that available age provisions of 59 to 73 years are intended for vesting of social security and related issues.

The retirement age in Ghana is 60 years; even though, governmental appointments can be extended to 65 years and in the particular case of the Church of Pentecost globally, the retirement age for ministers is 65 years. I will encourage the younger generation to maximize the learning phase of their lives as early as possible; because this will avoid the use of part of working life in learning as it was the case in my life. Yes, my situation has been different in many ways and I had to combine family life with lifelong learning.

The lesson I am passing on is for young people to accumulate as many credentials as possible before joining the workforce even at a younger age. The tendency for people to enter the job market with undergraduate qualification makes sense. Against the backdrop of the believe that it is difficult to get employment with higher qualifications. Sure, this can be true for most situations but not the case for all industries and workplaces. Whatever the situation or option used, there will be the need to further education to my proposed and desired qualification of a Master's degree, plus at least on professional certification. Likewise, there is the other consideration of developing skills and hobbies that will be relevant during the retirement years. While the typical years have been: (a) below 30 years for the learning phase, (b) between 31 and 60 years for working years, (c) beyond 60 years for retirement. These are not clear cut but it is left with the individual to chart a course for him or herself.

The following strategies and suggestions can be useful:

- Start preparing for retirement as soon as you begin working;
- Parents should avoid being completely dependent on children because that can constitute pressure with dire consequences;
- Furthering one's education can provide regular streams of income over time. Education does not necessarily make people rich but can provide opportunities for supplemental incomes and avenue for networking;
- Building a savings base to cover six months' expenses is a conservative guide. This can provide a buffer for lean seasons or eventualities in life;

- Life insurance products can be another vehicle for retirement; as well as, retirement funds involving 401K, 403b, and building portfolios having a blend of stocks, mutual funds, debt instruments in a diversified portfolio;
- Investments in long-term care through insurance and funeral insurance; instead on relying on the social insurance in African communities (Societal Vs. Financial Strategies);
- Fully paid up home and vehicles can be worthwhile;
- Downsize, downsize, downsize; and be prepared to let out portions of house if need be because of empty nesters. Commuting spare or extra time to profitable activities and events;
- Stay within budget; as you utilize knowledge and experience for consultancy, writing, seminars, seminars, and social commentaries;
- I have grown along with the Village of Ashongman into a conurbation. So, you can buy a plot in a village that has the potential to grow over time;
- Stay engaged regarding things you care about and take advantage of the provisions of the tax laws because there are good provisions to be tapped;
- Selling off or donating items not needed to the Missions field and also giving back to society is a good suggestion (Social responsibilities);

FOOD FOR THOUGHT

The 2020 Fall Edition of the publication of the Parks and Recreation Department of the Village of Romeoville has offered, the following:

> *Travel can be safe and convenient*
> *Time spent playing with children is never wasted*

- ➤ *Play is the work of childhood*
- ➤ *Be as active as you dare to be*
- ➤ *Everyone loves a good party*
- ➤ *Small groups can make a big impact*
- ➤ *Childhood is the most beautiful of life's seasons*
- ➤ *Do not waste your youth growing up*
- ➤ *If you don't leap, you'll never know what it's like to fly*
- ➤ *Dance is the joy of movement and the heart of life*
- ➤ *Mind and technique become one in true karate*
- ➤ *To succeed we must first believe that we can*
- ➤ *Sports never get easier; you just get better*
- ➤ *While you are young you have everything to smile about*
- ➤ *Growing old is mandatory, growing up is optional*
- ➤ *Be active, be healthy, be happy*

CHAPTER 13

FAILURE IS A MINDSET

A SIMPLE *GOOGLE* SEARCH RETURNS some striking descriptions of the phenomenon of failure. Some described failure as the best teacher, a learning process, and a part of life; as well as, success in progress and the courage to continue to the end; however, to others success is not final. Yet, failure is neither fatal nor a restriction or limitation. There is the urgent need to learn from failure to derive the desired outcome because failure can be a good preparer for life. Specifically, a few prominent people have weighed in on what failure is to them. For example, Henry Ford has asserted that "failure does not mean you are a failure; it means you have not succeeded yet." Consequently, "failure is only the opportunity to begin again more intelligently" (Henry Ford). Likewise, "failure involves emotions and thoughts; however, failure can make us stronger or wiser." Additionally, per Thomas Edison, "I have not failed" but I have found 10,000 ways that won't work. I am not discouraged because every wrong attempt discarded is another step forward" (Retrieved from http://www.expresscoaching.net – accessed on 05/30/2020).

There are different definitions for the word-failure and the Webster dictionary provides the following definition *inter alia*:

(1) *Omission of occurrence or performance;*
(2) *A state of inability to perform a normal function or an abrupt cessation of normal functioning;*
(3) *Lack of success;*
(4) *A falling short or deficiency.*

Other definitions include the following: "failure is an act or instance of failing or proving unsuccessful, or simply lack of success" {http://www.expresscoaching.net –accessed on 05/30/2020). Per Dr. Brons (n.d.), several people have given their perspectives to the meaning of failure, such as the following: "failure is an event, never a person" (Brown, W.D.); "you always pass failure on your way to success" (Rooney, M.); "you can't have any success until you can accept failure"(Cukor, G.). On his part, Bill Cosby had stated that "I don't know the key to success, but the key to failure is trying to please everybody"; as well as, F.S. Fitzgerald's take "never confuse a single defeat with final defeat" (Retrieved from http://www.ajourneytojoy.com -accessed on 05/30/2020).

IS FAILURE A MINDSET?

I have shared earlier on in the initial pages of this textbook about how my father taught me how to respond to failure early in my life. I am grateful for this nugget of truth I learned in my life from home. The key lesson learned is that failure is not the issue but the appropriate response to failure is what is critical. I consider failure as a mindset. Even though, Kurt Lewin had described failure as a feeling. In real life, challenges to be surmounted can offer opportunities at the same time. I know a medical student in Ghana who had to rewrite examination papers in Surgery seven times, but this gentleman had become a very good surgeon today.

There has been increasing ability to share findings and practices across disciplines and tradition; and for that reason, the focus of a life story narration is a logical sequence of biography relevant events, operating at the level of the individual narrator's often tacit knowledge, and the emphasis of analysis is on answering the explicit research question, working at the academic level of knowledge (Eichsteller,

2019). So, you see that failure is the mother of success and is not an option.

The Acronym for *failure* is as follows: Fundamental, Attitudinal, Involvement, Leverage, Understanding, Routines, and Experiential. **Fundamental**, means failure is based on a central or underlying point that has been missed in the first place. Failure should be pointed to the source before the right action can be taken to address the situation. The question to answer is: *What went wrong?* As a result, continued denial does not augur well for desired resolution. **Attitudinal**, suggests appropriate responses to failure regarding, posture, orientation, behavior, tendency or disposition. The proper response to failure is the best way of dealing with failure. People tend to appropriate success to themselves but will leave no stone unturned in apportioning blame to others when failure knocks at the door. **Involvement**, implies association and participation leading to failure. Suggesting that failure is somebody's responsibility and success is their personal achievement. The mindset should be that both success and failure are personal responsibilities because this attitude is a winning one.

Leverage, contemplates the exploitation of systems for one's advantage. However, failure results from the lack of taking advantage of systems and processes to achieve desired objectives. There are basic principles governing all aspects of life such as hard work, persistence, perseverance, and resilience; and as a result, until those principles are respected, failure becomes inevitable.

Understanding, covers appreciation and comprehension of failure with a view to having insights that can help to provide reliable judgment to the failed. Failure can occur in every sphere of human endeavor such as in business, education, politics, religion or ministry, and many more. Consequently, failure unfortunately is part of human life and this fact should be ingrained in young people early enough in their life for them to rise to the occasion.

Routines, bring to the fore that the same sequence of events and actions will lead to the same failed outcomes. As a result, regularly performed procedures that lead to failure must be reviewed for improvements and enhancements. A continued failure in human endeavor may be attributable to continued routines that do not get changed because most people do not like to change. Several people want to remain in their comfort zones even in the teeth of failure; and for that reason, rationalize all events leading to failure.

Experience is the combination of knowledge arising out of involvement and mastery of an event or actions. Many a time, experience is incremental because every failure can present an aspect of the puzzle and so a cumulative experience from failure or series of failures can help in the right diagnosis of the problem. I argue that implicit in every failure is an insight that can point to the right direction. In practice, people who persist and work very hard after failure are able to turn the fortunes around.

DEALING WITH FAILURE: MY POINT OF VIEW

The ability to handle failure is a capacity to be developed intellectually and experientially over time. For that reason, what we encounter in life is reinforced by what we experience. This implies that when failure occurs, we are not completely oblivious of what is happening because we are prepared ahead of time to deal with the phenomenon. In my humble opinion, some of the people who grew up in other environments tend to be able to handle life failures than some of those born into this environment. In the United States of America, most young people leave home when going to college or to the world of work and they are required to deal with real life issues at that time. Some feel overwhelmed and so parents are required to assist their young people navigate through life's journey.

Some African parents left the shores of Africa for greener pastures in their early twenties, tackling life challenges head-on and this experience cannot be discounted by any means. The older generation tend to do better at handling failure than the younger generation. Perhaps, due to experience acquired over time. For example, the older generation that grew up in other environments, were released to go to the boarding house at a tender age, outside the direct control of parents; learning how to follow daily routines and structured school rules. The principle "a breach of common sense is a breach of school rules" was learned at that stage of their development. As a result, real character formation took place during this era and several people remember events in the secondary or High School than even the university or college.

To the extent that permanent relationships are built at this time and not to mention the development of capacity to deal with life challenges and choices. The processes of dealing with failure in my opinion is phased as follows: *Formulation stage*-(1) Acceptance, (2) diagnosis, (3) disaggregation, (4) analysis and evaluation, (5) aggregation, (6) prioritizing; as well as *implementation*-(7) selection of appropriate strategy or solution, (8) feedback, (9) refection, and (10) lessons learned.

FORMULATION STAGE

The foregoing narration is the formulation phase of dealing with failure in life.

ACCEPTANCE- The initial and appropriate response to failure is to accept it as a reality. Life lessons tend to be similar and for that reason, with a heart of gratefulness we should consult with those who have gone before us. Ask more question but listen more and speak less. This will serve you well. Everyone wants to succeed, but few people understand why they fail over and over again (Manson, n.d.). The practice of refusing everything even where the fact points to actual failure does not help matters at all. In most cases, precious opportunity is missed when immediate response in acknowledgement of failure is not utilized to allow for the process of mitigation to begin. In my opinion, the acceptance of failure is the first step toward emotional healing because failure can have a very strong impression on people.

DIAGNOSIS-Failure can be diagnosed using discrete events models (Sampath, Sengupta, LaFortune, Sinnamohideen, Teneketzis, March 1996). This process is involved with the assembling of more information using *40-70 rule* because all aspects of the issue under consideration should be explored. The *40-70 rule* required decision makers to gather adequate information, however, the adequacy of information is the challenge. In this direction, a minimum of 40 percent of information is good for a start and a 70 percent information is a good gauge because it is not possible to gather 100 percent of information.

Neither is it practical for decisions to be taken in a vacuum. For that reason, the use of *trial-and-error* approaches are not very helpful because the absence of an intentional diagnosis of the events can lead to another failure. There are underpinning reasons that can account for failure; either in part, or in whole. Therefore, there is the need to answer the *whys* and *hows* questions. Comparatively, just as a medical doctor can fail in his or her administration of a cure when the right diagnosis is not obtained; the principle is the same.

The causes of failure are manifold but some of the reasons encompass the following: lack of- discipline, persistence, conviction, humility, networking, and relationship; lack of confidence for the things we want; rationalization, dismissal of past mistakes, doubting the reality of failure, poor self-esteem, fatalistic attitude; as well as, fear to stand out among the crowd, including distraction, tendency to argue against good advice instead of taking it in *good faith*, and not taking responsibility for actions (Manson, n.d.-Retrieved from www.success.com; www. Markmanson.net -accessed on 05/30/2020).

DISAGGREGATION-The process of disaggregation is involved with the identification of probable courses of action, through mitigation strategies, as well as, conducting emotional audits to come to terms with failure. The disaggregation process revolves around *demolition* in order to *reconstruct*. This process is just like a jigsaw puzzle because the process gets worse to get better with time. I am challenged by the story of *Abraham Lincoln* (a former President of the United States of America). Per Shryock (n.d.), a list of key events in his life is chronicled below to serve as a motivation for people who are experiencing any form of failure:

- *At Age 23 –defeated as a candidate for the legislature*
- *Age 24-failure in business (spent several years paying off debts)*
- *Age 29-defeated as a candidate for speaker*
- *Age 31-defeated as a candidate for elector*
- *Age 34-failure to receive the congressional nomination*
- *Age 35-lost wife in 1835*
- *Age 39-failure to be re-elected to congress*
- *Age 46-lost the race for the US Senate*
- *Age 47-failure to receive the nomination for Vice President*
- *Age 49-lost the race for the US Senate*
- *FINALLY, attained the satisfaction of being chosen President of USA (1860).*

By way of application, only a few people are capable of withstanding the disappointments and rebuffs of President Abraham Lincoln; and to the extent that the right personality could be developed for the presidency (Shryock, n.d.). Nevertheless, President Lincoln had developed the desired habit, coupled with his natural temperament of a melancholic trend; as well as, his sense of humor and the ability to tell hilarious and amusing stories emanating from his salvation (Shryock, n.d.). Consequently, the trick of seeing the funny side of things can work very well in dealing with depressed moods (Shryock, n.d.).

Most often, we see the greatness in people who ever lived but what we miss is the how they made it to greatness. One way of getting to know *how* people made it to greatness is to study *how* they surmounted challenges by reading their memoires and autobiographies. Yes, biographies are very good but they tell the story from a by- stander's perspective; occasionally, with inputs from the individual. However, memoires and autobiographies are straight from the horses' own mouths and dependable because the person who has the direct knowledge is the one who tells the story.

Likewise, Shyrock (n.d.) belabored on the critical milestone of age 40, as follows: "Life at 40: (i) *it is at about the age of 40 that two (2) lines cross; the ascending line, representing efficiency, self-discipline, and increasing influence and the descending line, representing decreasing mental and physical vigor.(ii) A person has to be about in early in life, then, if he is to accomplish something worthwhile; and (iii) the demands of modern life require that children receive training for some specific field of endeavor*" (Shryock, n.d., p.244). The above quotes from Shyrock (n.d.) is both instructive and insightful because of the controversies linked to it. There is an aged adage that states that "Life begins at 40", implying that the age 40 is the milestone that begins real life of man.

In the Biblical account of the descendant of Adam, they all live very long lives, with Methuselah recording 969 years. Likewise, the argument of the years allocated to man by God has been a debatable issue. While some support 120 years (Genesis 6:3) as the years granted by God to man, others also support the 70-80 years view (Psalm 90:10). Nevertheless, life expectancy is very critical because in some societies life actually begins at 40, yet in others life actually ends at 40. Additionally, we do not know the exact years we will spend on this earth because that knowledge continues to be a misery unto us.

I argue that the age 40 should only serve as a guide but the key is to identify your purpose in life and to work towards that purpose. I have seen people who have made great impact and died early and also people who have lived long but have nothing to show. For me, what one does with his or her life is the most important consideration. So, each day should be viewed as God's gift to us to make the most out of and for that reason, should not be taken for granted. Consequently, *efficiency, increasing influence, and self-discipline* (Shryock, n.d.) should be daily goals; against the backdrop that we shall not live forever because there will come a time when we will experience *decreasing physical* and *mental vigor* (Shryock, n.d.).

ANALYSIS AND EVALUATION-The process should revolve around the application of effective strategies on all alternative course of action; through the detailing out of specificities on available courses of action. In some cases, outside help should be sought. As a finance and accounting professional, I have been taught how to analyze and evaluate the merits and demerits of alternative courses of action using tools developed for analysis to take proper decisions. When I receive the financial reports of a business, I can apply the tools of financial analysis to dissect the entity to be able to interpret the numbers and also read the management discussion and analysis to glean qualitative information for decision-making purposes.

Investments are not taken lightly in businesses because of the huge capital outlay involved and so tools of investment analysis are utilized to arrive at the best decision. I consider failure as a very expensive phenomenon affecting many aspects of life and so the processes involved in addressing the root causes should not be taken lightly. I suggest that enough effort is put into the process of analysis and evaluation. I do not want to suggest any tool for analyzing and evaluating alternate courses of action regarding failure because each situation is different.

AGGREGATION-The process of aggregation encompasses the

development of possible strategies for success. On several occasion, considering a few options such as the best-case scenario and the worse-case scenario; as well as, the best desirable, the least desirable alternatives, and the optimal desirable alternative can be instructive in the analysis. In the process, it is not completely out of place to review the experiences from other people. The mind is capable of creating things from nothing. I have provided the resilience of President Abraham Lincoln to make a case for the possibility for turning failure in the short-term to success in the long-run. Today, the State of Illinois is proud to be associated with him as the "Land of the Lincolns" This achievement did not come on a silver platter. The Bible has recorded the challenges of the Apostle Paul, as follows:

> "Of the Jews five times received I forty stripes save one. Thrice was I beaten with rods, once was I stoned, thrice I suffered shipwreck, a night and a day I have been in the deep; in journeyings often, in perils of waters, in perils of robbers, in perils by mine own countrymen, in perils by the heathen, in perils in the city, in perils in the wilderness, in perils in the sea, in perils among false brethren; in weariness and painfulness, in watchings often, in hunger and thirst, in fastings often, in cold and nakedness. Beside those things that are without, that which cometh upon me daily, the care of all the churches. Who is weak, and I am not weak? who is offended, and I burn not? If I must needs glory, I will glory of the things which concern mine infirmities. The God and Father of our Lord Jesus Christ, which is blessed for evermore, knoweth that I lie not." (2 Corinthians 11:24-31, KJV).

The Bible (Philippians 3:5-6 and 2 Corinthians 12:9) provided for Paul as follows: **first,** he was circumcised on the eighth day, of the stock of Israel. A Benjamin and an Hebrew of Hebrews. **Two,** a pharisee in the matter of the law, blameless based on matter of righteousness; yet prosecuted the early church before his conversion on the road to Damascus. Paul authored more books in the Bible and also provided in sights on many Biblical controversies. **Lastly,** the grace of God was sufficient for Paul to perfect in weaknesses. Nevertheless, Paul was not perfect because he did not possess the *omni-qualities* (Omnipotent, Omniscient, and Omnipresent) of Jesus; and also had a thorn in the flesh (II Corinthians 12:9).

Dear reader, the grace of God is sufficient for us in our failure.

PRIORITIZING-This process speaks to the ranking of available solutions or strategies, involving some prioritization. There may be more than one way of addressing any failure and so the broader the preparation and consultation the better. When reasonable effort is put into the process, better outcome is assured. Choice is an integral part of the decision-making process and also choice contemplates the ranking of possible courses of action into more desirable at one's end of the continuum and least desirable options at the other end of the spectrum. In between these points are other possible actions to be considered. Consequently, prioritizing precedes the implementation phase of the entire process. It is not enough to go through all the above stages without a tentative plan for implementation.

IMPLEMENTATION STAGE

Implementation is very critical and for that reason, the lack of it may lead to procrastination. Typically, implementation takes the form of pilot studies, running parallel strategies, phasing, and confronting the issue of interest head-on.

SELECTION OF APPROPRIATE STRATEGY OR SOLUTION- Dear reader, when you are confronted with failure, try to spend quality time to diagnose the problem and once the diagnosis is right; then, the appropriate strategies can be employed to overcome the failure. Handling failure along the way:

- *Let Abraham Lincoln's example inspire you*
- *Treat failure as only temporary and the best way to learn from mistakes for success in life*
- *Recognize that "where there is a will, there is also a way"*
- *"Try again: if first you do not succeed, TRY AGAIN."*
- *Develop positive philosophy about yourself–I WILL ARISE*
- *Trust in God with all your heart and might and in everything give thanks to God.*

FEEDBACK-The process is linked to cybernetics and achieved through evaluation and re-evaluation of the above processes in dealing with failures. For the avoidance of doubt, it may not be necessary to go through each one of the above stages in every failure. While in some cases, some of the steps may not be necessary, in some other cases, every step will be worth considering. Manalo and Kapur (December 2019) postulated that failure benefits and/or comprises an integral part of effective teaching and learning practices in subject-specific disciplines or learning activities.

Many people go through struggles that are not known to others unless the stories are shared but the mode of sharing is another consideration because the knowledge may be circulated among a closed circle of friends and acquaintances. Some life experiences are better than others but each case can present a different dimension of solution to a problem. However, in some instances, the loudest voice may not necessarily present the best lessons. I have the unique opportunity to present my life lessons and experiences in this book to provide assistance to others who will be confronted with similar situations in future; as well as, providing guidance to all people who will be called upon to offer advice or counseling to others in any capacity.

The fifteen (15) things Paul survived per 2 Corinthians 11:23-27 include the following:

- *Paul survived a lot of pain.*
- *Paul survived dangers from disloyal people.*
- *Paul survived dangers from his own countrymen.*
- *Paul survived dangers from robbers.*
- *Paul survived dangers in the city.*
- *Paul survived dangers in the wilderness.*
- *Paul survived extreme exhaustion.*
- *Paul survived five beatings from the Jews.*
- *Paul survived forty-eight hours in the deep sea.*
- *Paul survived frequent imprisonments.*
- *Paul survived several journeys.*
- *Paul survived stoning.*
- *Paul survived the cold and nakedness.*
- *Paul survived three beatings with rods.*
- *Paul survived three shipwrecks.*

The concept of time can be used to solve many life problems because time solves most issues by itself. As a result, there is no point in worrying over unnecessary issues. Lafuente, Viailant, Vendrell-Herrero, and Gomes (October 2019) asserted from the sequential deductive triangulation analysis that *practical experience* is an essential pre-requisite for entrepreneurial learning and that *the resilience* of those with *negative entrepreneurial experience* induces the generalized *entrepreneurial leaning* especially suitable for subsequent intentionally-oriented ventures. Successful business people have been developed through failure.

REFECTION

I dare say that every failure provides some opportunity to teach life lessons; and as a result, the above process guide can help from start to finish. Sjastad, Baumeister, and Ent (May 2020) observes, as follows: One, the results suggest that what people want is restricted by what they can get, using the principle of adaptive preferences in philosophy and cognitive dissonance theory from psychology; Two, initial failure made people underestimate how good it would feel to succeed in the future. Lastly, a systematic tendency to down play the value of unattainable goals and rewards (Sjastad, Baumeister, & Ent, May 2020).

The effect of failure has to do with the immediate consequences of the failure on functionality, operation, function, status; and generally, as experienced or perceived by the user (Kiran, 2017). Throughout the entire book, one theme has become clearer than ever and that is the need to develop capacity to deal with failure in all forms. I have cited the names of different people as role models, including Abraham Lincoln and how he weathered the storm to the United States Presidency.

The names of John Agyekum Kufuor, Professor John Evans Atta-Mills, and Nana Addo Dankwah Akuffo-Addo (all of Ghana) proved that they all contested the Presidency of Ghana and successfully won at the third attempt. Likewise, the three attempts at winning the Democratic nomination had failed for Joseph Robinette Biden, Jr. until 2020, when he became the presumptuous nominee of the party at an older age. Now, sworn in as the 46th President of the United States of America on January 20, 2021. The list goes on and on.

On the personal note, I have discussed the lessons my father offered me early in my life, bordering on attitude to failure as part of my parental legacies. In Chapter 4 and 5, I touched on my re-sit of *Management Information System* and redo of my Doctoral Comprehensive Examinations at the Graduate School. Perhaps, for the good reason for encouraging others. In Chapters 6 and 7, I emphasized the low pass rate resulting in series of failures in professional examinations. Likewise. In Chapter 8, I have told the story of how my farming enterprise failed because of weather conditions in the 1980s. These are just to mention a few.

LESSONS LEARNED

The most important process in handling failure is the lessons and insights that are provided by the event or occurrence. The lessons can be *triple-fold*: (a) for personal application and meant for the individual in question; (b) for practical application and for the benefit of others; and (c) for both personal and practical applications. At times it pays to share your heart out with trusted persons. You would recall my interaction with Kofi Ofori in Chapter 6, when he shared with me the materials to use for preparing for professional examinations and this became a game-changing experience for me.

I remember on one occasion when I was sitting for the CPA examinations, when the Auditing results were released, I was not convinced of the mark I scored so I was seriously considering applying for a remarking. Around the same time, I happened to have discussed my intention with Mr. Albert A. Buabeng (now Dr. Albert A. Buabeng), who had just completed the CPA examinations. Based on the advice he had received from an instructor during a prior CPA Review session, he suggested to me to re-focus my energies on preparing to re-sit the Auditing part of the examinations. With the benefit of hindsight, I find that advice to be a good one. I summarize the lessons learned below:

There is Hope for The Tree- Failure is not an end in itself but rather a means to an end. Failure is temporary unless you want to make it permanent. A failure today can be a success tomorrow. Failure presents very good lessons for life and the Scriptures is very emphatic on the hope that can be brought to bear on failure. The tree is presented to man in a metaphoric fashion for human life and sanctity. The Bible stipulates as follows:

> [7] *"For there is hope for a tree,*
> *If it is cut down, that it will sprout again,*
> *And that its tender shoots will not cease.*
> [8] *Though its root may grow old in the earth,*
> *And its stump may die in the ground,*
> [9] *Yet at the scent of water it will bud*
> *And bring forth branches like a plant*
> (Job 14:7-9, NKJV).

The Bible describes the capacity for the tree to spring back to life after a setback. When a tree is cut down, it is an indication of a state of hopelessness but the Bible continues to emphasize the inner ability of the tree to grow out again. Most often it is quite evident that a tree may be cut for numerous reasons: as firewood in some societies, as lumber for construction purposes, as electricity or telephone pole, and other purposes. It turns out that a straightforward definition leads to unsoundness-A correct definition of a failed tree is given (Drabent, 1992). As a result, the cutting of the tree may suggest the end of the life of the tree but when all hope is gone, the tree begins to spring out again.

I have witnessed this myself when I cut the pine trees in my house. The trees were originally planted to provide wind breaks, as well as, improve the ecology through respiratory advantages. From my biology class, I was taught that human beings breath-in *oxygen* and breath-out *carbon dioxide* and to the extent that trees do the opposite. Consequently, trees co-operate with nature to make respiration of man a reality. Yet, the pine trees in my house grew in size and length over a 20-year period and threatening life and property. I had to spend a large sum of money to cut them down.

The negative effect of the pine trees was that the roots begun to affect the foundations of the fence wall of the house and some branches fell on the structures. In the circumstance, in spite of the benefits I have alluded to above I was compelled to cut off the pine trees which I have intentionally planted. Not quite long, I saw the pine trees growing off shoots again and this time around, I saw some of the stumps developing offshoots that produced two or more trees on the same stump. Indeed, *there is hope for the tree.*

Valued reader, I want to suggest to you that just as there is hope for the tree, there is hope for mankind. The passage continues to tout the reality of the challenge or failure in this case; nevertheless, with a change in its environment the tree can bounce back to life to fulfill destiny. If a tree can go through this; then, a human being is more than capable of rising to any challenge. Continue to keep hope alive because once there is life; because *faith* can keep *love* alive to produce *hope.*

The Power of Group Studies-I did not know the power of group studies in my undergraduate studies but it proved to be a very rewarding methodology for learning at the Graduate school in Ghana. At the Master's level, my group members included-Messrs Alex Cofie, David Ofantse, Henry Acquah, Mrs. Shirley Jiagge, and Dede. Within the group, individual strengths were identified for the benefit of the entire group. The major problem that confronted the group was the meeting place. Our meetings started from Madina (a suburb in Accra), to the back of the Great Hall of the University of Ghana, Legon; then, to the West Africa Secondary School in Adenta (Accra).

Following this success story, the group study methodology was employed in our preparation of the (ICAG) examination. I started with a colleague and later joined Assan Yakub (deceased) and Sulemana Zakari. We did individual studies from Monday through Friday and met on Saturdays (whole day) and Sundays (half-day) at the Baptist School Complex at Madina Zongo Junction (Accra). During those sessions, we held discussions, and solved many examination problems together, as well as, shared insights. As the examinations time approached different small groups came together to form a bigger group for the same purpose. The good news is that with time all the group members completed the examinations.

I recommend group studies to well-meaning and like-minded people, but the composition should be made up of serious people because it requires a higher degree of commitment and hard work for the desired impact.

CHAPTER 14

LEVERAGING TECHNOLOGY FOR TEACHING

LOVAT (2019) HAS EXPLAINED THAT the notion of 'self' pertaining to autobiographical writing has repercussions for the fact dichotomy inherent in autobiographical praxis. In this chapter, I am going to recount my exposure to the unprecedented technological advancement of all time. The term *technology* connotes the use of machines for practical application of scientific knowledge. The advancement in technology has revolutionized the world and has contributed to make the world a Global village. One of the best things that happened in the world is the introduction of computers and internet in the affairs of men. While those who lived before the introduction of technological breakthrough are grappling on daily basis to cope with the changing times to normalize life; those who have been born around this same era see things as normal. As a result, the younger generation cannot fathom the struggles their parents go through when confronted with the issues of technology.

My aim for including this subject as someone who lived before the introduction of the advancement in technology and the need that arose for me to respond to the change, whether by choice or design, is to shed lights on this phase of human development for the benefit of all.

THE PAST (Where We Have Been)

Information Technology (IT) was non-existent when I was born but I had to embrace the change along the line when it occurred in order to stay relevant. Information Technology (IT) or Information Communication Technology (ICT) will be used interchangeably in this book to mean the same thing. It is interesting to note that computers were not considered as part of machines used in the office in my Office Practice and Business Methods classes. I recall a statement that appeared in one of the *comprehension* sections of the English Language in our General Certificate of Education (G.C.E) Ordinary Level Examinations, as follows: *"We were all not born with a sliver spoon in our mouths. Neither are we to own a typewriter. A good handwriting is an asset-So keep it"* Suggesting that owning a typewriter is a luxury and beyond the reach of many and so the best approach is to focus on developing a good hand writing. Consequently, owning a typewriter was not to engage the attention of students but rather a good handwriting was the best alternative.

Good handwriting was intentionally taught in the primary school from Classes 1 to 6; and for that reason, specific books were designed to teach pupils about handwriting. The books were called-My First Copy Book for class 1, My Second Copy Book for class 2, My Third Copy Book for class 3, and so on. In these books, letters of the alphabets and complete sentences are provided for students to copy. To this end, teachers showed appreciation to students who have good handwriting. In times past, judges took case notes by hand and several medical doctors were mocked for poor handwriting.

I took my lesson and lecture notes by hand and extracted critical material from textbooks and references for course outline in writing. Most of the examinations were administered using *pencil and paper* format. In my working life, official communications were drafted in hand for typists to do the needful. This need helped in the creation of the offices of typists with different grades and secretarial class in the civil and public offices. With the passage of time, electric typewriters became the *talk of the town*, when business acquired these assets for improved outcomes. Prior to the advent of the electric typewriter, I saw the utilization of typewriters in banking in Togo in West Africa. While in Ghana deposit slips and withdrawal forms were completed in ink, the banks in Togo utilized typewriters to complete forms.

On communication, cell phones were non-existent as it is common today. Landlines dominated the telephony landscape. Telephones were deployed as analogue before the digital versions were introduced. The old handset for calling was the norm. International calls in Ghana could only be done in Kumasi in the Ashanti and Accra in the Greater Accra regions of Ghana. Precious time was spent to travel to these locations to book appointment for an intended call and another time to travel for the actual call. Later on, *collect calls* were introduced to allow for recipients to pay for the call but this turned up to be expensive because of the additional charges for the service. This did not stand the test of time.

Another area of interest is the advancement in Television sets (TVs). Growing up in Mampong Maternity Hospital in Ashanti region of Ghana, television sets were not common. Adjacent to the compound of the Mampong Maternity Hospital was the Saint Monica's Complex (Secondary/High School, Training College, Middle School). The opportunities to watch television was two-fold-(I) going to the bungalow of a nurse of the Mampong Maternity Hospital, and (II) going to the bungalow of a driver of the Saint Monica's Secondary School. The story was not different in the Mampong-Ashanti township because only a few homes owned television sets. Beyond that only a few allowed others to come to their rooms to watch television. One of my school mate's uncle, who was the Manager of the United African Company (UAC) in Mampong allowed me to come and watch television programs in his living room. I appreciate that gesture.

Likewise, one chemist also allowed the general public to come into his house to watch television. This man displayed his television set in the open court of the compound house for all to enjoy the entertainment programs such as the *Osofo Dadzie Group*, featuring the likes of Super O.D., Osofo Dadzie (Frimpong Manso), Kwadwo Kwakye, Fred Addai,

Beatrice Kusi, Akua Boahemaa, Mercy Offei, and S.K. Oppong. With the passage of time, Major General Kudjiku (the Ashanti Regional Commissioner), whose daughter became my classmate at the undergraduate level, donated a television set to the Mampong township for the benefit of the community. The donated TV set was displayed in front of the Mampong Silver Stool Palace for the community. I hasten to say that all the TV sets were in black and white color.

By the 1990s, accounting systems were purely manual with a few IT deployments. Likewise, teaching approaches involving- lectures, tutorials, workshops, seminars, and so on were undertaken manually.

THE PRESENT (Where We Are)

In my undergraduate studies at the University of Ghana School of Administration in 1986, a typing pool was available to permit students to learn the skill of typing on their own. Students registered and bought a typing manual and went ahead to schedule hours for practicing. The first shot at computer training was in *GW-Basic* and the instructor was Mr. Kwame Osei Sarfo. The syllabus of professional accounting bodies such as the Institute of Chartered Accountants, Ghana (ICAG) provided for IT bordering on hardware, software, and communication. Nevertheless, the knowledge remained theoretical because there was no corresponding practical dimension. At the Graduate School of the University of Ghana School of Administration in 1999, computers and internet have been introduced. A Graduate program in Management Information System (MIS) was created to prepare Graduate students, in collaboration with a foreign university that required MIS students to study abroad for one year as part of their preparation for the world of work.

I responded to the technological advancement by: (a) going to the *Osu-RE*, a suburb in Accra to familiarize myself, learn, and browse the internet by spending ¢6,000 per week; (b) I used the period between my Master's degree program and entrance to the world of work to learn how to use some computer programs, including *Lotus 123, D-Base 3+,* and many more. Later on, other accounting software, including- *Topaz* and the *Soft Tribes'* modules bearing local names such as Bimbilla (general Ledger) were learned. With time, the accounting software-*Tally* was promoted for clients by the Accounting firm-Deloitte in Ghana.

Around this time, a bank in Ghana migrated from manual banking unto the Online platform using the *ORBIT* and introducing *automated teller machines* (ATMs) in Ghana. I experienced this technological revolution as a customer of the bank at the time. Interestingly, all resumes prepared at this time for job searches specified "I have user-knowledge in computers" but now this is taken for granted. Some organizations used search engines such as Yahoo and Google for internal communication.

Internet development has been involved with the use of V-SAT and masts to capture signals and the utilization of fiber optics. In the process, bandwidth, routers, and modems have been dependable. My first ownership of a cell phone was in the Graduate school when my friend- Alex Cofie bought the Chip from the Winneba (Central region) Post Office for ¢360,000 and some change. The chip was not readily available and so I had to buy the chip for my mother at ¢1 million from somebody who had visited Ghana and was returning back. Unlike back then, cell phones abound and have become a household item. Interestingly, the influx of telephony companies has made it cheaper to use cell phones to make international calls in Ghana to other destinations such as the United States of America.

Similarly, other platforms such as Viber and *WhatsApp* have also facilitated international and local call because of internet-enablement. Another area I want to comment on is that of TVs. The revolution of technology has affected television sets from Colored TVs to Flash

Screen sets. I once chanced on a family in a Supermarket in Accra-Ghana, who have come to buy a black and white TV set and the smile on the faces of the children was illuminating and infectious. While several people had moved on to own colored TV sets, some are still grateful for the ownership of the black and white TVs-such is life. IT-supported teaching deployment has revolved around the use of Moodle platform and the utilization of Power Point presentations.

THE FUTURE (Where We Go from Here)

The past is known, the present is evolving but the future is unknown. In the United States of America, children are exposed to computers and video games early in their development.

It is normal for children to use computers from start of school and typing skills becomes a consequence of using computers for a period of time. The privilege of using computers at an earlier developmental stage should not be taken for granted by young people in the USA; but must be viewed as an act of grace.

The story is told of two boys who were given an old telephone handset to dial a telephone number, but they could not figure out how to dial the number. I do not blame them because it is not their fault. They did not live during those days when those handsets were prevalent. If care is not taken, the youth of today will take some of the opportunities in the land for granted. I remember one day, there was a total blackout in my office in Chicago for just few minutes and I saw all the staff on the corridor because no work could be accomplished. Nevertheless, I have come from a background where at a point in time in 2016 when specific plans were rolled out for load shedding exercise for the entire country-Ghana. This was popularly called- "dumsor"

Lest I forget, my bosom friend-Dr. Appiah was recounting his life story to his baby son regarding how his entire household in

Mampong-Ashanti had only two lanterns. So, he needed to stay late for everybody to go to bed so he can have a lantern to himself to study. His son looked at the father and said: "Daddy, you are a fat liar" At that moment in time, my friend called me on phone into the conversation to provide a contemporaneous confirmation or otherwise to the son. I confirmed the story as exactly right to the boy. He asked me if that was my story and I explained that I had light in my house but his father did not at the time. I went on the explain that I lived with his father in the same room in my house so we can study together. This conversation has taught me that there is the need to have cross pollination of ideas between parents of African descent and children born in the United States of America. By this, the young adults will not take opportunities around them for granted by any way, shape, or form.

The utilization of IT has revolved around the application of computer software and hardware in electronic accounting systems in some employment; through the preparation of source documentation and financial reporting; as well as, the setting and administration of examinations to students through the course unit system. IT cuts across sectors and industries. Computer laboratories have been provided to help students who cannot afford personal computers and laptops. Online learning protocols have evolved around the following: research and literature reviews, E-book, PowerPoint presentation, discussions, E-Library, auditing procedures, Databases such as ProQuest, Wiley, SAGES, etc.

My observation is that while the cost of printers can be low, the cost of replacement of cartridges can be very expensive. Moreover, the following resources have been developed for mankind, including- Application Tracking System (ATS) for evaluation, review, and selection of resumes; Turn-It-In, Write Check, and Grammarly for measuring similarity index and grading of written work; readability tests, and other models of prediction.

The future of IT will be characterized by greater use of IT in future and so I call on the younger generation to embrace the change brought about by IT; otherwise, such people who ignore this change will be left out. Knowledge has proved to be revolutionary and the younger generation should be part of the evolution; otherwise, remain irrelevant. Likewise, the advancement of technology is important but *spirituality* is also important.

TEACHING- A GIFT FROM ABOVE

I have narrated how I desired to have the teaching abilities exemplified by Emeka Nwapah, Esq (International Conference Speaker) in 1987 at Aburi in the Eastern region of Ghana; under the auspices of Pentecost Students and Associates (PENSA). I had forgotten about the prayer request until one day, I was assigned a preaching appointment at the Madina Central Church of Pentecost and after the delivery of the message, a lady told my late friend (Lawrence Larbi) that I was a teacher. I responded to a vacancy announcement for lecturing positions partly because of the feedback provided by this young lady. I also needed some flexibility in working hours because of my personal circumstances at the time.

The thrust of my teaching goals is making the student the center of impartation by emphasizing on the teacher, the learner, and the learning outcomes (TLO). My teaching goals include but not limited to the following:

1. *To see in my students a generation of business professionals who are knowledgeable and command respect in their chosen career.*
2. *To inculcate in students ethical standards and a high level of professional conduct.*

3. *To develop a world-class scholars and professionals in accounting and finance who can compete in every environment.*

4. *To ensure that students take positive outcomes from the classroom and look forward to coming to the next class.*

5. *To assure students that learning is part of growth of human existence.*

In approaching the teaching work and studies, I apply the following:

1. *I believe in teaching to the best of my abilities and that students continue to be the best testimonial of teachers.*

2. *There is the need to encourage students to combine both the academic and the professional aspects of their career. I encourage my students not to settle for anything below a graduate degree plus a professional certification as the minimum achievement.*

3. *I use different teaching approaches and delivery methods to achieve the desired objective.*

4. *I employed the Moodle, Backboard, Classe365, Google Classroom, and Brightspace technology platforms for the students to ensure interaction among students, advisors and faculty. The graduate students of the University of Professional Studies, Accra (UPSA) also created a group emailing system to promote continued flow of information in the learning process.*

5. *I updated my course materials regularly and improved on my teaching methods based on the evaluation of my students.*

6. *I provided career counseling to students by keeping them abreast with developments in the accounting profession.*

7. *I availed myself for meetings of Boards and Committees.*

TEACHING LESSONS

My teaching lessons were grounded in my teaching philosophy and characterized by: *One*, students' self-assessments, strategic checks for appreciation; appropriate interventions; as well as, students population dynamics and demographics, and differentiation. *Two,* students learning preferences, teaching approaches and methodologies, revised lesson plans, and standard attribution to students. *Lastly,* flexibility and strategic grouping, problem-based learning instruction, time management strategies and practices; and inquiry-based deployment and learning outcomes, and instructions

STATEMENT OF TEACHING PHILOSOPHY

My teaching philosophy is rooted in Galatians 5:22-23: *"But the fruit of the Spirit is love, joy, peace, longsuffering, gentleness, goodness, faith, meekness, temperance: against such there is no law"(KJV).* The thrust of my teaching philosophy covers a wide range of issues and spans over fourteen years (teaching accounting and related subjects in Ghana-Africa for about ten years and almost five years in the United States of America-as of December 31, 2020). I taught in a *brick and mortar* school in various environments: traditional, non-traditional, undergraduate, graduate, and professional streams. I have taught in the *Online* setting in the United States of America to graduate students; as well as, *blended* environments in both Ghana and the United States of America.

I have worked in various capacities and industries such as public accounting, private sector, governmental, and in the *not-for- profit* environment in Ghana and the United States of America.

I entered the teaching field to impact lives and also be impacted in my professional career. I had to study to teach my students, I also updated my knowledge which enabled me to prepare for my professional examinations as well.

The major satisfaction of a teacher is to make positive impact in the lives of students who look up to you as mentor, father, friend, and role model. The teaching job exposes the teacher to a network of students, scholars, and practitioners.

I taught the undergraduate, graduate, and the professional levels and ensured that I employed appropriate styles and techniques in the deployment of the courses to get the desired outcomes.

I diffused the misconceptions about accounting as a discipline because most students associated accounting with statistics and mathematics. I assured the students that, accounting is a set of principles and concepts to be applied to everyday life.

For instance, when I taught Taxation I to level 300 (undergraduate juniors) and Taxation II to level 400 (undergraduate seniors) students who are accounting major; as well as Taxation to Levels 300 and 400 as elective to students in other departments, I had to use different teaching styles to catch their attention such as applying a whimsical sense of humor, textbooks, tax laws, business examples, and professional debates on taxation. Lecture notes were combined with group work and presentations. I taught taxation as a tool for national development and this became my motivation to write a textbook on-*Taxation in Ghana: A Fiscal Tool for Development.*

When I taught Public Sector Accounting to level 400 students who are accounting major, I developed a study manual to assist the students because the area was not well-developed in Ghana. I employed the existing laws on financial administration and regulation, internal audit agency, public procurement, local governance, and the governmental budgeting systems. I introduced students to the United States governmental accounting systems.

When I taught Taxation and Fiscal policy to graduate students, my students were holders of bachelor degrees and professional certifications in accounting and auditing. The groups of students were combining work with studies and the classes were held in the evenings and weekends. I had to assist the students with course materials by uploading them ahead of time to enable them interrogate them before meeting in the classroom. The presentation of course materials took the facilitation approach and students discussed the issues thoroughly. The following teaching approaches were employed: course materials, group work, and class presentation, mid semester quizzes, and so on.

In the case of the professional programs, I taught financial accounting foundation to Certified Institute of Management Accountants (CIMA) level 1 students; performance management to Association of Chartered Certified Accountants (ACCA) level 2 students; corporate financial management to Institute of Chartered Secretaries and Administrators (ICSA) final level students; and taxation to Institute of Chartered Accountants, Ghana (ICAG) level 2 students, advanced tax planning and fiscal policy, and corporate reporting strategy to Institute of Chartered Accountants, Ghana (ICAG) level 4 students.

The teaching approach to this cohort was challenging because their preparation was based on prepared course manuals by the respective accounting professional bodies. The challenge with this group was that the final assessment of the student was done by the various accounting professional bodies, leaving my duties to teaching according to the manuals.

While teaching in the Southern New Hampshire University (SNHU), I taught federal taxation, as well as, advance auditing, and capital budgeting and financing to graduate students, using the Blackboard and Brightspace technology platforms.

The specifics of teaching students online encompass welcoming and having positive interactions, providing general and specific support to students especially to students with challenges, monitoring of performance to ensure success, and providing adequate feedback to reinforce teaching and learning.

As a teacher, research has engaged my attention and my research interests have revolved around: financial reporting, taxation and fiscal policy, accounting education, business ethics, corporate fraud, internal controls, and corporate governance. I have been following developments in these areas and that motivated me to pursue my doctoral program in advanced accounting, with research focus on *corporate fraud* and *accounting education*. The outcome of my dissertation has resulted in the writing of a book on-*Fraud Prevention and Detection Puzzle: Skills, Strategies, Competences, and Programs.*

TECHNOLOGY-DRIVEN DISCIPLESHIP CLASSES

I have been blessed to prepare young believers through discipleships classes. A blended approach utilizing *technology* and *in-class* formats to teach in the following courses: (a) Leadership Academy, (b) New Members Orientation Program, (c) Marriage Preparation Group. The discipleship classes were designed in response to the findings and recommendation of the National Youth Retention Research conducted by the Church of Pentecost U.S.A.,Inc., chaired by the Principal of the Pentecost Biblical Seminary in February 2018. The course was structured as follows: doctrine (60%), leadership (20%), current affairs (5%), church history (2%), church polity (8%), financial administration (5%).

The course materials encompassed articles and scholarly sources, the Bible, textbooks, discussions, lecture materials, Online resources, publication, selected cases, self-search, Special Church of Pentecost publications, specialized journals, and many more. The graduation requirements of the Leadership Academy was a total of 30 credits spanning a period of six months; composed as follows-7 credits for *in-class* instruction, 5 credits for class assignments covering short written papers and group work, 7 credits for term paper or project, 3 credits for class presentations, and 8 credits for attendance to presentations and engagements. A minimum of 15 credits is needed for graduation.

The first graduating class of the Leadership Academy- 2019 is made up of the following: (1) Schwarltcouf Sintim-Aboagye (Overall Best Students), (2) Bridget Mawuse Amenyo, (3) Charlotte Nkpe, (4) Freda Opoku Agyemang, (5) Hannah Afi Torsu, (6) Kwame Kyei Amoah, (7) Priest Kofi Bonsu, (8) Vera Osei, (9) Yaa Dufie Karikari, and (10) Nana Ama Nti. The first batch of the graduates for the New Members Orientation Program comprises of the following: (i) Solomon Awin-Ongya, (ii) Daniel Darko, (iii) Jeffrey Yiadom, (iv) Goldie Amoah, (v) Emmanuella Gyamera, (vi) Ella Okai, (vii) Michelle Duah, (viii) Josephine Brobbey, (ix) Derrick Boateng, (x) Lernard Donkor, (xi) Bryce Donkor, (xii) Randy Appiah, (xiii) Biance Akosua Jackson, (xiv) Michael Ameyaw, (xv) Abena Cofie, (xvi) Doreen Atakora, (xvii) Samuel Kissi Baah, (xviii) Kelsey Agyekum, and (xix) Fantasia Awuah.

LESSONS LEARNED

Few lessons are presented below for your guidance:

The critical competencies-In addition to the importance IT (myths, facts, and fiction) has assumed over the year, other distinctive competences to be developed include-critical thinking, teamwork, business communication, and many more (Appiah-Sokye, 2016).

The **COVID-19 Global Pandemic** that affected the entire globe in early 2020 had challenged individuals, organizations, and nations to take the IT utilization to a higher level; because failure to respond appropriately will cause them to be left out. Today, several workers are able to work from distance locations such as their homes, using *Virtual Private Network* (VPNs), *Team Viewers*, ShareFile, and many more. Likewise, meetings and conferences can be held via Virtual platforms such as the *ZOOM, Cisco, GoToMeeting*, etc. Likewise, online accounting software such as the NetSuite ORACLE can be accessed in any place on the globe where internet is available.

Yes, the pandemic took away a lot of human lives-(CNN News, 2021)-May their memories be a blessing! The electronic and the online platforms have been developed to support-education, travel, church, and many more human endeavors; with concomitant social distancing, wearing of face masks, and washing of hands. The lesson is that either you respond to change at your own pace; or you are compelled to change in this case by COVID-19.

Course Designs and Implementation- My active involvement in Church of Pentecost over the years has afforded me the privilege of attending many leadership and training programs; as well as, the holding of several positions including: Assistant District Financial Secretary, Assistant District Leader, PENTYEM; Presiding Elder (PIWC, Chicago), Member, National/Regional Audit Committee, Local Secretary; Member, District Finance Committee; Member, District Executive Committee (Chicago/Romeoville), and currently an Member, Chicago Regional Executive Committee, and Elder of the church.

I am well placed to give back to help develop lay leadership and the youth of the church. I have designed and implemented four blended courses (in-class and online courses, using *Google classroom platform)* in response to specific needs of leaders and young adults in my Church, as follows: (1) P.I.W.C Leadership Academy to train future leaders for the church; (2) P.I.W.C New Members Orientation Program to provide structured orientation course for new members of the church; (3) COP Training Platform for providing self-study opportunities to officers of the church in the Chicago region; and (4) P.I.W.C Marriage Preparation Class as pre-marital course for young adults.

While aggressive preparation characterizes the certification for various professional bodies, the certification provided for marriage is not deemed important by many. Several certifications come at the end of rigorous preparation and training but marriage certification is presented upfront. Think about this for a minute.

Again, the mode of teaching and learning in Africa in general and Ghana in particular is different from that of the United States of America. While the Ghanaian approach is skewed towards teaching, the United States' approach is based on learning. In Ghana, the teacher prepares to teach the student but the teacher in the United States facilitates learning. It is against this background that I consider the utilization of the Blended (Online and In-class) course approach the best to *intentionally* develop the youth of the church.

Typewriters have served us well- I encountered both the manual and electric typewriter in my working life. As I indicated earlier on that important official documents were typed by Personal secretaries of companies but most of the documents started as written drafts. I remember one of the typists I worked with used to be noted for typing full of mistakes (absence of proof reading), but I saw a strength in her work. Typically, she indicated the initials of the originator and typist below the document. When I told her how I like that style she opened up and explain that she was taught that in the typing school. Thereafter, she never submitted a typed document to me without proof-reading.

I recommended the buying of a typewriter to one of the typists whom I work with in the Ghana Internal Revenue Service in Cape Coast at her retirement as a way of making some money to support her in retirement. The work of public typists abounds in Ghana and continue to provide critical services to the public. Public typists can be found within the surrounding areas of Law Courts, Registrar-Generals Department, the Lands Commission, and other places. A few of the typist assist students in their project work. These secretarial and legal services continue to be relevant today just as they were in the past but some have responded to the advancement in technology by giving clients the option of getting output from manual, or electric typewriter, or from a computer. I have come to learn that giving praise where it is due can be very rewarding.

CONCLUSION

I have already impacted over one thousand students who are working in various fields of accounting and finance in Ghana, whilst others have pursued further studies. I continue to get former students who request me to write recommendation letters to employers and schools across the globe. In the United States of America, I have taught over 250 students and still counting in the graduate school category mainly in accounting and finance. I am currently exploring a new role as the Registrar of the Pentecost Biblical Seminary (PBS), since July 2020. Upon reflection, I consider myself successful as a teacher and for that reason, I was appointed the head of the accounting department between October 2006 and April 2007. My exposure to teaching has helped me to make the world a better place to live in and to impact future generations with accounting knowledgebase. My students have made me proud.

CHAPTER 15

MENTORED TO MENTOR OTHERS

THE PURPOSE OF THIS BOOK is to respond to my purpose-driven name-*Enough to be shared*-to provide the much-needed framework through the telling of my life story regarding lessons-usefulness to all who desire mentorship in one way or form. I admit that the lessons provided in this book cannot solve all human problems but can be helpful to some towards the untying of some knots in certain situations and circumstances. Mentorship revolves around the giving and receiving of insights or guidance or experiences over a time frame. Typically, the *mentor* is the experienced person who provide guidance to the mentee. The mentoring process can be a *win-win* situation. While the *mentee* learns and develops skills through counselling, coaching, cheer leading and consultancy; the *mentor* gets fulfillment and sense of accomplishment through the process.

WAYS, SHAPE, and FORM

Per Onyinah (2004),"You need to emulate David to remain the same, give credit to God and be focused"(p.32). Mentorship takes different forms and a few approaches will be discussed in this section of the book. *Apprenticeship*-This is the most widely used in preparing people for trade and vocations. In this arrangement, the master or mistress serves as the mentor and the apprentice becomes the mentee. The relationship covers a considerable period of time. While the mentor provides the training needs of the apprentice in exchange for a fee, the mentee in turn performs general duties for the master/mistress. The mentor determines that the mentee has completed the needed training and has achieved the level of competence desired for the vocation. I have come to observe that apprentices who self-graduate and leave without the payment of agreed upon fees do not prosper in their trade. I have seen at least one or two apprentices, who came back to confess to their mentors and to do the needful such that they could go back to succeed.

Pupilage-This form of mentorship appears to be utilized in some professional groups such as accounting, legal, and *full-time* Christian ministry. After professional examinations and certification, some professional bodies require new graduates to undergo practical training at the offices of experienced professionals before admission into membership of the professional body. In some churches, newly called ministers have to understudy experienced ministers and also function in the comfort of experienced lay leaders before progressing to the pastoral class.

Formal education-Another form for mentorship takes formal education format through the deployment of course contents, structured curricula, and the use of contact hours, and course unit system. The outcome is the award of certificates, diplomas, or degrees, and professional certification. All-in-all, mentorship can take the form of *one-on-one*, at the same location or at different locations; or *group approach* such as *one-to-many*, including distance, or one-to-group at the same or varied locations.

DUAL ASPECTS OF LIFE

Life is presented in a dual fashion and for that reason there is dualism or duality to most of the things we do in life; as a result, mentorship is no exception. For example, there are two sides to a coin-the head and the tail. The subject accounting is based on the double-entry principle which stipulates that for "every debit entry, there must be a corresponding credit entry" Additionally, the accounting equation ensures equality between the left-hand side (Assets-meaning resources owned) and the right-hand side (Equity or capital, plus liabilities-meaning ownership and claims on resources). Likewise, not only do the cardinal points have *north-south*; but also, *east-west* and many more. Similarly, there is the first (beginning or alpha) and the last (end or omega). Mentorship is from person (mentor) to person (mentee) and subject to duality. While mentorship can be direct, it can also be indirect; can also assume an intentional and unintentional dimension. Mentorship can be closed or remote; as well as, mentor-initiated or mentee-initiated. As a consequence, the experienced person is mentored to also mentor others and this is the sense of responsibility I carry.

JUSTIFICATION FOR MENTORSHIP

To whom much is given, much is expected (Luke 12:48). As a result, having received much from parents, teachers, society, and the church; it is required that I share my experiences with others for impact, effect, and relevance. Moreover, the Latin maxim: "Nemo dat non quid habet" implying that you cannot give what you do not have is also true. I seek to pose four question, as follows:

How much has been received?

The quantification of what has been received is difficult because some may be visible and others invisible, and several of them can be direct but others are indirect, a few may be obvious but others can be *less obvious. Some experiences are positive and others are negative, yet provide teaching* moments for both the mentor and the mentee. Arguably, some perspectives are personal and others are impersonal. Some endeavors are active but others are passive or inactive.

Who gives that much?

To answer this question, all well-meaning people can contribute to this process. In Chapter 8 of this textbook, I emphasized that every experience is relevant. The *development of expertise, competencies, and skills* is one area that mentors can respond to benefit mentees. Another area, *goal setting* has been an area that makes the relationship between mentors and mentees more important than ever before. Additionally, when mentors make their experiences relevant to support change that mentees are confronted with on daily basis, half of the *battle* is won. Likewise, *sustainability* over the long haul should provide the needed impetus for objective perspective, because no single solution is right.

Mentors should be satisfied that mentees have been assisted to navigate through the storms of life. As a result, mentors should stay connected to their mentees to reflect on actions. Consequently, mentees should respond adequately by co-operating with mentors, learn to be life learners and patients, develop positive philosophy in outlook, and be able to stretch beyond their comfort zone.

Who has received much?

Every mentor did not start as a mentor but had to be mentored in order to mentor others. A lot can be received throughout life journey, including-(i) formal and informal schooling for certification and certificates; (ii) participation and facilitation in conferences, workshops, training, and preaching; (iii) listening to radio and TV shows, (iv) taking part in blogging and social media conversations; (v) involvement through community engagement, (vi) reading of memoires, biographies, and autobiographies of other people; and many more.

How much can be given?

I can give back to others through several means such as sharing my life experiences in this book, teaching and research, counseling and advising, and mentorship. The perspectives I am able to share in this book includes but not limited to the following 60 points of view:

1. *I make no apologies for being a Christian in general and a Pentecostal in particular;*
2. *I consider my accountancy profession as a call of God upon my life;*
3. *I seek to impact others with my values and knowledge;*
4. *I view character formation as a critical success factor;*
5. *I argue that failure can be surmounted;*
6. *I contend that my life lessons can be told through this book;*
7. *I portend that life losses cannot be avoided but Can be managed;*
8. *I suggest that the learning of languages is a good idea. Consider Spanish, French, and Hausa;*
9. *Information technology adeptness is a necessary condition for success in this age;*
10. *Other competencies required are critical thinking, business communication, and teamwork;*
11. *I encourage the setting of challenging goals;*
12. *I argue that leaders must be developed with intentionality for every sphere of life;*
13. *I am of the view that young Christian youth should be prepared for marriage;*
14. *I think that people should know and respond to their God-given purpose;*
15. *I challenge young people to harness their potential. Parental accomplishments are not necessarily your personal achievements;*
16. *I suggest that people should endeavor to stay relevant so they cannot be discounted;*

17. *I have seen that decisions based on long gestation period tend to produce better outcomes;*
18. *I consider life experiences as bittersweet (positive and negative);*
19. *I recommend that impacting lives leads to fulfilled life;*
20. *I argue that failure to know your roots will permit others to define who you are;*
21. *I contend that there is an association between what concerns you and your purpose in life;*
22. *I suggest that you admit your weaknesses so you can seek help. Do not pretend;*
23. *I advise that you show gratefulness for little things;*
24. *I contend that you accept accountability in response to the grant of responsibility and authority;*
25. *I assert that you stay truthful to yourself at all time;*
26. *I portend that our faithfulness will be subject to test with time;*
27. *I am of the view that rewards can drive endurance. Cause and effect;*
28. *I have seen that society is identified with success. You suffer alone but rejoice with many;*
29. *I recommend peoples' skills because computers have hijacked technical skills;*
30. *I pray that you embrace challenges in life. "Life is how you make it"*
31. *I implore you to take training and professional development seriously;*
32. *I have seen that Visions developed needs to be sold and bought for positive outcomes;*
33. *I postulate that seeking honest feedback can prevent a lot of pitfalls;*
34. *Listen, listen, listen;*
35. *I have been taught that God's silence is also an answer;*
36. *I counsel that it is better to ask if you do know, rather than showing your ignorance publicly;*
37. *I have observed that every successful person can point to an unknown humble beginning;*

38. *I have learned that life is a journey, has an origin, has a destination, and full of experiences;*

39. *I have seen that values that are not cultivated cannot stand to be harvested;*

40. *I contend that the favor of God is key;*

41. *I argue that academic success can be infectious;*

42. *I have come to know that professionalism is society-focused;*

43. *I am convinced that faith produces the foundations for lives to be focused;*

44. *I admit that service to God is also service to mankind;*

45. *I have learned at firsthand that "It is a small world after all"(Credit Union Song);*

46. *I counsel that man will not live forever;*

47. *I have seen that no situation is permanent. Everything that has a beginning has an end;*

48. *I want to give this encouragement that denial is not the same as delays;*

49. *I consider opportunities in every bitter experience;*

50. *I view the family as the pivot upon which the wheels of society rotate;*

51. *I argue that divine provision and selection are sufficient conditions for success;*

52. *I agree that whatever you accept to do, do it to the best of your abilities;*

53. *I counsel that you learn to say-No, when the need arises;*

54. *I suggest that you learn to please God (credible) and not man because man is not predictable;*

55. *I suggest that you have your opinion on issues and be decisive on your progress;*

56. *I argue that both speed and accuracy are equally-important in responding to issues;*

57. *I contend that there is the need to be intellectual or academic for insights on some issues;*

58. *I suggest that you respond to change, otherwise, you will be compelled to change;*

59. *I consider success as a product of fulfillment of God-given purpose and destiny;*

60. *I contend that we are mentored to mentor; through- advocacy, coaching, guidance, counseling, role modeling.*

MY MENTORS

The most difficult challenge I have encountered is the attempt to single out mentors for my entire life because I am a beneficiary of the life of a lot of people such as school teachers, Sunday school teachers, church leaders; as well as, cheer leaders, family, and friends. In the course of telling my life story, I have mentioned the roles played by certain individuals in different phases of my life. In this section of the book, I want to recognize the roles they have played in my personal development. I acknowledge their contribution with grace and gratefulness. In this section, I am going to touch on only two in the interest of space; **one**, the late *George Emmanuel Appiah-Sokye* (my father) touching on parental ethos; and **two**, the late *Apostle Dr. Emmanuel Owusu Bediakoh, with* focused on Christian or Pentecostal heritage.

GEORGE EMMANUEL APPIAH-SOKYE (1922-1986)

I presented the life story of my parents in Chapter 2 of this book and so I do not intend to repeat the same information here. Readers are encouraged to go back to chapter 2 to refresh their memories before continuing the reading of this section. Every parent can transfer values and legacies to children and grand-children and my parents were no exception. **Personal qualities**- My mother was God-fearing, outspoken, hardworking, and truthful; as well as, dependable and focused on the big picture. Again, she was the first to convert to the Pentecostal faith in her family, which was predominantly Catholic. Now, a good number of her family members are Pentecostals. I possess some of my mother's values and qualities. On my father's part, he was the mentor-in-chief to me and I continue to be guided by some of the principles and values he inculcated in me from infancy. I used to ask him a lot of questions from Archeology (A) to Zoology (Z) and he took my questions as teaching moments to emphasize on critical life lessons.

In line with the theme of this book, I would want to share some of the lessons with readers, as follows: *One,* **teaching book**-The first admonition from my father is to take the Bible as a Sacred and teachings book, which has answers to all life questions. While the Bible is not confined to only history, it has perspectives for the present to affect the future. Consequently, the relevance of the Bible is not in dispute because it has been able to stand the test of the time. A very authoritative book to settle all arguments. By way of reflection, I can categorically state that the Bible has served me well and I recommend it to all readers to endeavor to learn, read, ponder over, meditate, and study the Bible at all times. The Bible was recommended to me as teachings book and my teaching philosophy is anchored in the Bible.

Two, **learning to the level allowed for by grace of God**-The words spoken by parents, especially, fathers into the lives of their children cannot be discounted. My father asked me to study to the level to be permitted by God and so that became the basis of my overall objective. I remember when one of our classmates decided to join the workforce after High School. At the time, he was earning ¢75 as an accounts clerk of a company. When I visited him, he had acquired some furniture and few basic personal items for himself and he could buy friends food and drinks. One day, as I was talking about my job prospects after my High School days, my father joined the conversation and told me that I should not worry about the earnings of the classmates working after High School but rather be focused on continuing my education because at the right time, when I join the working class, my first month salary will be equivalent to the savings of my classmates who decided to work earlier.

Upon reflection, this principle works now just as it did back then. When I completed the undergraduate degree and started working, all my classmates who worked with me in the same organization were below me in grade or rank and salary. While they needed a minimum of nine years to be promoted to my starting grade, the promotions were not automatic and some had to write and pass internal examinations to go beyond the junior level grades. Yet, it took me only additional three years of College level education to commence work as a senior officer, as compared to nine years of my Sixth-form classmates in the workforce.

The same principle is true for my classmates, who continued after undergraduate level education with graduate and professional level education. By the time, those who joined the workforce immediately after undergraduate realized, those in the other category were ahead of them and the pace has been maintained over the long haul. My recommendation is for the young people to consider completing graduate studies and preferably add at least one certification before joining the workforce. Otherwise, the same objective should drive the individual's career objective no matter how long it takes.

Three, **positive response to transfers**- People tend to be resistant to change and transfer is not different; and for this reason, my father advised me never to refuse to go on transfer, when the need arises. Yes, it is possible that your superiors might use transfer to punish you but they are not God. Perhaps, the new station will be the God-given destination in your life. The Bible states that all things work together for good for those who are the called according to his divine purpose. In life, I have come across situations where people have been transferred and initially, resisted but when they finally reported, they were reluctant to leave the same place they did not want to go in the first place. I have observed in Ghana that such people often decided to leave their families behind; others made those towns their permanent homes by building residential houses in those towns. My piece of advice to the young people is that, God controls the affairs of men in working his purpose through such transfer but people should see these instances as the hand of God at work to perfect things in our lives.

Four, **remaining in holy ground-** Per my father, whenever God's children meet at a place, the devil or the enemy goes around or patrols the area to see if he can unleash any onslaughts on the children of God. This view is consistent with Scriptures: *"Now there was a day when the sons of God came to present themselves before the LORD, and Satan also came among them" (Job 1:6-ESV).*The habit of aimlessly moving around the venue for Conventions, Crusades, Rallies, and many more should be reconsidered. Arguably, those venues constitute holy grounds and should not be taken lightly. If there are genuine reasons for leaving the place, I have no problem with that but the habit of just moving about aimlessly can be dangerous.

Five, **unnecessary agitations against ministers-** A related concept is the writing of letters, including anonymous letters about ministers of the Gospel. My advice is that one should speak his mind in all situations and at all meetings; as well as, all grievance protocols should be adhered to, including the Biblical formula for conflict resolutions. However, taking delight in writing letters about ministers should be discouraged.

Lastly, **attitude to failure-** Just as Kurt Lewin considered *failure* and *success* as feeling; my father seized on my failure of the common entrance examinations (an aptitude test for entering High School in Ghana) in 1976-77 as a teaching moment to guide me on how to handle failure as part of life. When I failed my common entrance examinations, I refused to eat and so when my father came home and learned that I was not eating because I had failed the Common entrance, he called me and ask me if I had eaten and I replied that I have not eaten and he asked the reason why I have not eaten and I told him I have failed the common entrance examinations. Then, he told me to go and eat and come back after eating, which I obliged. On returning to him, he sat me down and explain to me that failure is not against my person but against my work and efforts. What the failure means is that my preparation was either inadequate or the overall learning strategy was defective.

I have to go back and review the methods, processes, approaches employed with a view to determining what methods did not work and to also explore other alternative approaches. Then, this was re-enforced with the poem-*If at first you do not succeed, try again.* After several years, this lesson has served me well. I sat for the Institute of Chartered Accountants, Ghana (ICAG) professional accounting examinations with a pass rate of 25 percent at the time. The prior preparation by my father helped me a lot because the Institute used to provide-*BAD FAIL* for *F* grade, which was a note of discouragement for students. My father's lesson on how to handle failure provided me with the capacity to weather the storm. I remember our counter slogan- *They can delay us but they cannot deny us.* By this response, we considered failure as a delay in the graduation process and not a denial of our ultimate certification.

The story was not different, when I was sitting for the Certified Public Accountant (CPA) certification in U.S.A. After every failure, I have to rebound and go back to sit for the examinations as soon as possible.

May I state that young people should see failure as a springboard for success and there are many people, including: (i) Abraham Lincoln, whose persistent failure in life did not deter him to finally becoming the President of the USA; (ii) President Joe R. Biden, who has never won any presidential primary until 2020, won the South Carolina primaries; then, went ahead to win the nomination of the Democratic Party of USA. Now, the 46th President of the USA. (iii) President John Agyekum Kuffour of Ghana, whom the Opposition Parties stated that he had never been successful in business and law practice, yet defiled all odds to become the President of Ghana. Likewise, considering (iv) Presidents- John Agyekum Kufuor, Professor John Evans Atta-Mills, and Nana Addo Dankwah Akuffo Addo; the common thread for all these honorable men was the fact that they contested for the presidency and won after the third attempt.

Dear reader, *nothing succeeds like success* (Abraham Dumas-Retrieved from www.brainyquote.com -accessed on 03/20/2020). Ultimately, success will erode all the failure records. Whether you attempted the desired challenge once or multiple times, the most important thing is that you have finally passed or succeeded and failure records are remembered no more-YOU CAN MAKE IT!

By way of reflection, I want to credit my father with the following:

- *Minutes writing at home*
- *Reading of time from the clock using 5 times on the multiplication table*
- *Proper handwriting*
- *Motivation on attainment of specific milestones*
- *Pointing to long-range objectives instead of focusing on short-term goals*
- *Notes taking-Taking of copious notes from books sent to him by Oral Roberts (Tulsa, Oklahoma) and other ministries.*
- *Self-study- My father studied Electrical engineering at the Associate or Diploma level through correspondence from Bennet College in the United Kingdom.*

APOSTLE DR. EMMANUEL OWUSU BEDIAKO (1954-2013)

The next mentor I want to talk about is the late Apostle Emmanuel Owusu Bediakoh, whom I met in Mampong Ashanti in Ghana in the early 1980s. When I was growing up, a lot of the officers of the church occupied places of influence in the town but as a young adult the members of the church who were influential in the marketplace included the likes of Messrs. -Freeman M. Kagyah (a Principal Inspector of Taxes of the Internal Revenue Service), E.O. Bediako (a Manager of the Ghana Commercial Bank Limited), and many more. As a young adult, I looked up to these people as mentors but with time my association with the Bediakoh family was taken to a higher level and lapsing for a very long time. The profile of the late Apostle Bediakoh is presented below:

Apostle Dr. Emmanuel Owusu Bediako was born to Mr. James Kwame Owusu, a Kumasi-based Road and Building Contractor and Madam Dora Abena Dapaah on March 6, 1954 in Kumasi-Ghana. He pursued professional education in banking at the Institute of Banking in London and was awarded the ACIB and became a Chartered Banker. He pursued an Advanced Banking degree with the American Institute of Banking, New York from 1988 to 1990. He graduated with a PhD degree in Biblical Studies from Christian Bible College, North Carolina, USA. The title of his dissertation was: African Pentecostal Churches in Diaspora. He authored- Book of Books: A history of the Bible in 2008. He worked with the Ghana Commercial Bank and later joined Dick Scott Inc., New York, as the Financial Controller from 1990 to 1992. He responded to a call into full-time as a minister of the Church of Pentecost U.S.A., Inc. in January 1992.

Later, he served as missionary in Germany and Canada, after having served as District pastor from 1993 and Area head in 1998. He had helped many of the Churches in Japan, South Korea, and Switzerland. He was a conference speaker. For example, he responded to an invitation to present a paper on: Africa Doing Missions in Diaspora at the Conference organized by the Movement for African National Initiatives (MANI) in Abuja-Nigeria. He was elected as a member of the International Executive Council of the Church of Pentecost in April 2013. Apostle Bediako was a member of the National Clergy Association, USA; and Associate member of the Chartered Bankers Association, London. Apostle Emmanuel Owusu Bediako died on Thanksgiving Day, Thursday, November 28, 2013 at the MD Anderson University Hospital in Houston, Texas, USA. He left behind a wife-Faustina and children- Christie, Portia, Esther, and Eunice (Extracted from Funeral Brochure. December 2013).

Upon reflection, I can say many things about the late Apostle Bediakoh (popularly called *Apostle B*) but I want to mention a few, as follows:

- *Apostle esteem others more than himself. He called me "my learned brother" In actuality he was a people's person.*

- *When I told him of my appointment as the District accountant with the Internal Revenue Service in Cape Coast (Ghana) he congratulated me and held that was 'big post'*

- *Held himself accountable by communicating to all stakeholders about impending trips and also reporting back on the outcome of these trips. I remember his trip to Nigeria to present a paper on his doctoral dissertation, apostolic visitation to Trinidad and Tobago, and visits to Japan for pastoral and apostolic oversight.*

- *Known to be very generous. Supported retirees and widows in the church, including my mother.*

- *Visited me on campus at the University of Ghana on his return from the USA.*

- *Built a Sanctuary in his hometown of Kyebi (Chebi) in the Ashanti region for the Church of Pentecost. I joined him and some officers, his wife to inspect progress of work on one occasion.*

- *Very zealous for the work of God and prepared to sacrifice his banking profession for the call into the kingdom business.*

- *I spend four hours together with him in Ghana one-on-one in 2011 but little did I know he was going to pass on.*
- *The following people visited him in the Teaching Hospital in Canada on his sick bed–Elders–Dr. Albert Osei, Richard Osei, myself, and Deaconess Belinda Boateng.*
- *In recognition of his impact on my life, I have named one of my sons after him.*

In the next Chapter, I am going to concentrate on providing some guidance for the younger generation on one topical area- *The Choice of a Career.* My understanding is that a lot of people struggle in this area and it is my hope that the foregoing pages will be helpful to many who seek direction in this area.

CHAPTER 16

CAREER CHOICES

ECONOMIC THEORY TEACHES THAT CHOICE is as a result of scarcity of resources relative to the demand for them. Life is about the choices we make. While good choice can lead to positive outcomes; bad choices can also lead to negative outcomes. Nevertheless, to the extent that bad outcomes can serve as useful lessons and teaching moments, such outcomes can be good; yet expensive in terms of time and cost. In all aspects of human endeavor, a decision is required and the rational decision-making process contemplates a choice of an alternative course of action. A typical decision-making process is involved with the diagnosis of the problem, developing alternative courses of actions, analyzing alternative course of action, with a view to choosing an alternative course of action.

In my view, this is the most critical part of the process and must be taken seriously. Then, comes the implementation of the alternative course of action. The life journey from birth to death is involved with making choices in one way or the other, while some choices are minor, other choices tend to be major and can be game-changing. Implying that such choices should not be taken lightly. Doing nothing is also a choice and also subjecting issues to chance is also an option.

OVERVIEW OF CAREER CHOICES

Mankind does not have control over or does not have the right to choose parents, color of skin, the biological gender, and nationality at birth. In some cases, some have attempted to modify some of these characteristics at birth. This is the power of choice in life-*for better or for worse.*

Some of the major life choices revolve around: the choice of a marriage partner, the choice of a career, the choice of faith-based organization to provide the spiritual oversight and nourishment, In this section of the book, I will focus on the choice of a career to help the youth to make this transitional decision as early as possible. For those, who have made mistakes, I want to state that mistakes are part of life and corrective action can be taken to get back on track.

Interests and/or passion-Career choices can be driven by identified childhood passion or interests such as things that get done with ease. Some children are able to declare their career interests ahead of time in life. The identification of the career interests helps parents, family, and friends to frame the individual child's life along that path for success. I remember one of the children who died in the tragic Sandy Hook Elementary School shooting incident in 2012 in Newtown, Connecticut in the United States had identified firefighting as his future career and so the Fire Departments across the United States accorded him the honor that is the preserve for officers who die in the line of duty. This was reported on December 14, 2012 as follows: "*Daniel Barden, 7...killed 12-14-12 in the Sandy Hook school massacre. He wanted to be a firefighter when he grew up. and firefighters from NYC and all around came and stood guard at his funeral*" (Retrieved from https://www.nbcconnecticut.com; https:// www.pinterest.com -accessed on 06/06/2020). Wow, that was huge! May the souls of those 26 people, including 20 children who lost their lives rest in perfect peace, Amen.

Childhood preferences- The American system is helpful in chronicling the interest of children and exposing them to identify interest on time. In some African societies, the career choices of children are dictated by the interest parents have for their children. While not discounting the influence of parents towards life choices, most of the proposed choices are borne out of genuine desire of parents to see children succeed. Nevertheless, I argue that these proposals from parents, family, and friends should be part of the development and analysis of the alternative courses of action in the rational decision-making model; but the final decision should be left to the children to make for ownership purposes.

I remember one of my classmate's parents wanted him to be a lawyer and so when he did not make the required grade in one school, he was sent to my school to repeat a class with a view to helping him to make the requirement. At the university level, this classmate of mine pursued law and successfully qualified and practiced as a good lawyer but he met his untimely death in the line of duty. I am not blaming the parents for his death but it is also possible that if He had been allowed to choose a career, perhaps, he may be living today. Yes, it is possible that a child may come to accept the proposal from the parents, family, and friends; and as a result, I consider this acceptance as ownership and such decisions become that of the child.

Purpose in life- Some people are born to fulfill a divine and specific purpose in life. In this vein, parents tend to know and share this overarching purpose with these children right from birth. At times, the individual received an inner conviction of his or her purpose in life and this conviction drives life choices, including the choice of career paths. It is not uncommon to distinguish between born medical doctors from those who were just brainy and so could pursue any course of study and for some reason ended up as doctors. The same can be said about the ministers of the Gospel.

While the call of God in some are manifest, it is also possible that some may have responded to the call into ministry due to other circumstances. All calls can be categorized into- God-appointed or, man-appointed or, self-appointed. I have explained elsewhere in this book that I view my entry into the accounting profession as a *call* and for that matter purpose-driven and that explains why I have spent considerable time in impacting young accountants all over the globe. Likewise, that explains the reason why I focused an aspect of my doctoral dissertation on accounting education enhancements to influence accounting education in the world.

STEPS TO CONSIDER IN CAREER CHOICES

I propose the following *10 steps* in the choice of career for consideration by anyone who needs some basic information in this area. **Step 1**-*Purpose and passion*, I have identified only three possible ways supra of identifying a career of interest, namely-(i) purpose in life, (ii) childhood preferences, and (iii) interest and passion. I have mentioned the overall concern of parents in this regard. I beg to add that some parents have come to understand that some jobs are not readily available to minorities; however, opportunities abound in the information technology (IT), accounting, and other technical areas; as well as, the health sector, including nursing (RNs and BS Nursing), CNAs, LPNs, pharmacy, medicine, radiography, anesthetics, and so on.

The reasons for the opportunities in the health sector stems from the higher life expectancy in the developed world, coupled with the baby boom concept in the United States of America. In the other fields, there is stiff competition from indigenes, who tend to dominate specific fields such as the management and marketing sectors. Similarly, a few sectors tend to pay more than other sectors. All these considerations count.

Step 2-*Sustained interests*, I would suggest that High School graduates entering colleges or universities should enter with a clear sense of purpose regarding the desired course of study in mind. I counsel against entering with -undecided for your course of study. This can be a waste everybody's time and bear in mind that education is expensive. Some educational institutions have been designed as business enterprises, practicing business concepts such as price discrimination. To the extent that the same undergraduate certificate can cost different amounts to different students in the same classroom. Consider differences in room and board, meal plans, and many more.

Step 3-*Career objectives*, the process of developing a career objective begins with reading about the general area of interest, including buying and reading books in the area of interest. Another approach is also to research into the career field, with a view to acquainting oneself with the entry requirements, available routes such as academic and professional avenues, age and residence requirements, and restriction, if any. Likewise, read about people already in the field and their achievements.

Step 4-*Available routes and opportunities*, I want to touch on interest versus abilities. There are times when people have interest in specific careers; yet, they do not have the corresponding abilities to pursue that dream. This distinction should be drawn as early as possible. The common example is the intention by many science students to pursue medicine but the truth is that medicine is cut for very brilliant or 'A' students; suggesting that only a few average students do typically succeed in their pursuit of this dream. Most of my classmates (67%) at the sixth-form level in Saint Peter's Secondary School were science students; however, those who ultimately emerged as medical doctors were about 17 percent.

I contend that these people were good students. The lesson I present to young people is that interest should be aligned with individual abilities and capabilities. I have asserted that per the book of Job in the Bible, there is hope for even the tree and so any course can be good in the United States of America, but if the career does not have strong earnings potential, another option is to pursue the course to the terminal degree level. Career is not always about money but other considerations can equally be rewarding.

Step 5-*Preparation*, there are many ways of preparation such as the following: career fairs, job fairs, college tours and fairs, recreational and cultural activities, workshops, seminars, and conferences, field trips, and many more. This list is not exhaustive but a minimum avenue to be explored. **Step 6**-*Competencies and skills*, The opportunities for the identification of the needed skills and competencies for specific career path should be explored by young people. I suggest that the United States Labor Bureau website is visited with a view to exploring the different occupational categories, earnings potentials, and outlook for each occupational category. The role of mentors cannot be underplayed in the choice of careers but I want to caution against the typical advice given by college counselor to the effect that- follow your passion. Yes, passion can be followed.

I argue that passion needs to be directed. This is a head and tail issue or two sides to a coin. Moreover, skills and competencies can be developed by visiting career sites such as the following: careerbuilders. com; usajobs.gov; upward.net; HigherEdjobs; job leads, USA staffing; Next, hire accounting; neuvos.com; cybercoders; Zip Recruiter; Lensa; career marketplace; LinkedIn; Findjobmarkets, etc. Likewise, the practice of internships and volunteering is another way of developing competencies and skills. Some States offices such as Illinois WorkNet help job seekers with the needed resources.

Step 7-*Availability of courses*, It is obvious that there are plenty of career opportunities in the United States of American than in some countries such as Ghana. I propose the following areas for consideration no matter the choice of career path: entrepreneurship, venture capital, business plan preparation. There are occasions where the required skills and competencies for specific careers are not available locally; and for that reason, an alternative will be studying abroad to make up the missing skills or competencies. In some cases, the specific course may be available in other countries and should not be out of place to take advantage of the externally-deployed courses.

Step 8-*Costs-Benefits Analysis*, I contend that career choices revolve around passion and economics. Whatever has a benefit tend to have an associated cost. Most often, it is the benefits that get projected but precious time should be invested to explore the cost as well in order to make an informed decision.

Step 9-*Evaluation*, I suggest that the evaluation stage should be involved with the search for the type and strength of accreditation of institutions that prepare people for the career of interest. Beyond accreditation, the faculty, and alumni of the institutions of learning are also worth reviewing in the process. Implicit in this argument is the suggestion that school catalogues and hand books; as well, as review or information on institutions' website are critically important.

Step 10-*Reflection*, Peer pressure should not be the only driving force in the choice of career. Yes, collaboration can be sought in this endeavor but peer pressure should not be the driving force for career choices. I recommend other *languages* such as Spanish, French, and Hausa for consideration. Language can be one the best ways of going global in a career. Another area worth mentioning is in the area of *STEM* (Science, Technology, Engineering, and Mathematics). I suggest that the subject -*Mathematics* is taken seriously. The subject (Mathematics) cuts across many disciplines and most courses turn mathematical at higher levels of education. Arguably, only a few college courses is devoid of mathematics in one manner or form. I know the methods or approaches for teaching mathematics can be challenging in some jurisdictions, but that should not deter people from embracing the subject. I argue that the battle begins from the mind.

I want to repeat that temporary setbacks such as repetition in the process is not the end of one's life because all my classmates who were repeated for academic performance were able to rise to the occasion to ultimate achieve their purpose in life.

By way of illustration, **One,** I have seen one person who was academically suspended but was able to re-strategize to respond to his inner passion. He has now gone past the undergraduate level to complete the Graduate School. **Two,** I have seen some people who have remained concentrated and steadfast to achieve what they set themselves ahead to do and they have achieved just that. **Three,** I heard of someone who came from Ghana to the USA wanting to pursue architecture but his host asked him: "Look at the buildings, bridges, and roads of America. What at all can you add?"

To those wanting to pursue accounting, they are asked: "Who will give you his or her money to manage? Recently, one of my students migrated to the USA with his family. This gentleman had finished his bachelors and accounting certification in Ghana before coming to the USA. He has been advised to venture into nursing and at the time he spoke with me, he had finished the CNA and pursuing his LPN. Prior to this experience, one of my students seeking a career in Taxation in the USA had been advised to go into nursing.

This advice is common because I was advised once upon the time to go through the same route but I had to respond to my known purpose. I find a lot people who have been advised to go into nursing without any prior knowledge in science have ended up unenthusiastic because they do not want to be seen as going against the advice of respected family, including parents. They have developed indifference in the process because there is no passion, interest, and purpose driving their career path in the proposed career. **Lastly,** I conclude that when it is all said and done, the individual is expected to fulfill his or her own destiny and purpose in life. In this book, I seek to share what I have learned and experience with all.

WHO SHOULD BELL THE CAT?

The term *selflessness* connotes having concern, love, giving, and more concentrated on others more than one's own. If this definition is anything to go by; then, my Brother Willie had been selfless in the family over the years and his sacrifices for my siblings and family is hereby acknowledged. Actually, he considers himself as *hustler*-travelling initially from Nigeria and later to Gambia by air. From Gambia travelling by road to Libya through the Senegal and Algeria. He once recounted his experiences on the Sahara desert to my father who recorded on a cassette, especially, the encounter of a man who wore *a white robe* on a hill and gave direction regarding the route on the desert and passing along the edge of a valley or a deep cliff. While in Libya, he had the opportunity to travel by boat to Italy.

My brother later traveled and settled in France for a long time before finally ending up in Belgium. I can categorically state without equivocation that he had paid is due to the family. He financed the travelling cost of our elder brother to Germany before he later settled in France. He provided me with all my clothing needs through my undergraduate studies and specifically ordered books for my economics and business finance class; as well as, providing me with a sophisticated calculator and a tape recorder. Specifically, he gifted my father with a saloon car (Opel Record), my mother a taxi cab, a sister a car that was sold on her behalf. My father documents this as follows:

(I) *September 2, 1984-Received the LINER BILL OF LADING from William Appenteng Appiah, who is at present at PARIS, FRANCE about his Opel Rekord sent to Ghana in my name.*

Chasis: 1751.050.499;43.058,PL.FR.993 EXX 75; dossier 731. TEMA.1or.BL per ship's mail said to contain 1 spare wheelcric and repair-keys. Gross weight 850,K.Place and date of issue 26-7-84 Antwerpen. Registration No.023168(84wv).

January 23,1985–William Appiah Appenteng Remitted us an amount of fifteen thousand ¢15,000.00 on the Christmas tide.

January 31, 1985–Received one hundred thousand (¢100,000.00) through …from one…of Kyeremfaso to day to take delivery of the Opel Rekord exported by William Apenteng Appiah, who is at present in PARIS, FRANCE.

Earlier on, he had offered to give me a Peugeot 504 salon car but I asked him to sell to complete his building project because I was not in a position to maintain a vehicle as a student. At his own cost, he enhanced my mother's house at his own expense before our mother passed and so during the funeral of our late mother, we offered him help to defray some of the cost he had incurred. In 2004, he shipped to me a car (Suzuki Swift) for my private use, for which I remain eternally grateful.

On my part, I started earlier in life to support some of my nieces and nephews to the extent possible for them to find their feet in life. It was challenging financially at the time to combine such laudable responsibilities with the normal family responsibilities but I thank God that we were able to do these little things to help the family. As regards to the nuclear family, I had to forgo the potential and prospects I had in Ghana. I had been ACCA Course head and the first Head of Accounting Department of the Ghana Institute of Professional Studies with the inception of the degree program. There was room for progression within and without the institution; especially, when one comes to think of the emerging universities in Ghana at the time. I had to leave practice for academia in January 2004 to combine both scholarship and professionalism. The Ghana Institute of Professionalism Studies was the best for me because my career objective coincided with the organizational direction. Later on, I migrated with my family to the United States of America, but I wanted to continue with my career path in Ghana after my initial two-year leave of absence in Ghana, I returned to continue my work.

The need for me to move back permanently to the United States became apparent due to some circumstances beyond my control. In addition, there was the urgent need to sacrifice my future prospects in Ghana in the meantime in order to support the family, especially, providing support for the children to enable them go through their education successfully. I did not grow up in the United States of America so I did not have specialized funds such as Sections 401K, 403B, 529 education funds or ESA, and other investment vehicles. I needed to build my credit from the scratch and the initial applications were rejected on the grounds that I did not have adequate credit history. As a result, I approached a bank and deposited $300 for a credit card.

The education of the children at the Elementary and High Schools was not very difficult but the undergraduate education was very challenging financially if I consider cost of attendance vis-à-vis the available grants and loans to students. Parental components have been met through parent plus loans and out of pocket payments. This is against the backdrop of financing my professional education and certification through *out-of-pocket*, with the support of my wife. However, with regards to my doctoral education, it was financed mainly through students' loans (both subsidized and unsubsidized).

I accepted my current job as a temporary independent contractor and later on as a permanent employee just to put food on the table and to also get health insurance benefit for the family. This job permitted me to carry on with my academic work and after graduation, pursue other interests. For that reason, I decided to remain on the job because the objectives of the organization (giving a second and best chance to at-risk students) resonates with me; while exploring adjunct faculty positions to supplement my income. I know at some point I will move on with my life.

I am convinced that the sacrifices of forgoing my prospects in Ghana to provide the needed support both directly or indirectly will allow for my children to pursue their God-given passion and career and to meet the minimum threshold of a Master's degree and a professional certification standard I have set for all who come into contact with me. While I guide my children in their career choices, I leave the ultimate decision to them to make and own. I appreciate the wise counsel given to me by the late Reverend Maxwell Kofi Kusi, who admonished me to refocus my energies on my children over my career in Ghana in order not to regret in the future. This suggestion was corroborated by my late mother and Mrs. Matilda Mensah (former Nursing Supervisor of the Church of Pentecost). I have learned that throughout generations, it takes the selflessness of one person to change the trajectory of a family and I believe the trajectory of my family will be changed with my sacrifices in the long-run.

CHAPTER 17

FAVOR OF GOD IS KEY

SOME PRIVILEGES IN LIFE ARE difficult to explain and the best way to respond to them is what I am referring to as the *favor of God*. In Chapter 12, *grace* was defined to mean-*the unmerited favor of God*. The question that arises for determination is: *what is the meaning of favor?* Typically, *favor* connotes a preference or approval that facilitates likeness for a particular person. Consequently, commendation for a particular person implies a possible rejection of others. Approving a person is accomplished by overlooking others. Likewise, approbation or holding one in higher esteem can suggest the show of disapproval for others. Life revolves around choices, which is why we discussed career choices in chapter 16 of this textbook. I mentioned divine *selection* and *provision* in chapter 12 to emphasize the favor of God upon my life.

We should encourage dialogue on the use of multiple methodologies in the biographical narrative field as well as a more comprehensive overview of the similarities and differences between them (Eichsteller, 2019). In this chapter, I will mention divine *appointments* and *callings* as components of God's acts of favor towards me. For that reason, all opportunities I have accepted to explore is considered as a favor that has been bestowed upon me by my creator. Afterall, there are always other people who are better placed to occupy those offices and positions. Consequently, *divine appointments* should shape our perception regarding: (i) the willingness to seek education, (ii) technological advancement in the marketplace, (iii) attitudinal modifications, (iv) the evolving dynamics of population and structure, (v) competitiveness in the global space, and (vi) having a bigger picture of issues. As a result, *divine callings* can be linked to the Pareto's (20:80) rule, because less time and energies (20%) should be committed to less urgent and least important issues; thereby, allowing for considerable time and energy (80%) to be focused on very profitable and rewarding assignments.

I argue that my life composition and for that matter the composition of a person is shaped to a larger extent by the favor that is made available to the person in life. Suggesting that man is molded by situations and circumstances to fit into a particular space or position at the right time.

DESTINY CHANGING GOD

My father's wish was for me to be in full-time ministry. I do not know the motivation but I can speculate that it was to make up for his own inability to enter full-time ministry when he was growing old. On the contrary, my interest was to enter the foreign service. While the reasons may be difficult to explain fully, I can authoritatively state that a sermon preached by a deacon, who was a police officer in the Mampong-Ashanti church might have influenced this resolve. The message was based on the caption: *"You are an ambassador of Christ"* (II Corinthians 5:20).

The Police inspector and deacon of the church at the time, expounded on the Word of God by comparing the Christian and the ambassador in *real-world* and illuminated insight into the privileges of ambassadors. As a boy in elementary school, I desired to be an ambassador when I grow up and so used the qualities provided in the message to organize my life. As I have explained, I obtained an admission to Switzerland to read Post-Graduate studies in international relations. At first sight, I thought the admission letter was an answer to my purpose; but that never materialized because of lack of sponsorship. Therefore, the lack of sponsorship became a nightmare for me.

THE ACCOUNTING PROFESSION

The paradox was that while I desired to be an ambassador, my father would have wished that I entered the full-time ministry. As if this dilemma was not enough, God called me into accountancy through a word of knowledge that was delivered to me by a close relative and friend; and that was a corroboration to the case made to me by Emelia Hanson (my senior at the UGBS). I have recounted aspects of this story in other parts of the book. Consequently, I view accountancy as a calling on my life to bring about value-addition to humanity. Initially, I resisted this direction because I evaluated myself to be more of qualitative than quantitatively-endowed person. This personal assessment was consistent with my interests in subjects or courses in secondary and sixth-form schools.

I once applied to Ghana Institute of Professional Studies (IPS) for Institute of Chartered Accountants, Ghana (ICAG) program in 1995 because it was becoming increasingly difficult to combine work, family life, and studies but I did not get study leave for the purpose. I applied for study leave with pay to pursue professional accountancy at the Ghana Institute of Professional Studies (where I would later become a lecturer). I followed up on my application at the Ghana Internal Revenue Service Headquarters. I met Mrs. Bigah in the Administration Department, who read to me the minute on my application letter from the Office of the Commissioner. The Commissioner was the late Professor J. E. A. Mills, who later became the President of Ghana. The ruling indicated that I should serve for seven years to qualify for study leave.

I contemplated resigning to go back to school but for the timely intervention of Mrs. Bigah, who counseled me against the decision and suggested to me to continue to work while preparing and writing the professional examinations privately in order not to bring untold hardships to the family in the short-to-medium term. Unknown to

Mrs. Bigah, my wife was pregnant with our second son. At the time, the Ghana Internal Revenue Service was grappling with a high number of staff wanting to pursue further studies. To give a context to this development, the Central Revenue Department (CRD) in Ghana was re-organized into the Internal Revenue Service (IRS) in 1986, the Service employed many university graduates and other professional class. At a point, the Internal Revenue Service was used to recruit professionals such as accountants for other Civil and Public Services in Ghana. This category of professionals was referred to as "Non-IRS staff"

In 1999, I got admission into the Graduate School of the University of Ghana to read my Master of Business Administration (MBA) with a concentration in accounting. *Divine Intervention*-I want to recount one story during my MBA program at the University of Ghana, where I became aware of some people were moving behind me to get me dropped out of school. I had applied for *study leave with pay* but did not receive any response before the university re-opened for registration of freshmen. I went to register pending the outcome of my application of study leave with pay.

I applied for part of my accumulated leave to enable me attend lectures while waiting for an official response to my application for study leave. Later, I gathered that a letter had been sent to the Registry of the university to enquire about my status; but through the assistance of a colleague, I was able to continue with my program under *leave without pay*. Interestingly, while I had admission for the graduate program, I was given *study leave without pay* but another colleague who was granted *study leave with pay* did not have admission in the first place. The study leave was granted in anticipation of admission. The old adage-*Some want they do not get; and some get but they do not want* was true in this case. Ironically, I had served the required seven years with the Internal Revenue Service, so I applied for study leave *with* pay but

I was compelled to take a *study leave without pay* to maximize the rare opportunity. Nevertheless, I view education as an investment in myself.

THE LAW PROFESSION

When I was growing up and during my secondary school days, I used to spend some days in the Courtrooms of the District Magistrate Court and the Circuit Courts in Mampong-Ashanti for my own curiosity. I enjoyed the Court proceedings relating to the calling out of cases, interpretation services for parties, taking of plea deals, out of court settlements, judgments deliveries and sentencing. I listened to prosecutors laying facts patterns of cases before the courts and intervention of attorneys or lawyers.

I will narrate a few aspects of the cases I listened to in the lower courts. *One,* there was an oldman (name withheld), a money lender in town who was regular litigant and known by Court officials and lawyers operating in the area. Most of the cases he presented to court centered on people who defaulted on money lending agreements and could not redeem their indebtedness.

In this particular case, he was complainant in a case involving another man (name withheld), alleging that the man has uprooted some oil palm trees for palm wine tapping. He asserted that the land was not his, but the oil palm trees were his but could not convince the court how the oil palm trees became his property.

In the process, a lawyer who opted to a friend of the Court argued that even if the oil palm trees were hanging in the skies, the owner of the land beneath is deemed to be the owner of the oil palm trees. The friend of court wondered why this oldman continues to bring frivolous cases to court in spite of his familiarity with the court system. *Two,* a case involving a man who did not restrain his flock of sheep in a village and in the process caused destruction to food crops of some villagers.

His lawyer relied on a section of the law, which was read in court with the permission of the trial judge. The provisions of the law he read provided a detailed list of towns in Ghana that stray animals should not be allowed and the lawyer contended that the village in question was not on the list mentioned and so his client was not guilty of any offense.

Three, another experience I had at the High Court in Kumasi was when a prominent lawyer gave his *address* before the court in a chieftaincy case revolving around the 'Oath' The lawyer quoted copiously from authorities such as Professors- K. A. Busia and Idohu regarding the sanctity of oath in chieftaincy. I must admit that I was very impressed with the display of legal knowledge encompassing the quotes from the law, case law, and anthropological scholarly sources. I compare this address to the Court to the case made by Moses before God in Numbers 13 and 14 in the Bible.

While in Cape Coast in Ghana and working for the Internal Revenue Service, I nurtured the desire to study law so during one of my visits to Accra, I went to the Ghana Law School to inquire about how to get to the Law School. I was advised to register and sit for the Entrance Examinations before going for interview to enter the only Law School in Ghana located near the Supreme Court building in Accra.

It was after this initial preparation that my wife queried my motive for wanting to pursue law as a profession and felt that it might just be in response to my family litigation. Perhaps, my perceptions have been deepened because of my involvement in the protracted litigation discussed in this book. Additionally, she averred that pursuing law in addition to my human temperament would make it difficult for her to cope; and thus, encouraged me to concentrate on accounting. Nevertheless, I have come to accept that accountancy is my calling and endeavored to be focused. Consequently, I know anything I pursue will not come on silver platter but if I stay focused success will crown my efforts. This has paid off in the long-run and that explains why I have all my qualifications in accountancy and related areas.

TOPICS OF INTEREST

This section of the textbook is devoted to some personal topics of interest and I hope that readers will find them useful; for application to daily lives through the life lessons presented.

MASTER OF CEREMONIES (MCs)

I know that God has granted me eloquence and oratorical prowess but I have not taken to Master of Ceremonies (MCs) as a vocation. However, I have handled a couple of opportunities offered by the church and other entities. I have been privileged to be the Master of Ceremony for some important church-related programs both in Ghana and United States of America. I can recollect a few as follows:

1. Send-off Service in honor of the call of one of our elder into full-time ministry at The Church of Pentecost-Madina Central.
2. The Church of Pentecost U.S.A.,Inc.-Chicago Regional Easter Conventions.
3. The Church of Pentecost U.S.A., Inc.-At funerals of a few members.
4. Welcome Service for one of our pastors and family to the Romeoville district of the Church of Pentecost U.S.A., Inc. on July 21, 2019.
5. Book Launch of Apostle Sampson Ofori Yiadom on *the Meaning of Life* at McKeown Worship Center-Romeoville, Illinois on February 22, 2020.

6.   The Church of Pentecost U.S.A. Inc.-*Chicago Regional Virtual Recognition and Graduation Ceremony* (under the auspices of the Youth and PENSA Ministry) held on Sunday June 7, 2020 at 6:00pm (amidst COVID-19) for graduates of the Middle School, High School, Undergraduate, and Graduate School categories.

7.   25th Anniversary Dinner Dance and Awards Night of the Chartered Institute of Taxation, Ghana at the Golden Tulip Hotel in Accra-Ghana on Friday, September 16, 2005 at 7:00pm, under the Presidency of Mr. E. E. Kwesie. My Co-MC was Ms. Aisha Tiwaa Gyasi (FCITG).

PRESENTATION OF A PASTOR TO SACRAMENTO

I remember my first visit to the State of California was at the instance of the Pentecost International Worship Center (PIWC)-Chicago. I was given the responsibility to accompany and to introduce our Pastor and family on behalf of the Church. The Man of God had been the Youth Pastor with Pastoral responsibility for the youth of the Chicago region of the church. After a short period of time, he was transferred to the Sacramento district of the Church of Pentecost U.S.A.,Inc. While at the Sacramento Airport, I was picked up by one brother, who together with the wife acted as my host family during my period of stay in Sacramento. I met the then presiding elder and other leaders of the church. I do not take this opportunity for granted.

The Welcome Service was officiated by Pastor Samuel Amponsah (now Apostle of Jesus Christ) of Oakland. The National head of Guinea-Bissau at the time was also in attendance; as well as the wife of one of the Executive Council members. After the ceremony, I met the Out-going minister, the wife, and mother. Later on, I was told by one of the members of National Audit committee that the married couple, who hosted me at Sacramento had relocated to San Diego district of the church. I appreciate their hospitality very much and I trust that they will continue to grow in the Lord. Likewise, one of the Praise Team members who made a lasting impression on my mind was a brother of Sierra Leone origin, who tried to sing a *Twi* song on the greatness of God, as follows: *Onyame Krokrokro, Onyame Krakrakra, Onyame krokro, Onyame krakrakra.* While the lyric of the song was great the words were mixed up. I applaud the brother for the effort at the ministration at the rehearsal.

BENEVOLENCE OF PEOPLE

I have enjoyed the benevolence of several people. I appreciate the late Professor S.Y. Sarfo, former Pro-Vice Chancellor of the Kwame Nkrumah University of Science and Technology (KNUST, Kumasi) and family for bearing the transportation and feeding of guests cost components of my wedding in January 1993. I am eternally grateful to Professor Sarfo and Mama Jane. May the soul of Professor Sarfo rest in perfect peace and may his memory by an inspiration.

VOLUNTEER AUDITOR

I have been provided the opportunity of serving on the National Audit Committee of the Church of Pentecost U.S.A, Inc. I know I will not do this work forever but I thank God that I could be used in this ministry. In the first term, spanning 2015 to 2019, I served with the following: Elders-Oti Akenten (Chairman), Amos Martey, Christian Bimpong, Noah Gyimah, Deacon Albert Abaaho, and Deaconess Vida Amiah. In the second term from 2020 to 2024, I am serving with the following members-Elders- Joseph Oppong (Chairman), Dr. Eric Osei Kwarteng, Amos Martey, Daniel Ohemeng, Robert Ocran, and Deacon

Harry Obeng-Boafo. I thank God for the lives of Elders- Oti Akenteng and Fred Asare Addo for providing the internal auditing needs of the church in the United States of America during the formative stages. At the regional level, I was appointed to the Regional Audit Committee to join Elders- Joseph Oppong and Fred Addo, when Elder Mark Amponsah relocated to Ghana. I assumed the Chairmanship of the Regional Audit Committee in 2019, when Elder Joseph Oppong was elected the Regional Deacon for the Chicago Region. I must say that these people are fantastic and professional, thorough, and incredibly knowledgeable.

DENIED TO BE APPROVED

The ability to identify the will of God early in life is the most important thing to know so you can stay according to his divine purpose. For me, the purpose of God concerning my life has evolved over time. During the time of my journey through education also saw military regimes that ruled in the affairs of Ghana. The political terrain was dominated by military rule. As a result, the period was marked by uncertainties and hardships to the extent that a lot of people sought *greener pastures* in other parts of the world. A lot of Ghanaians traveled to Nigeria and other African countries; as well as, other European and the Americas. To this end, traveling to seek greener pastures was the order of the day. It was not uncommon for graduates from the universities to leave the country for any available destination. In my case, I had two brothers and some family and friends outside of Ghana and most of them were willing to assist me travel for the same purpose.

In furtherance of this objective, I got denied on four occasions for visa applications: *In the first place*, when I applied to the British High Commission in Accra for visitor's visa as part of a student group for the

Summer of 1988, my application was denied together with 29 others out of 40 participants. My subsequent appeal to the Home Office in United Kingdom got lost in the process. *In the second place*, on completing my undergraduate education, I wanted to further my education into international relations; and as you have learned that I wanted be an ambassador and to work in the Foreign Service of Ghana.

I was denied visa because I could not find the much-needed financial support to cover my Post-Graduate education in international relations in Switzerland in the 1990s. As I was going about my working life in Ghana and working for the Ghana Internal Revenue Service, one of my good friends sent me an official invite to come visit the United States of America, the Consul Officer determined that my salary at the time was not sufficient to encourage me to return to Ghana on the expiration of my visa; and for that reason, I was denied the Non-immigrant visa.

In the third place, in 2001 after my graduate school, one of my brothers-in-law and the wife officially invited me to Canada to help me re-organize myself after a hard time of studying and recovering from the loss of my better half in 2000. I got denied. *In the last place*, I got approved in 2007. Between 2001 and 2007, I focused on work, family, church, and professional education and came to the realization that perhaps, God's will for me was to prosper in Africa.

To be frank, when the time came, I was hesitant to travel due to the experiences I have recounted above and the fact that I had resigned myself to fate and for the reason, I was not willing to pursue traveling any longer. I was doing quite well in Ghana. It would interest you to note that I have visited almost all the countries I purposely applied to visit in the past but got turned down. The key here is knowing and understanding the times. As King Solomon in the Book of Ecclesiastes points out, there is time and season for everything under the sun. Consequently, delay should not be misconstrued to be denial in life. I got denied to be approved!

THE RADIO TEACHER

Technology was not characteristics of my life growing-up but there was the semblance of technology-driven learning system in my lower primary school era. On specific days and times in the school week, all pupils in the same class congregated in one place to listen to *"The Radio Teacher"*; who taught us songs and lessons each week. As children during the early 1970s, we looked forward to learning from the *radio teacher*. It was when I reflected with time that I determined that the *radio teacher* back in the days was a class recorded on tape for us. We did not know of the technology back then.

In 1978-79, when I went to the Mount Mary College (an institution that trained French teachers) in Somanya in the Eastern region of Ghana, I was exposed to an analogous concept in their Language Laboratory, where students learned the correct pronunciations of French words and terms from recordings on tapes by repeating the same words and later re-playing to listen to yourself as a learning moment. Technology-driven education has been in existence in the past but it is a question of prominence and advancements in recent times. I remember in 1983, I took pains to record some of my class notes on tape, which I played from time-to-time to reinforce the contents. Instead of reading over and over again, I played some of them on tape from time to time.

LOOKING UNTO JESUS (Hebrews 12:2)

The development of my writing skills started in response to an altar call for writers in 1986-87 at one of the Campus-based Students Ministries called Ghana Fellowship of Evangelical Students (GHAFES), an umbrella body of all Christian organizations on the University campuses in Ghana. My first writing was a *poem* captioned: *"Looking unto Jesus"* which was published in the Official magazine of the Legon

Pentecostal Union (LPU) during the 10th Anniversary celebration. The basis was that there was the need for fixing our eyes on Jesus as both the pioneer (author) and the perfecter (finisher) of Christian faith; because of the following reasons: (i) for the joy set before Him; (ii) enduring the cross; (iii) scorning the shame; and (iv) sitting down at the right-hand side of the throne of God.

Dear reader, God is greater than every problem you are currently going through. Continue to look unto Jesus as the pivot upon which the wheels of solution rotated.

MARRIAGE COMMITTEE

My involvement in the workings of the marriage committee of the Church of Pentecost has provided me with a very rich experience to be passed on to others. I served on this committee with the following: Elder Nsafoah Boakye (Chairman), Deaconess Beatrice Asare (member), and my good self as a member/secretary. All-in-all, the committee received 30 cases from the local presbytery regarding couples wanting to enter marital relationships. While two of the cases never resulted into marriage; another two couple had problems maintaining the union and ended up as separation or divorce. Beyond these four cases, the remaining 26 marriages are working as far as I can tell. I am pleased for this assignment.

Typically, members who plan to get married inform the presiding elder about their marital plans and because of the sensitivity of personal information and privacy issues, the marriage is referred to the marriage committee instead of dealing with the application at the entire local presbytery level. A form is administered to permit the couple to provide basic information that will facilitate the interview and counseling process. Meetings are scheduled by the marriage committee to deliberate on all issues central to the marriage. The number of meeting is not fixed but depends on how the proceedings go.

The entire marriage committee process can lapse three to six monthly meetings. A report is completed, and recommendations are forwarded to the presiding elder. Upon review, the presiding elder makes a recommendation to the minister or pastor for subsequent counseling and finalization of the plan. When the pastoral counseling is completed, the presiding elder can announce the details of the engagement and wedding to the church public and the same is documented on the monthly preachers' plan for the church.

While American law provides for ordinance, Ghana law provides for three types of marriages as follows: (i) marriage by ordinance, implying one man one wife; (ii) customary marriage, which can be polygamous, and (iii) the Islamic marriage, involving a man being allowed to marry up to four women, if he has the ability and the resources so to do. These marriage types do standalone but the church encourages the performance of the customary rites (engagement) to be combined with the blessings (wedding). Consequently, the engagement in the Western world is not synonymous with the customary rites in the African context.

The engagement in the West is involved with the man asking on his kneels with a ring, as to whether the woman will agree to marry him. In the traditional African context, marriage is a contract between two families through their representatives-man and woman. The involvement of the extended family is a critical component of the association. For that reason, we marry into a family and the father loses a daughter to gain a son and vice versa.

FACE to FACE with DEATH

On Sunday November 22, 2020, I stood before the congregation of the McKeown Worship Center (MWC)- Pentecost International Worship Center (PIWC)-Romeoville and also before the saints of MWC -Central church to give thanks to God for sparing my life and giving me a second chance to live. I do not take this opportunity lightly. On Thursday, October 15, 2020, my primary doctor requested me to present myself to the Emergency Room (ER) because of acute blood deficit emanating from bleeding arising out of two hemorrhoids. I got to the ER at 4:15pm and received the first blood transfusion in my life. Around 11:00 pm I was transferred to the Ward for admission. There, I received another pint of blood and I was also prepared for the procedures for the second day, including the following: Endoscopy, Colonoscopy; and ultimately, a surgery to remove the two hemorrhoids in my rectal region.

I was discharged on Saturday evening of October 17, 2020 after my hemoglobin percentage had stabilized and reached the minimum tolerable level. Thereafter, I followed the discharge instructions such as the taking of medication as directed by my medical team. On *Saturday, October 24, 2020,* while attempting to respond to nature's call, there was a period of uneasiness all over my body. So, I decided to reach my bed to relax my body.

On my way out I *fainted,* and the impact of my fall was felt downstairs. Thereby, causing my wife to rush to the scene because she heard an unusual noise emanating from the floor. I could have lost my life in the twinkle of an eye. Just like that. The lesson is that as humans, we do not have control over our very lives. Consequently, every day should be viewed as God's gift to humanity and whatever good thing that can be done, should be accomplished. I am grateful to Doctors-Seth K. Osafo (Primary, Board Certified-Internal Medicine), and specialists-Sameer A. Barkatullah (Gastroenterology), and Stephan G. Wyers (General Surgery); as well as, doctors' office and hospital staff who attended to me. I appreciate their care.

CONCLUSION

I have explained to the younger generation that they should take their personal development seriously and endeavor to convert more of the learning years to their advantage. I have no objection to the combination of work and studies provided there is a corresponding discipline to stay focused; but the more learning that is done in the early part of life is key. Likewise, there are two categories of work approaches, as follows: *first,* **working with your shoulder**-the mode of working is characterized by the use of physical efforts, very strenuous, energy consuming, higher toll on physical body, no or less span of control and influence, and low earnings capacity. S*econd,* **working with your head**-the alternative puts a higher demand on the brain, with less physical strain, existence of span of control, greater influence in the marketplace, and higher earnings. These should be viewed as alternative approaches available in the marketplace. As used by the Times Higher Education in 2020, the key metrics have revolved around: teaching and research, citation, and industry income. The young generation should endeavor to pursue certification and to either: establish their own business as the first option, or allow their monies to work for them through aggressive savings, investments and retirements schemes; as well as, generating decent earnings through work.

CHAPTER 18

FAITH, FOUNDATION, AND FOCUS

IN THIS CHAPTER, I WILL be talking about the *3Fs-faith, foundation,* and *focus.* The focus of my life has been grounded in the foundation I have received over the years because it is rooted in faith. The Bible stipulates that faith comes by hearing and hearing of the Word of God (Romans 10:17). Therefore, the Word of God is both active and sharper than a two-edged sword (Hebrews 4:12); and for that reason, has become the basis of our faith. Nevertheless, the Word of God is both *written* (the Bible is the written Word) and *living* (Jesus Christ is the Living Word). Consequently, a simple obedience to the written word and a relationship with the living word is all faith is about. There is a link between writing of own life story and conscious empowering, arguing that the author becomes more conscious about own personality after having analyzed the past decisions from the perspective of present times (Dadashova, 2018).

I consider the Christian life as a cycle, encompassing the following phases- (a) the Initial Stage, (b) the Growth Stage, (c) the Maturity Stage, (d) the Plateau Stage, and (e) the Declining Stage. The Christian lifecycle will begin from the initial stage and end with the declining stage, which culminates into death. The doctrine of *entropy* dictates that anything that has a beginning also has an end. With this mindset, I am able to *number my days* (Psalm 90:12) because I am a mortal being. As a result, every day is considered as a gift from God because this is the day the Lord has made and so we cannot help but to rejoice and be glad in it (Ephesians 2:8; Psalm 118:24).

INITIAL STAGE

I was born into the Pentecostal heritage because my parents were Christians. I was dedicated on the eighth day by the late Reverend T.A. Addo. I was introduced to the Sunday School in the church early in my life. The Children ministry was not formalized as we have today across the length and breadth of the church worldwide. In 1971, a Christmas Convention of the Church of Pentecost was held at Mampong in the Ashanti region and the children in the church were organized to present Bible recitals to the meeting. I did not play any important role during this time. Later on, Brother Johnson Agyemang Badu (*Teacher* as he was affectionately called) came into the scene to strategically establish a Sunday school whilst in Mampong Ashanti. He later furthered his education at the Saint Andrews Training College in Mampong Ashanti. Teacher was granted permission to come to town to assist with the Sunday school in the church. Teacher Agyemang Badu was endowed and gifted as a teacher for the ministry.

I will share only four stories during this time. The first was that one day we went to Sunday school in the morning and we were served with beverage and because of this we always looked forward to the class. We were not fed at the Sunday school as we have in most churches now. The second story is linked to the relationship Teacher Johnson built with the late Pastor David and Mrs. Margaret Mills. Mrs. Mills was deeply into the Children's ministry and so she collaborated with our local church and Teacher Johnson to prepare us for Children's days celebrations; as well as, camp meetings, which were characterized by singing of songs, acting of plays, and Bible recitals. Mrs. Margaret Mills used to present prizes to *deserving* children who performed creditably.

The third story is in regards to the Sunday School's involvement in the August Convention that was held at Nsuta-Ashanti of Ghana. Here, I offered my Bible Recitals to the admiration of the convention participants. In the process of my recital, I remember the ministers provided a table on the platform for me to stand on so most people could catch a glimpse of me. In those day, Bible recitals by children was not very common and the fact that the recital was in English was very huge. Freewill offerings were given by individuals in response to the Bible recital. Lastly, a children's convention involving all children in the Ashanti region was held at the McKeown Temple (Asokwa, a suburb of Kumasi in Ghana) and it was at this convention that we were presented with the late Pastor J. K. Appiah (former Pastor of Obuasi) as the Regional Leader of the Children Movement in the region. The formalization of the Children's Movement was around this time.

EPICENTER OF PENTECOSTALISM

The Ghanaian township of *Asamankese* in the Eastern region has been referred to as the *Jerusalem* of Ghana by Pastor Joshua Yirenkyi-Smart (retired). This characterization is related to the role this town played towards the growth of Pentecostalism in Ghana. Unlike the *centripetal* arrangement where people of faith converged on Jerusalem as a Center of worship; the outpouring of the Holy Spirit has allowed for Pentecostalism to breed along a *centrifugal* fashion. In the process of time, the Pentecostal *fire* engulfed the Ashanti region of Ghana and Mampong-Ashanti played a critical role in this development. Consequently, the town has been central in the growth of the church. I cannot tell exactly the date on which my father joined the Apostolic Church but I know it will be in latter *1940s* but as for my mother, she joined the church on marrying my father. The available records show that my parents got their marriage registered in 1952.

As I informed you in Chapter 2, several ministers have been stationed in one point or the other in Mampong-Ashanti. The names of ministers of the Gospel I can recollect in order of posting include the following: Pastors- Bimpong, D.Y.A. Owusu, T.A. Addo, Amponsah, Isaac Kwasi Adu Mensah, Samuel Opoku Adipah, F.T. Obuobi, J.E. Ameyaw, and so on. One Joseph Owusu Sarpong (the son of Apostle D.Y.A. Owusu, now deceased), whom I worked with in the Ghana Internal Revenue Service in Cape Coast in the Central region of Ghana told me that they were transferred from Mampong in 1963. Pastor T.A. Addo replaced Pastor D.Y.A. Owusu; and having regard to the fact that I was dedicated in Mampong-Ashanti in the church, I beg to speculate that I was dedicated by Pastor T. A. Addo. Interestingly, Pastor T. A. Addo is the father of Elder Fred Asare Addo of Cincinnati in Ohio. I know that Apostles - Joseph Egyir Painstil, J.C. Quaye, Alphonse Wood, and many more provided apostolic leaderships; but I did not see them because I was either not born or very young.

The Regional Apostles of the Ashanti region I can recollect include the following: Apostle- F.S. Safo, A.T. Nartey, Aninkorah, and S. K. Ansong. I was present at the service in Kumasi that welcomed Apostle F.S. Safo to Kumasi as the Regional Apostle for the Ashanti region from Togo, where he was stationed for a decade as the National head. A prophetic song was released through Deaconess Manko (Mrs. Sarfo). The translation was as follows: *"I have chosen you as a life stone; You will be used for the building of my house; and in the house life abound"*

The Mampong-Ashanti district was upgraded to the status of an Area in the church's administrative structure. I attended a number of conventions (Christmas, Easter, August, Movements/Ministries, Rallies, Crusades) in Ankaasi, Agogo, Kumasi, Amanteng, Kwame Danso, Agona Swedru, Juaben, Banko, Nsuta, Atonsu, Kwamang, Nintin, Nwadan, etc. To mention just a few.

The first Area head was Apostle B.K. Swanzy (the father of Apostle Abraham Sam Swanzy), combining both the role of a district pastor and a regional head. Thereafter, there has been district pastors and area heads. Some of the district ministers are: Pastors- Nana Ofori, Asihene, Debrah, and many more. Other area heads include: Pastors- Tetteh, Joseph Mensah; Prophet Aniakwah; as well as, Apostles- E.K. Apea, A.L. Angoh, Asare, and others. Today, there are 5 ministers (comprising 1 Area head, 1 PIWC/PENSA ITI Secretary, and 3 district pastors). This is huge because if someone had ever mentioned that the church was going to dominate the entire township and beyond, the person would have been tagged "a false prophet"

Today, most of the local assemblies in the then Ashanti region have become districts and several of the districts have become areas in the church's administrative set-up. I dare say that this development did not happen by accident, a lot of work had been done by the pioneering people of God. I will highlight a few in this section of the book. The pioneering role of Prophet Ankomah (the father of Elder James McKeown-*A good one there*) and wife (Awo Krah); both of blessed memory and natives of Atonsu in the Ashanti region should be recognized. It is very instructive to observe that during the time of Pastor D.Y.A. Owusu in Mampong, the power of God was demonstrated in causing a dead woman to come back to life.

I was not born by then but I came to meet Maame Achiaa in her advanced age in the church. Dark in complexion, Maame Achiaa used to come to church in her white cloth when her health and strength permitted. I witnessed her 'second death' I am told the church grew in number after this spectacular event; causing the church to move into a spacious place of worship. However, I grew up to find the church in a rented storefront in the late Opanin Kwarteng's house at Tadiem. Opanin Kwarteng was the father of Honorable S.K. Sarfo (MP-Mampong, deceased) and sisters-Janet, Comfort, Salomey, Sarah, and others.

In the latter part of the 1970s, it took the courage of Pastor Sam Opoku Adipah (father of two ministers-Samuel and Timothy) to motivate the church to go back to continue the sanctuary that Pastor T.A. Addo had left off in the preceding decade. Here, additional financial support was provided by some elders outside of Mampong, who regularly contributed to the fund-raising efforts. They include: Elders-Clottey (Area Manager for the United African Company's (UAC) Northern Sector of Ghana), Gyimah (a former Regional deacon of Ashanti region), J.K. Asante (a former Regional deacon and father of Mrs. Mary Kusi, Apostle S.O. Asante and another minister), Safo-Kantanka (transport owner in Kumasi), and many more.

My mother catered for them during their visits and they dined in my father's living room. The building in question is the one currently being used by the Pentecost International Worship Center (PIWC) in Mampong. I want to add that my father was involved in the design of the building, which was according to the pattern of the Church building located on the Mampong Maternity Hospital, where my father worked.

Pastor Sam Opoku Adipah caused the Mampong Central assembly to be further broken down into units to allow for the neighboring villages to have local assembles. I must state that he faced stiff opposition from the members and officers commuting to Mampong for regular services on Sundays and also during mid-week services. Some insinuated that because they were coming from villages that is why the pastor was cutting them off; however, with time people bought into the vision.

With the passage of time, zonal leaders were put in place to oversee a number of assemblies. I remember my father became a zonal leader over the Appiakrom area and had very young elders such as Elder Sarfo (electrician) under him. The team performed functions such as officiation of the Lord's supper, naming of children, and conduct of funeral services in the absence of the minister. Similarly, the ministry of Pastor Isaac Kwasi Adu Mensah (he used *Joe Boye* in his illustrations) was focused on individual members. He spent quality time with his members in the Mampong market, sitting behind them on rotational basis. Pastor Mensah will leave no stone unturned to get members back on track. I remember at times he used to hold all-night prayer sessions in homes of officers.

On his part, Pastor Fred Tetteh Obuobi (father of Apostle Samuel Gyau Obuobi) brought punctuality and following strict time regimes and this endeared the hearts of the members because members were seen running to be part of the church services because if you come late you would come to meet the church closed after the stipulated time. On the Church of Pentecost, my father's daily journal stated as follows:

On September 25, 1982-Mampong District Presbytery held this day. I was appointed to take charge of Bosofour Assembly as from 3ʳᵈ October,1982

On June 9, 1983, Regional Prayer Week held at Kumasi. Prophet Yeboah and Apostle D. K. Anang, the Church's Secretary attended. Overseer E. Ofori has been ordained as Pastor, my wife prayed for as a Deaconess.

December 14, 1983-Ashanti Regional Apostle, Pastor E. D. Aninkorah visited Mampong Assembly and its District assemblies today.

December 23,1983-Attended Christmas Convention at Agogo Asante Akim on the 23ʳᵈ day of December 1983 and closed at 26ᵗʰ arrived home on the same day.

April 17-23,1984-EASTER-The Good Friday Tide was held at Atonsu, which was headed by Elder G.E. Appiah-Sokye as Chairman and Elder S.K. Amponsah as Vice chairman. The Mampong Ashanti District was divided into three (3) Zones by the District Pastor F.T. Obuobi: Zone 1 was headed by Pastor and Elder Osei and Zone C headed by Elder Odame-Kofiase and the surrounding villages.

April 27,1984- Pastor E.K. Kyei who died on the 24ᵗʰ March 1984 and whose wake-keeping was held on the 27ᵗʰ of April 1984 and burial at Kumasi on the 28ᵗʰ instant. The founder Pastor James McKeown and the Chairman of the Church did attend the funeral

Weddings:

April 29, 1984–Elder Odame weds Sister Helena Ntim on the 29th April 1984.

May 27, 1984–Brother Jones Gyimah Agyekum weds Sister Ernestina Okrah on the 27th May 1984.

Bailed one Brother…a Tractor Mechanic from Ejura Sunday night of 15th April 1985 from Police Headquarters, ACP Office, Mampong Ashanti. He was re-bailed on the 16th to appear before the ACP's office on 29th of April 1985.

Pastor J.E. Ameyaw's (affectionately called *Yensiamoah*) ministry brought financial upliftment to the church in Mampong; leading to the purchase of the first district saloon car for ministry. This vehicle served the first Area head of Mampong (Apostle B.K. Swanzy) because his official vehicle was more than ten years and needed to be replaced by the church's headquarters.

The evangelistic drive of the church in the wider Mampong area encompassed the entire Sekyere Area up to Yeji (the border of the Volta river) and towards Kwame Danso both in the Brong-Ahafo region of Ghana. The local assemblies in Nsuta, Kofiase, and Atonsu were very strong at the time. There were other local assemblies including-Appiakrom, Amoaman, Ankamadoa, Bonkrong, Kyebi, Kyeremfaso, Aboatem, Abonkosu, etc.

Later on, Kwamang, Asaam, Nwandan, Nintin, and many more were added. The strategy involved reaching out within the suburbs of the town and into the surrounding villages; as well, as wider coverage of places for church planting. I remember I was part of the area rally that was organized to get an assembly established at Agona-Ashanti. Prior to that time, the surrounding towns like Asamang and Wiamoase had local assemblies. The establishment of a church in Agona, resulted in the stationing of Pastor Rockson at Agona. The rally was the collaborative work of the churches in Kumasi, Mampong, Ejura, Effiduasi, and many more. The ministers present included, Pastors-Sam Opoku Adipah of Mampong, Forson of Ejura, Tiako (father of Apostle Tiako) of Effiduasi, and so on. Pastor Gyekye Ampem of Bekwai- Ashanti used to join the evangelism outreach programs in Agona and Kwamang.

At the Agona rally, Pastor Forson of Ejura ministered during the Saturday retreat and traced Pentecostalism from Jerusalem to the Martin Luther's reformation era to the present day. Pastor Tiako led the congregation in prayer for the release of one Pastor Mawuko of Togo, who had been arrested as part of the persecution of the church back then. A prophetic song was released through Pastor Forson in Twi; translated as follows: "*The foundation of Pentecost is our Lord Jesus Christ; So, who can overcome the church; while Jesus is alive?*"

I will attribute the transformation of the church in Mampong to Pastor Samuel Opoku-Adipah for the bold and ground-breaking initiatives he took as the district pastor. At the time, he was misunderstood but most of the initiatives have been rewarding in the long-run. Nevertheless, the actual expansion of the church in Mampong township was the outcome of the pioneering *apostolic* work of Apostle Swanzy and later 'watering' by other ministers. These narratives are just to mention a few. I cannot say a lot after Apostle Swanzy because I was not physically present in the town, except for regular family visits.

HISTORY OF THE CHURCH OF PENTECOST

The public information on the beginnings of the Church of Pentecost is linked to the ministry of an Irish missionary by name-Pastor James and Mrs. Sophia McKeown, who was sent in 1937 by the Apostolic Church, Bradford. I have provided a historical account of the Church of Pentecost in Chapter 66 of my book on: *Taxation in Ghana: A fiscal policy tool for development.*

The purpose of Pastor McKeown's arrival was to help a group led

351

by Peter Newman Anim, encompassing believers of the Apostolic Faith. The first station was a town in the Eastern region of Ghana known as Asamankese.

In 1939, the group was split into the Christ Apostolic Church and the Apostolic Church, Gold Coast. The reason for the split was attributed to differences emanating from divine healing, without recourse to medicines. By April of 1940, the attendance during the first General convention was over 400 participants. The literature on the history of the Church of Pentecost has adequately covered the *doctrinal crisis* that plagued the church back in 1939; however, much is not known about the *constitutional crisis* that engulfed the church in 1953. I was personally asked about this in one of my New Members Orientation Program of the McKeown Worship Center (MWC)-Pentecost International Worship Center (PIWC), Romeoville, Illinois in the first quarter of 2020. What we do know is that a constitutional crisis led Pastor James McKeown to start the Gold Coast Apostolic Church. I present the narratives from Yirenkyi-Smart (2017) below:

- Pastor James McKeown left the Gold Coast to attend the General Quadrennial Conference Meeting of the Church in UK; which commenced on May 1953 in Braford;
- The merits and demerits of the practices of the Latter Rain were discussed and the meeting came to consensus and requested every member present to re-affirm his faith and belief in the Doctrine and Practices of the Apostolic Church;
- All participants at the meeting with the exception of Pastor James McKeown and Cecil Cousen made the affirmation; and when asked to make the affirmation offered: "I cannot conscientiously accept this"
- McKeown was dismissed from the Apostolic Church;
- Pastor McKeown explained later on his return that the affirmation would mean that Missionaries posted abroad

would have nothing to do with the Latter Rain Movement. Additionally, he was against the fact that an African apostle was to be an apostle to the blacks alone but not over whites; whereas the white apostle could be an apostle over both blacks and whites;

- Initially, Pastor James McKeown sought constitutional amendments before discussion on the Latter Rain and the black and white apostle issue, however, these were refused;
- McKeown did not see any wisdom in the affirmation;
- This attitude of Pastor James McKeown proved that he abhorred racial discrimination; and further demonstrated that though a 'white man', he had a black heart" (Yirenkyi-Smart, 2017, pp.148-150).

Pastor Joshua Yirenkyi-Smart, writing in 2017 on "Pentecost from Jerusalem to Asamankese-The Journey of Pentecost and the Untold Story of Pastor James McKeown and The Church of Pentecost (1937-1982) elaborated, as follows:

A Resolution by the Church in the Ashanti Region

The Council of Pastors, Overseers, and Elders of all the districts in the Ashanti Province convened a meeting at Wiamoase on December 26,1953 under the chairmanship of Apostle Anaman. The meeting was attended by six pastors including Pastor F.D. Walker of Kumasi (1952-56), Pastor S.T.W. Frimpong of Kumawu (1953-55) and Pastor J.A. Bimpong of Juaso (1950-54). Six overseers including the 21-year old, Fred Stephen Kwasi Mensah Safo, resident minister at Wiamoase (1952-54), where the meeting took place, attended.

*The meeting was deemed so important that 82 elders from all the assemblies in Ashanti and Ashanti Akim attended. They included Elders Erasmus Stephen Ntim and **Appiah-Sokye** of Mampong; Plange, Amanyina, Adane, Safo Kantanka, Osei, Kusi, Asiedu, Asienie, Gyimah, and Manu-all of Kumasi; Nkansah Brempong and Amponsah of Juaso, Enyan and Wiafe of Agogo; Ofori of Konongo, T.W.O. Korsah of Konongo-Odumasi, and a host of others.*

It should be noted that there were some elders who were, at the time, in a dilemma, not so clear, as to whether to back the mother church or McKeown. They included Elders Esssandoh, Karikari, Duku, and Biritwum.

The points raised on which the meeting reached a consensus were:

That we reserve to ourselves the right, as a church to invite any Latter Rain Team, or and Team of Evangelists, to visit us, be they from Europe or America.

That Pastor Seaborne, Hammond, and Rosser should kindly communicate with Bradford to reinstate Pastor McKeown.

That should Bradford refuse to reinstate Pastor James McKeown, we in Ashanti will continue to work with him as before.

The mother church in Bradford, UK did not heed to the resolution (pp.157-158).

I did not know Apostle Anaman personally but from the list of elders, I can categorically state that *Elder Appiah-Sokye* is my father and Elder E.S. Ntim is the father of the *Ntims* (Pastor Phillip and Sammy). Elder Enyan is the father of Apostle Michael Agyemang Amoako (the current National head of the USA). I knew Elder Karikari who became my father's friend and also stayed in Mampong and had a son in ministry; Elders Safo Kantanka (Mama Manko's husband) and Gyimah (once upon a time a Regional deacon of Ashanti region) were natives of Mampong but stayed in Kumasi. Elder Asiedu (Paa Asiedu used to interpret for Pastor McKeown) and Papa Plange. I remember the names of Elders Duku and Amponsah.

Ghana attained independence on March 6, 1957 and the changes of Ghana's name, necessitated a corresponding change in the name of the church from the Gold Coast Apostolic Church to the Ghana Apostolic Church. On August 1, 1962, the Ghana Apostolic Church was replaced with the new name- *The Church of Pentecost*. This name had earlier on been adopted in 1961 on the admonition of the then President of the Republic of Ghana, *Osagyefo* Dr. Kwame Nkrumah to foster harmony and peace on the Pentecostal front.

Table 11 shows the most important historical dates for the Church of Pentecost, as follows:

Table 11: *Important dates in the history of the Church of Pentecost*		
Dates	**Important Events**	**Remarks**
September 12,1900	Founder's Birthday	Children's Day
1937	Arrival of Founder	As a missionary of the Apostolic Church, Bradford, U.K. to the Apostolic Faith led by Peter Newman Anim (one group)
1939	Doctrinal Differences on Divine Healing	The Christ Apostolic Church; and the Apostolic Church, Gold Coast (2 churches resulted)

1953	Constitutional Differences	The Apostolic Church, Gold Coast; and the Gold Coast Apostolic Church (led by Ps. James McKeown) emerged
1957	Change of Name (Ghana's Independence)	The Apostolic Church, Ghana; and the Ghana Apostolic Church (Ghana replaces Gold Coast)
1961	New conflict ensued after the 1953 crisis	Dr. Kwame Nkrumah advised the leadership of the Ghana Apostolic Church to change their name to preserve the unity in the Pentecostal front
August 1,1962	A new name was adopted-"The Church of Pentecost"	"The Church of Pentecost "officially replaced the Ghana Apostolic Church

Source: Created from the literature on the history of the Church of Pentecost

Pastor James McKeown and all the selfless workers in the Church of Pentecost deserve our commendation. Per I Corinthians 3: 6-8:

"I have planted, Apollos watered; but God gave the increase.[7] So then neither is he that planteth anything, neither he that watereth; but God that giveth the increase.[8] Now he that planteth and he that watereth are one: and every man shall receive his own reward according to his own labour"

CONVERSION

I have listened to very impressive testimonies of people and how they came to faith in Jesus Christ. Some came to faith after chronic sicknesses and life threating events; as well as, appropriate response to an altar call. The Bible has records of how different people were called by God, including the calls of: Samuel, Saul who later became Paul, the disciples of Jesus such as Peter, John, James, and many more. While the identity of the one who calls is not in dispute; the circumstances, the purpose, the timing, and the approach differed for each person. As a result, conversion is not important until it is inextricably linked to the purpose of the call. I trace my conversion as a Christian to December 30, 1979 when I accepted the Lordship of our Lord Jesus Christ as my personal Savior at the time of my baptism by immersion; symbolizing my death, burial, and resurrection with Jesus Christ. Consequently, while April 15,1964 is my physical date of birth; the Spiritual date of birth is *December 30, 1979* and my baptism was officiated by Pastor Sam Opoku-Adipah (District Pastor) in the *Sumanpa* River at Mampong-Ashanti.

GROWTH STAGE

The growth stage will be focused on the period of my young adulthood. I want to categorically state that I have gone through this phase of life as every human being does and susceptible to all the challenges of the youth, including peer pressure. I do not claim to be perfect by any means but I can say that the Lord has been with me through it all. May His name alone be praised now and forever. Amen. I will narrate my story in a *triple-fold* fashion as follows: (i) pre-college, (ii) college, and post-college.

Pre-College- This period is characterized by my faith after leaving home into boarding schools for my secondary and sixth-form education. I was not very active in any faith-based activities except the formal Sunday services organized by the School. One of our tutors (Miss Comfort Acheampong-Agricultural science) took a key role in the organization of the church services. She substituted for preacher who were unable to take up preaching appointments. Reverend Kwakye (now a bishop) was posted to Juaben as the resident minister of the Methodist Church and he was assigned to teach us Bible Knowledge; for this reason, he became the chaplain of the school. Prior to my undergraduate education, I had attended schools owned by different churches, as follows: Evangelical Church (Nursery), the Anglican Church for my elementary school, the Methodist church (secondary school), the Catholic church for my sixth-form education.

I do not remember much about the activities of the Evangelical church at my day nursery but the Anglican church imbibed in the students their liturgy and hymns. We went in processions to the cemetery during the *all souls' days*. In the secondary school, the Methodist church had its turn to inculcate values in students. The church services were organized in the evenings of Sundays. Initially, various churches were allowed to group in different classrooms but there was no seriousness attached to the services by our seniors; so, management had to cancel them. Several seniors joined the Pentecostal group.

Tables were used for drumming during the praises session and when prayers are being said, a few will be calling the names of Elijah, Nebuchadnezzar, Moses; Others pretended to be possessed by shaking their bodies. After offerings are taken, some will opine that the offerings should be shared. I cannot tell if the offerings were actually shared. The morning denominational services were discontinued.

Saint Peter's Secondary School, as a Catholic institution allowed for Catholics and Protestants to meet simultaneously at different locations; except during the first, last, and retreat weekends, where all students attended the Catholic church. The retreat periods were memorable because a Retreat Father is invited to engage students over the weekend and the occasion also translated into our feeding patterns. The campus hosted the *Fathers' house* on the Kwahu ridge, where Catholic fathers resided and serviced the churches on the ridge. The school held a morning assembly of students and prayer time after the evening studies sessions. Our headmaster, the senior housemaster, and the chaplain were all Catholic priests on one hand and tutors for regular classes on the other. On campus were also *brothers* of the Catholic faith.

THE FORMATION OF PENSA

The Pentecost Students and Associates (PENSA) was birthed in the early 1980s. The introduction of PENSA and the Pentecost International Worship Center (PIWC) concept are the best things that have shaped the trajectory of the Church of Pentecost and has helped the youth of our time. Until then, campus ministry was dominated by the Scripture Union (SU), which have trained many Christians in Africa; but they reached out to students of many denominations. Some leaders of the Church including Apostle A.T. Nartey felt the need to reach out to students on the university campuses and beyond and so were instrumental in the formation of PENSA in the church. I was present at PENSA conferences, as follows: two at Prempeh College in Kumasi, two at the Wesley College in Kumasi, and one in Aburi Girls Secondary School in Eastern region. A number of both students and associates at the time have played critical roles in PENSA. I know the former Chairman of the church (Apostle Professor Opoku Onyinah) had recognized some of the pioneers at one of the Church's Council meetings, especially the first National Executive Committee members of the ministry. For that reason, I will not attempt to give names here.

At the Aburi PENSA Conference, the meeting mooted the idea

for the church to acquire its own conference center because of the large sums of money paid for Conference venues. Individual pledges were made. I redeemed my pledge through one of the elders who worked at the church's head office. I received an official to that effect. The meeting suggested to the leadership to impose a levy of ¢1 on every member of the church as the seed money for the construction of the Center. The Lord has given the Church an awesome Conference Center in His own time through His own resources and provision. May His name be praised.

At the PENSA conference of the Ashanti region in 2001 at the UST Campus, a suggestion was made to the church to consider building a Sanctuary in any one University campus of the choice of leadership to deepen the presence of the church in the Universities. I have not followed up on this suggestion ever since. I want to state that PENSA has gone a long way to help in the growth in faith through the discussion of very topical and contemporary issues at conferences. The associates also served as mentors to the youth. Those of us in the secondary and High schools looked up to those in the universities; and those in the universities also looked up to those in the world of work.

In the interest of self-disclosure, it was at Aburi that the Guest Speaker (Emeka Nwapah); a seasoned conference speaker and a lawyer from Nigeria expounded the Word of God to the admiration of all. Apostle Noble Atsu described him *as a man who knew the Bible more than his law books*. An awesome and knowledgeable speaker of the Word. He gave the minutest details to the Scriptures he expounded on. During prayer time in this 1987 Conference, *I prayed specifically for a quadruple portion of this man's teaching anointing*. I know this prayer has been answered because I received the gift of teaching from the church and not from the classroom. This gift has helped to put food on the table for my family over the years. I know the Lord is not done with me yet because my teaching grace is not up to the quadruple level, I asked for; So, I have to continue to work on this grace gift I have received from on high.

In 2019, after the Chicago Regional Holy Ghost Convention, Yoke Town, Illinois, I was talking to one elder of Chicago and he talked about his experience at the Aburi PENSA Conference. He was also at the conference but I did not know him back then.

College- This phase is concentrated on my life on campus as a believer while in the University for my undergraduate education. I took advantage of the resources available in the University to equip me as a person of faith. I was exposed to some of the finest minsters of the Gospel in Ghana through their ministrations when called upon to preach. I guess because they were mindful of the fact that the audience were university students, they gave a very good impression through the Word and prayer ministration.

At the University of Ghana, all Pentecostals had one group called the Legon Pentecostal Union (LPU). The LPU Campus ministry blended both Charismatics and Pentecostalism under one umbrella. This group has produced several giants in the kingdom of God and other spheres of human endeavor. In addition to the specific group (LPU), there was the general non-denominational group called at different times as University Christian Fellowship (UCF) or Ghana Fellowship of Evangelical Students (GHAFES). While LPU responded to the needs of Pentecostals and Charismatics, GHAFES catered for the needs of all Christians on campus. There was also meetings organized by the Chaplaincy Board of the University.

With time, most of the minister who used to preach to us on campus have responded to higher callings and are now bishops and apostles of different church denominations. In the Church of Pentecost, some of the products of the LPU are: Apostles Asabereh (International Executive member of the Church of Pentecost), Apostle James McKeown Quinoo (Canada); Reverend Professor Nana Anto Adubofour (Barea Academy), Pastor Jojo Forson (Jamaica); as well as, Elder Dr. Chris Ampadu (Samaritan Strategy), Dr. Koomson (USA), Dr. Isaac Painstil (Oasis

Church-Chicago), Pastor Joseph K. Painstil (formerly of Pentecost Biblical Seminary), Mr. Kobina Ampofo, Pastors- Akoadjie and Ahlijah, and Ms. Lydia Kobia Amanfi (France), Mr. Boama Agyei, Sister Victoria Sonekan, Ms. Abigail Aryee; Mr. Samuel Sampah, and many more.

The plurality of programs covered the following: Saturday Retreats at the Legon Botanical Garden, Tuesday one-hour non-stop prayers at M-Block, Late Night Prayer sessions on the Soccer Field, Bi-weekly Half-Night sessions, *Jesus March* on campus; participation in Crusade by Archbishop Benson Idahosa of Nigeria.

At the 10th Anniversary of the LPU, the late Reverend Derrick Prince was invited as the Special Guest for the celebration. Per the conversation we had with him, he explained that he had a financier who received his budget for traveling ahead of time and provided the resources in the course of the year; but since our invitation came late, it could not be included. Consequently, Reverend Derrick Prince could not honor the invitation.

I must state that I missed the opportunity of seeing Reverend Derrick Prince in person. I have studied under his feet as his student of the Word. He mailed to me books for study as a young Christian. Some of the collections include but not limited to the following: *Laying on of hands, repentance, appointment in Jerusalem, Resurrection of the dead, Fatherhood, God's Medicine Bottle,* and many more. I used to give some of these books to a few of my elders, who later became ministers and two have retired (one as an apostle and the other as a pastor of the church).

Post-College- The era is characterized by going out from the protected academic environment to the wide world of work and also to demonstrate values in a practical way. I consider this stage of my life as incremental to the experiences offered by the pre-college and college phases of my faith life. I began to play vital roles in the church and ministry during this stage and to brighten the corner where I found myself. I stayed in Accra after graduation to offer my second-year national service. Initially, I worshipped with the Madina Central assembly of the Church of Pentecost but it was a very big congregation, so the personal touch of ministry was missing.

One day, I got home quite late, and I was running late for the mid-week service and so I went to the Madina West (now Ebenezer Temple) assembly. Indeed, the people were welcoming and I felt at home and the young ones started visiting and checking on me. With time, I started attending church at that assembly. I remember a lot of the people such as: Elders and Deacons-Maxwell Bremang Darko, Nartey, Nicholas Darko (all presiding elders at different times), Osabutey (retired), Archurst, Obeng Boateng, Vincent Donkoh, William Owusu Yamoah, Titus Adjei, Asiedu, Paul Bidim, and so on. Just to mention a few.

BAPTISMS

As recounted above, the baptism by immersion was received on December 30,1979 but I received the Baptism of the Holy Spirit in 1985. I cannot recollect the exact date, but I can recount the events leading to this experience. Prior to this experience, I had received the baptism of the Holy Spirit with the evidence of speaking in tongues in one of the Children's movement retreats but due to lack of appreciation at the time, I doubted the experience and did not pay attention to spiritual nourishment needed to sustain the experience. I can say I lost the experience and so it was not until the 1985 encounter that I could confirm within my Spirit that I had been baptized in the Holy Spirit.

In 1985, as I have recounted elsewhere, I was providing my first year National Service at the Mampong District Hospital. My cousin was given oversight of the Assemblies of God Church in one of the villages called Bonkrong near Mampong-Ashanti. So, one weekend, I was invited to give a talk at a retreat organized by this group on the topic: *Sanctification.* I honored the invitation and spoke for some 45 minutes using *John 17:17* as the Scriptural text. During the afternoon prayer session, there was an outpouring of the Holy Spirit and I resumed speaking in tongues and since then, my life has never been the same. Praise God!

MATURITY STAGE

The initial and growth phases discussed above have helped to nurture and prepare me for the kingdom business. I have had to receive adequate development from the opportunities offered by the University of Ghana and PENSA. For this reason, I could no longer remain obscure but to respond to the exigency of the kingdom enterprise. In this phase of *faith, foundation, and focus*- I will cover my involvement in the following local assemblies- Social Security and National Insurance Trust (SSNIT) flats, Madina West, Madina Central (all in Ghana); and Pentecost International Worship Center (PIWC)-Chicago.

ELMINA DISTRICT- Around this time, the Elmina district had 31 assemblies but did not have quite many workers. Pastoral oversight had been provided by Pastors M.N. Wiredu and J.K. Appiah. I do not know most the ministers who came before and after these ministers. Elder Napoleon Anang presided over the Bantama assembly as a deacon, but the two of us were the youngest, called into eldership the same day, and quite very vocal in the presbytery.

Some of the church workers in the Elmina district, as of September 1995, included the following: Reverend M.N. Wiredu, Reverend Joseph Appiah-Kubi; *Elders*-Christian Darkwah (Number 1), P.K. Mensah (Central), Benjamin Yankson (Number 2), John Osei Akowuah (SSNIT Flats), J.K Mensah (Ayensudu), Samuel Michael Boham (SSNIT Flats), Isaac Awotwe (Number 1), George Appiah-Sokye (SSNIT Flats), S.K.

Mensah (Ankwanda), Philip Conduah (Abayee), J.K Otoo (Abayee), and George K Essuman (Number 1)

Others were- Glara, Tetteh, Amissah, John Elliamo, Peter B. Duntu (Essaman), Alex Dabi (Number 2), Emmanuel Asamoah (Bronyibima), Elijah Eshun (Brenu Akyinim), John Ackon (retired-Number 1), Isaac Kwesi Nyarko (SSNIT Flats), Youche, Baah, Cobbina, Gyan, Philip; as well as, *deacons*-Matthew, Quayson, Boadu, Amponsah; and *deaconesses*-Mary Agyemang (Number 2), Angelina Awotwe (Number 1). *Brothers*-Christian G. Quaicoe (Bantuma), Joseph Arthur (Abayee), Francis Tawiah (Essaman), John Esson (Bronyibima), Joseph Cobbina (Pershie), Joseph Eshun (Pershie), George Saikum (Essaman), Alfred Sagoe (Essaman), John Duntu (Essaman), Paul Essel (Number 2), Samuel Sam (Number 2), Joseph Abaka Otoo (Number 2), Comfort Boham (Bronyibima), John Boah (Ayensudo), Joseph Bassaw (Number 1); and *Sisters*-Janet Elliamo (Essaman), Gladys Duntu (Essaman), Mary Mensah (Essaman), Grace Owusu (Bantuma), Elizabeth Awotwe (Number 2), Rose Koomson (Number 1), and many more.

SSNIT Flats Assembly-My involvement with the SSNIT Flat assembly in Elmina of the Central region of Ghana is provided below. The SSNIT flats were constructed by the National Pensions Body as part of the diversification of investments in their portfolio. The flats were allocated to organizations for purchase and the entities had the option of either allow employees to buy them or keep the ownership of the properties on the balance sheet and rent it out to employees. When I went to stay at the SSNIT flats in 1991, the members of the community either went to Cape Coast (about 15 kilometers) or the Elmina township (about 3 kilometers) for worship. With time, about seven families were identified as members of the Church of Pentecost, but have now come to reside in this community.

The two headmasters of the Methodist Elementary School located within the SSNIT flats were contacted with a view to getting one of the classrooms to be used as place of worship. The request was submitted to the Church board and approved. The leadership approached the district minister (Pastor M.N. Wiredu) on the idea of starting a nursery assembly. The proposal was agreed and six months was granted for the assembly to keep the money raised to finance the needs of the church. With this arrangement, the church was able to finance the connection of the school to the national electricity grid to help the church run *mid-week* services; and also permitted the students of the school to attend classes in the night.

The SSNIT flat assembly had good human and material resources for ministry. I remember I had to stand in for the three elders for the evening services because the nature of their work did not allow them to get home early. Typically, I got home by 7:00 pm; and for that reason, I was actively involved as a young man full of energy, I participated from opening prayer, worship, prayer sessions, word ministrations, and so on.

In January 1994, I was called to the office of elder at an Officers Retreat held at Kisi near Komenda and my ordination was performed by Apostle Rigwell Ato Addison (Central Regional head). Just after my ordination, I was assigned preaching appointments every week in my local assembly and also sent to other 30 assemblies within the district. Some of the names I can remember include the following: Elders-John Osei Akowuah, Aggrey (Prisons officer), Samuel Michael Boham (a teacher), Koomson (a banker), Isaac Kwesi Nyarko (a tax inspector); Deaconesses- Esther Hagan, Ernestina Nyarko, Christina Nyarko, and Doris Fosua. Other members- Davi, Kingsley, Auntie Nana, and many more.

The local church was community-focused and provided for the financial needs of a few members with critical needs. The church re-capitalized one elderly lady who lost her stock-in- trade (fish) during the fish smoking process. Another lady's total medical cost was fully covered by the church. She developed a serious infection after childbirth at home and the family looked unconcerned. The church was informed and action was taken. The church stepped into the situation and helped.

I can say that I was a beneficiary of the generosity of the SSNIT flat church because the church supported the maintenance of my children in Kumasi with a monthly stipend of GH¢50 when I was in the Graduate School on leave without pay. This gesture motivated me to donate substantially towards the fund-raising ceremony in aid of church building in later period.

I actively took part in the preparation of the Timothy class (those graduating from the Children's movement) before their integration into the regular adult church. The preparation class centered on the tenets of the church (Statement of Our faith). The participants asked very good questions. The preparation culminated into a graduation ceremony that took place at one of the district Joint Services. The church presented the participants with baptismal certificates and a gift of the Bible with a citation inscribed in them. A group photograph was taken with the District Pastor (Pastor J.K. Appiah-Kubi) and the leadership of church and the participants showed off their baptism certificate in their Bible. Family picture- taking followed because each student was allowed to invite two family members. It is gratifying to note that during my next visit to this assembly, I was delighted to see some of them playing key roles in the Church.

I want to recount one event which took place when I was in the SSNIT flat assembly. I woke up early on a Sunday morning to prepare for church and I documented the thoughts as they came to me and went ahead to prepare a sermon in my sermons' book. I went for this district Joint Service and as Pastor begun to expatiate on the Word of God, the message veered into the exact message I had prepared just that morning. The difference between my pastor's message and my written message which I showed him after the service was only a sentence.

What I did not like was the fact that at district leadership ministry (movement) meetings which was held on a rotational basis was characterized by drilling local leaders for low performance. While I appreciated the accountability aspects; the attack from all fronts was also a disincentive to local leaders who were doing their best in the circumstance. Some local movement leaders had to use monies received from weeding of farms to pay movement dues back then. To give you an idea of what I am talking about, a few local assemblies were assigned with huge tracts of land by their local authorities but they did not have the means to build sanctuaries. When you visit some of the local assemblies, the zeal in their service is unparallel; yet they do not have money for kingdom business.

I went to the Central region as a member of the church but I returned to my previous assembly as an ordained elder, with hands-on ministry and leadership exposure. Against the background of a *militant* presbytery-the presbytery meetings erupted into serious arguments but the interesting thing is that just after the meeting everything was about normal. Presbyters spoke their mind freely and openly. I am eternally grateful to the Elmina district pastor and leadership for conducting a send-off service (Joint Service) in my honor after I was transferred to Accra after staying five years in the district. By then, the district had been divided in two districts (Elmina and Komenda). I did not deserve such a treatment and I appreciate the local assemblies and my local assembly for this gesture.

The next discussion will cover the Madina district. A lot of ministers have had oversight of the Madina district and notable among them are-Pastors-Ammon, S.K. Baidoo, P.K. Awuah, Asamoah, E.K. Apea, Nicholas Siaw, Edzii Davidson, Appianing, and Adjatey; as well as, Prophets- J.O. Amaniampong, Appiah Agyekum, and Kankam Beditto. The list goes on. A countless number of elders have served the Madina district. The former Madina district has grown to become the Madina Area with most assemblies attaining district status. Some of the elders are-Appiah Dankwah, Koranteng, Okoe Barnor, Asante (Ashaley Botchwey), Asamoah Manu, E.O. Kissi, D.F. Anang, Professor Kwabia Boateng, Appiah-Mensah, Abeiku, and many more. A few of the elders have responded to the call to become minsters of the church and a few have passed on. The Madina West and Central assemblies will be discussed below.

MADINA WEST- I felt completely at home at the Madina West Assembly (now called Ebenezer Temple); and as a result, when I returned from Cape Coast after a five-year duty tour, I could not help but come back to this very assembly as my new place of worship. The fellowship of the brethren was awesome. The church had increased in number on my return and a lot of people had to stand outside the church during Sunday services because the size of the Sanctuary could not contain the growing number of members.

A business meeting was held to consider two options: either (a) the assembly adapts a shift system, or (b) carved out a new assembly from the existing church. The membership favored the creating of a new assembly because the church had an ongoing church building under construction on a land in the Madina Zongo. While the new assembly was named *Madina West* because the original Madina West assembly started from the Madina Zongo; and the existing assembly was re-named-the Ebenezer Temple (symbolizing how far the Lord had brought the assembly). The new assembly was born during the presiding eldership of Elder Nicholas and Mrs. Mabel Darko (now Reverend Dr. Nicholas Darko- former Finance and Administration Director (FAD) of the Church of Pentecost). The Accra-Madina-Adenta road became the boundary but covered the entire Madina *Zongoland*.

The following officers were transferred to the new assembly, as follows:-(i) 4 elders- David Kwabena Mensah (Presiding), William Owusu Yamoah, Samuel Bekoe. I was assigned to the new assembly as the first local secretary. (ii) A few deacons, but (iii) there were no deaconesses posted initially to this new assembly. The existing deaconesses at the Ebenezer Temple serviced the new assembly on rotational basis until new deaconesses were called. Later on, other elders were called and other also joined from other assemblies such as: Elders-Agyemang Dugbatse (who assumed the presiding eldership after the expired term of Elder Mensah), Alfred Vaeta, Lawrence Baidoo Larbi (see also Chapter 10), Dovia, and others joined from other assemblies. The deaconesses that were called were: Mama Dankyi (the local women's leader), Mama Asiedu, Mama Gifty Owusu Yamoah, Mama Agyemang Dugbatse, and others.

My involvement with this assembly related to my role as the local secretary. Apart from the traditional role of taking minutes of meetings, I brought creativity to the role of the secretary in the local assembly. Firstly, I introduced education on church practices and business promotion into our weekly announcements. I also introduced humor to the delivery of the announcements because the announcements came at the tail end of the service when members were tired.

The impact of this was felt when a family transferred out to another assembly in another part of Accra. After a while, we saw the lady attending church on three consecutive Sundays. After service, we were interacting with the sister and the presiding elder asked her if they have not moved yet. Surprisingly, this lady told the presiding elder that the announcement delivery at the new assembly is not good as compared to ours and that is the reason why she has been coming back to join our services. So, it means people are ministered to differently. The lesson I have learned here is that different people have different needs in the church.

Secondly, I took the local reporting to a new level. I developed a reporting template for reporting on the local. A standard reporting protocols were adhered to and the packaging of the document endeared the heart of the district presbytery. Third, I caused the local office space to be furnished and also provided a suitable venue for local presbytery meetings; as well as, four, I re-organized the Welfare Fund by:(I) writing a Bye-law or a Constitution, (II) causing the opening of a bank accounts, (III) selecting collectors for the groupings in the church (Faith, Love, and Hope); as well as, (IV) publication of statements on the notice board. The fund was run strictly as a restricted fund but after my transfer to the Central assembly, I learned later that the welfare fund was transferred into the local fund. End of story.

Fifthly, I caused a register of members to be created for the local church. A sheet of paper was distributed to members to solicit responses on basic information for church's database. I remember on one occasion, when one of our sisters passed. The church's tribute contained the correct information as compared to those provided by the family because our information was provided by very sister before she was called to glory. Lastly, I served on the foundation stone laying planning committee, putting together the history of the assembly, the history of the church building; as well as, the cost of construction to date.

On this item, I want to acknowledge the grace of God, through the provision of handymen. The church had a lot of masons, who helped in no small measure in raising the superstructure of the gigantic edifice. On some chosen Sundays, we started the church services early and closed by 10:30am to allow for construction work to go on voluntary basis because it was difficult getting a lot of hands for the building project during the weekdays and Saturdays were market days for Madina. The men mixed the mortar or concrete for the construction project, and some men using wheel barrows and the women carried the mortar/concreate using head pans. The young adults fetched water. The communal spirit was at its best. No wonder the actual construction cost lesser than anticipated. The masons were paid a daily wage but they worked more than expected.

I quite remember when we got to the roofing stage of the huge building against the backdrop of most of our members being petty traders. The initial quote for the entire roofing project was ¢70 million and the faith of the leadership and members was tested to the full. The reality was that we did not have the financial strength to make it happen. The leadership organized series of prayer sessions towards this project. We invited my brother the late Elder Dwomoh Amaniampong (former Chairman, National Finance Board of the Church of Pentecost) to lead us in the raising of funds. To the glory of God, this church raised funds that was impossible to raise. On this realization, the Area head (the late Apostle F.E. Antwi) and his executive provided us with all the roofing sheets costing ¢30 million at the time and the local church covered the rest of the cost. Now, in 2020, this Sanctuary has been re-decorated into an ultra-modern edifice.

Praise Report-The testimony I want to share here is that the special offering was held just at the time I had started my Graduate program and I had made some savings to buy a used car to help me with my commute to school. I went to negotiate for a car, and I requested for a discount so I can use the discount amount for the offering. On the night before the special offering, I received a message from the Lord to give the money for the offering. I struggled with this all Saturday night and so on Sunday morning, I gave the amount to the Lord. I felt a relieve after the service but I had more problem-How I was going to inform my wife about this because we had planned together for the used car but not on the offering because she had gone to Kumasi to visit the children. I went back home to pray to God to convince my wife for me.

On her return, when I told her of the move of God in the offering and the fact that I have given the money out from the promptings of the Spirit, she said that was alright because if God requested for the money for the used car, he was going to provide a better way for us. At this word, I felt a great sense of relief. Thank you, Jesus! Yes, I went three years after this offering without a car (ride); when the time came,

I was there and a loved one called me from Europe and told me he has purchased a car for me and was wondering if I could raise the money to pay the duty and clear it from the port of entry. I answered in the affirmative.

In chapter 9, I mentioned the role of this church during the period of my devastation in prayer and in deeds. I do not want to repeat the goodness of this church to me. I appreciated their love and support and May God continue to bless them. The church which started with 97 people at the maiden service had grown to 276 at the time I was transferred to the Madina Central assembly. Most of these people now own homes. This church has become the Koonaa District of the Madina Area in Ghana.

MADINA CENTRAL- I was transferred from the Madina West assembly to the Madina Central assembly together with the late Elder Lawrence and Deaconess Rosina Larbi, and one Deaconess Millicent Koomson (now in United Kingdom). I guess my appointment as *Elder for Special Duties* (ESD) is partly to be the purpose of my transfer. My duty was to help in the re-organization of the District Office (Administration). The Central church is a very big one with a typical attendance of 500 to Sunday services. If the attendance drops to between 300 and 400, leadership is concerned. The total number of adult members is 1000. The Madina Central Sanctuary has three floors. The first two-floor seats 1000, when the district meets, when two floors are occupied. The whole building is packed to capacity when the Area meets during evening programs. Now, the original area has been split into many such as Dome, Haatso, and others.

I remember some time ago. We were recording 450 attendance of members to church on Sundays. When we did further analysis, we discovered that most members were attending church every other Sunday and the total membership number was validated during one

Cross Over Service. When we took the count and invited those visiting us and did the mathematics, we realized that the number was correct.

At the Madina Central assembly too, I was tasked with the Welfare Fund and I wrote a Bye-law or constitution, and caused the various groups to choose dues collectors for the fund. As usual the fund was run strictly as a restricted fund but the welfare fund was kept within the Local fund with a budget and accounting line items created. A circular was received from the church's headquarters to the effect that no dues should be collected towards welfare funds. In compliance with this directive, the balance of ¢13 million was handed over to the local presbytery, with a suggestion to apply the balance to the welfare cause. The welfare scheme was discontinued.

The Madina Central assembly had a total presbytery of over 50, comprising: 20 elders (with 2 retired elders), over 25 deaconesses, and about 5 deacons. Some of the officers of the Madina Central include-Elders-Obeng Boateng, Rexford Adomako Bonsu, Joseph Kwaidoo, Dr. S.D. Boateng, Emmanuel Asante (former Area deacon), Richard Asamoah, Lawrence Baidoo Larbi (deceased), Provencal, Quist, Eric Adarkwah, Addai, Addo Wontumi, Armah Kesse (deceased), Nyame Boame, Richard Boateng, Adu Gyamfi, Adade Yeboah (we called him International Evangelist), and so on. Later on, other elders were transferred to the Madina Central assembly, including Elders-Chris Dorgbadzi, Ing. Ashia, and so on.

My usual seat was between the two retired elders (Elders Asiedu Dade and Andah) at the back but I must say these fathers of ours spoke positively into our lives from time to time and gave us evaluations after ministrations. We did not have many deacons. Interestingly, this presbytery contributed more that 60 percent of the church's tithes. Suffice it to say, the membership had the same professions and vocations in the presbytery. I can only speculate that these officers were very faithful with their dealings with the Lord.

The problem I had in the Madina Central assembly had to do with the timing for evening services. Some of us stayed very far from the Madina township so preferred to go straight to church just from work but most of the members and officers lived within a very close radius. When they close from work, they go home to eat, take their bath and take their time to get to church at their own pace. Time was not important to some of them and were not worried about the closing time. We got home very late affecting our daily routines.

As I told you about the day, I had a verbatim message while in the SSNIT flat assembly, history repeated itself. Unlike the Elmina case where the occurrence was during a district joint service, in the case of Madina Central assembly, it was also a district joint service but in honor of one of our beloved elders who had been called into full-time ministry. As Pastor E.K. Apea was ministering the message, the second part of message coincided with the message I had prepared that weekend. I was the conductor for this farewell service and after the service, one of our fathers and retired Police Commissioner called Elder Asante (the father of Pastor Seth Asante) called me aside and told me that I conducted the service professionally. I did not know that there was a professional way of conducting a service. These types of fatherly motivations are very refreshing in the development of the younger generation.

Another lesson I learned from the late Elder Asante was his words of wisdom that settled a serious problem. One day, we received a message to the effect that there was going to be a Special presbytery meeting immediately after church service. When we met the agendum was that the minister had used available district funds in the reconstruction of the fence wall of the parsonage. In addition to this, there was an outstanding debt of ¢8 million to be apportioned to the local assemblies. That is what broke the back of the camel.

The environment was fully charged because the project was not budgeted for and the minister had also not sought authorization to do the project. To the extent that the outstanding debt is being allocated to local assemblies. When enough arguments have been made, the late Elder Asante stood to his feet and asked for attention to speak. Elder admitted that the amount was not budgeted for and the authorization was not sought. A lot had gone wrong; yet, an elder or family head does not sit aloof while the family property is being destroyed. To the extent that the money had been used to preserve the property of the church, we can pardon the minster and see the way forward. This statement calmed the nerves of all the presbytery. I have not found this in any textbook and so I am grateful to our fathers. I pray that God will continues to teach us through them.

The next event I want to recount is in regards to the day I was ministering in the Word of God but I cannot recollect the exact words I uttered but all of a sudden, I saw almost all the congregation up on their feet. I had not experience this before. To borrow a friend's phrase "the divine Charisma was very present" Likewise, it was through one of such Word ministrations that one of the young adult ladies told my good friend that I have the gift of teaching and so it was based on this testimony that I responded to an advertisement for the appointment of lecturers, when my personal circumstances warranted some flexibility in working.

The last experience I want to talk about at the Madina Central assembly is what I will refer to as: the *uncommon praises*. On this particular Sunday, I was the conductor for the service and before the start of the service, a deaconess (name withheld) approached me and told me that she was to accompany the husband to a regional program but she is billed to lead the call to worship and was wondering if the part of the program could be modified for her. I told the presiding elder that there was the need to modify the order of service and he gave me the latitude to do so. After opening prayer, I invited our deaconess to continue with the worship segment of the service. As the deaconess was walking towards to podium, I heard some elders on the platform reminding me of the praise and testimonies before worship. Just after the worship, I felt a strong edge for the ministration of the Word to follow so I invited the preacher man (the late Elder Lawrence B. Larbi) for the day. Unknown to me, the caption of the message was-*praises*. After the Word ministration, there was the need for appropriate response to the message so I invited all the local song leaders upstage. I asked one of them to lead the team into congregational praises. In fact, I have never experienced the like praises because of the impact on the general membership. The lesson here is that, God is not limited to a specific order of service.

CHICAGO DISTRICT-The Romeoville district was carved out of the Chicago district. The Bolingbrook assembly was part of the Chicago district, which had other assemblies such as: Chicago Central, PIWC-Chicago, Detroit, and Milwaukee. Later on, the Hanover Park and Greater North assemblies were added. Ministerial oversight has been provided by Pastors- Omane Yeboah, Emmanuel Owusu Bediakoh (deceased), Samuel Yaw Aidoo (deceased), Maxwell Kofi Kusi (deceased), Michael Agyemang Amoako, Jehu Gyimah, and Francis Agyapong. A number of district executive committees steered the affairs of the district at different times but the Committee, I was a member of was composed, as follows: Reverend Michael Agyemang Amoako (Chair), Deaconess Grace Williams (secretary), Elders-Albert A. Buabeng (Area deacon), Jake Ameyaw (financial secretary), Dr. Albert Osei, Maxwell Owusu, Dr. Barimah Sekyi, Gerald Osei-Bonsu, and myself.

PIWC-Chicago-The last assembly to be discussed under the growth stage of my faith, foundations, and focus is about the one year and a half I spent with the Pentecost International Worship Center (PIWC)-Chicago. I was transferred from the Bolingbrook assembly to the PIWC-Chicago. This was in response to a re-organization of the

Center. I was privilege to have 7 elders, 7 deacons, and 7 deaconesses (total presbytery of 21) but the membership was around 50 adults. The elders were: Joseph K. Painstil, Richard Osei, Francis Agyei, Isaiah Ayiku, Nene Ofori McCarthy, Stephen Anokye, and my good self. The deacons were-Mark Williams, Joseph Gyan, Rockson Acheampong, Hayford Asare Baffour, Edmund Boateng, and Edmund Mensah. The deaconesses were-Eunice Antwi-Nsiah, Grace Yannum Kenney, Gloria Dzidey, Grace Williams, Beatrice Asare, Hannah Anokye, and Dr. Adufah.

Around this time, the Chicago church operated a shift system, where the PIWC worshipped between 8:30am to 11:00am and the Akan service was held between 11:00am to 1:30pm. The assembly did not have many members because the presbytery was about half of the total membership. For that reason, ministry leaders did not have assistants let alone other executive members. The plague I received during the 20th Anniversary of the Chicago Church had the following citation:

The Church of Pentecost U.S.A.,Inc-Chicago District
Presented to:
Elder George Appiah-Sokye
For Your Outstanding Leadership and Tireless Service as a
Presiding Elder at PIWC Assembly
Chicago District from 2008-2009
Your Work in the Lord's Vineyard has Not gone unnoticed and
we pray that your territory be blessed and expanded in the will of God
On June 30, 2013
By: Reverend Michael Agyemang Amoako
District Pastor

During this time, there was the involvement of all officers; especially, the eldership was exposed to all aspects of ministry. I remember, when I assigned an elder to perform the naming of a baby, he thought that was the preserve of the presiding elders. A new level of financial transparency and reporting was pursued. I thank God that the Center was able to manage its finances well to be able to raise the down payment for the acquisition of the church van. I also thank God that almost all the deacons are now elders and a few presiding elders and some of the young adults have finished Colleges at different levels. Those who were in the children's ministry are in colleges. One of the deacons has been called into Full-Time Ministry of the Church of Pentecost in 2021. To God be the glory!

Bolingbrook Assembly-I was not around when the Bolingbrook assembly was established but I joined the church from Ghana in May 2007. In Part I of my relationship with this church, I worshipped with the Bolingbrook Assembly of the Church of Pentecost U.S.A., Inc in the United States of America. As discussed above, I was transferred to the PIWC-Chicago during the 2007 End of Year Presbytery Meeting held in Chicago at the 8600 South Kilpatrick Avenue. I met the following officers-Elders- Albert A. Buabeng (presiding elder), Amoh Broni, James Boasiako, Augustine Williams; the deacons were-Hayford Asare Baffour (financial secretary), John Appiah, Nii Cudjoe (secretary), Nicholas Agyemang, Emmanuel Darko, and Sarpong. The deaconesses were- Francisca Buabeng, Adelaide Appiah, Angelina (Kesse) Eshun, Juliana Saka, Beatrice Asare, and Esther Ankobiah. I returned on transfer back to the Bolingbrook assembly in 2012 after returning from Ghana. In 2012, the opportunity to purchase a 20,000 square footer building was presented to this church, which had spent over a decade in worshipping at different locations. A request for permission to acquire this building was made in the same year, followed by a special purpose submittal to the Village of Romeoville.

PLATEAU STAGE

This phase of faith, foundation, and focus is presented to give meaning to my involvement in the Church of Pentecost in the United States of America in general and the Romeoville district in particular. I highlight my role in church building from the local level to the national level. The acquisition of the new building for the Bolingbrook provided a lot of opportunities involving the creation of a district but the building was located in Romeoville so the church could no longer be called Bolingbrook. Consequently, the user-friendly building was named after the founder of the Church of Pentecost-McKeown Worship Center (MWC) and instead of one assembly, the available facility permitted the creation of two assemblies from the existing branch with different focus. While *the MWC-Central* continued the legacy of the Bolingbrook assembly, *the MWC-PIWC* was established with a concentration in the development of the young adults of the church and also to reach out to other nationals.

ROMEOVILLE DISTRICT- The Romeoville district was created in 2014 by the General Council of the Church held in Accra. I was privilege to serve in the very first District Executive Committee, composed of the following- Pastor Benjamin Dankyi (Chair), Elders-Nana Adjepong (District secretary), Nicholas Agyemang (District Financial Secretary), Gerald Osei-Bonsu, Hayford Asare Baffour, Eric Heduvor, James Boasiako, Albert A. Buabeng (Regional/National deacon), and my good self. A plaque was given to me at the Dedication of the McKeown Worship Center on July 20, 2014 with this citation:

The Church of Pentecost U.S.A., Inc.
*** Leadership Appreciation Award***
Presented to:
Elder George Appiah-Sokye
In Recognition of Your Generosity, Dedication, and Special Skills

On Behalf of the Chicago-Romeoville District
May God Bless You
McKeown Worship Center Dedication-2014

McKeown Worship Center (MWC): Central- As I indicated above, the MWC-Central is the offshoot of the Bolingbrook assembly. The presbytery members I have worked with in the MWC-Central is composed of the following: Elders- Hayford Asare Baffour (Presiding elder), Nsafoah Boakye, Amoh Broni, John Appiah, Augustine Williams, Dr. Nana Appah Dankyi, Oheneba Boadi, David Antwi Boakye, James Boasiako, Kofi Ferguson Haizel, and Eric Heduvor. The deacons were-Emmanuel Darkoh, Charles Aborah, Peter Attakorah, Paul Fosu, Willies Owusu, and Francis Atobrah. In addition to the list of deaconesses listed above, including- Francisca Buabeng, Adelaide Appiah, Angelina (Kesse) Eshun, Juliana Saka, Beatrice Asare, and Esther Ankobiah The other deaconesses are as follows: Cynthia Amoh Broni, Florence Boasiako, Rebecca Modey, Roseta Cann, Faustina Fiankoh, Nana Yaa Poku, Gladys Humedo (Awonye), and Hagar Yeboah.

For the period that I have been with this assembly, I have served as a secretary of the Local Marriage Committee, under the able chairmanship of Elder Charles Nsafoah Boakye and Deaconess Beatrice Asare. Indeed, we served at least 6 years, handling about 30 cases. Out of this number, 2 cases did not end up in marriage and we have had 2 unfortunate separations (divorce). Likewise, I have been a Bible Study teacher and also a Bible study Co-Ordinator for the church. I have been involved with the training of financial officers in the district and beyond. I was actively involved with membership database administration (MWC Special Communities Project), and was assisted by Elder Kofi Haizel and Brother Nelson Koomson. Similarly, my strategic role has revolved around providing *liaison* to support both the front and back offices. The Romeoville School of Ministry also

381

presented another opportunity to be involved in the training of leaders of the church. On the eve of my transfer from the MWC-Central to MWC-PIWC, I received a plaque with the inscription:

The Church of Pentecost U.S.A., Inc.
The Church of Pentecost U.S.A., Inc-Romeoville District-
McKeown Worship Center
Plaque of Appreciation
Elder Dr. George Appiah-Sokye
Member of the Local Finance Committee (2012-2018)
Thank you for Your Dedicated Service to God and the Church
2019
Presented by
Reverend Benjamin Dankyi

I portend that we should not allow accomplishments to define who we are; rather our faith in God.

MWC-PIWC-I assumed duty at the MWC-PIWC on March 17, 2019 on transfer from MWC-Central. I am focused on the development of the next crop of Christian leaders; through – (1) Leadership Academy, (2) New Converts Orientation Program, and (3) Preparing Sons and Daughters for Marriage. These discipleship programs are deployed by leveraging technology for development (see also Chapter 14). My passion is to encourage young adults to combine both education and spirituality, fashioned along the Pauline and Mosaic models.

I contend that there is the need to allow the young ones to lead and make all the mistakes for us to correct them while we are alive so that we will not be thinking about the future of the church in our old age. Again, at times when you have discussion with the young ones on marriage, there appears to be a disconnect in their worldviews and so we need to ingrain in them that the Church is still interested in marriage because it is Biblical.

The leadership structure at the PIWC is as follows: (I) Elder Dr. Nana Appah Dankyi (Presiding elder), Elder Nana Agyapong, Elder Albert Osei Afranie, and myself; Deaconesses- Anita Adjepong and Clara Attimuh; and Deacons-Isaac Amanor. (II) Other leaders include the following: Brothers- Dr. Schwarltcouf Sintim Aboagye, Michael Nyarko (Assistant secretary/Secretary), and Kwame Kyei Amoah; Sisters- Bridget Mawuse Amenyo (Secretary), Yaa Dufie (Treasurer), and Hannah Afi Torso (financial secretary). The membership list of the McKeown Worship Center (MWC) Pentecost International Worship Center (PIWC) of Romeoville, Illinois as of April 15, 2021 is provided in the table below.

	THE CHURCH OF PENTECOST U.S.A., INC. PIWC-ROMEOVILLE						
	LIST OF MEMBERS AS OF APRIL 15, 1964						
	S/No.	Name			S/No.	Name	
	1	Agnes Amoh			65	Lydia Acquaah	
	2	Sally Buabeng			66	Michael Attakorah	
	3	Prince Jeffrey Boadi			67	Miles Afriyie	
	4	Keziah Buabeng			68	Nana Dickson	
	5	Jared Buabeng			69	Nana Osei	
	6	Nana Ama Nti			70	Nana Yaa Dufie	
	7	Elder Nana Appah-Dankyi			71	Natasha Donkor	
	8	Sharon Nkpe			72	Nii Okine	
	9	Elder Nana Adjepong			73	Obedina Gyamera	
	10	Rita Ayisi			74	Orgetience Appiah-Sokye	
	11	Mcjane Yeboah			75	Priest Bonsu	
	12	Nana Pokuaa Nicole Cann-Duah			76	Priscilla Adobah	
	13	Gabriel Nkpe			77	Priscilla Koomson	
	14	Carmen Awinongya			78	Rebecca Poku-Adusei	
	15	Schwarltcouf Sintim-Aboagye			79	Richard Effah-Appiah	
	16	Yaa Karikari			80	Richard Ofusu-Hene	
	17	Emmanuel Yiadom			81	Sally Sintim-Aboagye	
	18	Noel Princess Yiadom			82	Samuel Acquah	

19	Sebastian Ofori Yiadom		83	Sophia Frimpong
20	Jeffrey Ofori Yiadom		84	Stephen Pianzina
21	Elder George Appiah-Sokye		86	Sylvester Poku Adusei
22	Mrs. Appiah-Sokye		87	Vetona Ama Sarpong
23	Joann Asare		88	Vera Osei
24	Priscilla Asare		89	Veronica Osei
25	Jesse Asare		90	Doris Appah-Dankyi
26	Adwoa Coffie		91	Nana Kwame Appah-dankyi
27	Alex Bonsu		92	Nana Yaa Appah-dankyi
28	Andrew Nelson		93	Chief Appah-Dankyi
29	Andy Aborah		94	Sequita Bonsu
30	Deaconess Anita Adjepong		95	Randy Appiah
31	Audrey Eshun		96	Ama Dankwah
32	Austin Adjei		97	Tracey Moreland
33	Beatrice Okine		98	Fantasia Berko-Awuah
34	Bernard Eshun		99	Emmanuella Gyamera
35	Bill Bedell		100	Abena Coffie
36	Brandy Antwi-Boachie		101	Michelle Duah
37	Gladys Baffour		102	Lernard D
38	Bridget Amenyo		103	Ella Okai
39	Bridget Amponsah		104	Afia Acheampong
40	Charlotte Nkpe		105	Derrick Boateng
41	Clement Yeboah		106	Biance Jackson
42	David Okai		107	Solomon Awinongya
43	Daasebre Appah-Dankyi		108	Elder Albert Osei
44	Drew Sintim-Aboagye		109	Priscilla Boadi
46	Enoch Antwi		110	Goldie Amoah
47	Nana Emmanuel Acheampong		111	Emmanuella Akua Okai
48	Esther Darko		112	Daniel Darko
49	Eric Sarpong		113	Michael Owusu-Nyarko
50	Eric Nyantekyi		114	Freda Opoku-Agyemang
51	Freda Poku Agyemang		115	Sebastian Yiadom
52	Junior Frimpong Sintim-Aboagye		116	Josh Aborah
53	Geopat Appiah-Sokye		117	Deacon Isaac Amanor
54	Gideon Okai		118	Emmanuella Abena Gyamerah

55	Gloria Awinongya		119	Obedina Gyamerah	
56	Halle Agyemang		120	Gideon Awinongya	
57	Hilda Gyeduah		121	Michael Ameyaw	
58	Joel Boasiako		122	Halle Agyekum	
59	Juliana Durowah Coffie		123	Samuel Kissi-Baah	
60	Jesse Agyemang		124	Chelsea Agyekum	
60	Josephine Brobby		125	Shekainah Okai	
62	Kevin Amponsah		126	Gladys Ama Baffour	
63	Kwabena Ankobiah		127	Kwame Asante Ababio	
64	Kwame Kyei Amoah		127	and Many More.	
Source: Membership Database					

DECLINING STAGE

The declining phase of my faith, foundation, and focus will actually *start from the period of my retirement as an elder*. I have not hesitated in letting my intentions known that I plan to retire as an elder at 65 or in 2029 (if God grants me the grace). After my retirement my relevance will be to support and advise the new generation of leaders. Additionally, I will serve as the Spiritual grandpa to the children of current youth in future. I will not be very active but spur the next generation to lead the way and to be allowed to be used by God for His own glory. Meanwhile, my pre-occupation is to help develop the next generation of Christian leaders.

I argue that should be done with intentionality.

OFFICES HELD IN THE CHURCH

I have been actively involved in church activities with the Church of Pentecost. I have assumed a lot of positions including: Presiding Elder (PIWC, Chicago); Assistant District Financial Secretary, Assistant

District Leader of PENTYEM, District Finance Committee, member; Local Secretary; Member, District Executive Committee (Chicago/ Romeoville), Member, National/ Regional Audit Committee, etc.; and an Elder of the church. Apostle (Professor) Opoku Onyinah is quoted as saying: *"we must not be afraid for the church of tomorrow. The simple reason is that <u>we hold the key of tomorrow's church today</u>. What <u>we sell to the church today is what the youth will apply</u> in various forms in the future"* *(Emphasis mine).*

I dare say that the church of today holds the key to the transformation of the youth. The future generation of the church should be at the very center of actions, policies, and practices. When this is done the glory will be unto God and we will be rewarded with the corresponding blessings.

CHRISTIAN DISCIPLINE

Christian discipline is traced to the creation story in the Bible. In the Garden of Eden, man sinned through rebellion and was disciplined by God. In the process, not only was man disciplined but the serpent was also disciplined. Per Galardi (2015, 2006), there are four main reasons for Christian discipline as follows: *purge* out of leaven (1 Corinthians 5:7); *honor* Christ (Psalm 51:4; I Samuel 12:14); *redeem* the believer who has fallen into sin (I Corinthians 5:3-5; II Corinthians 2:6-8); and *deter* others from sin (I Timothy 1:20; I Timothy 5:20). In the Church of Pentecost, discipline is a factor of church survival and has been identified as a variable accounting for the growth of the church by Professor Kingsley Larbi (2001).

Some have argued that the church is not forgiving but the church disciplines and does not punish. I have seen the church evolve over the years by moving away from isolation of disciplined members to that of engagement with disciplined members. By isolation, a separate seating was provided at the back of the church auditorium with some of benches painted in blue or black. The disciplined member was not allowed to participate actively in church activities such as giving testimonies, giving of offertory, and many more. Perhaps, this hard line was in response to the church's covenant with God, which requires the church to purge out the leaven, otherwise, God will step in to purge the church from time to time.

THE 'TALE' OF THREE DEACONS

The caption of this section can be misleading because true stories have been recounted, except that I have concealed the real identities of the persons involved. Mistakes can be committed by anybody and so nobody is immune to human error; irrespective of social standing and position. Barely a day passes without the mention of the name of a prominent person in society falling into a scandal in one shape or form. The question that is often asked is: *Why did the person commit this mistake?* Society is quick to pronounce judgment at the least opportunity, forgetting that if care is not taken such acts can happen to anybody. The noise tends to be loudest if the person involved is considered to be a good Christian or influential person in society. As if errors committed by the least in society is not an issue. In one of the churches, I worshipped in the past, I met a few deacons of the church. In the spate of a decade, three deacons have found themselves in one trouble or the other. I am using the pseudonyms-Deacon 1(D1), Deacon 2(D2), and Deacon 3(D3) to tell the stories.

Deacon 1-This deacon was very serviceable to all members of the church and as part of the follow-up of new converts of the church; got involved in one way or the other with a new convert in the church who was a lady. Deacon 1 attempted to have an amorous relationship with this lady, but the lady countered the advances with the Word of God she had received from the pulpit. In an attempt to succeed at all cost,

Deacon 1 told her that having sexual relationship was normal because all the elders in the church have their sexual *partners* aside their wives in the church.

The lady trusted the deacon of the church and gave in to his advances. However, the lady continued to live in guilt because the messages she received from the pulpit was incongruous with the information given her by the deacon who was following her up. Additionally, she could not fathom why the same elders whom she has been told to be sleeping around with sexual partners in the church could also be speaking on holiness, purity, righteousness. One day, she presented her dilemma to the leadership and gave all the details of what has transpired between herself and Deacon 1. The matter was investigated and both parties were given hearing per the laws of natural justice and the deacon was disciplined. The lady was not disciplined because she was a new convert and also took the right action by reporting the matter the leadership.

The lesson is that officers visiting the opposite sex should endeavor to be accompanied by other people such as their spouses or other officers because the perception of people and the need to protect one's integrity. This measure might not necessarily prevent any wrongdoing, but it can be a good way of protecting oneself.

Deacon 2-This deacon was the longest serving deacon among the three deacons under consideration. The family had a domestic help and the deacon made sexual advances towards this young lady, but the lady was afraid because of the messages she had been hearing from the pulpit; as well as, the respect for her madam (wife of the deacon). Deacon 2 assured the lady that he will buy her a sowing machine and pay for her to learn a vocation. Upon this assurance, it paved the way for the deacon to be sleeping with her during the period that the wife of the deacon had given birth and also anytime, the wife went for all-night services. On few occasions, the deacon will sneak into the hall in the middle of the night to have a quick one with her.

This situation continued for a while, but the lady was not comfortable with what was going on. So, she approached the senior apprentice of the deacon to plead with the deacon on her behalf to stop having sex with her because she deemed it as a sin. The senior apprentice came to report the matter to the leadership. The matter was brought before the leadership and the lady's account was determined to be accurate and truthful. At the end of the day, the deacon was disciplined. The lesson borders on the need for self-control, involving restraining of one's sexual passion. Additionally, *masters(mistresses)* should not exploit the vulnerabilities of their *servants(maids)* to their advantage; but should see the opportunity as their God-given privilege to influence them positively.

Deacon 3-This deacon was transferred to a new assembly and later became the presiding elder of the church. I know this deacon commanded a lot of financial resources but I cannot tell if that contributed in any ways towards the problem. It came to light in the process of time that this man has been sleeping around with the single ladies in the church. Not one, not two, but quite a few. The matter was investigated and he was disciplined. The lesson learned is that the people we lead and, keep in the church and other capacities as leaders do not belong to us. Per Exodus 3:1, the flock that was tendered by Moses belonged to Jethro (the father-in-law) and so the church members entrusted to church leaders belong to God. There is going to be a day of accountability; So, leaders have to be careful how the members entrusted to them are handled.

SUSPENDED LADY RISES TO THE OCASSION

I worshipped in an assembly of the Church of Pentecost in the late 1990s, where one of our young adult ladies got pregnant out of wedlock. The lady admitted to her mistake and was taken through counseling before been disciplined. Interestingly, the young lady did not relent in her involvement in church activities. You would not know that she had been suspended if you are not privy to her disciplinary action. After the young lady delivered, the young man who impregnated her agreed to marry her and that led to her restoration into the church. I describe this lady as the one who caused the presbytery to regret the suspension meted out to her. The purpose for telling this story is to explain that Christian discipline is not pleasant but it is intended to build up and not to destroy. As humans we have our frailties, which can be attributed to the fall of man in the Garden of Eden. It calls for carefulness and getting constantly in tune with God.

In recent times, church discipline has been characterized by *grace, love,* and *mercy.* For that reason, the church celebrates with restored members for making it through the process; through the extension of the right hand of fellowship and in few cases such persons have been allowed to take part in communion with the presbytery or leadership. Discipline has been viewed as an essential component of overseeing Christ's sheep to help troubled believers. Consequently, discipline is provided for in the Bible, the Constitution of the church; as well as, Ministers' Handbook to *regulate* the officers and members of the church. The glory of God in the church is considered paramount because it is believed that the purity of the church is intricately linked to the presence of God in His church. Likewise, the spiritual benefits for members are enormous because it could avert reproach upon the name of Christ; as well as, repentance of the transgressor due to the warning to the congregation.

LESSONS LEARNED

One, *Celebrating specific Christian leaders for specific cause-* I want to celebrate the following Christian leaders: (1) **Reverend Eastwood Anaba-**For establishing his ministry in Northern Ghana; but unlike other ministries, which started in other parts of Ghana but had to be moved to the Capital city of Ghana for whatever reason(s); the headquarters of Reverend Anaba's ministry has remained in the Northern part of Ghana. Another case in point is Reverend Anaba's officiation of the burial (funeral) service of his two children involved in a car accident. This is an uncommon grace to be mentioned. (2) **Pastor Mensah Onumah Otabil** is mentioned for keeping title-*Pastor* throughout his ministry. This unique characteristic is not common because as the leader and founder of the International Central Gospel Church (ICGC), he could have chosen any title to befit his status. I am not against the use of appropriate titles but I find this commendable.

(3) **Apostle James Smith Gyimah** (retired) is mentioned for exercising all the *five-fold* ministries or ascension gifts (apostle, prophet, evangelist, pastor, and teacher) at different times of his ministry. I have seen other believers exercise one, or two, or three; but all the five is not very common. (4) **Apostle Patrick Eninn** (retired) is celebrated for his selflessness. Throughout his ministry he had given financial proceeds from transfers and retirement for greater cause of God and the church. I have followed him keenly from Merry Villas to Agona Swedru, to Nigeria and to Ashiaman. I am not suggesting that everyone should emulate this gesture but I applaud his extra-ordinary graceful heart of giving.

Two, *Writing skills*-Unknown to most people, I actually responded to an alter call into the writing ministry in one of the Half-Night services on campus at University of Ghana, Legon. I wrote the poem on: *Looking unto Jesus*- in the official magazine of the LPU in the 10th anniversary edition. For this reason, writing comes to me naturally. I thank God for the grace of writing. **Three,** *Expanded Vision of the Church of Pentecost*- The logo of the church had given a sense of the expansion of the vision of the church over the years. When I was growing up, the dove symbolizing the Holy Spirit was seen in the logo descending on Ghana. Later on, the dove was seen descending on Africa; and currently, the dove is seen descending on the entire globe. There is no doubt that the church has the entire world in view now.

Four, *Giving God quality time is key*-I battled a lot in 1994 when the call to eldership was unveiled to me. At the time, I had started working after College and had a lot of plans for my future, including furthering my education, exceling in career, and traveling, among other things. Growing up, I saw the toll ministry had on my parents. To give you a sense of what I am talking about, my father regularly went to church on Sundays without taking breakfast but returned after 4:00pm. My parents attended meetings, conventions, funerals relating to the church. After some time, my mother attended Easter conventions (national) and my father attended Christmas convention (regional); however, August conventions were attended by either of them to ensure family stability. My father was the church secretary for over three decades. The church minutes records were kept on his writing desk so I learned minutes writing at home.

When I was called into eldership, I battled with this having regards to what I have alluded to above. I raised three fundamental objections on the basis of the foregoing: (a) I was going to prepare for professional examinations; (b) I am very outspoken for the liking of the church; and (c) the nature of my work does not allow me much time; however, my presiding elder (Elder John Osei Akowuah) gave me words of wisdom by: (i) encouraging me to give quality time to God even as I pursue my purpose in life. To the glory of God, I entered the eldership with an undergraduate qualification but I have gone on to accumulate other academic and professional qualifications. (ii) I was called upon to speak my mind on issues if I feel strongly about them; perhaps, I may be speaking for God; (iii) when God calls, he equips and facilitates.

These pieces of advice have been helpful to me over the years. I must confess that it has not been easy combining ministry with education because at times you are given assignment to perform from both school and the church-equally important. I have seen that some people choose either education or ministry; but I have *combined* both. Yes, some of my dream got delayed by human standards but God has made all things beautiful in his own time (Ecclesiastes 3:11). I encourage the younger generation to combine both ministry and education; as well as, family life.

Five, *Divine provision has been made for the church-* I have come to appreciate that enough financial and human resources have been made available to the church to use. In the process, I think the church should continue to develop systems instead of relying on personalities. Yes, systems are run by personalities; however, systems outlive persons. I want to emphasize that both the front and back offices of the church are equally important.

A lot of people are interested in the front-office ministries because the back-office ministries tend to be obscure. I see the back office as the pivot upon which the wheels of front-office ministries rotate. There is the need to avoid the over-burdening of a few, leading to dwindling efficiency and effectiveness in outcomes. Consequently, the right and available people should be allowed to function in areas of value to the church. A robust system can be a legacy to be bequeathed to the next generation of leaders.

Six, *Transfers-*Transfers are common in the church and different reasons are given but I want to associate myself with the notion that when Men of God are transferred, it the gifts that are transferred and not the persons. The ministers that have been identified in this book brought varied dimensions to ministry because no two ministries are the same. The missing link is the buying and selling of visions. Visions are of less value unless they are sold and bought.

Seven, *Politics and the Church-* I have witnessed countless number of politicians in Ghana joining church services during the period they canvass for votes; yet when these people are voted into office and they do things that attract criticisms from the church, they defend themselves by saying the church is becoming political. The question is: *Accountability and voting, which one is political?*

Eight, *Writing of Books by Ministers of the Gospel-* I view the writing of books as another way of extending the tentacles of the church to a wider population. Literacy works goes beyond the typical congregation reached by the minister. **Nine,** *Discipline with human face-*Growing up as a child, the children sat with suspended members on a bench at the back of the church during services. The disciplinary regime at the time was very stringent. No wonder, discipline was dreaded. The process involved commending the souls of the one being suspended to the devil. This is a very necessary but difficult stage because responses from a few of the people who have been disciplined in past indicate that the effects are unpleasant both physically and emotionally. In recent times, there has been some improvements in the administration of discipline but the overriding consideration should be restoration.

Ten, *Few take away-*I have learned a lot of lessons during the faith, foundation, and focus phase of my life such as the following: (I) the call to eldership has helped to hold my life in check because of the higher standard linked to the calling of God. I do not take lightly God's assigned role of-*custodian of the faith.* I see it as a privilege and a challenge at the same time. (II) I came across a presbytery that was quite *militant* but soon restored normalcy immediately after meetings. I have come to appreciate that disagreements are not the same of enmity. (III) I have also learned that an elder does not allow God's property to be destroyed under his watch; (IV) the church services and programs can be conducted professionally.

(V) The late Elder Professor Kwabia- Boateng (Sychar-Madina) told me that time management is critical for ministerial success, when one is swamped with a lot of responsibilities. (VI) Elder Armah Kesseh

(Madina Central) also spoke on the need to-*Think about stakeholders such as the family and church in all our actions.* (VII) Apostle Amegatcher also ministered on: *What do you do when your child goes wayward?* He offered (a) pray for him or her, (b) teach him or her, (c) love him or her; and (d) provide for him or her. I thank my parents for bequeathing the gift of faith to me. I am eternally grateful. Thank God!

CONCLUSION

Loren Larson writing in the June 2020 edition of *the Evangelist* asserted that *Christian growth and maturity are to be constant in the life of the believer.* Quoting from Joshua 13:1, which stipulates as follows: *"Now Joshua was old and stricken in years; and the Lord said unto him, Thou are old and stricken in years, and there remaineth yet very much land to be possessed"*

Larson (June 2020) provided five points as follows: (1) *The initial victory,* our spiritual growth might be considered as the land that is yet to be possessed; (2) *Growth never ends,* believers must come to terms that the potential for growth is endless; (3) *Applying what we have come to know,* as Christian experience victories upon victories and move from glory to glory.

The truth embraced validates its continued placements in the life of the believer; yet (4) *The process takes time,* some Christians become discouraged and divert from the object of faith. Though it tarries, wait for it, for victory and relief will come! (5) *Acknowledge your inability,* there is much land that needs to be possessed, but we have no strength or faith (keep in mind that Joshua was old by natural standard and diminishing in vitality) in ourselves (Larson, June 2020). I am grateful to Brother Larson (as he is popularly called) for sharing the above insights. I find them very deep and educative.

I wish to comment as follows: *first,* Joshua was *mentored* by Moses before he assumed the reign of leadership in Israel, however, there are no known *mentees* of Joshua in the Holy Scriptures. I stand to be corrected. If this assumption is correct; then, there was the need for him to respond to the unfinished business of possessing additional land even at an advanced age. I guess if he had trained others people, the divine assignments and responsibility could have been shared because delegation is founded in the Bible (Moses and Jethro).

I contend that all the apostles and prophets I came to meet in the church during my childhood are dead with the passage time. Likewise, I have seen very great ministers of God from start to finish in ministry in my life time. I can cite Apostles-Albert Amoah, J.S. Gyimah, Ackah Baidoo, Isaac Amoako; as well as, Pastor Robert Odame, and many more. Likewise, I have seen elders, deacons, and deaconesses, and members phased-out. Consequently, the reality of old age and death is inevitable. I have the mindset that I will not live forever.

Second, I agree that Christian growth is endless but I argue that under this *life cycle* of faith, foundation, and focus framework; Christian growth increases at an increasing rate initially and later increase at a diminishing rate. Suggesting that human life has an end. As a result, *third*, the entire Christian life cycle takes time because it revolves around processes, experiences (both positive and negative); and for that reason, honesty is required in acknowledging weaknesses, shortfalls, and inabilities. As humans, it is the grace of God that propels us into greater heights.

Lastly, there is the urgent need to apply what we have come to know through experiences and knowledge and this is the driving force behind the writing of this book. To God Be the Glory!

CHAPTER 19

※

SERVICE TO HUMANITY

THE OVERARCHING PURPOSE OF LIFE is to gravitate towards service to God and service to humanity. Arguably, while service to mankind is deemed as service to God; contrarily, service to God does not necessarily imply service to man. The duality in service can be linked to the whole concept of man- as a body, soul, and spirit. The apparent contradiction arises because we strongly ascribe different levels of reality to autobiography and to fiction in experience, privileging so-called 'reality', when in effect there is only one consistent level of fiction (Lovat, 2019). Humanity exists to *create* and *solve* problems. Consequently, once a problem is solved, another spontaneously emerges. Just as economic theory teaches about the insatiable needs of man; when a person aspires and achieve a feat, a corresponding burden surfaces, begging the question as to why the problem was addressed in the first place.

By way of illustration, suppose an individual staying in a rented room decides to buy or build a house. Just as this goal is achieved, other issues begin to crop up such as the provision of security, maintenance of the landscape, repairs and maintenance of the property; as well as, meeting new bills that are linked to property ownership. This same argument can be made for people who enter the world of work at any level of education. Initially, very excited because of the experience and financial benefits associated with the job but all too soon come to realize that the position or role occupied could have been better. For that reason, decides to go back to school or go through continuous personal or professional development to make up for the knowledge gap.

I am well placed to offer service to humanity in varied forms because of exposure to the following: professional audit, taxation and fiscal policy, accounting services, internal audit outsourcing; as well as, finance, accounting and tax training services, and business support. Furthermore, involvement in customer care strategy, business planning, budgeting, and forecasting, resource audit, and internal control projects. Likewise, special financial and operational audit, preparation of manuals-operational and financial, and review of internal controls. More so, financial management training, valuation of assets, audit of fixed assets and register, and how to manage delinquent loans.

Leadership coaches are needed for the younger generation with some of the following skills: *first*, leadership, communication, analytics, problem-solving, moral values, and tolerance. *Second*, guidance and counseling, respect, pursuit of excellence, ownership, singular achievement, and implementation. *Third*, overcoming compulsion, incredible engagement and execution, robust life trajectory, ramping up the pieces, unyielding commitment to improvement, and obsessiveness to purpose of life. *Four*, flattening the life cycle curve, immersing oneself in activities with a mission, counter-mediocrity, and going for margins that exceed expectation. *Lastly*, value-addition and collaboration.

As shared in chapter 3, I was school prefect and house prefect in secondary school (High School) and sixth form days. I have benefited from many leadership coaches, including my headmaster Daniel Atakora (now deceased) who took advantage of our morning assembly sessions to impact knowledge to our taught on some philosophical teachings from Plato, Aristotle, Socrates, and many more. At the time we did not appreciate the *life skills*. While we can control some things, there are others that cannot be controlled. For example, I was the District secretary of the National Service Personnel Association from 1985-1986 before I entered College.

TOPICS OF INTEREST

This section of the textbook is devoted to some personal topics of interest and I hope that readers will find them useful; for application to daily lives through the life lessons presented.

LESSONS FROM THE ANIMAL KINGDOM

The theme that runs through the creation story in Genesis is *"And God saw that everything he has made was good"*; culminating into the creation of fishes, birds, livestock, small animals, and wild animals (Genesis 1:20-25). The critical interplay of the creator and the creation is demonstrated in the creation story; and as a result, the role played by some animals in the life of human beings is instructive. Arguably, some animals from different classifications can present useful life lessons to mankind. In this section, a few of the animals which stand out will be explored: (1) In the *bird category*, *the fowl* is considered as an animal with a short-sighted view of things. Fowls fly at very low level and get back to the ground immediately; consequently, do not maintain buoyancy in the air. Additionally, the fowl is fond of always looking down and does not look into the horizon to explore the environment. A characteristic of low achievers.

Comparatively, (2) another bird-*the eagle* presents a different perspective to humanity. The eagle is characterized by visual acuity, supersonic speed, flying at higher altitude, and preparation for endurance. The eagle is known to fly at higher altitude and moves at a supersonic speed while coping with buoyancy. This is symptomatic of setting of higher objectives backed by long-range goals; as well as, setting one's eyes on the ultimate (higher) goal. Again, from time to time, the eagle has been determined to shake off its feathers to allow for new feathers to develop and emerge; thereby, developing capacity for pain and endurance. This virtue in the eagle is needed in the human race now than ever before.

(3) The *peacock* or *the turkey* is another bird I want to mention. This bird symbolizes arrogance and pride. The suggestion is to be mindful of pride, which has been established without doubt to go before destruction. It pays to be humble because pride can spell doom for people. In *the creeping category*, (4) I will mention *the ant* for effective planning. The ant is believed to gather adequate food during the summer or dry season in preparation for the *evil day* (Proverbs 6:6-7) for the day that it is not able to go out in search of food because of the vagaries of the weather. Keep in mind the size of this creature. In the *wild life category*, (5) I want to comment on *the Giraffe*, as the kind of animal who feeds on the fresh shoot of trees; and for that reason, reaches out to the top. The giraffe is a motivator for high achiever to crave towards self-actualization.

In *the amphibian category*, (6) I will consider *the toad or frog*. The true length of this creature can only be established at death. While hopping on daily basis, it becomes difficult to establish its exact length. By implication, the correct assessment of a person can be determined when the person is no more. I remember a story of a man who was known to be very rich in Mampong-Ashanti (Ghana). When he died a lot of nephews were bracing up to succeed the uncle but it turned out that this uncle was living on past glory, meaning that he was living on bank overdrafts. The extent of his indebtedness came to the fore when he died.

In *the reptile category*, (7) I want to discuss *the snake or serpent*. The snake has been described as subtle in the Scriptures in Genesis (Origin) of the Bible; but what is in-sighting about the snake is its ability to hide; while flourishing. A snake can live obscure life such as hiding under uncompleted buildings, trees near human settlements, in holes, or even in unassuming locations to avoid spotlights. By the time, it is seen it has grown in size and multiplied in number. A good strategy in life is to do a lot of things behind the scenes and by the time you are exposed in the limelight, you are ready for your purpose in life. Many times, when people are exposed pre-maturely, if care is not taken; they tend to fall by the wayside. In today's job market, recruiters have been accessing information about prospective employees through social media platforms. The youth is admonished to be circumspect in the nature of exposure to social media.

RESPONSIBLE FATHERHOOD

The United States Census Bureau has established a father absence debacle in America because 19.7 million children live without a father in the home, translating into 1 in 4; and as a consequence, a case can be made for a father variable in every social ill in America (National Fatherhood Initiative-Retrieved from http://www.fatherhood.org -accessed on 08/24/2020). The number of births which occurs to unmarried parents has been increasing over the years; from 4 percent (1940) to 11 percent (1970) to 33 percent (2002). Fatherhood is under serious threat.

Eighty-five (85) percent of all children who show behavior disorders came from fatherless homes; because 43 percent of United States children live without their fathers (CDC; United States Census Bureau).

Yet, *"children need a dad to be anchor that stabilizes their youth as they are pulled in every direction"* (*The consequences of the absent dad*, retrieved from http://wwwallprodad.com -accessed on 08/24/2020). However, the salutary effects of being raised by two married, biological parents depends on the quality of care parents can provide (Jaffee, Moffitt, Caspi,& Taylor, February 2003). The natural order of the family is for the man to have authority to lead and when that authority is abdicated, a vacuum is created that will certainly be filled elsewhere (*The consequences of the absent dad*, Retrieved from http://wwwallprodad.com -accessed on 08/24/2020). Historically, men are expected to assume their rightful place in the family because they are deemed the image and the glory of God.

My remote ancestry has been discussed in the beginning pages of this text (Chapter 1), as well as, my Christian parentage (Chapter 2). In a conversation with one of my cousins, he offered: *"George, you came from a stable home"* and that can contribute to a balanced Christian living. Several young men structure their personal goals and their relationship with families and partners in terms of providing emotional and financial stability for them (Enderstein, & Boonzaier, October 2015). The ramifications of absent dads are *increased chances of behavioral issues, depression, higher dropout rate, insecurity, bad grades, and many more* (*The consequences of the absent dad*, Retrieved from http://wwwallprodad. com -accessed on 08/24/2020). The variables accounting for absent dad have been discussed below.

There is a higher drop-out rates in high schools; and for that reason, 71 percent of high school dropouts come from fatherless homes per the National Principals Association Report on the State of High Schools (*The consequences of the absent dad*, Retrieved from http://wwwallprodad. com -accessed on 08/24/2020). Likewise, the Department of Health and Human Services estimated that 71 percent of pregnant teens have no dad present in their life (*The consequences of the absent dad*, Retrieved from http://wwwallprodad.com -accessed on 08/24/2020). Similarly, the accelerated odds due to the absence of dads leads to substance abuse, which stems from the feeling of abandonment; and as a result, the use of drugs becomes an attempted way of escape (*The consequences of the absent dad*, Retrieved from http://wwwallprodad.com -accessed on 08/24/2020).

I argue that dads should be present in the life of children such that they can provide guidance, leadership, and trust to stem the tide of higher dropout rates.

The absentee father has resulted in the following: **first**, (a) lower job security, (b) increased mental and social behavior issues, (c) seven times more likelihood to becoming pregnant, and (d) five times the average rate of suicidal tendencies. **Second,** (e) more likelihood to face neglect and abuse, (f) increased rate of divorce and relationship issues, (g) consistently reduced mean income levels, and (h) twice the greater risk of infant mortality. **Lastly,** (i) thirty-two (32) times the average rate of incarceration, (j) four times greater risk of poverty, (k) more likelihood to committing crime, and (l) two times more likely to suffer obesity (National Fatherhood Initiative, n.d.-Retrieved from http:// www.fatherhood.org; *The 9 devastating effects of the absent father,* June 2015-Retrieved from http://www.thefathercode.com; cdn2.hubspot. net -accessed on 08/24/2020).

McKenna Meyers (Therapist and Grief Counselor in Oakland, California), writing in February 2020 on *"Fatherless daughters: How growing up without a dad affect women"* observed as follows: **One,** growing up without a dad shape who you are; because;

"Fathers provide their daughters with a masculine example. They teach their children about respect and boundaries and help put daughters at ease with other men throughout their lives...So if she did not grow up with a proper example, she will have less insight and she'll be more likely to go for a man that will replicate the abandonment of her father" (Retrieved from http://www.wehavekids.com -accessed on 08/24/2020).

Two, the negative effects of *fatherless daughters* revolve around susceptibility to addiction, as well as, eating disorder, low self-esteem, and depression (Retrieved from http://www. wehavekids.com -accessed on 098/24/2020). Specifically:

- *Per Debora Moskovitch (author and divorce consultant),fatherless daughters have self-esteem issues;*
- *According to Denna Babul and Karin Louise (authors), fatherless daughters are more prone to depression;*

- *Pamela Thomas (author of fatherless daughters) asserted that fatherless daughters struggle to maintain and build relationships;*
- *Fatherless daughters are more likely to become sexually active earlier but girls who are close to their dads are less likely to get pregnant as teens; and*
- *Marcia Herrin and Nancy Matsumoto (authors) find that fatherless daughters are more likely to have eating disorders.*

Many of the men in Kavita's (2007) study assumed the same gendered parenting roles and responsibilities of their fathers from both men and women to conform to established gender norms; fulfilled and justified a range of irresponsible fathering and fatherhood practices by drawing upon prevalent gender ideologies and pressures from both men and women to conform to established gender norms. Against this background, I call on men to stand in the gap to provide the hedge for the family; especially, their children to advance into the unconquered territory in parentage. As a result, men should provide leadership in the family. Likewise, men should be dependable to shun any apathetic tendencies associated with the raising of their own children; as well as, those children who look up to them for mentorship.

Several men have spoken about the tendency for parents to bring their children to live with them in the towns so as to take advantage of better education prospects as well as to conform to nuclear household ideologies propagated by the church (Kavita, 2007). The mindset of some traditional African men is that:

(I) *Children belong on the spouse's family*; especially, among those who inherit matrilineally. Some young men deliberately shift focus and actively renegotiate their identity through the choice to take responsibility for their children (Enderstein, & Boonzaier, October 2015).

(II)   *A child without a father has an English name called <u>bastard</u>,* but there is no such name for a child without a mother. Existing studies tend to paint a picture of young men as subjects of risk factor vulnerability and negative outcomes who become uninvolved fathers (Enderstein, & Boonzaier, October 2015). Nevertheless, Bock (February 2000) finds the following: *One,* that single motherhood can be by choice, those who feel entitled to enter solo motherhood because they possess four essential attributes of *age, responsibility, emotional maturity,* and *fiscal capability; two,* that single mothers by choice can utilize *economics, moral,* and *religion* as justifications to further legitimize their decisions; and *lastly,* that the single mothers by choice can present themselves as *ethical, competent,* and *mainstream* mothers (Bock, February 2000).

(III)   *A child will ultimately look for the father when (s)he is grown.* Some men have questioned the gendered parenting roles that they were expected to perform arguing that the role of disciplinarian harmed their relationship with their children.

Marriage may not be the answer to the problems faced by some children living in single parents' families unless their fathers can become reliable sources of emotional and economic support (Jaffee, Moffitt, Caspi,& Taylor, February 2003). However, there is evidence that children who grow up in families headed by a single parent have worse socioeconomic outcomes than do those raised by married, biological parents (Waller, 2002). Unfortunately, there is no heavy price paid in African societies for men who fail to take responsibility for their children. As a result, the system tends to condone the practice of neglect of children by fathers. Consequently, some policy makers have called for society to increase the number of paternities established for children born outside marriage and to promote tougher enforcement of child support orders (Waller, 2002, p.3).

I intend to provide the next generation with a lasting legacy through the writing of this book so that when everything is said and done, the family would be acclaimed as the center of gravity as the caption of Chapter 27 has suggested. I say so because I have identified some of the factors partly responsible for the debacle, as follows: (i) *some men wanting to be fathers but not husbands because of economic consideration; (ii) experimentation in youthfulness; (iii) maturity in age vs. emotional maturity; (iv) lack of appreciation of fatherhood; (v) lack of self-control; (vi) irresponsible character developed from childhood;(vii) cycle of broken homes; (viii) institutional breakdown involving-the church, schools, marriage, and society; (ix) absence of role models in society; and (x) societal value system vulnerabilities.* I will leave further explanation of these variables for the reader to explore.

I have recounted in other Chapters, I have 8 siblings and the count in the family is over 100, involving nephews, nieces, and their off springs. I have witnessed at first hand the absence of some dads in the life of a few of the members of the family. Contrarily, I have been a beneficiary of the wise counsel of my father, who had admonished me to learn to the level permitted by the grace of God, providing me a blueprint towards the handling of failure, adding the teachings book (the Bible) to my courses of study in school, and not taking part in unnecessary agitations. I am refocusing attention on the phenomenon to offer valuable lessons to be taken seriously because irresponsible fatherhood is more than just a phenomenon but it is part of a grand scheme against the sanctity of the family.

THE WEEPING BRIDE

I sincerely appreciate the trust reposed in me to walk to the altar one of our own. Before the wedding ceremony of one of the members of my local church by name- *Akosua* (not the real name) on one beautiful

Saturday in year 2000, I was signaled by one of the deaconesses of our local church to come out of the Madina West Sanctuary of the Church of Pentecost in Madina, Accra (Ghana). Just as the wedding service has commenced, I was brought to a waiting vehicle carrying the bride to the church and I saw a weeping bride for the first time in my life. Weddings are expected to be joyous occasion for the marrying couple, especially the bride; yet in this particular case, it was a sorrowful experience for this bride. I learned that the father of the bride had refused to accompany and walk the daughter to the altar because he claimed that the son-in-law had been insolent to him. For that reason, an aura of uncertainty surrounded her fate.

Prior to this day, the church had witnessed the performance of the customary marriage rites, during which the same father received the *bride price* of the daughter from the family of the son-in-law. Traditionally, that was when the marriage was established. In my opinion, the purpose of the wedding is to invoke God's blessing upon the couple as they begin their lifelong marital life. Therefore, the acceptance of the bride price by the father and the abandonment of his duty to walk the daughter was a contradiction. As a *spiritual father* of the members of the church, coupled with the witnessing of the marriage rites during which the father collected the items on the list provided by the family from the groom's family; I was in a better place to step into action to walk *my daughter* to the alter on behalf of the church to the glory of God. I remain grateful for this role to bring smiles back the face of this bride.

FINANCING ASPECTS OF EDUCATION

My desire has been to deduce routine daily applications from sophisticated concepts and for that reason, furthering my education was key to the achievement of this objective. **Step 1**- I applied for a three-year study leave dated January 27, 1995 to pursue Master of

Business Administration (MBA) at the University of Ghana School of Business Administration, or Institute of Chartered Accountants, Ghana (ICAG) in the Ghana Institute of Professional Studies (IPS). Later on, I forwarded my admissions letter WBD/MA/IPS.2 of December 4,1995 to the Commissioner of Internal Revenue Service per my letter C8244 of December 27, 1995. My study leave application for 1996 was recommended by the Chief Inspector of Taxes' CRC 2181 of November 22, 1995.

Step 2-An application for a three-year study leave with pay was based on admission letter from the Ghana Institute of Professional Studies dated June 5, 1997. **Step 3**-An invitation letter was received from the IPS dated November 11,1998 to attend interview for admissions on December 14,1998. I had deferred my prior 1996 admissions to 1998. **Step 4**-Another letter of mine *viz.* C8244 of February 10, 1999 was sent to the Commissioners and I informed the Commissioner of IRS of my admission and also attached a copy of my Graduate Admission letter DGS:1 of September 7, 1999 per my letter LTC 8244 of September 1999; as well as, the IRS' of December 22, 1999. **Step 5**-I re-applied for study leave per my letter of February 17, 2000 to pursue Master of Business Administration (MBA-Accounting Option) at the University of Ghana. On March 28, 2000, a request for permission to pursue a course of study per my letter C8244 of March 28, 2000 was sent to the Commissioner of the Internal Revenue Service setting out the facts as have been enumerated above.

An old adage states that "if you think education is expensive, try ignorance" My paternal grand-mother owned a lot of farmlands, which were available to the children so my father released some out for production sharing or share cropping arrangements and the monies realized from some of those arrangements helped in paying for most of the cost of secondary school education. I was also involved in farming as I have explained. At the undergraduate level, the financial support came from subsidy from the Government of Ghana. I have provided a narrative of how some aspects of my education was financed. For example, I have mentioned my own brother, William Appenteng Appiah for providing me with financial and material support in diverse ways, including clothing and footwear; as well as, educational materials such as textbooks, scientific calculator, radio cassette player, and so on. Likewise, Brother Willie gave me a slightly used vehicle for my comfort in the early 2000s.

I applied to the School of International Relations of the International University of Japan (IUJ) to read International relations. My statement of purpose gave: (1) a brief background about myself, (2) my reasons for choosing international relations and also Japan, (3) future aspirations, (4) research interest, and conclusion.

On three occasions, I applied to University of Ghana Business School (UGBS) for the Master of Business Administration (MBA) with accounting concentration. The sponsorship of my education came from myself and the support of friends during the loss of my first life partner.

Similarly, my doctoral education was mainly from my family and student loans but my professional pursuits have been financed entirely by myself and family. The Ghana Stock Exchange (GSE) course I attended in February 1998 was sponsored by the Ghana Internal Revenue Service (IRS). Nevertheless, the workshop, seminars, and training I have attended have been sponsored by my employers; as well as, the Ghana Co-operatives Credit Unions Association (CUA) Ghana Limited and the Church of Pentecost (COP) in Ghana and the United States of America.

DEBORA'S CONFRONTATION

I was not good at memorizing names so I usually call people by pseudonyms such as calling men-*Kwaku* and varying the names for ladies-Yaa, Ama, Esi, and so on. I soon discovered that ladies will not just accept any name you call them but will go ahead to give you the correct name to use. On one occasion, I called a lady by one of the usual names at church but not knowing that this lady had taken note of my lack of interest in learning names of the church members. She responded: *"Elder, that is not good enough. You are fond of calling people by different names without taking pains to learn their names. My name is Debora (not the real name)"* I must confess that this feedback has been helpful to me over the years. I have experienced times when I went to the bank and the teller said: *"Happy birthday, George"* In actual fact, I had forgotten that the day was my birthday. In some of the banks I transacted business regularly with in Ghana, some of the staff greeted me by name. As a result, it pays to call people we associate with by name.

THE 40-70 RULE

The *40-70 rule* was introduced to me by Professor John B. K. Aheto in the Graduate School in Ghana and I have come to find the concept very useful in life applications. We are told that when data is processed, information is provided. When information is processed, knowledge is the resulting outcome. Then, the application of the knowledge is what is established as wisdom. Consequently, decision-making is best when it is information-based; but how much information is considered adequate is a legitimate question. The *40-70 rule* provides for a *floor(40%)* and a *ceiling(70%)* for the quantum of information to be gathered in any important decision-making adventure in life.

By way of application, I have met a couple of young ladies in my experience on the Marriage Committee of the church, who appear to have very scanty information about the man they want to marry. To such people, the term: *"I love you"* is deemed adequate and nothing else is important. Keep in mind that Christian marriage is a lifelong undertaking so to speak and so to have some basic information or knowledge about the person you are going to marry will not be out of place at all. Consequently, responding: "*I don't know*" to almost all questions is not helpful to anybody. Against the background that "*not all who wonder are lost*"; the *40-70 rule* has general applicability to every sphere of life.

THE ABIGAILS OF TODAY

In 2001, I was processing the Life and Survivors Benefits from Social Security and National Insurance Trust (SSNIT). I visited the Gulf House Branch often and during one of my visits, I was referred to the Pension House (Headquarters) for some issues regarding membership data. After going through the protocols at the Reception, I was directed to an office upstairs. After providing the necessary information, I was told that my enquiry could be done at the Archives/Data Center at the Industrial Area. I spend time in traffic so I was angry for them to be tossing me from one location to the other. When I finally got to the Archives/Data Center, I met an officer who asked me of my mission.

After waiting for a while, I got to know that the officer had left for lunch break. I got furious and started complaining about the treatment meted out to me by the organization at the Reception area. Not quite long, a middle-aged woman emerged from a door with a bottle of water on a tray and brought it to me and said: "Sir, I know you are tired and thirsty. Please take this water, drink, and relax; and we will meet your need before you leave" I thanked her and took the water and drunk. Truth be told, I was actually very thirsty. In a moment, she came back with a gentleman and introduced him to me as the officer to attend to me. Within a few minutes, all my enquiries were addressed. I do not remember the name of the lady but there is one thing I know that we still have the 'Abigails" of our time.

GOD ORDERS OUR STEPS

The steps of the righteous are ordered by God (Psalm 37:23). I have passed through many towns and cities in my life including: Mampong and Juaben (in the Ashanti region of Ghana); Nkwatia-Kwahu in the Eastern region of Ghana; Cape coast and Elmina in the Central region of Ghana); Madina and Ashongman in the Greater Accra region of Ghana; as well as, Romeoville and Chicago in the State of Illinois. Each of the locations presented me different learning and working experiences to enrich my overall life perspectives. I have had the opportunity of visiting different countries and States in the United States of America and still counting.

I have been presented with several opportunities to explore in life and in the church, the opportunities include but not limited to the following: Assistant District Pentecost Youth and Evangelistic Ministry (PENTYEM) Leader, Local Secretary; Secretary, Foundation Stone Laying Committee, Elder for Special Duties, Chairman of History Committee; Member, Estates Committee, Patron of Sophia McKeown Singers, COP-Chicago; Marriage Committee Secretary, just to mention a few.

I have invested (mostly financial and physical energy in a few circumstances) in building projects in the Kingdom of God, as follows:

- *The interior works of the old Mampong Tunsuom Church building(now being used by the PIWC);*
- *The foundation of the Mampong Tunsuom Central Church building in the Ashanti region of Ghana;*
- *The fund raising for the acquisition of land for the SSNIT flats assembly in the Elmina district in the Central region of Ghana;*
- *The interior works of the Ebenezer Temple in the Madina Central district in the Greater Accra region of Ghana;*

- *The construction of the church building in the Madina West from lintel level to roofing in Accra-Ghana;*
- *The re-modeling of the Madina Central Sanctuary in Accra-Ghana;*
- *The Madina Estates building project in Accra-Ghana;*
- *The Chicago Sanctuary project at 8600 South Kilpatrick Avenue in Chicago, Illinois;*
- *The McKeown Worship Center-Romeoville in Illinois, USA.*
- *The Sanctuary building project of the Paradise Assembly of the Church of Pentecost in the Ashongman, Accra.*

All-in-all, the opportunities offered have presented me with learning moments. I am grateful for the exposure.

MINDING OWN BUSINESS

My attention was first drawn to the Biblical admonition below by my bosom friend (the late Lawrence B. Larbi-May his memory be a blessing):

"And to make it your ambition to lead a quiet life: You should mind your own business and work with your hands, just as we told you, [12] so that your daily life may win the respect of outsiders and so that you will not be dependent on anybody"(1 Thessalonians 4:11-12-NIV).

At first, I was surprised to learn of the advice to mind one's own business and the leading of a quiet life, however, the part that recommended hard work in order to be independent did not surprise me. I felt leading a quiet life will not bring about fulfillment until I learned the power of gleaning (Ruth 2:17), which can help people get noticed in the process. Likewise, I thought that to mind one's own business was misconstrued to mean-inward looking tendencies; but I have come to appreciate that concentration is *sine qua non* to the attainment of purpose. I recognize that it is all about interpretation of terms, concepts, and principles.

The critical elements encompass the following: career, family, values; as well as delight, disillusion, and depth. For that reason, the implication of the parable about the talents in Matthew 25:14-30 and Luke 19:12-26 is very instructive, concerning the servant who was given five talents and gained additional talents (5:5); the other servant who received two talents from the master and also gained two more talents (2:2); and the lazy servant who was unprofitable enough to gain nothing on the one talent received from the master (1:0). The principle established by Christ is that: *"For unto everyone that hath shall be given and he shall have abundance, but from him that hath not shall be taken away even that which he hath?* (Matthew 25:29). As a result, the master's trust becomes the basis of the master's test to measure our faithfulness. Consequently, societal pressure should not lead us into conformity behavior.

CONCLUSION

My involvement in the credit union system and professional affiliations have been rewarding over the years. The more openly we discuss the strengths and limitations of biographical methods, the more we can defend and improve our analysis and findings in dialogue within our respective fields of interests and with other research methodologies (Aurell & Davis, 2019; Eichsteller, 2019). My involvement in the credit union concept is fully discussed in the next chapter of this book. I have been Chairman, Board of Directors of the IRS Co-operative Credit Union Cape Coast and Greater Accra, and also member, secretary and chairman of the Supervisory Committee of the Ghana Co-operative Credit Unions Association (CUA) Limited (an apex body of all credit unions of Ghana). I have six years' exposure in the supervision and handling of funds and auditing of the society's books of accounts. The supervisory committee reported to the Board of directors quarterly and the biennial conferences; as well as, ensuring that required reports were sent to the Registrar of Co-operatives in Ghana.

CHAPTER 20

CREDIT UNIONISM

MY ASSOCIATION WITH THE CREDIT unionism dates to the early 1990s, especially, in 1992; while working with the Ghana Internal Revenue Service in Cape Coast, where the need to start a credit union in the Service was determined. The Regional Inspector of Taxes (Mr. Emmanuel K. Nyamordey-then-Chief Inspector of Taxes) invited me to his office one early Monday morning. I thought the discussion was going to be focused on matters arising out of the "Bring up (BU) diary" as it was the routine administrative style to be updated on the progress of outstanding assignments. For some reasons, this discussion was different and turned out to be one of the most important meetings, which shaped the events of history.

The issue of lone voices in society can be weighty because sometimes, some people have to stand for the truth and what is right but not to be intimidated. In response to the regular requests for financial assistance from the Office of the Chief Inspector of taxes, Mr. Nyamordey mooted the idea of forming a credit union in the office to address the financial needs of the staff.

Consequently, I was assigned the responsibility of looking into the credit union concept. I contacted Mr. K.A. Otu, the Central Regional Field Officer of the Ghana Co-operative Credit Unions Association (CUA) Limited in the Co-operative House in Cape Coast for informational sessions, as well as, educational materials. A staff meeting was held in 1992 to discuss the formation of a credit union in the Ghana Internal Revenue Service-Cape Coast in the Central Region of Ghana. At that meeting, a decision was taken to start a credit union with fourteen staff indicating their preparedness to become members.

An interim Board was put in place to steer the affairs of the society until the First Annual General Meeting, where the composition was ratified.

The Concept of the Credit Union

The credit union concept revolves around the following:

> "*The credit union concept is such that people with a common interest come together in a society, mobilize funds regularly so that after six months, when a needy member applies for a credit facility (s)he would be offered with a minimum interest rate payable within a period of time. At the close of a financial year, management declares profit and shared among members contributions. The concept is good and appreciated and need to be promoted in workplaces, parish, and communities*" (Retrieved from http://www.cuagh.com -accessed on 02/15/2020).

The implication of this concept is quadruple-fold, as follows: *first, a credit union is formed by people with a common bond or interest.* Typically, common bond or interest has revolved around three ideas-*workplace, community*, and *parish*. Examples of credit unions in the Greater Accra Region of Ghana encompass: (1) In 1997, Internal Revenue Service (IRS) Employees Credit Union Limited was registered as a workplace credit union; (2) in 1984, the North End Credit Union was established as a community credit union; and in 2004, the Church of Pentecost-Darkuman established a parish or faith-based credit union (Credit Unions in the Greater Accra Chapter of Ghana Co-operative Credit Unions Association (CUA) Limited-Retrieved from www.cuagh.com -accessed on 02/19/2020).

By way of illustration, the Numark Credit Union has been serving Countryside, Crest Hill, Joliet communities, Tinley Lark, Bridgeport,

Aurora, New Lenox, Plainfield, and Warrenville in the Southwestern suburbs of Chicago in the Illinois for over six and half decades (Retrieved from www.numarkcu.org -accessed on 02/19/2020). The Energy Credit Union Limited in Canada was established to meet the financial needs for over seven decades to serve active and retired employees of Toronto Hydro Corporation; Signal, Electric, Communications (SEC), Southlake Regional Health Center, Gerdau; as well as, individuals employed in any health care facility in Ontario (www.theenergycu. com -accessed on 02/19/2020).

The Parishioners Federal Credit Union of the United States of America also has been established to serve the financial needs of Catholic families since 1961. Once upon a time, Monsignor J. Augustine O'Gorman of Saint James Parish in Redondo Beach realized that a member-owned financial co-operative would understand his parishioners' needs and share their values as no commercial bank could (www.parishionersfcu.org -accessed on 02/19/2020). *Second, credit union is a vehicle for the mobilization of savings.* I find that one of the most effective ways of mobilizing savings is through the credit union system because the usual minimum deposit requirement by traditional banks is non-characteristic of credit unions and in areas where traditional banks consider non-profitable, credit unions have filled the vacuum easily. The individual contributions start small but grow over time.

Third, credit unions allow for the granting of loans to needy members. Surplus units provide deficit units with financial resources to meet pressing personal, commercial, and business purposes. In a typical credit union in Ghana, members get twice their contributions as loans up to a limit set by the society and half of the loan is guaranteed by the member's own saving and the remaining amount is covered by other members who voluntarily guarantee with portions of their savings.

Four, a credit union is a financial co-operative. The credit union is best described as a financial co-operative and not a bank. However, in advanced countries, there is a thin line between a bank and a credit union. Nevertheless, concepts such as statutory reserves, risk management, central finance facility or Federal Deposit Insurance Corporation (FDIC) are common to both banks and credit unions. *Lastly, a credit union is member-owned and member-managed.* The uniqueness of credit union is that it is both *member-owned* and also *member-managed*. This presents a challenge and opportunity to the society and the membership. The net surplus of the society at the end of the year can either be ploughed back into the society or declared as dividend to the members. The challenge is getting members with adequate management skills and training to run the societies effectively and efficiently.

Credit Union Activism at the Primary Level

The Board of Directors of the Internal Revenue Service (IRS) Employees Co-operative Credit Union Limited was composed of the following: Mr. George Appiah-Sokye (Chairman), Mrs. Aisha Molley (Secretary), Mr. Mark Kwofie (Treasurer), and Mr. Peter Abaka-Davis (Assistant Treasurer). Additionally, the Loans and Supervisory committees were also established. Credit union education and membership covered the following: (i) visit to the *Western region*, including Takoradi, Tarkwa, Asankragwa; as well as, *Central region* covering-Cape Coast, Assin Fosu, Dunkwa-On-Offin, and Agona Swedru.

Technical advice to the society was provided by Mr. K.A. Otu, Central Regional Field Officer and Kristin Johnson (a Canadian Credit Unions Association (CCA) intern). The society was duly registered with the Registrar of the Department of Co-operatives and Ghana Co-operative Credit Unions Association (CUA) Limited in 1996. I had been the Chairman of the Board of Directors of the I.R.S. Co-operative Credit Union- Cape Coast from 1992-1996. I was transferred from Cape Coast to Accra in 1996 and at the Annual General Meeting held by the society in the Basement of the Court House in Cape Coast, the *Credit Union Sterling Management Award* was presented to me and below is the citation:

Mr. George Appiah-Sokye

*The Internal Revenue Service (IRS) Employees Credit Union Limited considers it an opportune moment to honor you at its 4th Annual General Meeting not only as a member but also for your **meritorious and sterling services** which saw the birth, weaning, and nurturing of the society to its 4th milestone.*

Not only did you take the society as your baby but that you regarded it as if your whole life depended upon it.

You devoted a greater part of your leisure, virtually all your energy and knowledge, notwithstanding risks and other demoralizing instances you stood resolute to ensure the growth of the society–Your tenacity to increase the membership is still–"Talk of the Town"

Your stewardship as a chairman has been unparalleled, taking into account the virtual ignorance of the management of credit unions. With your display of qualitative management, this young society ranks among the few best in the Central region.

Your rather unexpected transfer from the region has left a big gulf within the society, which may be difficult to fill.

Again, the society applauds and honors you today for the <u>principles and integrity</u> displayed in the performance of your duty.

May God bless you and your family.

Barely a year after settling down in Accra, several employees approached me in June 1997 to start a credit union in the Greater Accra Region, following the success story of the IRS Employees Co-operative Credit Union Limited in Cape Coast. Series of meetings were held, backed by a number of consultations with the Ghana Co-operative Credit Unions Association (CUA) Limited. Finally, a decision was taken to start a new credit union for the staff of the Internal Revenue Service (IRS) in the Greater Accra region because the Cape Coast society had a limited *common bond* covering only employees in the Central and Western regions.

The credit union membership covered the following units (districts, Head office, Regional offices): (a) Internal Revenue Service *Headquarters*, (b) *Districts*- Kinbu, Osu, Adabraka, Tema, Teshie-Nungua, Achimota, Legon, Kaneshie, and Agboblorshie; (c) *Regional Administrative Offices*-Legon and Agboblorshie. I am listed as Number 0015 on the Membership register of the IRS Employees Co-operative Credit Union Limited as of January 7, 1998. The Membership Database span from January 7, 1998 to May 31, 2000; involving a total of 278 with a few cessations.

The Board of Directors of the Internal Revenue Service (IRS) Employees Co-operative Credit Union Limited-Greater Accra comprised of the following: Mr. George Appiah-Sokye (Chairman), Ms. Buela Nutsugah (Vice Chair), Mr. J.E. Amoako Kusi, Esq. (Secretary), Mr. B.K Christian (Assistant Secretary), Mr. Gabriel Alifui-Segbayah (Treasurer), Mrs. Cecilia Botsio Manison (Assistant Treasurer), and Mr. J.K. Ghunney (Member). Later, Mr. D. Saka Ashong took over from Mr. Christian and Mr. Amoako Kusi was transferred to Kumasi. So, he was replaced by Mr. D. Saka Ashong, who was assisted by Mr. Leslie Mark-Hansen. Likewise, Mr. A.T Koduah was co-opted as a Board member. Technical support was provided by the Department of

Co-operatives and the Regional Field Officer of Ghana Co-operative Credit Unions Association (CUA) Limited.

The Executive Committee is made up of the Board of Directors, all committee members, and representatives of the IRS Branch Offices (Co-coordinators). At a meeting of the Committee held on March 5, 1998 in Room 11 of the IRS Headquarters, the following were in attendance: **One,** *The Board*-George Appiah-Sokye (Chairman), Buela Nutsugah (Vice Chair), J.E. Amoako-Kusi (Secretary), D. Saka Ashong (Assistant secretary), Cecilia Botsio (Assistant Treasurer), J. K Ghunney (Member). **Two,** *Other committees and Co-coordinators*-Rebecca Larnyo (member), A. K. Yankson (Member, Adabraka), Anthony Owusu (Member, Osu), Daniel Nuer (Member), Harrison Baidoo (Member), J.K. Appiah-Kubi (Member, LTO/Kinbu), Sylvester Akpilima (Member, Tema), Margaret Asheetey (Member, Makola), Richard Lamptey (Member), Timothy Ashley (Member), A. Tweneboah Koduah (Member), Cecilia Takyi (Member), and Minta Afari (Member)

On December 10, 2010, the Ghana Revenue Authority (GRA) Credit Union was inaugurated to replace the IRS Employees Co-operative Credit Union Limited. The change in name was in response to the promulgation of the GRA Law (Act 791) of 2009. The history of the credit union has been captured, as follows:

Login | My Account | Help

Ghana Revenue Authority
Co-operative Credit Union Ltd

HOME　　ABOUT US　　SERVICES　　MEMBERSHIP　　NEWS & EVENTS　　GALLERY　　CONTACT US

How We Began As a Credit Union - Our Story

In June 1997, some staff of the erstwhile Internal Revenue Service, Head Office, led by one Mr. George Appiah-Sokye met in one of the lecture rooms of the Internal Revenue Service, Headquarters Annex 'B' to discuss the formation of the I. R. S Co-operative Credit Union. This meeting was preceded by a series of informal meetings held with this Mr. Appiah-Sokye who first mooted the idea of forming a Credit Union. Mr. Appiah-Sokye was the Chairman of the Central and Western I.R.S Credit Union before he was transferred to the Head Office; thus he came with a wealth of credit unionism experience to bring to bear on the formation and organization of the Credit Union at the Head Office.

At this maiden meeting, a firm decision was taken to form a Credit Union under the name I.R.S Co-operative Credit Union – Greater Accra. It had a founding membership of about eighty (80). With the informal resolution to form a Credit Union, the necessary contacts were made with the umbrella organization which has the oversight responsibility for Credit Unions in Ghana that is the Credit Unions Association of Ghana (CUA). Consequently, the necessary ground work was done and a formal approval was sought from the then Commissioner of the Internal Revenue Service, Mr. David Adom, for its formation.

In July 1997, the first input was made for the deduction of members' contributions at source. The first cheque that was given to the union in early August, 1997 was a mere GH☐170.00 and this included members' savings and payment for shares and registration fees. After a few months of operation, the then Management Committee applied for registration with the Department of Co-operatives and also for affiliation with the Credit Unions Association of Ghana (CUA), the National Association and with the Regional Chapter of the Association, having met all the conditions necessary for registration and affiliation.

There was no formal launching or inauguration of the Union in I.R.S. but by holding the first Annual General Meeting in 1999, the union was deemed to have been formally launched. A vigorous membership drive was embarked upon by the Board of Management both at the Head Office and in the Districts and in no time membership grew and the I.R.S. Credit gained popularity among staff all over. As at the time when it was though necessarily expedient and absolutely imperative to apply for a change of name to Ghana Revenue Authority (G.R.A) Co-operative Credit Union in March 1,200 and 1,300.

Immediately after the last Annual General Meeting in February this year, the newly constituted Management Board, upon expert advice, both legal and administration, decided to apply for change of name in view of integration of the Revenue Agencies and the promulgation of Act 791 which established the Ghana Revenue Authority (GRA). The necessary consultations were done and based upon an enabling board resolution a formal application was made to the Department of Co-operatives for change of name from the IRS Co-operative Credit Union Ltd, Greater Accra, to the Ghana Revenue Authority Co-operative Credit Union Ltd (GRACCU).

The change in name was immediately followed by a very aggressive membership promotion drive at all the division of the GRA and the result is what we are seeing today, the birth of the Ghana Revenue Authority Co-operative Credit Union. Mr. Chairman, at this point I wish to formally say that we are launching the GRA Co-operative Credit Union. The cardinal reason for doing so is to fully integrate the union so as to bring on board all interested staff of the Ghana Revenue Authority (GRA). We believe that we will have strength in numbers which this integration will bring to enable us achieve our objectives as summarily captured in the theme for this launching; "GRA.Co-operative Credit Union, the Key to our Sustainable Future".

Mr. Chairman, I wish to salute all our founding fathers, particularly Mr. George Appiah-Sokye (no longer with G. R. A) and Mr. Gabriel Alifui-Segbaya – led Management Team for the solid foundation laid for us to build on. It is worth mentioning that from a modest beginning of GH☐170.00 as contributions, the assets of the Union grew to GH☐1.2million with a monthly deductions total of GH☐105,000.00 at the time we took over in February, 2010. This was no mean achievable by all standards. We wish to state that the new Management Committee took over office hitting the ground running. We have started vigorously to build on the foundation

424

bequeathed to us. As I speak now, I can, in all humility, say that our total assets as at 30th November, 2010 stood at GH☐2.2million.

We want to mention just a few of what we have been able to do:

- ☒ We have a fully equipped office with the required human resource as for now.
- ☒ We have required and installed the Credit Unions approved Software – known as CU-SOFT. This is fully operational and members can now access their statements at will.
- ☒ There is quarterly distribution of interest earned.
- ☒ We have added a product line to include the following:-
  - ☒ Sale of Computers to all Staff
  - ☒ Sale of Consumables to all Staff

This is part of the drive to argument our income for the benefit of all members.

Formation of the Credit Union National Association (CUA) Limited

In terms of opportunities available to us as a Union to explore, the achievements numerated above is a drop in the Pacific. There is a very large room for improvement. What the Management Committee envisages to do is to afford members, depending on their individual ability, the opportunity to own property (moveable and immoveable) whilst in active service on retirement. This is their vision and this has informed the choice of the theme for our launching today.

In this regard, I want to encourage all staff of the Ghana Revenue Authority, both Management and non-Management to come on board. There is strength in Unity, so goes the old adage; but we say there is security in numbers. We believe, having regard to the staff strength of the GRA which is about 7,000 by our estimation, that if we can pool our resources together we can conveniently dispense with borrowing from the banks at very high interest rates to carry out our individual pursuit. I therefore appeal to all staff particularly those who are already members that at any time their disposable incomes increase they should also commensurately augment their savings, for that is where our future and lifer after age sixty lie.

As we have always done, our commitments and obligations to the various organizations including the Greater Regional Accra Office of the Department of Co-operatives and our own caring mother association CUA to which we relate or are affiliated. The change in name does not signify a change in commitment or a dereliction of existing or future obligations. We will be up to our responsibilities with our usual candour and vivacity. I thank the Almighty God for taking the Union this far. I wish also to thank fellow Management Committee members for throwing all their support behind me as **PRIMUS INTER PARIS** in all that we have done so far.

Fellow Co-operators, the future of this Happy Family is in your bosom. Your position of being the owners and customers of the Association at the same time makes you unique. I therefore implore you to fully participate in all spheres of the Union's collective endeavors to enable us achieve our objective of a healthy and a happy life after retiring from active service.

Finally, on behalf of the Management of the Credit Union, I wish to express our gratitude to the Commissioner –General and his lieutenants, the Commissioners, for the platform given us to outdoor the GRA Co-operative Credit Union Ltd.

Connect with Us

425

The above publication-*How we Begun As a Credit Union-Our Story -* was published on the website of the Ghana Revenue Authority Credit Union on April 28, 2014 (Retrieved from www.graccu.org -accessed on 05/15/2014). The following information was obtained from the public domain:

- *A society which started with about 80 members has grown in membership to over 4,000 and first contribution of GH¢170 covering savings, shares, and registration. The total assets stood at GH¢1.2 million* (Retrieved from www.graccu.org -access on 04/28/2014).

- *As of June 2013, total membership stood at 4,219 and the total asset registered GH¢16.9 million. There was an agreement with JMET Corporation for 300 mini-buses for members to own and operate as commercial vehicles* (GRA Credit Union holds Annual General Meeting-Retrieved from www.ghanaweb.com -accessed on 02/20/2020).

- *The Ghana Revenue Authority Credit Union commissioned 40 housing at Pampaso in Nsawam in the Eastern region, with an additional 60, expected to be completed by the end of the year for GH¢75,000* (GRA Credit Union Affordable Housing Units Commissioned, Ghana New Agency-Retrieved from newsghana.com.gh -accessed on 02/20/2020).

- *The chairman of the Board of Management of the Ghana Revenue Authority Credit Union Limited reveals that most members have made huge withdrawals from savings with credit union and invested same in Menzgold and other Ponzi schemes. The withdrawal increased from GH¢700,000 to GH¢1.5 million per month. He assured members that despite the financial tsunamis in the financial sector, the GRA Credit Union is robust and safe* (Emmanuel Ajarfor Abugri on GRA Workers Collapse Accounts to Invest in

Menzgold-Union-Retrieved from modernghana.com -accessed on 02/20/2020).

- *At the 7th Annual General Meeting of the GRA Credit Union, the total asset was GH¢17 million in June 2013 as compared to GH¢4.4million in June 2011*(Emelia Ennin Abbey wrote on GRA Credit Union Records Growth on January 11,2014 -accessed on 02/20/2020).

- *At the 9th Annual General Meeting, there was a plan to set up a bank that will cater for the needs and wants of the union members* (GRA Credit Union to Establish Own bank-retrieved from www. allafrica.com -accessed on 02/20/2020).

- *Peacefmonline.com reported that GRA Credit Union Gets 150 minibuses for members. The expectation is for a total of 450 mini-buses and 200 saloon cars by the end of September under the Credit Union Car Loan Scheme* (Accessed on 02/20/2020).

- *The Chairman of the GRA Credit Union, Mr. Godwin Monyo has cautioned that... "the demand for withdrawal by members who are servicing loans poses a threat to the continued existence of the union" He observed that while the total membership stood at 4,219,the total asset recorded was GH¢16.9 million* (Retrieved from africanbusinesscommunities.com -accessed on 02/20/2020).

By way of evaluation, I am thankful to God for the grace to be of service to humanity. To Him be all the Glory! A review of the Report to the First Annual General Meeting of the IRS Employees Co-operative Credit Union Limited shows:

a. *The membership of the society stood at 132 as of June 30,1998, made of 79 males and 53 females. As of June 30, 2000, the membership had grown to 278.*

b. *The meetings were as follows: 9 of 12 Board Meetings, 3 of 4 Executive Meetings, 5 of 5 Loans Committee Meetings, 2 of 4*

Supervisory Committee Meetings, and 3 of 4 Education Committee Meetings.

c. *The following attended the 10th Biennial Conference of the Ghana Co-operative Credit Unions Association Limited at Bunso in the Eastern region of Ghana: George Appiah-Sokye (Chair, Board), D.S. Ashong (Secretary, Board),and J.L. Appiah-Kubby (Chair, Loans Committee.*

d. *The society was affiliated with:(i) Ghana Co-operative Credit Unions Association Ghana Limited with CUA/191 of March 5,1998; and (ii) Greater Accra Chapter of CUA as 136 of March 5, 1998.*

e. *The State of the Union was as follows: Total assets stood at ¢37.4million; Loan's outstanding was ¢9.1 million; Central Finance Facility (CFF) savings stood at ¢1.0million; Membership savings amounted to ¢28.1million; Membership shares was ¢3.8million; Investment in Treasury Bills was ¢23million; Total loans granted was ¢11.9million; and the average savings per member per month was ¢17,796.58;*

f. *The meeting received proposal for other loans, including(I) Special loans (¢1million, 5%, 12months); (II) Project/Development loan (¢5million, 60months, subject to other conditions). (III) Commercial loans (¢3million, 36months, subject to other conditions).*

g. *Other products were:(a) Leave grant, school fees, special X'mas savings; and (b) welfare scheme with dues of ¢5,000 per member and Live and Death benefits.*

h. *The Committees were composed as follows: One,* **Loans Committee-** *J.L Appiah Kubby (Chairman), Harrison Baidoo (Secretary), and Daniel Nuer (Member). Two,* **Supervisory Committee-***Seth Kye (Chairman), K.W. Minta Afari (Secretary), and Cecilia Takyi (Member); and three,* **Education Committee-***A. K. Yankson (Chairman), Rebecca Mark-Larnyo (Secretary), and Anthony Owusu (Member)*

I am appreciative of the Vision of Mr. Emmanuel Nyamordey (Deputy Commission-Retired), which culminated into the formation of the first credit union in the Internal Revenue Service in Cape Coast. The name of Mr. E. J. Barnerman (Chief Inspector of Taxes-Accounts) cannot be spared mentioning because he registered as members and also facilitated the deductions through the Payroll system. *First*, I want to register my sincerest thanks to Mr. Acquaah for taking up the mantle of the Chairmanship of the Board of directors of the IRS Employees Credit Union-Cape Coast on my transfer to Accra in the Greater Accra region. Likewise, I thank Mr. Gabriel Alifui-Segbayah and his team, who took over from me after leaving the Internal Revenue Service in 2000. I am grateful for the remarkable performance of Mr. Godwin Monyo-Chairman, Board of Directors of the Ghana Revenue Authority Credit Union for taking the credit union beyond our dreams.

Second, I thank the Government of Ghana for merging the three Revenue Agencies (Internal Revenue Service, Value-Added Tax Service, and The Customs, Excise and Preventive Service). The amalgamation of the three institutions has provided the GRA Credit Union with a potential of 7,000 employees (see also *How we Begun as a Credit Union-Our Story* -Retrieved from www.graccu.org -accessed on 05/15/2014). Implying that there is still about 2,800 employee who are yet to be roped into the union. Perhaps, an aggressive membership outreach should be pursed and dubbed- *No Employee Left Behind (NELB)*.

Third, I cannot agree more with the Chairman of the Board that credit unions remain *robust and secure saving* and investment vehicles. The GRA Credit Union has been able to meet the wants and needs of members-*personal, commercial,* and *business loans*, including the provision of mini-buses, saloon cars, and housing units at reasonable interest. For that reason, It is not fair for members to use the credit union as a vehicle to mobilize saving over the long haul only to withdraw the saving over time to invest in *Ponzi* schemes, which appear to promise abnormal returns. The simple logic is that if members want higher interest on their savings; then, they should also support the charging of very high interest on loans. Keep in mind that credit unions are both member-owned and member-managed.

Four, I am delighted at the involvement of the management of the Ghana Revenue Authority (GRA) as exemplified in their participation in Annual General Meetings over time. When the credit union started, the concept was new to the management as a body except few individuals who identified themselves with the new concept. We had to use our personal time to conduct some of the credit union businesses such as educational tours and participation in national and chapter activities. I applaud the management for the recognition given to the union.

Lastly, I am grateful to all members who have believed in the credit union concept from the beginning; as well as, others who joined when they began to see signs of progress. For example, Gender and Development (formerly Women in Development) organized a seminar for the female members of the IRS Co-operative Credit Union Limited for 50 female members but only 18 attended. The seminar was facilitated by Mrs. Grace Sarpong (GAD Coordinator) and the topics covered included the following: (a) Steps for doing feasibilities, (b) How to organize a business, (c) costing and pricing in business, (d) Profit and loss; (e) Buying and selling on credit, (f) Communication in business, (g) Time management, (h) Reproductive health (Education Committee, IRS Credit Union Newsletter, June 2000, 1(3), p.1).

I thank all stakeholders, who have nourished and sustained this credit union in particular and all other credit unions in general. The overarching goal of the credit union that resonated with me from day one is the pulling of financial resources into a pool from which members in need can be helped. Upon reflection on how far the GRA Credit Union has come-*I am pleased with the achievement in the financial upliftment of workers above the poverty line.*

Credit Union Activism at the Regional Chapter Level

The Central Regional Chapter of the Ghana Co-operative Credit Unions Association (CUA) is the umbrella organization for all societies. While the membership of the credit unions was made of individual members, that of the chapter was composed of credit unions or societies. My involvement in the affairs was associated with participation in meetings, events and activities. I was elected to the Chapter Board from 1996 to 1998. The membership of the Board comprised of the following: Nana M.A. K. Essamoah (Chairman), Mr. S.K. Banson-Member, Ms. Christina Nyarko (Popularly called Honorable)-Member, Ms. Jane Kinful-Member, Mr. Charles Hagan-Member, and Mr. K. A. Otu (Field Officer).

During our tenure, we organized the *International Credit Unions Day* on October 25, 1996 in Agona Swedru in the Central region of Ghana, with a brass band procession through the principal streets of the town to create awareness of the credit union concept.

Credit Unionism at the National Level

The Ghana Co-operative Credit Unions Association Limited is the umbrella organization for all credit unions in Ghana (financial co-operatives) with the responsibility of mobilizing savings and giving loans for the financial upliftment of members. My involvement in the credit union system was felt at the national level. While serving at the primary level in both Cape Coast and Accra, I was also serving in a different capacity at the national level. On starting the IRS Employees Co-operative Credit Union Limited in Cape Coast in 1992, the same year coincided with the Biennial conference of the group. Initially, the conference was to take place in Tamale in the Northern region of Ghana but due to the eruption of an ethnic conflict, the meeting was re-scheduled for Accra.

The IRS Employees Credit Union limited nominated Messrs.-Emmanuel Sackey and Mark Kwofie; as well as my good self to represent the society at the conference. We all attended the meeting as observers because our society had just started but there was the need to attend all this important meeting as part of the learning process for the society. I participated fully in the deliberations of the meeting and when the Supervisory committee was invited to present its report in line with the business of the meeting, no report could be rendered. Members expressed disappointment in the development.

Surprisingly, during the election of a new Supervisory committee, my name came up and I was duly elected to the Supervisory committee of the Ghana Co-operative Credit Unions Association Limited at the Legon Biennial Conference in 1992. The Supervisory committee was responsible for the handling of funds; and ensured that the required annual reports were filed with the regulators. Also reported on the financial affairs using internal auditing standards, involving compliance, operational, governance, and financial processes on quarterly-basis to the Board of directors using planning, fieldwork, and reporting; audited and reported on the Central Finance Facility, Risk Management Scheme, Gender and Development programs to the Bi-annual Conferences of the association. Ensuring that required reports were sent to the Registrar of Co-operatives.

The membership of the Supervisory Committee of the Ghana Co-operative Credit Unions Associations (CUA) Limited, into which I was elected, was composed as follows: Mrs. Beatrice Hammond (chairperson), Mr. Akwasi A. Ankomah (secretary), and Mr. George Appiah-Sokye (member) from 1992-1994.

After the day's session, I was standing by the decorative pond of the Legon Hall of the University of Ghana and a gentleman approached me to congratulate me on my election and said: *George, I have confidence in you to deliver on your mandate on the supervisory committee. For 25 years,*

432

the Supervisory committee of this association has not been effective. So, don't let us down. I later got to know that he was from the National Film and Television Institute (NAFTI) Credit Union in Accra. Likewise, another person I knew also came to congratulate me and also told me that: *"You are new to the credit union system, so I want to let you know that…also understand the politics of the system"* I dare say the words of these gentlemen provided me with the initial guidance and became the driving force in my call to duty.

The Ghana Co-operative Credit Unions association (CUA) Limited provided training to equip committee members; and for that reason, I was privilege to participate in a seminar on Principles of Management in Accra-Ghana in 1994. At the end of the term, the Biennial conference of the association was held in Tamale in the Northern region because uneasy calm had been restored in the place after the conflict. The Supervisory committee was able to report to the meeting and during the election, the following were *re-elected* to the Supervisory committee for the period 1994 to 1996: Mr. Akwasi A. Ankomah (chairman) and Mr. George Appiah-Sokye (secretary) and Mrs. Janet Kinful (member) was elected.

Ghana Co-operative Credit Union Association (CUA) Limited organized another seminar on Principles of Management in Accra-Ghana in 1996 to equip committee members for proper function of duties. I was a participant of this seminar. Similarly, I participated in a course on Principles of Management in Accra, Ghana in 1998: as well as, a workshop on Strategic Planning, Lobbing, and Financial Management in Accra-Ghana. The facilitation for the workshop on lobbying and strategic management was provided by the Canadian Credit Union Association (CCA). During this period, a seminar was organized by CUA to refresh members of the credit union on the responsibilities of the Supervisory committee and best auditing practices. The facilitator was Mr. Emmanuel Darko, a consultant attached to the Country Manager (Bob Bildfell's) office. Mr. Bildfell was from the CCA.

The next Biennial conference was held 1998 in Bunso in the Eastern region of Ghana, where the supervisory committee presented its report to the meeting. During the election of the supervisory committee, the results were as follows: Mr. George Appiah-Sokye (Chairman), Mrs. Sethlina B. Donkoh (Secretary), and Mr. Ebenezer Aryee (Member). While Mrs. Sethlina Donkoh was my senior and the Girls School Prefect in the High School, Mr. Ebenezer Aryee was a lecturer at NAFTI.

The two themes of the Biennial Conference were as follows; *One*, **Legal framework**-the Ghana Co-operative Credit Union Association (CUA) Limited was advocating for a separate law to regulate credit unions because the credit unions in Ghana were registered under the ambit of the Ghana Co-operative Decree (NLCD 252) of 1967. However, the Financial Institutions (Non-Banking) Law (PNDC 328 of 1993) had been promulgated to categorize credit unions as non-bank institution. Internally, the Legal framework of the credit unions in Ghana encompassed: (i) The Credit Unions Association (CUA-Registration Number 4032) Bye Laws and Articles of Association-Revised, Amended, and Approved on March 27, 1991 at Cape Coast; (ii) Model Byelaws and Articles of Association for Ghana Co-operative Credit Unions.

The credit unions held the view that the law was inimical to the development and survival of credit unions. *Two*, **the funding from CCA**- CUA was coming to a close on attaining self-sufficiency status and so there was the need for strategic planning for the organization to be able to stand the test of the time. At the end of the session on strategic planning, participants were able to craft a Vision and Mission statements for the organization and a national lobbying committee was established to respond to the credit union laws. The biennial conference for the year 2000 was held in Ho in the Volta region of Ghana and I had the singular honor of presenting the report of the Supervisory committee to the association.

CONCLUSION

Writing on Poverty Trap-Taking Responsibility in 2002, Emmanuel O. Darko elaborated as follows:

> *Unfortunately, most people in our society fail to manage their money wisely. The moment someone starts a new business, he or she tries to act big and join peer groups who are already well established with a sound capital base. These people want to enjoy all the fruits of success before working hard to earn them. Quickly, these people are drawn into highly expensive social functions and begin to waste all the money on things they don't need at all. Capital cannot easily be accumulated and under such conditions"* (p.32).

CHAPTER 21

ASHONGMAN: A VILLAGE TO A CONURBATION

A CAREFUL READING OF SEVERAL chapters of this book shows that I have stayed in different towns and cities at one time or the other. By law, residence is associated with a period of 183 days. By implication, most of the places I have stayed over the years may qualify me for a residence status. I have decided to write about Ashongman for a number of reasons to be discussed in this chapter. I worked with the Ghana Internal Revenue from 1991 and I was transferred from the Cape Coast in the Central region of Ghana to Accra in 1996; and desirous of not renting or leasing an accommodation but to acquire a plot and build a place of my own. There were indigenes in Ashongman at the time of residence, however, I met a few settlers and others moved during the period as and when their building became habitable.

Some of the early settlers included but not limited to the following families: Mr. Obuobi, Honorable Walter Blege (former Deputy Minister of Education), Auntie Anna and husband, Auntie Gladys (formerly of Barclays Bank Ghana Limited), Lawyer Kofi Mensah, Mr. George Amfo (Airport Cab Service), Mr. Elle Blue (former Finance Director of the Ghana Health Service), Mr. and Mrs. Vulley, one George, Mr. Akorli (formerly of the Ghana Health Service), Owner of Damfo Domino Production (whose wife operated Down Town Bakery), Madam Toroo and family, the Amenuvors, Mr. Ernest Akoto Bamfo (Second hand vehicle parts dealer), Auntie Rose and husband, Mr. Mawuli (Carpenter), Sister Pat (USA) and mother (Old lady in memoriam), a professor of the UGBS, and many more. More importantly, a number of caretakers occupied uncompleted buildings at the time and they became neighbors such as Maame Fanti, Wofa Yaw, and so on.

ASHONGMAN AS A VILLAGE

The name -*Ashongman*-comes from two words-(i) *Ashong* (name of a person), and (ii) *man* (town in Ga dialect of Ghana), or the town of Ashong. Located in the Ga East in Greater Accra Region of Ghana and part of the Ga East District Assembly of the Local Governance System of the Republic of Ghana. Ashongman is surrounded by the Ashongman Estates, Agbogba, Ablor- Adjei, and Teiman. The traditional rulers of Ashongman are part of the Odawton Family of Teshie in Accra. At the time of my moving into the Ashongman village, the chief was the late Nii Ayi Anang.

Prior to my assumption of duty in Accra, I called on the late Mr. Albert Nsiah at Madina Zongo Junction to discuss the possibility of selling one of his plots to me on installment basis to enable me to prosecute my plan of house ownership in Accra. Mr. Nsiah was my brother Willie's father-in-law. He promised to get me a place at another location and gave me a site plan of a plot he was contemplating for me. At my next visit, I was introduced to one of the princes of Ashongman.

In response to my personal plan of moving into my own house, I negotiated to pay for the cost of the plot in four equal installments of ¢500,000 each. A photocopy of the indenture was released to me and the original copy was to be released on full payment. Under this understanding, I was permitted to commence development almost immediately. The cost of building my Boys' Quarters or Outer house was assessed by my architect at ¢8 million and the cost of my plot was ¢2 million (totaling ¢10 million). In fact, I did not have the ¢10 million on hand but I calculated that the money to be used in renting accommodation in Accra could be invested in this project over time to realize my vision.

At the time I went to inspect the plot, there were dispersed settlements (new developments) and bush fire had ravaged the entire area. So immediately, I was able to move most of my building materials such as sandcrete blocks, sand, and concrete stones to the site to commence the construction of the Outer house. There were three uncompleted building located near the vicinity of my house. After the rainy season, I discovered that my house was in midst of a thick bush, where the people from the village hew firewood, burn charcoal, and collect snails. Others used portions for farming. Finally, I arrived to assume duty in Accra and I put up with Kwame Asafo Agyei (my nephew-in-law) at the Madina Zongo Junction for about two years. I visited the site every other weekend to inspect the progress of work. As soon as the building was roofed, I provided burglar proofing and doors and moved into the partly completed building in New Ashongman on *Saturday, September 26,1998.*

ASHONGMAN AS A TOWN

The New Ashongman is a peaceful community and stealing was not a characteristic of the fabric of society. The New Ashongman was well-laid out in proper town planning and executed under a deed of assignment. Ashongman is composed of the following: (1) the Ashongman village proper; (2) the Ashongman Estates; (3) Ashongman New Town; and (4) the New Ashongman. While the Ashongman Estates is the most popular, the Ashongman village is the least popular. Most people do not know of the existence of the Ashongman village, and they mistake Musuku (a village closer to the Estates) for the Ashongman village.

Major problems confronted the early settlers mentioned here but discussion is deferred to the latter parts of this chapter. The land is clayey which allowed for certain portions of the land to flood after persistent downpour or rain. The water table is very shallow, and the salinity is very high so sinking of wells or the construction of septic tanks was challenging. There was no pipe- borne water and no electricity. Transportation was not dependable and the community school was not the best.

ASHONGMAN AS A CONURBATION

The town has grown to be a conurbation with buildings depicting sophisticated architecture and now there is a taxi rank, where cabs or taxis ply from Pure Water to Madina Market. Private Elementary Schools have sprung up in the area. The Golden Avenue School started by one -Afriyie, whose elder brother is Bishop Dr. Peter Akoto (we grew up together in Mampong) has grown to become a very good school in the entire area.

Over time, convenient shops and stores for electrical parts, plumbing materials, chemical shops or pharmacies, and students' hostels have abounded. The community has benefitted from the installation of street lighting by the Member of Parliament, Professor Aaron Mike Ocquaye (the then Member of Parliament of Dome-Kwabenya). Nevertheless, Owners of buildings in my area had to provide street lights in front of our homes and we had to also purchase electric poles to extend electricity to our homes.

The major problem confronting the area is rugged terrain of the road from the Ashongman village to Pure Water (my area and from the Ashongman Estates to the Village and Pure Water. The 2020 Budget Statement of the Government of Ghana mentioned the construction of these road in 2020. The construction of the roads will go a long way to alleviate the plight of the people and bring relief to the community at large.

LIFE LESSONS

The stories told by the autobiographical narratives in this issue are already part of history and continue to nourish a more direct approach to history and consequently, our understanding of history (Aurell & Davis, 2019).

LONELY VISION PATHS

I have included my experiences in living in Ashongman as part of my personal growth stories. I was privileged to learn early of strategic planning under the pupilage of Benie Barparte (a Canadian facilitator) for one of the credit union workshops in Accra, which culminated into the crafting of a Vision and Mission statements for the Ghana Co-operative Credit Unions Association (CUA) Limited. Even though, I learned of strategic planning in the Graduate School, the practical touch received during my credit union days was very instructive. The facilitator used the vivid account of the specific steps (timelines and actions) used by President J. F. Kennedy to strategically land Americans into Space.

My decision to own a house in Accra (the Capital City of Ghana) was informed by planning for retirement earlier on in life. I determined that in Ghana, the compulsory age for retirement is 60. So, *I was going to retire in the year- 2024.* The lessons drawn from those who went to retirement while I served in Ghana was an *eye-opener* to me and I did not want to find myself in the situations some of them found themselves in. I do not want to cite names here, but the lessons were quite instructive.

I remember my architect in the process of designing my building plan told me that the project was going to be costly and wondered how I was going to put the project up. I viewed the project as a life-long project and that in life at times when you are asked to produce ¢100 you cannot;

but at other times you could produce ¢1 million. In the USA, people acquire a home through mortgages over 20 to 30 years at rate of interest (fixed or viable) using amortization process to allow for both principal and interest to be paid over time. My neighbor recently finished paying fully for the home after 30 years on living and paying for the home. My question is: *How is the USA approach different from my approach of investing funds from time to time to finance aspects of the building project?*

The specific aspects of the project revolved around the following: (I) foundation, flooring, super-structure, lintel level, roofing level, actual roofing, fixing of frames for window and doors, electrical wiring and fittings, plumbing system and fixing of fittings, and plastering. (II) Others covered- ceiling joints and ceiling, tiling, painting, compound work covering drainage, and septic tanks construction. Additionally, (III) underground water reservoir to harvest rain water, connectivity to national electricity grid system, provision of additional poly tanks to provide water to specific areas of the house. The project has taken over 20 years to complete but the story is the same.

UNWAVERING DETERMINATION

I have discussed the overarching Vision of home ownership in the section above. In this Section, I am going to talk about the discouragement I received from people, including family and friends. The basic theme of discouragement centered on (a) the place is too far (about 26 kilometers from Central Accra); and (b) the house is located in the bush. Yes, facts were accurate but I did not allow these sentiments to discourage my resolve to reach the ultimate goal in the long-run. We had to allow our children to be enrolled in the University of Science and Technology (UST) Primary School in Kumasi in the short-run, staying with the late Grandma for about 5 years. I stayed in the house with my wife (in memoriam) and our trusted dog (Mavis-1998 to 2011). Mr.

Kwame Asafo-Agyei (my nephew-in-law) spent the weekends with us for some time until 2000.

TIMELY ENCOURAGEMENT

One day when I visited Mampong-Ashanti in the early *2000s*, I met my late mother (Afia Amaniampong-the mother of the Amaniampongs in the Church of Pentecost family) and he said: *"Papa, I hear your house is located far from the Accra City Center. Don't be disturbed about the location. The rate of growth and development in Accra is very fast. Somebody gifted your elder brother…a plot of land in a remote location in Accra. There was a narrow path that led to the house but today, as you know, your brother's house is located right in town. You would soon see your house in town"* Wow! This was very huge for me. May *Old lady* rest in perfect peace. I can confirm that my old lady's prediction has been fulfilled in just a matter of two decades, as of December 31, 2020. The one-time village of Ashongman has been transformed considerably, with the area almost built up and having associated amenities.

PROBLEMS ARE SURMOUNTABLE OVER TIME

In this section of this book, I would like to address how the major challenges I faced in Ashongman were surmounted. (1) **Transportation**- There were no public vehicles available early in the morning before 8:00am and after 8:00pm because of demand and supply for transportation services. Only few workers staying in Ashongman at the time utilized transportation services. The option left was to walk for about 2 miles to and from Ashongman to Agbogba (the next settlement). With time, two *trotro* (private passenger minibuses) became available in Ashongman because the drivers lived there. So, travelers had to make it early to catch any of the 2 buses.

To give you a sense of how far Ashongman has become, I can recollect about 28 *bus stops* for pick-ups and drop-off of passengers, as follows: *(i) Madina Market, (ii) Madina Zongo Junction, (iii) Masalatchi (Mosque), (iv) Firestone, (v) Atomic Junction, (vi) North Legon Junction, (vii) Agbogba Junction, (viii) Chari (Charismatic Evangelistic Mission (CEM)/ Wisconsin University, (ix)Adjei-Mensah, (x) Selasie, (xi) Flowers, (xii) Dar Es Salam, (xiii) Top Herbal, (xiv) Lotto Kiosk, (xv) Koliko Junction, (xvi) Cossway/GOIL Filing (Gas) Station, (xvii) School Junction, (xviii) Fitting Shop, (xix) Agbogba Last Stop, (xx) Agbogba Cemetery, (xxi) Assemblies of God, (xxii) Antch, (xxiii) Ahmadiyya first gate, (xxiv) Ahmadiyya second gate, (xxv) Down Town Bakery, (xxvi) Obuobi, (xxvii) Alloway (All the Way), and (xxviii) Ashongman Last Stop. Wow!* Interesting names and landmarks.

The question is: *If you get to any place where any of the signposts bearing any of the names are removed, how do get the correct location?* This state of affairs gives an idea as to how the addressing system was in Ghana in the past. The Government of Ghana is commended for introducing the Digital Addressing System for the development of the country. With the passage of time, most of the earlier settlers of Ashongman owned private vehicles. Most of the vehicles parked overnight at the compound of *Pure Water* before getting good surfaces that facilitated driving vehicles home.

The vehicles of the early settlers became a pool that assisted our movements outside of the area in the mornings. Community support at its best. *Isn't it refreshing?* In the process of time, *trotro* became available from the Madina Market through Atomic Junction to Ashongman. Taxis (cabs) plied between Atomic Junction and Ashongman. Later, some *trotro* served from Abokobi through Ashongman to Accra Central.

(2) **Water supply**- The immediate problem that needed attention was the availability of water. We engaged one person to fetch water from a stream (Onyinase) in the vicinity; this stream is believed to be

the source of the *Odaw river* in parts of Accra. The arrangement was to fill our barrels and jerry cans with water over the weekend for general purposes but portable water was brought from other parts of Accra for cooking. The water for drinking was through bottled and filling of bottles.

Ashongman is located at the leeward side and not very far from the foothills of the Akwapim ranges. Contrary to geographical knowledge, rainfall is rampant as compared to other parts of Accra. With the passage of time, we begun to explore the harvesting of rain water. A security man with one of the Pentecost Clinics offered to dig a bore hole for me in Ashongman but due to the higher salinity levels in the soil, I did not pursue that option.

I approached my bankers back then and took a loan of ¢300,000 to construct an underground water reservoir, measuring- 15feet (length) X 10feet (width) X 10feet (depth). Designed like a septic tank with two compartments, having opening to allow water to be distributed between them. Painted in white oil paint to enable regular cleaning of the floors and the walls to be undertaken before the rainy season started. There are two openings with metal coverings.

Water is drawn by lowering a plastic bucket tied with a plastic rope. Currently, two huge poly tanks have been placed on concrete stands to receive the pumping of water from the underground reservoir and supply from private tankers services for distribution in the three overhead tanks (one on top of the porch for bathrooms), another on top of the kitchen to supply water to the *powerhouse* and the other on a metal overhead stand to service the Outer house. With six (comprising underground tank and five poly tanks) water reservoirs in the house, the water needs of the house has been addressed.

(3) **Electricity supply**-There was no electricity in parts of Ashongman. Suffice it to say, the wider surroundings such as Adenta, Legon, and Ashongman Estates had electricity and this was displayed

in the night. The Ashongman was seen as a *dark spot* surrounded by light. Later on, there were pockets of light in the dark spots. The connection of Ashongman to the national electricity grid begun as explained below. The Ashongman locality was deem as part of Rural Ga in the Greater Accra Region.

In one election cycle, a political party delivered several electric poles to *bait* the people to vote for them. Nothing was done after the election when the party came to power. On the occasion of campaign for re-election, when the same party came back to solicit for votes, the people categorically told them that they would not be taken for granted the second time. As a result, the party asked all those in the village who wanted electricity to submit their names and their homes were connected to the national grid free of charge.

When the residents in other parts of Ashongman got to know this information and approached the appropriate quarters; we were told to apply but I paid ¢2 million cedis for my connectivity to the national grid. It took a period of three years before the provision of electricity became a reality to me in Ashongman. I gave some of my electrical gadgets to a close person but when I needed to collect them back, was reluctant to release the items to me when I finally got electricity in the house. I had to reacquire some of the very item again with time. I used to send my clothing to chez Larbi in Agbogba for ironing. I thank my son-Benjamin Kwasi Larbi who did the ironing for me most of the time.

(4) Security- My first loyal dog (Mavis) provided me with some security of the property because of the reputation she had in the area as a wild dog. She escorted me from home by accompanying me to a point where I instruct her to return home. In the evening, she left the house to meet us and returned with us to the house.

In the year 2000, when the exigency of my circumstance required me to move to the Campus of the University of Ghana, this dog survived because I later learned that my caretaker was not staying at home most of the time. Keep in mind that the dealings with pets in Ghana (Africa) is not the same as those in America. Currently, my crossbreed dog-*Terror* and off springs have kept security in the house. *Terror-T* as I call her, was given to me as a gift by one of my neighbors (Mr. Ernest Akoto-Bamfo) on learning of the death of Mavis (first dog). I am grateful to him for this gesture.

(5) **Education**-The problems I encountered at Ashongman did not deter me from furthering my education. I stayed in Ashongman to commence my Graduate School but had to move to campus to complete due a major change in my family circumstance (discussed) elsewhere. I continued my professional education in Ashongman. As far as the children were concerned, they enrolled at a private school near Ashaley-Botchwey in Accra from Kumasi.

The school bus picked and dropped them off at Mr. Obuobi's place by the main road. They had to walk to and from Mr. Obuobi's place for 20 minutes to get home. The walking distance between the Ashongman Estates and the house and from the house to Mr. Obuobi's place was 20 minutes. The walking was a daily affair but when I leave the house around the same time; then, I will drop them off at Obuobi's place or send them to school if for some reasons the bus does not show up or breaks down.

In retrospect, I am of the belief that problems can be solved with time and so human beings have to discover the relevance of time in the wider scheme of things. I have suffered some setbacks overtime. The huge one being the call to glory of my better half during these periods. Other minor setbacks encompass the following:

Stealing of Aluzinc roofing sheets, I contracted out the roofing of the Boys Quarters to a carpenter (name withheld) from Kwamekrom in the Volta region of Ghana to roof my house. At the time, he was attending Church at Agbogba and known to my nephew-in-law. The roofing sheets were carried to the project site from the church location, where they were kept.

In the final day of roofing, the carpenter came for 17 pieces of roofing sheets and moved towards the site and later branched off to the place where he was staying and that was the end of the story. An eye witness saw him branching to his place. He was never seen again. When we went to check at his place, he had packed off. An official report was made to the Madina Police Station.

Removal of vehicle battery, one Saturday morning, my good friend (Late Mr. Larbi) asked me to bring along the children to his place so we can have a brief cerebration of his birthday. When we got ready to go and sat in the car, I started the car but it would not start so I was wondering what was happening because the battery was fairly new. When I opened the bonnet or engine compartment, I discovered there was no battery in place. Upon further inspection of the car, I saw a dent arising out of a tool used to force the bonnet open. I was down because such practices were alien to Ashongman, but I had to move on.

Cross Country (SUV) get stuck, One day, after our peak season in the office, the official vehicle that brought me home got stuck in the soil because of the clay content. The driver applied all skills acquired through long years of driving trucks but did not work throughout the whole night. The driver did not want to sleep because he did not tell the family that he will not come home. Communication was not as it is now. He toiled from 9:00pm to 1:00 am but to no avail so he gave up and came inside to rest. In the morning, I arranged for a tractor in the area to pull the vehicle out and it took only a few minutes to bring it out.

Exposure of bad deeds, I used to clear the weeds on plots and roads surrounding my house from time to time and I chanced on a couple of dried mortar (mixture of cement, water, and sand). Not knowing that masons and their laborers threw the remaining mortar and concrete (mortar plus building stones) into the nearby bushes at the end of day to prevent discovery. In addition to these, I have come to understand some schemes by construction workers in Ghana.

Failure to return materials in custody, There was a caretaker in the area I met and I used to give him minor jobs to do for me and to help him as well. I kept the first batch of my personal belongings in the basement and corridors of my good friend (Evans Boakye) at the Ashongman Estates because of proximity and because my house was also not ready. Later on, I brought the second batch of items from Cape Coast covering all doors for the Outer house, and a few household items. I kept the remainder of roofing boards such as 2x6x16 and 2x2x16 in the house where one of the caretakers was staying. After releasing the doors for fixing, he could not account for the remaining items. I complained to one or two relatives in my church but that was the end of story.

Accident that was prevented, One day I decided to go to campus in the afternoon because my last lecture was going to end at 9:30pm. You recall I was teaching at the Ghana Institute of Professional Studies. Meanwhile, my daughter had gone to Madina to buy stuff from the market. She had the key to the main gate in her possession because I was going to meet her on my return in the night. When I started my vehicle, everything seemed alright until I got close to Pure Water (close to about a kilometer), I heard a strange noise under my vehicle. I stop to observe the under part of the vehicle but did not notice any problem. Then, knowing that I was going to come home late, I decided to return to park the vehicle in the house so I can take a cab or taxi to and from school.

I drove to the gate of the house but I could not get in because my daughter had the keys to the gate. While waiting for my daughter who was by then returning home, a neighbor of mine handed to me a wheel knot and told me that it fell when I passed him on my back home. I thank him and decided to inspect all my tires. To my amazement, four out of five of wheel knots of one tire have fallen off. Only one was

449

in place. I went back the route I have taken towards *Pure Water* and fortunately, I found the remaining three knots along the path. It was at this point that I appreciated the reason for the strange noise. Anything could have happened.

This negligence was caused by a mechanic who took my vehicle to *Abossey Okai* to replace all the tire. The knots were not tightened well. I invited my regular mechanic to work on the vehicle for me at home.

By way of summary, all major problems have been solved through the gift of time. Nevertheless, the outcome of the solution is the same but the approaches have varied. In this section, I am going to discuss how some problems have been resolved: **One,** *Solo*-Some the challenges such as the solution to water crisis was addressed mostly by myself and with financial support from my bankers. The application is that in life some problems can be solved by you; but not in all cases. In other situations, alternate approaches should be explored. **Two,** *Collaboration*-I am humbled by what collaboration can achieve if harnessed properly. In Ashongman, five of my neighbors collaborated by buying one electric pole each and paying for one-fifth of the cost of connecting to the national electricity grid. Instead of the cost falling on one person, was borne by many in this case five landlords.

Three, *Private partnership*-I have benefited from a private partnership with one dealer in building and construction materials from water tanker service to supply of stones and sand, cement, iron rods, sandcrete blocks, and other building material. I had an arrangement that allowed me to deposit moneys from time to time towards agreed-upon building materials at a price and quantity. No matter how long it takes, I just had to produce my receipt to schedule a date for the delivery of the item. By this arrangement, I provided him funds to do his business at no interest and he intend afforded me the opportunity of saving towards the purchase of specific items without recourse to price level changes. The arrangement was a win-win for all and his honesty was the talk of the town. No wonder this man has *waxed* stronger in the area and continue to increase.

Four, *Communal*-I have explained how the transportation needs of the early settlers of Ashongman were met. I quite remember once upon a time I was returning home very late after work around 10:00pm and I saw a lady-neighbor, whose brother was known to me. I stopped to give her ride home but she refused. I sensed she was afraid so I had to introduce myself and provide details about the brother who was personally known to me before she agreed to join us home. In another development, I was involved in an accident with a couple at the Atomic Junction. While the man worked with the IT department of an Examinations body; the spouse worked as a librarian. We all survived.

I want to recount the gesture of an unknown sweeper of my house compound. When I returned from the Graduate School, I was initially, staying alone and on some days, I returned home to see my compound completely swept. I was wondering who might be sweeping my compound because I had not contracted anybody to do so. I discuss with my good friend and we decided to allow a family to stay in the house with me. That was how a family came to live with me.

After about two years, the boy and girl left because they came to Accra to raise money to further their education. The boy worked as an apprentice cobbler and the girl fried plantain chips for sale. The woman sold meat pie on commission basis and the man was a painter. Later on, the woman told me she was going to take care of the sick mother but never returned. Until then, I thought they were marriage couples but got to know that they were co-habitating.

A woman in my neighborhood lodged a complaint to my friend to the effect that she had given the man in my house an amount of ¢500,000 as her contribution towards the electricity connectivity project without our knowledge. She discovered that the project had been completed but her house was not connected. She learned the man had given her money to replace the monies the boy and girl had been saving with him over time.

My friend requested him to raise some money so he can lead him to plead with the neighbor for time to repay the balance. The man agreed but later on I realized that I was not seeing him in the house. The door of the room he occupied was opened and his radio was on. I checked and nobody was in the house, so I went to my friend and traced his biological daughter in a nearby village and she told us that he has gone to his hometown. I went to the Police Station to report the incident and I was told to pack his stuff into any safe place and make use of the room.

Five, *Agent of transformation*-It will naïve on my part if not absurd and I cannot continue to be silent to let people know that the process I went through in Ashongman has motivated other people who owned building plots around my house to speed up construction to move in with families. Others have been incentivized to acquire plot and gone ahead to complete them for occupation.

Dear reader, no matter how it takes it can be done. So, people are scared but it is not difficult, when I was building, the cost of a bottle of beer could buy 5 sandcrete blocks but there are people who were drinking every day and buying for friends as well. Such people were investing their building projects in their stomach. One Professor of the University of Ghana Medical School remembered this analogy when I met him and the family in Amsterdam Schiphol Airport in Holland around the year 2010.

Again, 2500 sandcrete blocks can build a two-bedroom self-contained house, with a hall, kitchen, bath, and toilet. Additionally, as an elderly man taught me, if you acquire 10 building plots at different locations, you can sell 7 of them to build the first house for rental. Thereafter, you can build a new house every 3 years. Likewise, a lady in one of my local churches, collected just enough money(advance) to build a room for a tenant at a time and after a few years she had a completed building that provided her with income in her old age.

Six, *Governmental*-The neighbors have done communal labor to fill parts of roads with boulders or stones because of the deep trenches created by tipper trucks. On my part, I have invested in the weeding of paths. I cleared plots closer to my home to prevent reptiles from coming to my compound. We have killed two snakes at different times-the first was seen by my nephew-in-law as hanging on a ceiling joint. This one was traced to an Oil palm tree that was behind the house. The tree was uprooted immediately. The second was when I got home from work one night and saw a black snake folded close to the door. I saw there was a small space under the main door so I had to immediately seal off the space.

The construction of the main and neighborhood road cannot be handled by individuals and so we continue to look up to government (both Central and Local) to help in this regard. If the Budget Statements and Financial Policies of the Government of Ghana for 2020 is anything to go by then, the construction of the roads in Ashongman will see the light of day.

Lastly, *Social responsibility*-While in Ashongman, I used to give food items such as rice, cloth, cooking oil, and geisha, etc. to my immediate neighbors during Christmas. On this particular year's Christmas, I decided to reach out to new people who have moved into my immediate neighborhood and in the process, I did not serve one or two of the old neighbors. After about three months, one woman met my daughter and wondered whether she had offended me because she did not receive the usual Christmas blessings from me. In fact, I did not know she was looking forward to this small gesture. I have learned a lesson from here.

CHAPTER 22

LIFE IN PICTURES

IN THE INTEREST OF SELF-DISCLOSURE, I am not a fun of taking pictures but on this occasion, I present a few for this book.

461

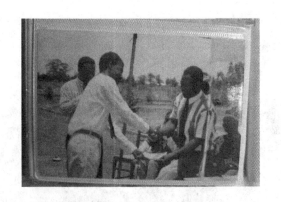

CHAPTER 23

CHALLENGES

A LIFE STORY OF 57 years as of April 15, 2021 cannot be deemed complete without problems. I consider life problems as surmountable challenges. As a result, instead of wallowing in self-pity towards problems, all efforts should be made to see challenges as possible opportunities to be harnessed for progress. In the *real-world*, successful people tend to be societal problem-solvers. Almost all human beings have problems; the difference is the attitude towards the handling of the problems. So, I have had my share of challenges in life. I have recounted elsewhere in this book some challenges I have encountered as part of my narratives under specific themes and I do not intend to belabor the points in this chapters. While some do nothing or amplify their problems to earn sympathy from others, several people confront the challenges head-on. To this end, rational approaches can be utilized to surmount most challenges.

The starting point is to acknowledge the existence of the problem (diagnosis); followed by gathering of facts and information about the problem, with a view to developing and evaluating alternative courses of action. For the avoidance of doubt, doing nothing is a choice and choice leads to consequences. All actions have consequences, yet consequences can impact our future- for better-for-worse. The grace of God should be sufficient to take us through challenges (II Corinthians 12:9) and that problems and trials produce in us- patience, endurance, and perseverance (Romans 5:3-NIV, NLT, KJV).

The extent to which autobiography is viewed as fictional depends on legitimate claim that the person to whom an event happened can easily show that the same opinion, attitude, or tastes may have changed over time. As a result, a genuine anecdote about the period when retold in the present, seems as if it happened to 'someone else' (Lovat, 2019). I will consider a few challenges with life applications. Just to refresh your memories, I have discussed a few of the losses I have suffered in life in Chapters 9 and 10.

I touched on my encounter with failure in Chapters 2, 6 and 15 among others. Likewise, I have talked about the conditions I lived with in the Village of Ashongman in the Greater Accra region of Ghana in Chapter 21. Generally, life events have been phenomenal, including: Corona Virus (COVID-19) pandemic era in 2020/2021 that has been characterized by the passing of loved ones, including those not diagnosed with COVID.

Similarly, terrorist attack of September 11, 2001 has produced consequences for air travel for example and has succeeded in shaping history through hardships. I also experienced the 1983 draught in Ghana. Nevertheless, in all these, we have emerged stronger more than ever before. While the impact of challenges cannot be denied, we take solace in the fact that-*We are in it together.*

Per the Millennium Project, the 15 challenges facing the world are the following: clean water, peace and conflict, energy, the gap between the rich and the poor, science and technology, status of women, transnational organized crimes, global ethics, education and learning, health issues, resources and population, global decision-making and foresight, global convergence, climatic changes, and democratization (Retrieved from http://www.millenium-project.org -accessed on 09/29/2020). The impact of these challenges on people across the globe differ considerably.

IGNORANCE MORE EXPENSIVE THAN EDUCATION

Education has been deemed to be one of the most effective ways of breaking away from the shackles of poverty because education produces knowledge and knowledge is considered as power. I have enumerated my specific personal financial model for my education to encompass the following: (i) family and friends funding, (ii) employer sponsorship for the Ghana Stock Exchange (GSE) Course in 1998, (iii) FAFSA/ Student loan, (iv) training offered by the Credit Union System; as well as (v) benevolence of people during the time of my loss, (vi) personal loans, (vii) proceeds from consultancy, and (viii) many more. While education is determined to be very costly; the cost of ignorance is even more expensive. Consequently, education empowers and enables wealth creation.

WOES OF THE FAVORITE CHILD

A major challenge in life is in regards to the favored or favorite child. I consider myself as a favorite child of both my father and mother. I have learned some useful lessons in the process and I wish to share with the reader in this section of the textbook. The most popular and well-known favorite child of all time is the Biblical character by name-*Joseph*. The Scriptures record that Joseph was born to Jacob by his beloved wife-Rachael. The preferential treatment is exemplified in the *coat of many colors* that set him apart from the other brothers. For the purpose of this discussion, a favorite child is distinguished from an overprotected child referred to in Ghanaian parlance as- *Dadaba* (literally meaning the son of a daddy). In *real-world* situation, it is possible for parents to have a favorite among the children; even though, the parents might argue they love all the children alike.

A few of the reasons that give rise to the phenomenon include but not limited to the following: (a) *circumstance of birth*, the story surrounding the birth of a particular child may trigger an emotional attachment; (b) naturally, some children are inclined to follow the instructions and guidance offered by the parent than others and that might lead to parents being pleased with them. (c) Natural endowments such as talents or innate abilities of a child may inure favor to his or her benefit; (d) some people are traditionally named after specific loved ones of the parents and that may cause the parents to automatically love such children; and (e) parental insight into the purpose of life of a particular child through discernment or intuition.

The favorite child concept is not bad per se because God has several children (Romans 8:16; John 3:16; Matthew 5:9; Galatians 4:7; John 1:12; Galatians 3;26; I John 3:1); but has only one *begotten* or *beloved son*, in whom he is well pleased (Matthew 17:5; Luke 9:35; Matthew 3:17).

Per Romans 9:13, the Holy Scriptures stipulate that "Jacob have I loved and Essau have I hated" The decision to show mercy is the prerogative of God (Romans 9:15; Exodus 33:19); as extended to the Virgin Mary-You are highly favored (Luke 1:28). There are advantages to both the favorite child and other siblings; because the other children take advantage of this reality to get favors and privileges extended to all. At times, the other siblings use this favored brother or sister to make a case for the benefit of all.

The negative payoffs can be huge. The disadvantages relate to: *Relationships*- The existence of apparent favoritism in the family can breed division that has lasting consequences among siblings. The consequences encompass the following: (i) *apathy*- This can create apathy and indifference in the family. (ii) *Alienation*-Many a time, there is the tendency for siblings to isolate the favored child from events and activities. Furthermore, (iii) *loneliness*-The intentional or unintentional approaches for ignoring the favored child in the grand scheme of things can lead to loneliness in his or her own home. (iv) *Conspiracies*-At times conspiracies can cloud good judgement; thereby, deepening the rift in the family; (v) *suspicions-* leads to (vi) *hatred-* Translating to generations unborn.

Patriarchal Privileges-I argue that patriarchal privileges should be exercised with utmost due care because of the lasting ramifications on generations yet unborn. The Biblical Jacob through deceit took the birthright of Essau (Genesis 27:1following); leading to Jacob's escape from the wrath of his brother, which lasted over 20 years and what is more not seeing his beloved mother until she died.

My advice to parents is to try as much as possible to treat all children alike. Yes, I agree that each child has unique circumstance but an explanation about certain courses of actions would not be out of place because the children are able to identify favoritism if one exists. Make every effort to offer the same courtesies as much as possible to all children. You cannot pick and choose and consider yourself to be fair.

I have seen children who have been ill- treated overcoming their barriers to become influential to bring about change in the family. Actions have consequences yet the so-called curse of Essau contained a *provision* for change, as follows: "When you have dominion (grow restless), you will break his yoke off your neck" (Genesis 27:40). I have observed that some siblings are able to overcome their difference before, during, and after the death of parents. Sadly, a few of the families are disintegrated forever. We are humans and are not able to judge correctly at all times. So, the child you invest all your resources into might not necessarily become the most successful in the end. As a result, poor performance in school and specific grace should not be the discriminating yardstick. I have seen at first hand, children who were considered 'hopeless' rising to the occasion to turn things around. Parents should not limit any child but should provide the required and enabling environment for all children to flourish and be fruitful.

INTEGRATED FAMILY MODEL

The Integrated Family Model (IFM) is presented in Chapter 27 on Family as Center of Gravity. Implicit in this model is a blend of the nuclear and extended family systems. A combination of two systems also carries a mixture of both negative and positive payoffs of the two systems. I find that the positive payoffs of the integrated family model encompass, the following:

- Provision of support at difficult times
- Giving of a sense of belongingness
- Availability of cost savings avenues
- Surplus units supporting deficit units in families and society
- Enablement of impactful moments

The negative payoffs cover the following:

- The model can be very expensive to maintain-Providing for both nuclear and some if not all extended family is expensive relative to the available resources; thereby, putting pressure on people
- There is also the perception of favoritism because the choice of a few members of the extended family also suggests the abandonment of others. Yet, it is impossible to ratably provide for all. As a result, it is the intention that those who have been helped will also go and affect others within the family.
- There is a possible rivalry among members of the extended family joisting for inclusion. I once observed a disagreement among two nieces (cousins), which ended up extending to cover their mothers.
- There is the need for management and the upholding of the unity of the family in the light of limited and available resources.

LOSS THROUGH DEATH

One of the challenges of life is the fact that the longer one lives, the more one has to cope with loss of close associations. I remember one of my paternal great grandfathers lamented about the departure of nine of the siblings (he was the tenth born and the only survivor) and he had lived to witness the death of all of his siblings and as he was recounting his loss, he was very emotional about the phenomenon. Death is very devastating and the effects are very difficult to measure in quantitative and qualitative terms. More so, unlike Muslims, Pentecostals tend to be ill-prepared for death. When I was growing up, the number of deaths in my church was extremely low. Arguably, our church population was youthful as compared to the orthodox churches with more elderly population. I can count the number of members of the church who died in my local church back then.

The impression was created that people of the Pentecostal faith were *immune* to death and that God has to heal every Christian at all cost. This implied that the dead were people of less faith. As a result, preparation towards final departure was alien to people of Pentecostal faith, who refuse death in Jesus' name; yet, the truth of the matter is that Pentecostal do die. Nevertheless, the response to death has been inadequate. It is against this backdrop that I applaud Apostle Dr. Alfred Koduah (a former General Secretary of the Church of Pentecost) for touching on the preparation for death, and offering *16 things to be done to be able to face death* courageously, as follows:

a) Accepting and fighting the sickness
b) Getting as much information as possible about the disease
c) Engaging in prayer for healing and restoration
d) Preparing a will if that has not already been done
e) *Preparing the minds of family members and loved ones*
f) Giving hope to the family and loved ones

g) *Recounting all the blessings in life*

h) *Not feeling disappointed with God in any way*

i) *Singing encouraging and heaven-oriented hymns*

j) Preparing psychologically to face death

k) Utilizing the situation to share the Gospel with others, if possible

l) Rejecting all negative thoughts

m) Taking medical advice and medication seriously

n) *Encouraging yourself in the Lord*

o) Knowing you need Spiritual, physical, and emotional support from all

p) *Expressing appreciation to God, family members, and loved ones* (pp.114-130).

I have witnessed at first hand some of the items listed supra in relation to the death of some people known to me. For example, (I) my bosom friend-the late Elder Lawrence K. Larbi (Chapter 10) adequately prepared his wife and children before his demise as if he knew he was going home. This has made the management of the matters arising out of the death a bit bearable although the loss is replaceable.

(II) My mother a year before her death recounted to me regarding the blessings of God and extended her gratefulness to God, family members, and loved ones. I perceived that she was engaging with the life hereafter. (III) I have seen a dying nursing officer at the Korle Bu Teaching Hospital (KBTH) singing Presbyterian hymns; and later joined by family and friends before dying in the process in the presence of loved ones.

(VI) I have also narrated the story in 1986/87 of a dying elderly man, who questioned God for the *unfair* treatment because he argued that he had spent all his life serving God as a Catechist yet suffering in sickness. He died short after he had stopped talking aloud at the Legon Hospital. His ward was next to the ward I was admitted. I was very sad and I have reflected on this for a long time. As a result, Apostle Dr. Koduah's admonition is fair-*Not to feel disappointed with God in any way.* Lastly, (IV) Encouraging oneself in the Lord is applicable to all life challenges in general and preparing for death in particular.

LITIGATING TO POSSESS POSSESSIONS

I am opening up for the first time regarding the family litigation we went through for over three decades ago; and the litigation itself evolved from January 13, 1987 to January 25, 1996. The purpose of telling this story is to illuminate in-sights into realities of life and also to shed lights on beneficial life lessons to be learned. The process and the aftermath had had a very dire consequences on my family (father's house) through enduring suffering and pain. Through it all, I can state without any reservation that we have been able to move on with our lives for a very long time due in part to the following reasons: (1) Christians have been admonished to forgive; (2) the Lord had blessed most of my siblings with their own residential property; (3) my mother reiterated to me of her forgiveness before she died and also in response to the apology rendered by one of our uncles for the wrong done by their family towards her and the children; and lastly, (4) we have developed capacity throughout the process and the period.

On one fateful day, I was invited by my father into his living room in the company of my mother, where he told us of the existence of his *will* and explain that: (a) wills are only effective after the death of the testator and supported his point with the Scriptural text- Hebrews 9:16; (b) handed to me for safe-keeping an *official receipt* for the deposit of the will in the High Court of Law, the receipt shows the reference numbers in the Court database; (c) that the receipt should never be shown to anybody other than the lawyer because if it gets into the hands of people they might tear it into piece; thus, making it difficult if not impossible for action to be taken on it; (d) that a copy of the *will* has been deposited in the Regional office of the Church of Pentecost in Kumasi in the Ashanti region; and (a) that confidentiality was needed.

Several years later, my father passed. I have recounted my father's passing in Chapter 9 of this textbook. I do not intend to belabor the point here. After the final funeral rites and before the fortieth day celebration, I went to Kumasi to follow the lead my father gave me. I went to the Church of Pentecost Regional office in the Ashanti region (at the time the whole of the Ashanti region had one office). The Regional office was located in the McKeown Temple in *Asokwa* in Kumasi and I was pleased to meet the then Regional head- Apostle Abraham Tetteh Nartey (of blessed memory). After asking and listening of my mission, he called one elder and asked him to take me to the Chambers of the late Elder F. K. Atuah (Esq) in the Asafo Market Building. At the time of my visit, Elder Atuah was not in the office but the wife exposed me to the necessary processes.

Just to digress a bit, I want to add that Elder Atuah has been called to glory but the wife who was in charge of administration at his chamber is alive. When my mother died in 2016, we placed on record the legal services Elder F. K. Atuah offered the family virtually free of charge partly because lawyer knew my father and was also moved by the fact that my mother was a widow. Our family is forever grateful to the family of Lawyer Atuah. I have come to know some of the children-Jean, Laura, and Kwasi. I have been to their residence in Kumasi, and we have hosted Elder and Mrs. Atuah in our house during our last Regional Christmas Convention. I recently had conversation on LinkedIn with one of the daughters, a professor in the Faculty of Agriculture of the Kwame Nkrumah University of Science and Technology, Kumasi. She told me that her mum was 85 years now. I thank God for her life.

Now, the necessary steps were taken by the Chambers of F. K. Atuah (Esq) to permit the reading of my father's will at the Registry of the Kumasi High Court. Invitation letters were sent by the High Court to my mother, the children, and members of my father's extended family. On the day set aside for the reading of the will, I accompanied my mother to the Kumasi High Court. We set off early on the fateful day and on our way to Kumasi, on reaching *Pankrono* (a suburb in Kumasi between Ahwiaa and Old Tafo), my mother decided to call on her son; then, district pastor of the Old Tafo. When we were returning from the Mission House (Parsonage) that was when we saw my father's siblings on their way to the High Court.

I am telling this story because later we learned of speculation from some quarters that they saw my mother and I coming from a possible place where the *so-called will* of my father was prepared. Interesting! My father's testament or *will* was dated on the 14th day of December 1982 signed by Reverend Minister 1 and Reverend Minister 2. The Trustees and Executors were the late Elder Osei Kwaku and another (name withheld). The Probate showed Gross Value of Estate as ¢160,000 (Collected vide CR. No. Z.544484 of June 23, 1988).

The reading of the last *will* of George Emmanuel Appiah-Sokye dated October 20,1986 was per the Registrar of the High Court's (Name withheld) 53/vol 23/86/1476. The *will* was deposited on December 17, 1982 with receipt number 489396. The reading was slated for Monday, November 3, 1986 at 2:00pm. The distribution covered the following: Opanin Kwaku Duah, Okyeame Kofi Badu, Opanin Osei Kwasi, Madam Abena Agyakomah, Madam Akua Kontoh (All of Mampong-Ashanti of Ghana and *now deceased*).

When it got to our turn, the Registrar of the High Court invited us and brought the book containing the *will* and pulled it out in a sealed envelope and opened the envelope in our presence and read the contents to the gathering. My father graciously bequeathed all his property to the wife and children and there was no mention of any sibling in the *will*. This turn of events did not sit well with my uncles and aunty and they told the registrar that they object to the contents because the property mentioned in the *will* is not for my father.

A *will* is a legal document that sets out the wishes of the testator regarding how pertinent matters should be handled such as where to be buried, how his or funeral should be handled, issues of succession of family businesses; including the opportunity to bequeath property to the next generation. At least two witnesses are required to sign off without necessarily knowing the contents of the documents. The testator should be a person of sound mind and the property under consideration (if applicable) should be free of conflict of inheritance; and for that reason, should be the *bona fide* property of the testator. Executors are appointed by the testator to ensure that the contents of the document are implemented according to the dictates of the documents. In the case of my father's will, while the witnesses were two Ministers of the Gospel, the executors were both elders in the local church in Mampong-Ashanti, Ghana.

A 'Conspiracy theory' was put out that I have connived with my mother to prepare the will because that *will* could not have come from my father. Later, when that narrative was not convincing, there was personal verbal attacks and confrontation on the two elders in Mampong-Ashanti church, whom my father had appointed as executors and trustees of his *will*. In the circumstance, one of the elders was not willing to fulfil the duties reposed in him by my father in his *will* because he was afraid of the threats of the family. Nevertheless, the late Elder Osei Kwaku (one of the longest serving elders) stepped up to do the needful throughout the application process for the probate from the High Court. May his memory be a blessing!

A law suit (Writ of Summons) was served on my mother after several days from the Kumasi High Court. While Lawyer Ampratwum (now deceased) represented the plaintiffs; my mother (the defendant) was represented by F. K. Atuah Esq. This case became known as- ***Opanin***

Kwaku Duah Agyemang vs. Akua Kontoh (LC 8/87). The original action was brought on 13th day of January 1987. The plaintiff in this case is the head of family and younger brother of my father; bringing this action on behalf of his siblings. The defendant in this case is the widow of the late George Emmanuel Appiah-Sokye; and also representing her children as beneficiaries of the estate. I do not know the exact reference of this case in the Ghana Law Report. From our copy of the Official Record of Court Proceedings, the fact pattern is as summarized below: *first*, **Statement of claim** – The Plaintiffs averred that the property numbered-*T.87* located in Tunsuom in Mampong in the Ashanti region was the property of their mother- the late Madam Amma Agyenkwah, who is also my paternal grandmother. For that reason, my father cannot bequeath the said property to the wife and children.

Second, **Statement of defense-** The defendant countered this by arguing that the building in question was *bona fide* property of the late husband and not the property of the mother-in-law as being claimed. *Third*, **Court proceedings-** In the course of the trial, the plaintiffs relied on oral evidence by utilizing associated persons to give testimonies to the Court. The defendant (my mother) was illiterate but fortunately for us, my father was literate and an excellent records keeper. A search through his personal files returned, a considerable number of documentations to support the defense, including-(i) a copy of written application for the plot on which the building was erected, (ii) allocation letter from the Mampong Local Council for the plot in question, (iii) payment of pegging fees, (iv) statement of accounts in his own handwriting on the building project, (v) a copy of the building plan, and (vi) many more. All the associated documents were tendered in Court and marked as Exhibits to the docket. Additionally, the Mampong Local Council was subpoenaed to provide details on file regarding this property. The evidence of the Mampong Local Council corroborated the defense case.

Four, **Leave to amend initial statement of claim-** In the course of the proceedings, the plaintiffs applied to the Court for leave to amend the statement of claim. Around 20th day of June,1988-The plaintiff's Motion on Notice for leave to amend the Writ and Statement of Claim was granted without any limitation as to time to file his amendments, pleading pursuant to the said order. *Five,* **Amended statement of claim-** The amended statement of claim suggested that it was my grandmother who asked my father as her first-born to put his name on the records. *Six,* **Defense and counter claim**: The defendant rejected this argument because by Asante custom such request would have be made to her only daughter (my auntie) because Ashanti's inherit matrilineally. The trial judge granted the amendment to enable proceedings to continue. Refresh your memory on Danso vs. Addai (1954) GLR 376 -Case heard on summons for directions stage. Wrong. Trial *de novo* ordered.

The judgement- The trial judge, sitting in Court 4 of the High Court in Kumasi in the Ashanti region of Ghana, after three consecutive adjournments; entered judgment in favor of the plaintiffs. **Stay of execution-** The defendants *respectively disagreed* with the judgment of His Lordship because the judgement was against the weight of robust documentary evidence but rather reliance was placed on oral evidence. Cases-(1) *"Where evidence on record, say documentary weights against facts found, Appeal Court can set it aside"* (see also Fynhaut Production Limited Vs. Kwayie & Anr (1971) 1 GLR 479; (2) Atadi vs. Ladzekpo (1981) GLR Digest 15; (3) Kessie Vs. Nami & ORS (1981) GLR Digest 40).

Likewise, **Notice of Appeal** was filed against the Judgment of the 17th day of May 1990 to the Court of Appeal in Accra. *"In a case where H claimed title to land based on oral tradition evidence, the Courts of Appeal held that the claim of title based on documentary evidence prevailed"* (Hayfron vs. Egyir, 1984-86, GLRD 79). An application was brought before the same judge for a stay of execution. "In the High Court of Ghana held at Kumasi on 27th day of July 1990 Before His Lordship- Suit Number LC

8/87-Plaintiff-Opanin Kwaku Duah Agyemang of Mampong-Ashanti Vs. Defendant-Akua Kontoh of H/No. T.87 Mampong-Ashanti".

Matters arising out of the judgment-Before the motion of stay of execution could be moved, Court bailiffs and law enforcement persons stormed our house one early Wednesday morning to effect eviction. One of my late uncle's affidavit dated 29th day of August 1990 read in part: "That early in the morning on the 8th day of August 1990 at Mampong Ashanti news reached me in my house that some people from the Circuit Court had entered the house Number T.87 in the town and were ejecting the inmates from there" (Paragraph 4). "That there one of my grandchildren (name withheld) informed me he sent a letter from the Kumasi High Court Registrar to the Mampong Circuit Court Registrar to suspend the execution, but this had been ignored" (Paragraph 5). The affidavit of my nephew of 29th August 1990 and that of the witness by name- Lisa (not real name) corroborated my uncle's declaration. Furthermore, a Certificate of search by Solicitor for the defendant/applicant dated at 'His' Chambers Kumasi on 22nd day of August 1990 shows:

(a) Date when *Exparte* Motion was filed for Writ of Possession-
    Response: *8/6/90*(August 6)
(b) Date when motion for Writ of possession to issue was granted-
    Response: *Motion still pending.*

Additionally, a Copy of Registrar of High Court's letter to the Registrar of Circuit Court Mampong-Ashanti dated 7th day of August 1990 and signed by Registrar stated:

"With reference to my letter Number 982/W.P.3/90 of 3rd August 1990, I have to inform you that Motion on Notice for Stay of Execution has been files at Court of Appeal in Accra. The Motion has been fixed for hearing on the 22nd October

1990. Please Stay Execution until the final determination
of the Motion"

The actual eviction was on a Wednesday, the *market days* for
Mampong-Ashanti; as a result, it was a spectacle. The throwing of
our belonging outside the house attracted a lot of people to the scene.
All-in-all, 11 out of 13 room were evacuated, the two rooms left were
my parent's living room and bedroom. By the afternoon, neighbors
and relatives came and offered to keep some of the property in their
homes for us in the meantime. Keep in mind that there was nothing
like storage facilities in Mampong-Ashanti at the time. We are grateful
to our neighbors for their help during this period. Unfortunately, most
of the property were damaged in the process, especially the electronic
gadgets-some belonging to my two brothers in France at the time.

In an affidavit CS1625/90 and filed on November 6, 1990 at
3:30pm on behalf of three occupants as plaintiffs and the family head:
as well as, deputy sheriff, registrar, and bailiff as defendants (all of
the Circuit Court Mampong-Ashanti) through the Judicial Secretary
Ministry of Justice, Accra. The Statement of claim set out the items
damaged while ejecting us from our rooms. The total damages of the 2nd
plaintiff amounted to ¢350,000, the 3rd plaintiff's total items damaged
totaled ¢212,000 and my total items damaged was ¢591,000. The items
included some valuables received from relatives abroad back then. Table
12 shows details of damaged items as indicated in the Statement of
claim, as follows:

Table 12: *Damaged Items*

S/No	Type	Quantity	Description	Amount(¢)
1	Damaged	1	Coloured TV set	40,000
2	Damaged	1	Soundz system	20,000

3	Damaged	1	Chop Box	5,000
4	Damaged	1	Wardrobe	3,000
5	Damaged	1	Writing Desk	1,000
6	Broken	18	Pairs of China Plates	50,000
7	Broken	4	Drinking Glasses	32,000
8	Broken	1	Plastic Flask	5,000
9	Missing	1	Engagement ring	20,000
10	Missing	2	Wedding rings	50,000
11	Missing	4	Shirts	15,000
12	Missing	5	Pairs of Trousers	25,000
13	Missing	1	Kitchen set	20,000
14	Missing	2	Kente clothes	40,000
15	Missing	4	Car tapes	120,000
16	Damaged	1	Furniture set	30,000
17	Damaged	4	Pairs of shoes	100,000
18	Missing		Cash	15,000
19	Missing	2	Personal files	-
TOTAL				¢591,000

The Ruling on the Stay of Execution stipulated: *"As the respondent is prepared to accommodate the applicant, I order that she should be given two rooms and a hall to stay in pending the hearing and determination of the appeal. It is ordered that tenants put in possession by the defendant should either attorn tenancy to the plaintiff or vacate forthwith. No order as to costs* (Signed, Trial Judge).

The Appeal-A notice of appeal was filed and the entire docket on the case had to be typed and bound into a booklet; because in the past, judges in the Courts in Ghana had to write Court proceeding verbatim and by hand. A copy of the booklet on the case is available in our family records [Opanin Kwaku Duah Agyemang vs. Akua Kontoh (Suit Number LC8/87). Record of Proceedings. Exhibits 1-10, Index 1-55, 80 pages].

The Grounds of the Appeal were as follows:

1. *The trial judge erred in law by failing to compare the form of applications sent by the late Appiah-Sokye to the Council with the alleged order by his mother for him "to go to the Authorities to REGISTER HER NAME" and make a finding thereon as to whether or not the two issues are the same or similar to each other.*

2. *The trial judge erred in law when he failed to make a finding of fact as to whether or not the Plot no. T.87 was vacant in the year 1954 at the time of granting it to the late Appiah-Sokye.*

3. *The trial judge erred in law in failure to consider one of the main issues affecting the question as to whether or not the plan alleged to have been used by Kwame Buor (P.W. 2) is the same one as the one the Council office tendered as Exhibit 5.*

4. *The judgment is against the weight of the evidence on record. Additional grounds to be filed after receiving the Record of Proceedings*

An *Application for a Building Plot* dated 4/2/1953 was sent by Mr. George Emmanuel Appiah-Sokye (Faith Provisions Store, P.O. Box 23, Mampong Ashanti) to the Town Development Committee, Health Board, Local Council Office of Mampong-Ashanti). A copy of the said letter is provided below:

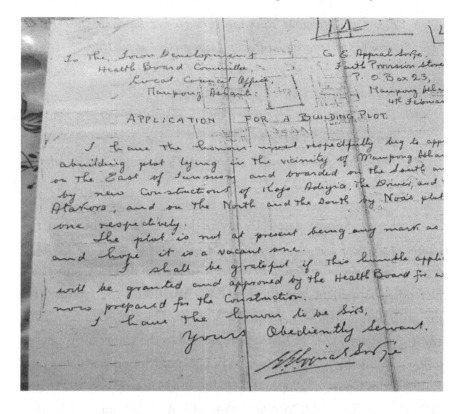

Counsel for Plaintiff/Respondent's Reply

On November 14, 1995, the Counsel for the Plaintiff/Respondent, replied, as follows:

1. *Trial judge was right. Had to choose between two. Preferred Plaintiff's version;*
2. *Complete history from 1951;Defendants starts from 1954;*
3. *Appears to know nothing about pre-1954 of the land;*
4. *Evidence was corroborated by witnesses especially 1951–1954.*
5. *There was a curious gap in defendant's case because she could not tell the Court when the Husband built the house.*
6. *ONUS was on the parties the same.*
7. *She could speak of events after the building had been finished.*

8. *Hearsay-Defendant claiming through her husband (p41-PW 6 family confrontation). Husband was present at meeting.*

9. *"He sware not to give away the family property". These bind defendant.*

10. *Defendant is claiming under a will as a volunteer-not as a bona fide owner-Will is VOID.*

11. *Defendant failed to rebut the plaintiff's evidence. She is claiming under a void will?*

Notice of Appeal dated 1st day of June 1990 sought from the Court of Appeal-*For the reversal of the judgment of the lower Court in favor of the Defendant/Appellant on her Counter claim.* The Counsel for Defendant/Appellant was the late F.K. Atuah and the Counsel for Plaintiff/Respondent was Adumuah Bosman. The case -*Opanin Kwaku Duah Agyemang Vs. Akua Kontoh*, progressed to the Court of Appeal as follows: While Steps in Affidavit in Support of Motion was dated June 5, 1990, the Court of Appeal's 346/180/90(M) of 6th day of August 1990 per Ag. Registrar; Motion was set down for hearing on Monday, 22nd October 1990. Likewise, (I) on November 13, 1995, the Appellant argued; (II) on November 14, 1995, the Respondent argued; and (III) on January 25, 1996, judgment was delivered by the Court of Appeal. The appeal was dismissed.

Decision to discontinue-Prior to the hearing for the appeal, we had decided to leave matters as they are and to continue with our lives; whatever, the outcome. As a result, Maame Afua Amaniampong offered my mother accommodation, as recounted in the tribute of the Appiah-Sokye family to Maame Amaniampong in her funeral brochure and the tribute of the children in my mother's funeral brochure. *More is her due than we can pay.*

REFLECTIONS

In the interest of self-disclosure, I was not present on the day of the eviction but I came back from Accra to find the house evacuated. Nevertheless, there are a cloud of witnesses available to confirm or disconfirm the events of that fateful Wednesday and beyond. My friend and I had to sleep on the varander in front of our room because the rooms were locked, and keys taken away by the plaintiffs.

Visits to the Police Station-There were series of police station visits by the plaintiff and defendant families arising out our resolve not to breach the peace. The Police came to appreciate the family relationships that subsisted and resolved most issues amicably; except one involving one my distant aunties and a niece of mine. I was the principal witness but when the case was called in the Magistrate Court (housed on the first (ground) floor of the plaintiff family house); the lawyers resolved the case with the trial judge.

Petition to the District Organizing Assistant-I petitioned the District Organizing Assistant of the Sekyere West District Council at Mampong-Ashanti on June 15, 1990 and copied the PNDC District Secretary, the Station Officer-Ghana Police Service and stated inter alia: "*The information reaching me from my mother says that, in spite of all these legal steps pursued so far, she continues to receive these threats. Considering the fact that, my mother is a hypertensive patient and respects the laws of the land, thereby submit my humble petition*"(Paragraph 10). In response, the District Organizing Assistant wrote to invite me at my earliest convenience per DS/CDR/Vol 6/135/90 of June 28,1990 and signed by one Antwi Bediako. I proposed the 9th or 10th of August 1990. One officer wrote per DS/CDR/vol 6/152/90 dated July 16, 1990 and copied to the PNDC District Secretary-to explain that the proposed date for the discussion is not convenient.

Pouring of liberations in house to invoke curses- One of my distant aunties by name- Leticia (not real name) died and my mother attended the funeral. During the course of the funeral, the plaintiff took the microphone as the head of the family and announce that my late father was not their brother but was from a certain place (name withheld) and so my mother has no business being in attendance at the funeral so she should leave the funeral ground. My mother left and came home and as if that was not enough, in the evening after the funeral several people from my father's extended family trooped to the house. A few gave what I will call optional speeches with intention to infuriate us but we did not respond. In the end, they poured *liberation* to invoke curses on wicked persons to die in a vehicular accident at the *Mampong Scarp*.

Lightning strike- As provided in my mother's funeral brochure, just around this same time, my mother was struck by lightning but she shouted the name-JESUS! Fortunately, she survived and her complexion was impacted for a long time. I am not accusing anybody here because I have no proof; yet, this occurrence was part of the chain of events. *Critical sources from inner circle-* The truth of the matter is that not everybody in my father's extended family supported the actions of my father's siblings. Some within the inner circle provided us with 'intelligence' that were very helpful in our daily response to issues and events. So, we are grateful for the *inside* sources. We learned at first hand two of our cousins who called out on their parents regarding their disagreement with their actions. The major financiers of the litigation were also revealed to us; as well as, those who *fanned the flames*. Most of the parties are dead so I do not intend to provide further information on this.

LESSONS LEARNED

We accept the rulings of the Courts of law on the case but we respectively disagree. I have provided the reader with a copy of the application for the building plot above. We argue that it was the application for leave to amend the original statement of claim that resulted in the judgment outcome. For example, Papa's Signed Application for Electricity Supply letter was dated May 29, 1968 and response to Service House Number T.87 Tamale Road-Mampong Ashanti with Reference Number SE 5/199fs/2662 was dated July 17, 1968 and signed for by the Senior Electrical Engineer with comments or minutes, as follows; F/S I 82 of 15/8/368. Receipt for N¢24 vide Receipt Number 152517 of 14/8/68 Account Number 730/948. We have moved on.

Involvement of close relatives in projects- Spouses and children are called upon to answer critical question after the death of the partner. Additionally, the lawyer of the plaintiff/respondent stressed on the number of "I do not Know" answers provided by my mother in the High Court docket to suggest that my mother lacked sufficient knowledge of the property. Invariably, the appeal was dismissed. For that reason, the era where spouses kept critical issues close to their chest is over. Married couples should adequately equip members of their family with the needed knowledge.

Good record keeping practices-The practice of keeping records is a noble act to be emulated by all. I have studied that discipline under my father so I am a good record-keeper. For example, my father left behind 7 important files that served us well. Beyond that, he documented most information in a diary or journal. At minimum, I recommend that the following specific files be kept by the younger generation-either hard or electronic but access is the most important consideration. The personal files should encompass the following: (1) Bank correspondence and statements, (2) Credit cards, (3) Bill payments, (4) Taxes, (5) Vehicles, (6) Health, (7) Children Education-General and specific for each child; (8) Travel, (9) Property and Improvements, (10) Students Loans, (10) Employment, (11) Permanent files for each member of the household; and (12) many more.

NEW DEVELOPMENT

Taken Up To Be Given Out– Granted that the property in question was for our grandmother and having regard to the fact that our father was the son. The question is: *Are the children of my father not entitled to part of the property of their grandmother?* In a strange turn of events, we learned that the plaintiff had bequeath the very property we were dispossessed off and given it to his children after his siblings preceded him in death before he also died. There was a call on us to avail ourselves of the opportunity to join in litigation to reclaim our property. We have declined to join in any such action. Afterall, the beneficiaries are also our kinsmen and most of our siblings have our own personal property.

REFLECTION

I consider challenges as teaching moments or lessons for life. I have come to appreciate that people who faced challenges in life in one way or the other tend to enrich their experiences for a better outcome. Problems can be created by the actions of man *for better-or- for-worst*; but no rational person invites challenges; yet at times, human beings have no control over some life events and occurrences. Another lesson, I have learned is that time is able to solve a lot of our worries and concerns. Indeed, several of the things we care much about never materialize. Is it not fascinating?

CHALLENGES BUILD CAPACITY– Problems helps us to develop inert abilities that we did not have or that did not seem obvious until that time. Therefore, challenges can produce the best in us. Several people become prominent as a result of surmounting critical obstacles. Going down memory lane, history teaches that great people start small but it is the challenges they overcome that make them stand out. As human beings, we can only rely on past and present events to extrapolate the future. We may get it right or wrong but we need to live one day at a time because life can present a puzzle that may be difficult to unpack. At times, the experiences we go through help us to strengthen others in the future because it becomes easy for them to relate to our experiences. If you are going through difficulties, please hang in there because help may be on the way earlier than you think.

OPPORTUNITIES IN ADVERSITIES-As people go through challenges, the concentration tends to be on the weight and magnitude of the problem; yet, implicit in every challenge is an opportunity to be harnessed and explored. As a result, I want to encourage as many as go through problems, irrespective the shape or form to make conscious efforts to look for the possible opportunities embedded in the situation. In some cases, the opportunities may be obvious but in others, it takes time for the opportunities to come to the fore. Be on the lookout for the opportunity when the challenge surfaces.

WE ARE ON EARTH TO CREATE AND SOLVE PROBLEMS- Life challenges should be accepted as an integral part of life. The human race is buffeted by challenges and as some of the problems are solved, others are created. This is comparable to a situation where a medical doctor diagnoses a problem and prescribes a medication; just as the sickness is cured, side effects appears. In the process, the side effects of the medication are evaluated in association with the cure of the sickness to make a determination. If you have a need for a means of transport, it becomes a burden and the need sets in a disequilibrium until a vehicle is acquired. Just as this need is met; then, the responsibility of maintaining the vehicle such as changing of oil, buying gas or petrol, signing insurance contracts, renewal of license plates, and so on becomes the emerging concern. Several examples can be cited on this.

ELIMINATION AND SUBSTITUTION-In our High School mathematic class, we learned that both sides to an equation should be equal, suggesting that the right-hand side of the equation should be equal to the left-hand side of the equation. However, the equality is achieved through the **re-arrangement** of the elements of the equation such as isolating or grouping of like-items. By way of application, just as simple equation can be attained by re-organization of element; several life challenges can be solved through the re-arrangement of the variables. Keep in mind that from Information System standpoint, when data is process, information is obtained; and the processing of information produce knowledge, which when applied to the situation produces the desired solution to problems. Nevertheless, the simple equation approach cannot be used to solve simultaneous equation for example. In this type of equation with two unknowns, the approach is through **elimination** and **substitution**. Consequently, life challenges help us to eliminate certain bad attitudes and behaviors and substitute in place of that better ones because you cannot get new results from the same old things.

CONCLUSION

The purpose of this chapter is to equip the reader with a few nuggets of truth to help calibrate by taking other variables of interest into account in dealing with life challenges that are inevitable. It has been established above that life challenges helps to amplify the best in us through every nuance in behavior or action. I am not overpromising solution to all problems but I do not want the reader to underperform in this area because some of the life challenges when not attacked properly can destabilize the entire equilibrium of life. I want to end with the words of the following song: *I owe it all to Jesus; If I am ever have anything; Giving praise to Him; If I have offered anything to somebody; I owe it all to Jesus; If I have been used in a small way; I owe it all to Jesus.*

CHAPTER 24

—✤—

ACCOMPLISHMENTS

HANSSEN (2019) HAS OBSERVED THAT researcher-initiated autobiographies were well-written texts in terms of language, fluency and coherence, thus making it easy for me to find good quotations to support my arguments, and can be a plausible explanation for the frequent use of quotations (pp.316-317). I want to associate myself with the Apostle Paul in asserting that:

> *¹² Not that I have already attained,[a] or am already perfected; but I press on, that I may lay hold of that for which Christ Jesus has also laid hold of me. ¹³ Brethren, I do not count myself to have [b]apprehended; but one thing I do, forgetting those things which are behind and reaching forward to those things which are ahead, ¹⁴ I press toward the goal for the prize of the upward call of God in Christ Jesus"* (Philippians 3:12-14; NKJV).

Per Unger's Bible Handbook (1966), the Apostle Paul is widely considered to be the writer of the book of Philippians dating back to around AD 62 while he was in prison (jail); with the overarching theme- Christ for all the experience of life, including hardship, preservation, deprivation, suffering (including COVID-19); as well as, prosperity and popularity. As a result, the four ways to view the joy of Christ are in association with (a) *Life* in Chapter 1 (b) *Example* in Chapter 2, (c) *Goal* in Chapter 3, and (d) *Sufficiency* in Chapter 4 (Unger's Bible Handbook, 1966).Therefore, the joy of the Lord has been the guiding principle of my life; thus, providing me with sufficiency and examples towards the attainment of my goals. Consequently, I will apply *Philippians 3:13-14* to the discussion under this Chapter of the book, as follows: (1) My contentment; (2) Telling my story; (3) Stepping into my destiny; and (4) Fulfilling my divine purpose.

MY CONTENTMENT

Not that I have already attained,[a] *or am already perfected; but I press on, that I may lay hold of that for which Christ Jesus has also laid hold of me.* [13] *Brethren, I do not count myself to have* [b]*apprehended* (Philippians 3:12-13). I have lived a fulfilling life throughout the 57 years, as of April 15, 2021, I have been on this planet and I am pleased with what the grace of God has helped me to accomplish. I am *proud* of my record. I am not by any means suggesting perfection; but the risks I have taken in life and the choices I have made, backed by my faith have enabled me to minimize on my threats and to maximize my opportunities. I am excited to stand in solidarity with all whose plan is to gain some practical life experiences. Likewise, my knowledge and convictions have helped to shape my sense of usefulness and relevance in the marketplace of influence. I have come to appreciate that being truthful to yourself can illicit astuteness to make the desired impact and substance.

I have been a pacesetter in several spheres of life. I have been guided by the Pentecostal worldview and heritage, as well as, the useful parental instructions received along with varied nuggets of wisdom imparted to me by my mentors and people in my inner circle. I am incredibly elated to contend that being a pacesetter does not make me the last to achieve these *feats* but to allow for as many people as possible to believe that these achievements are doable.

For example, to the glory of God, my pioneering role and pacesetting record from my mother's side; include the following: (i) first to complete bachelor's degree in 1989, (ii) first to complete master's degree in 2001, (iii) first to complete a doctoral degree in 2016. At the professional level,

(iv) first to complete professional certification in taxation (MCIT in 1995, FCIT in 2011); (v) first to complete professional certification in accounting (CA) in Ghana in 2006; (vi) first to be awarded professional certifications in Internal controls (CICA) in 2009; and (vii) first to complete professional certification in accounting (CPA) in the USA in 2010. First to be called to the office of an elder of the Church of Pentecost, and many more.

TELLING MY STORY

"Forgetting those things which are behind"(Philippians 3:13c). I have narrated my life story from the beginning but mine is not different from most stories that have been told in one way or the other; yet different in many respects. The similarities and differences are in the details of experiences and perspectives, successes and failures; achievements, growths, obstacles; as well as, memories and fantasies from events and phenomena. As a result, there is the need to reach out into the future from past rich experiences and events to make impact.

AWARDS- I have been *proud* recipient of a number of awards such as the following: (a) A fellowship by the Chartered Institute of Taxation, Ghana; (b) Credit Union Sterling Management Award by the Internal Revenue Service (IRS) Employees Co-operative Credit Union Limited-Cape Coast, (c) Supervisory Committee award from the Ghana Co-operative Credit Unions Association (CUA) Limited ; as well as, (d) awards by the Church of Pentecost (Chicago District) for Leadership appreciation in generosity, dedication, and special skills; (e) outstanding leadership for tireless service; and many more.

ACADEMIC-I am unbelievably grateful to have graduated from the University of Ghana School of Business Administration, with bachelor's and master's degrees with concentration in Accounting in October 1989 and May 2001 respectively. My terminal degree was pursued at the Northcentral University of Arizona in the USA, where I graduated with a Doctor of Business Administration degree in October 2016, with a specialization in Advanced Accounting. **Professional CERTIFICATIONS**- I have been (i) a *Certified Public Accountant* (CPA), since 2010 from the American Institute of Certified Public Accountants, USA; (ii) *Certified Internal Control Auditor* (CICA), since 2009 from the Institute of Internal Control, USA; (iii) *Chartered Accountant* (CA), since 2006 from the Institute of Chartered Accountants, Ghana; as well as (iv) *Chartered Tax Practitioner* (MCIT), since 1995 from the Chartered Institute of Taxation, Ghana.

Member of PROFESSIONAL BODIES- I belong to the American Institute of Certified Public Accountants and the Institute for Internal Control in the United States of America, and the Institute of Chartered Accountants and the Chartered Institute of Taxation in Ghana. I am a member of the Delta Mu Delta and the Golden Key International Honour Society. **LITERARY WORKS**- The thrust of my writings has revolved around the following thematic areas-(I) Public Sector Accounting; (II) Taxation as a fiscal policy tool for development; (III) Fraud detection and prevention- skills, strategies, competencies, and programs; and (IV) Accounting theory and practice. Likewise, (V) the development of taxation; (VI) the assumptions underlying financial reporting; (VII) the standards for financial reporting.

My RESEARCH INTERESTS have covered-(i) Occupational fraud and abuse in general and corporate fraud in particular, (ii) Tax compliance, and (iii) Accounting education.

While in the University of Ghana at the Graduate School, the major deficit I had was in regards to the cooking of rice using the electric stove. My cooked rice looked like rice porridge (popular called rice water). I was concerned about it so I told my study mate-Shirley Seidu (Jiagge), who outlined the steps to be taken, as follows:

1. Measure 1.5 cups of water to 1 cup of rice
2. Boil on Number 4 on the electric stove

3. Reduce to Number 3 on the electric stove after 5 minutes
4. Boil till cooked
5. Time the boiling time to the cooked time; So, you will know when to switch off the cooker to allow to cook on residual heat.

I prefer to call these steps as the "Shirley's Formula" and I find *step 1* to be the most instructive.

STEPPING INTO DESTINY

"Reacting forth unto those things which are before" (Philippians 3:13d). Sharing of life stories encompasses not only successes and failures but also apprehensions and challenges. I have indicated that my teaching career was in response to my personal circumstance as a single father, who needed flexible time to manage work and domestic responsibilities. When I went into teaching, I observed that most of the lower-level professional courses had been taken up by existing lecturers. As a result, I was left with higher-level courses for the Professional examinations. I took up the challenge and rose to the occasion. I remember taking Institute of Chartered Accountants of Ghana (ICAG) examinations with some of my students because I entered the teaching profession with a Master's degree, certification in taxation (CITG), partly-qualified at the ICAG (Part 2 of 4). I have taught financial accounting fundamental in the Chartered Institute of Management Accountants (CIMA) program; corporate reporting strategy at the final level of the (ICAG) program; and corporate financial management (ICSA).

SOME EXPERIENCES: I have recounted stories regarding my teaching experiences in Ghana to include the following:

a) A student who presents case for C+
b) A student presents envelope and matters arising-re-sit students and failed another paper

c) A student who attempted to bribe me when his attempt to register a colleague failed

d) A student who approached me for his grade to be changed

e) A student who called to say hello

f) A student who divulged scheme for registration after failing to get registered.

g) A student who fixed a personal phone issue

h) A student who provides name of an item I did not know

i) A student who was persistent in getting admission

j) A student whose sponsorship was through the sale of family property

STUDENTS MADE ME PROUD- The students who have made me proud include but not limited to the following:

1. *Dr. Benin Ibn Wahab-Was a class captain-pursued Masters and Doctorate at Coventry University in United Kingdom-I recommended him;*

2. *Mr. Emmanuel Ajene's project work at the bachelor's level was supervised by me –Completed Master degree-I gave him recommendation;*

3. *Mr. Martin Ayamborigya-Chartered Accountant, ICAG*

4. *Mr. Samuel Nubligah-Chartered Accountant, ICAG*

5. *Mr. Dominic Naab-Chartered Accountant, ICAG*

6. *Mr. Isaac Agyiri-Danso (Currently studying in Oxford University)– Chartered Accountant, ICAG, LLM, MBA, CITG*

7. *Mr. Michael Seshie-Chartered Accountant, ICAG*

Others: ICSA

8. *Mrs. Florence Blankson (CEPS)*

9. *Mrs. Larmie (SG-SSB)*

10. *Miss Jennifer Hammond Eshun (IPS)*
11. *Mr. Anthony Forson (LECIA)*

FULFILLING DIVINE PURPOSE

"I press towards the mark for the prize of the high calling of God in Christ Jesus" (Philippians 3:14). The fulfillment of divine purpose is the ultimate call of man. The challenge is to be able to identify accurately *la raison d'etre* and to answer the question: *Why am I here?* We are on this earth not only to solve problem but also to create problems. I have proposed a *master's degree, plus at least 1 professional certification* as the overarching goal for my students. Likewise, the Southern Illinois University, Edwardsville in Illinois' *Rule 1-2-3-4* is relevant: 1-*Join one voluntary association; ...;3-Maintain a minimum GPA average 3.0 over 4.0 scale; 4-Complete the bachelor's degree in 4 years.*

I encourage teachers to endeavor to build up students because a teacher does not have to destroy students. I have had occasions where students made mistakes but I had to overlook the errors because to err is human and to forgive is divine. Mankind is on this earth to fill temporary position as a way by which one's impact can be measured. As a result, it calls for a renewed level of analysis and strategy.

Call to ELDERSHIP- I am a man of faith, the converging point for hope and love. One of the far-reaching hallmarks in my life has been my response to serve as an elder of the Church of Pentecost in January 1994. Initially, I was reluctant in accepting this call partly because I saw at first hand the responsibilities placed on my parents and the high price associated with the office. As I have indicated, my father typically left home on Sunday mornings before 9:00 am at times foregoing breakfast and returning late in the evening. In other days, he travelled to the surrounding villages and towns to preach. Yes, my father was the church secretary for decades. I quite remember at a point in time, he was the Zonal elder for a geographical area covering a number of towns and villages and had younger elders and deacons under his charge for impact; where they organized programs including officiating burial services of departed members in the zone.

So, I had an idea of what the office required and I felt I could not combine those functions with my personal plans; but through it all, I can emphatically state that the call has been beneficial because of a few of the following: (i) I have combined this role with my academic and professional pursuits. At the time I was called into eldership, I had a bachelor's degree but I have gone further to accumulate more credentials to the glory of God; (ii) Elders are the *custodians of the faith* in the Church of Pentecost and this responsibility is onerous because this office is charged with jealously guarding against false teachings that are incongruous with the Biblical doctrine of the church. For this reason, the elder must be abreast with the doctrine before he can defend and protect them. This leads to a higher level of Spirituality.

The elder must be teachable to be relevant in this call. (iii) The call contemplates a disciplined lifestyle because the Church of Pentecost holds its members to a higher standard of moral expectation and so the elder cannot afford to live his life anyhow. In the process, the elder becomes a vessel of honor, ready for God, the church, and the society at large. (iv) An opportunity is presented to the elder to serve both God and Man and that is very refreshing. (v) There is abundant blessing (spiritual, financial, and material) implicit in the call but it is not obvious. Many a time, the elder might be required to lead by example through giving such as tithes and offerings but the blessings associated therewith is enormous but only experiential.

Involvement in setting a SAVINGS SCHEME-I have been instrumental in the introduction of the Senior Staff Savings Scheme as a Provident Fund (Employer and Employee)-Tier 3 under the New Pensions Fund in the University of Professional Studies, Accra (UPSA).

I chaired the team that developed the legal framework for the scheme. **Pioneering role in the formation of CREDIT UNIONS-** I have documented my pioneering role in the formation of the now Ghana Revenue Authority (GRA) Credit Union in Ghana in Chapter 20. My participation in these schemes was in response to my desire for the financial upliftment of the average worker.

Election to the SUPERVISORY COMMITTEE of the credit union movement in Ghana-I have become a teacher and practitioner of auditing partly because of my election into the Supervisory Committee of the Ghana Co-operative Credit Unions Association (CUA) Limited. At the time of my first election, I was working as an accountant and my practical experience with auditing was limited to my working relationship with internal auditors, external auditors and tax examiners. My new role on the Supervisory Committee (equivalent of internal auditing) developed me practically over the six-year period I spent on the Committee.

Currently, I am doing a similar task for my church, involving internal auditing and investigations on voluntary bases. The same experience has served me well in my current job as a fiscal compliance auditor. I can say that the Supervisory Committee in which I was a member is one of the best if not the best in the very existence of CUA in Ghana. My hard work in the Committee paid off in the subsequent re-elections. Keep in mind that I was elected as an observer in the most part.

TEACHING as a way of impacting others-One of the best ways of affecting lives is through teaching. Teaching is a passion and not a profession. Money is never the overriding consideration. It was once upon a time established that the rewards of the teacher were in heaven but come to think of the fact that it is possible some teachers will not make it to heaven. So, what happen next? As I described in my teaching philosophy in Chapter 8 and 14, my desire is to have students who will get better than me and also strive to go beyond what I have accomplished so far.

Christian LEADERSHIP DEVELOPMENT- I have also recounted the design and implementation of *four* blended (in-class and online courses, using *Google classroom platform)*courses in response to specific needs of young adults in my Church, as follows: (1) P.I.W.C Leadership Academy to train future leaders for the church; (2) P.I.W.C New Members Class to provide structured orientation for new members of the church; (3) P.I.W.C Marriage Preparation Class as pre-marital course for young adults; as well as, a Regional Training Platform to provide lay leaders with training material for personal development.

REFLECTION

In this chapter, I have recounted to the best of my ability how my divine purpose has served me well, by shaping me and bringing me to a place of contentment. To the extent that my passion has been directed by my purpose in life; thereby, helping me to step into my destiny. From the year 2021 and beyond, I am trusting God to help me channel my energies towards the promotion of five broad areas, as follows:

- *Development of a new level of Spirituality, grounded in Pentecostal ethos and theology;*
- *Encouragement of higher education, through career counseling because the benefits of education encompasses–investment in oneself, helping in rationale decision-making, enjoyment of life to the full at retirement, built-in inner confidence, and growth and productivity;*
- *Promotion of entrepreneurship, with a focus on small–medium–sized enterprises (SMEs) and business start-ups;*
- *Leveraging mentorship for leadership development; and*
- *Sharing knowledge and experiences to benefit many young people.*

I entreat the younger generation to continue to make the older generation proud. The suggestions for consideration include, but not limited to the following:

- Practice equips to leave one's comfort zone;
- Define for yourself happiness and learn not to compete with others;
- Acknowledge your efforts, strengths, and passion;
- Benchmark with the best and do not settle for mediocrity; and
- Do not quit at the least provocation but continue to try until you see results.

May God Bless you!

CHAPTER 25

LEGACIES

HUMANS CAN ABIDE FOR A season or live for a period of time on this planet. There is certainty for death because the probability of death is equal to one (Hebrews 9:27); however, the mystery lies in the timing of death. The question arises: *How come some people are remembered after death but other are not?* In William Shakespeare's writing in Julius Caesar, the famous speech by Antony *"The good is oft interred with their bones..."* Suggesting that the positive deeds of people are buried with them but the negative deeds are remembered into perpetuity. Yet, in *real world*, there are people who have been remembered for spectacular deeds. All over the world, there are records of famous and notorious people remembered for different reasons.

Legacies are simply the impact one makes on the surface of the earth. As a result, legacies are impressions or footprints of significance that brings transformation to life journey. According to Deuteronomy 6:23: *"He brought us out to bring us in"* Implying we are preserved for bigger divine purpose. For that reason, a researcher-initiated autobiography's position uses a method of producing data and a methodology that offer illuminating insights into how we as humans and nonhuman actants interact in networks, and how effects of these interactions and associations produce knowledge (Hanssen, 2019, p.321).

In the traditional sense, naming practices have been used to preserve the lineage. Typically, children are named after good people with a view to honoring the memory of the older generation such that their names will live on after their death. At the society level, monuments and national assets are erected for people of consequence to preserve their legacy. Future generation begins to enquire about such personalities when they come into contact with them; but at times, the accomplishments of such respected personalities do not resonate with the younger generation. Consequently, they consider only the historical dimension of the stories associated with them.

The plurality of legacy can be envisioned from the following: *first*, legacy can be property or money bequeath in a will to loved ones or for the benefit of the larger society. The legacy I intend to leave for the benefit of society is provided below-namely, a library and a scholarship scheme. I have chosen a smaller community to allow for greater impact. *Second*, legacy can just be as simple as life stories such as the subject-matter of this textbook. For example, Taylor (2016) categorically stated that "Sam Jonah is in the gold business" (p.1).

Three, lessons learned in life can be shared with others; thereby, constituting a legacy because the experiences of life can be a critical key that has the potential to unlock another's door. As a result, mistakes made by such persons are not repeated but positive actions can be emulated to reduce the need to build back things of negative consequences.

Four, legacy can be handed out to the future generation through the inculcation of positive values to guide actions. For example, the American society has inculcated in the younger generation the virtue of honesty and the Ghanaian society has imbibed respect for the elderly in the body fabric of the younger generation. My active involvement with the Church of Pentecost; resulting in the assumption of several roles, including but not limited the following: Local Secretary, Assistant District Financial Secretary, Presiding Elder (PIWC, Chicago); Patron of PENTYEM, National/regional Auditor, District Finance Committee, member; Member, District Executive Committee (Chicago/Romeoville); as well as, the office of an Elder of the church are part of my legacies.

Five, any good thing that has been started for which you would wish to outlive you can be a legacy. In Chapter 20, I recounted my exposure with the birth of the Internal Revenue Service Employees Co-operative Credit Union Limited in Ghana in the 1990s but now the association continues to grow some twenty years after leaving the organization. The Ghana Revenue Authority Credit Union Limited continues to make me proud and I am pleased to have been associated with the success story of the union.

Six, I am leaving a legacy regarding the sharing of family stories, traditions, pictures from Chapters 1 and 2, where I shared information about my ancestry, the extended family; as well as Chapter 27 devoted to my integrated family model and framework and Chapter 22 displaying life in pictures. *Seven*, the building of relationships and interaction in life is also a way of leaving a legacy. I have taken pains to research thoroughly to provide very detailed information including actual names to make a strong case for the conversation.

Eight, the telling of my life story itself is the best legacy to be left behind because elaborate information is available for processing. *Nine*, the desire to see the younger generation succeed is the driving force for my life purpose and for that reason, the willingness to pass on skills along to others through teaching, leadership, and mentorship. Afterall, *"I am enough to be shared"* Between 1985 and 1986, I began my practical leadership as a District secretary of the National Service Personnel Association.

I served in the capacity as School Prefect in the High School and House Prefect in my Sixth-form days. The leadership skills are transferable. I have enjoyed teaching because of the satisfaction of the impact on human lives. The students I have taught at the undergraduate, graduate, and professional levels in Ghana (Africa) and the United States of America bring me closer to my purpose in life.

APPEAL FOR SPONSORSHIP

As part of the legacy to extend knowledge to the next generation, I plan to set up two major projects: (1) the construction of a library, and (2) the setting up of a scholarship fund, as follows:

CONSTRUCTION OF A LIBRARY

My mother comes from a village in the Mampong-Ashanti area called Asaam. In the interest of self-disclosure, my mother was buried in her holy village. The Village is surrounded by Kofiase, Naama, and Nwadan. My ancestors settled at a place called Atwampumah (meaning no one cuts a walking stick longer than the height) by Asaam but there is no settlement there now. It is now being used as farmlands. One of the citizens (Son of the Soil, SOS), a philanthropic has provided the village with: (i) a Community Center, (ii) a Police Station and accommodation for the Police officers, (iii) Sanctuaries for two religious denominations including the Church of Pentecost, and (iv) an ambulance for the Health Post.

I propose to construct an ultra-Modern Library to provide the learning needs of this village and the surrounding villages. Just as the Health Post and the Police Station have been beneficial to the surrounding communities. The Library will be called Atwampumah Learning Center. The Library will have STEM (Science, Technology, Engineering, and Mathematics) Center, where patrons will be given help in mathematics and other areas. This is the physical property I want to leave as a legacy to society.

SETTING UP OF SCHOLARSHIP FUND

I am excited to share that life is a journey, with ups and downs but it is hope that keeps faith alive. In *Job 14:7, the Scriptures stipulate that:* "At least there is hope for a tree: If it is cut down, it will sprout again, and its new shoots will not fail. Consequently, the tree cannot abide when it is uprooted but once it is cut down, there is the inherent capacity to grow again. As humans, there are phases or seasons of life but all things can work for the better in the long run. Excuses cannot be given for non-performance in every human endeavor; and just as the different parts of the tree work for the general good of the tree; the varied components (body, soul, and spirit) co-operate for the overall good of mankind.

The roots provide the much-needed support or anchor to support the stem and branches and the leaves help with the very survival of the tree using the process of photosynthesis to produce fruits or the desired outcome. We are fortunate in life that everything that has a beginning also has an end and there is nothing new under the sun, says the Wise King in the Book of Ecclesiastes. Opportunities should be harnessed for creating, possessing, accumulating and dispossessing what is ours within the environment.

I believe it is a matter of time for solutions to be found for life problems and challenges. A renewed sense of urgency is required to surmount life challenges. Several people encounter problems and consider them as the "end of the road" but in actual fact problems are to be viewed as speed bumps on the highway of life.

I desired to pursue further education in the 1990s, which led me to pursue enquiries in some of the following institutions of learning: The Graduate School of Northern Illinois University; Graduate School of Management, The State University of New Jersey (RUTGERS); Office of Academic and Master's Admissions, Georgia State University; as well as, other Bodies such as Vermont Student Assistance Corporation

(VSAC), Office of Postsecondary Education, Research and Assistance, Government of the District of Columbia, The British Council, World University Service of Canada, and State Board of Education. I did not find sponsorship in all these pursuits.

My educational journey has not been easy as I have recounted in other parts of this textbook. Often times, the dreams of brilliant but needy students never materialize because of financial problems, they are compelled to abandon their dream *ab initio*. The proposal is to set up a scholarship fund with a Seed Money, to be managed by a Board of Trustees to be selected by the community from the area and beyond. The Seed money or corpus will be invested by the Board of Trustees and the earnings will be used to provide scholarship to support brilliant but needy students. Some scholarship schemes have been administered from the seed money and as a result had not been sustainable. The fund will be both merit and need-based. The Scholarship Scheme will be named after my mother-Christiana Appiah (a.k.a. Akua Kontoh).

ASTUTE PROFESSIONALS HOME

My interest in establishing businesses started in 1991,when *Zero On Mount Zion Enterprises Limited* (ZOMZEL) was incorporated as a company limited by shares under the Companies Code (1963) Act 179, with the Certificate of Incorporation Number 42,654 of June 14, 1991 and Certificate to Commence Business with effect from September 17, 1991. The authorized shares were 50 million and the objects of the company were as follows:-trading, import and exports, road transportation, business consultancy and secretarial services and catering; building construction, Audio-visual and photography, dealer in foodstuff, travel and advertising agency, entertainment and recreational services, and undertakers. My other endeavors have not permitted me to devote much attention to this business. My intention is to build a family business-*Astute Professionals Home LLC*, as a Series to allow this *stem* to produce *branches*; based on the professional focus of family members.

CONCLUSION

I contend that life should be lived with the end in sight. So, the type of legacy one wants to leave behind should inform the choices and actions to be taken. I have been hesitant in making a public appeal for these initiatives but I am sharing this vision so that others can also buy into the vision. I have carried well the name of my father-Appiah-Sokye thus far; however, my expectation is for my children and the generation yet unborn to carry the name-Sokye(as enough to be shared). I am calling all well-meaning persons who share in this vision to make it a reality. I am highlighting the incredible Vision because the Vision is not about me but it is for a greater purpose.

CHAPTER 26

PREPARATION IN LIFE

"PLANNING ENCOMPASSES: (1) OBJECTIVES AND policies, basic controls, plans and programs, and budgets; (2) Cash requirements, markets, and growth and development; (3) products improvements and staffing needs; and lastly, (4) a summary report " (Planning, CUA Workshop Document, p.17). Preparation involves planning for very important milestones in life. "The destiny of business enterprises, an industry, or a community, or a nation, is directed by the thinking and the planning that is done by the men who govern its affairs. Good management starts with viewpoints, investigations, and planning" (Planning, CUA Workshop Document, p.1). Preparation cuts across all spheres of life-from birth to death. In this Chapter, I will discuss preparation in relation to –(i) birth, (ii) education, (iii) marriage, (iv) building a house, (v) retirement, and (vi) death.

BIRTH

Typically, showers and outdooring are organized as part of the preparations to welcome the unborn into this world. Human pregnancies take about nine months, suggesting that a nine-month notice is provided the family to make the necessary preparation to receive the unborn baby. It should be possible for couples expecting a baby or babies to begin to buy the baby care for the children from the very onset in bits and pieces. To this end, preparation for receiving children in the family should be part of the pre-marital counseling process to allow for couples to commence such preparations just after marriage. While the contribution of family and friends are welcome, that should not be a substitute for our own preparation.

COLLEGE

Some parents are unprepared towards the education of their children. To some, college admission comes to them as a surprise. Currently, parents organize graduation and trunk parties as a means of raising monies to support the children going to college. I have no objection to supporting one another but parents should include the support of children in college in their preparatory plans. Consequently, parents should begin to think about college preparation when children are in the High school with a view to buying some of the following items-fridge, suite cases, clothing, beddings, and many more.

I contend that college preparation should begin from the birth of the child when funds are raised from the christening. Funds realized from the naming or outdooring of children should be treated as a restricted funds to be invested in products such as ROTH IRA, S.529, and ESA products to finance the education of the children. Additionally, children are listed as exclusions on tax returns Form 1040 and it should be possible for parents to invest portions of the tax refunds into the college funds for specific children. Likewise, the children can also put funds aside for the purpose from time-to-time from part-time and teen limited working opportunities.

The parents should make the library as the go-to for children. Likewise, parents should support children and to allow them to work during holidays so they can focus on maintaining a good GPA of 3.0 minimum to meet the requirement for some of the programs and courses. In practice, when students work full-time and study full time, one aspect suffers. Either the focus is place on money to the detriment of the course or vice versa.

To the students, I want to postulate that your excellent academic performance will be tested in college when all products from varied High Schools meet to study. Consequently, your performance in the High School should not provide assurances of continued success. Keep in mind that you do not know what other prospective classmates know and do not know. When learning, my suggestion is to learn for the bigger picture and not the performance at the High School. Way back in my secondary school in 1978, one of my tutors asked us to introduce ourselves and when we had finished the introduction, he said: "Perhaps most of you were the first in your respective classes before coming here. We are going to find out who will be the first here" I have been guided by this saying of this tutor of mine. I offer the following suggestion for the consideration of students:

- Make your books your friend and try to maintain a GPA of 3.0 over the period of the program;
- If we are looking for you on campus, you should be found at the Library;
- Attend lectures and do all your homework and assignments and on time;
- Join only one voluntary association to make time for a holistic education;
- Make it a point to complete your undergraduate program in four years. Review the handbook or catalogue carefully to know the credits required for graduation. Make up the difference through Summer classes or Community college if the credits can be transferred;
- Take advantage of available resources, including contact hour of professors and teaching assistants;

- Networking is part of college education and so take advantage of them;
- Appreciate your cheer leaders-parents, friends, and church leaders (These people should not be taken for granted);
- Trust in God and do not lean on your own understanding (Proverbs 3:5-6).

I recommend that a career is chosen early to be focused and I propose a minimum of a Master's degree, plus at least 1 professional certification; because a bachelor's degree is no more the desired level of education. The advantage is to possess a blend of academic and professional qualification.

MARRIAGE

In the United States of America, certification is deemed important in almost all vocations, occupations, and profession. Certification connotes qualification and recognition because of the regulation associated with it. Consequently, certification comes after a long period of training and development. I remember one of my friends (a medical doctor) had to submit himself for Board examination after ten years of practice. In other professions, continuous professional education is an important requirement for the maintenance of membership of professional association. While professional certification is awarded after rigorous training and subject to further continuous professional education or development; marriage certification is awarded upon the declaration of a vow. Some married couples get offended when churches try to help them in their preparation towards the marital journey.

No wonder several marriages do not stand the test of time. It has been established without doubt that there is a correlation between Christian maturity and sustainability of marriages. In the absence of formalized programs to prepare younger couples for marriage; the youth should invest precious time in learning about successful marriages in the Bible for the Christians, reading good books on the subject-matter, engaging with matured married couples, and picking the good aspects from parental marriages. Important questions should be asked and honest answers should be provided to settle all misconceptions, ambiguities, controversies, debates, and arguments.

Bridal shower has come to help young people getting married, yet marriage preparation should start as early as possible such as just after school such as undergraduate studies. Marital preparation begins with emotional maturity. I call on young people to explore opportunities that come their way prayerfully including possible suitors with a view to seeking counseling if the need arises. I want to caution against the habit of just driving away every person who comes our way.

Several people marry from the people they know already; even though, people can get married to people they did not know initially. I have seen other people marry to people recommended to them by people they trust. In all these, budgeting is key, where provision is made for wealth creation through savings and investments. Regarding people of African descent, young ladies should come to the table with financial contribution to support the gentlemen before, during, and after the marriage; the contributions should go beyond beauty.

RETIREMENT

Most people have in mind Medicare, Social security, and Medicaid as the surest support systems in old age. While these programs are good for the aged, they should not be the only programs to depend on. For example, social security pays retirees above the poverty line because while incomes decrease on retirement; the living expenses such as health cost increases because of possible comorbidities associated with old age.

Unlike *defined contributory plans* such as 401k, 403b and many more; the social security is a *defined benefit plan* and based on solidarity that our children will work to support us just we worked to support our parents.

I have seen people retire in misery both in Ghana and the USA. A few who lived in affluence ended up as paupers in retirement. The question is: *What went wrong?* I call for investments in both physical assets such as residential and commercial buildings and financial assets involving stocks (shares), debt, and marketable securities to create a solid portfolio. Similarly, people should develop hobbies and past times to keep them busy in old age.

BUILDING A HOUSE

A few young undergraduates have asked me about how is it possible to put up a house in Ghana having regard to salaries that are not commensurate with the cost of living. My answer is simple: *Where there is a will, there is a way.* Everything is about preparation. I will put the following suggestions across for consideration:

First things first-Begin with the acquisition of building plots-You can arrange for installment payments. If you do not have enough money to begin with: then, accept to go to places that are far off and start small and by the time development catches up with you, you are almost done. There may be some initial inconveniences but it is worth the future benefits. This is the model I used and it has paid off. Land appreciates in value so a piece of land that was sold for ¢2 million(GH¢ 200.00) in the late 1990 is now selling for GH¢100,000.00.

Sustained discipline-I was advised by the late Mr. Albert Nsiah to buy up to 10 plots and then sell 7 of them to put up the first house. Thereafter, it should be possible to build a new house at regular intervals of three to ten years. Even if you do not achieve this, it is worth the trial.

Do not compete-Someone stay in Ghana and completes his or her building in 20years. Another goes abroad for 15 years and comes to complete is building project in a year. Do not consider the length of time used to complete the building but factor in how long he stayed abroad before coming to complete in record time. The most important thing is that you are all property owners, who qualify to attend Landlords Association meeting in the community.

Phase the project-Construct the building project in phases such as foundation, flow level, blockwork, lintel level, gabble, roofing. Up to this point, it is standard for builders but the difference between a rich man's house and a middle-class person's house is in the "finishing" components, such as: fixing of windows and doors, ceiling and joints, plumbing, electricals, tiling, painting, compound work and many more.

Do the Math- Compare the price of a bottle of beer to one piece of sandcrete blocks to see how many blocks you are foregoing in consuming drinks on regular basis, plus those bought for friends. Consider the alternative forgone from basic economic theory.

Observe the rules of finance-There are several rules in finance that are critical in our pursuit of life, as follows: (i) the power of compounding and time value of money; (ii) pay God first but pay yourself second; (iii) align long-term financing with long-term projects and vice versa. (iv) Residential building and private vehicles do not generate cash inflows so business capital should not be invested in them but rather profits and returns.

One residential accommodation rule- I contend that you need only one residential accommodation to lay your head but all other investments should be channeled into income generating ventures or projects.

Effective land use-It is difficult to come by land so effective land use should be employed to get the best out of the property. Initial planning should be done upfront. Make provision for future development even if you do not have the financial resources now.

Downsize- The concept of *empty nesters* will catch up with you as you advance in age and your children leave home for the world of work. At retirement, while your income is bound to decrease, your expenses are likely going to increase. Design your residential accommodation with old age in view. Interestingly, the children whose interest are considered paramount in our building decisions are often not enthused about such projects because of a number of reasons such as: disconnect with architectural design, location of project, lack of privacy arising out of sharing space with other siblings. Yes, living in the house for holidays may be fine with them but continued residence may not be appreciated.

In contributing to the *Lecture Notes on the Annual Themes of the Church of Pentecost regarding-Tell the Next Generation*, the late Apostle F.E. Antwi (Area Head-Tema) provided nine steps in strategizing a project, as follows:

- *Receiving a God-given vision: visions come before strategy, Visions need time to mature, and visions will be tested. (2) Taking inventory, contribution versus resources; (3) Setting goals that are SMART;(4) Setting priorities, (5) planning, (6) organizing, (7) directing-staffing, communicating, delegating, decision-making (8) Controlling and supervision; and (9) evaluating.*

Apostle Antwi combines the functions of Management with Strategic Management to provide basic guidance to strategize projects in the church. Reverend Professor Kwabia Boateng (a Labor Economist) shed lights on development as follows: *"Business development and resource development in general, implies growth at a sustainable rate, a process of elevation to higher levels of activity. Development is necessary to maintain life. If natural resources are not developed, they cannot contribute effectively to human well-being"* (p.72). As a result, *"Making it happen for others is the final aspect of a vision. It gives vision meaning"* (Ashimolowo, 1997, p14).

DEATH

The doctrine of entropy as mentioned elsewhere in this book implies that whatever has a beginning has an end. Arguably people do not want to discuss issues affecting death, it is said that death is inevitable. The African community in the United States of America still rely on *social insurance* to support one another to bear financial burden in times of loss and other eventualities. *Social insurance* is the practice of making voluntary financial contributions to support others in times of funerals, weddings, outdooring, and parties. Implicit in this arrangement is reciprocity because we all support the one who is in need in exchange for support for us if gets to our turn. The concept works just like insurance but does not necessarily have the principles of insurance, including insurable interest, utmost good faith, indemnity with contribution and subrogation, and the doctrine of proximate cause.

I argue for a blend of social insurance in line with African culture and practices and financial insurance products. I have been told that "we do not plan for death' in response to a suggestion to make monthly contributions to be used in the event of death of friends and family. Likewise, while death can terminate a lot of legal contracts and agreements; death does not automatically terminate our relationship with the Internal Revenue Service (IRS) because our estates can be subject to taxes. My suggestion is that insurance product such as life and disability insurance products can take care of loved ones to mitigate funeral expenses and cost of death.

CHAPTER 27

FAMILY AS CENTER OF GRAVITY

THE IMPORTANCE OF THE FAMILY unit in the life of a person cannot be overemphasized. I am privileged to have a splendid family, where each person brings a different dimension to the table. I can speak to varied persons bringing unique talents, giftings, and endowments to the equation. I know where to tap specific resources from when any need arises. The telling and sharing of stories is synonymous through our personal histories; can help to make sense of who we are in the present and already use these stories anecdotally, at school, on dates, over coffee, in the local, to make connections with people and our social worlds (Moriarty & Adamson, 2019). Beyond God, the family has been the pivot upon which the wheels of my entire life have rotated because it has always been at the center of all I do. Actually, it is this family that bear my name across the globe. In Chapter 1, I presented my ancestry and discussed the life story of my parents in Chapter 2; as well as, my family tree. In this Chapter the focus will be on the Appiah-Sokye (Enough to be shared) family. As a result, I have given my children the opportunity to present themselves to the reader in the specific section allocated to them. Enjoy your reading! Some family pictures can be found in Chapter 22 of the book.

INTEGRATED FAMILY MODEL (IFM)

The *Integrated Family Model* (IFM) is a framework that underlines my family philosophy. The Bible is emphatic that: *"Anyone who does not provide for their relatives (own, KJV), and especially for their own household, has denied the faith and is worse than an unbeliever"* (I Timothy 5:8 NIV).

As a result, to be countered as a believer and to hold fast to the faith, the provision for *relatives* and *household* is paramount. Whereas the nuclear family system is practiced by Western societies, the African societies are characterized by the extended family system. At times, the *modified* nuclear family system is an expansion to include parents, grand children, and others.

Interestingly, the term *cousin* is frowned upon by members of my extended family. For that reason, most cousins are *brothers* and *sisters*, and maternal aunties are viewed as *mothers* and paternal uncles are considered as *fathers*. This understanding is critical for family cohesion. In my opinion, the nuclear and extended families make up-*relatives*; whereas, the term- *household* is made up of members of the nuclear family and other members who may be relatives or outsiders, who may be viewed as part of the family unit.

My Integrated Family Model is a variation of the household to encompass the following: (i) myself as head of family, (ii) Spouse as my better half, (iii) children and offspring, (iv) other identified relatives, (v) domestic help; as well as, (vi) mentees, and (vii) Spiritual children. Indeed, this model is not very different from my father's because in my father's Family Integrated Model, he provided for the spouse, children, grandchildren in general but three in particular; as well as, a younger brother, a niece, other children of a friend and relatives, who stayed with us from time to time to attend school or learn a trade and those for short to long-term stay and visits. The members of my Integrated Family Model discussed in this Chapter cover: myself (the subject-matter of this textbook), spouse, our children and grandchildren, a nephew and two nieces, and a domestic help. Each will be introduced to the reader in the section below:

MA CHERIE

My wife was introduced to me by my good friend-*Kwame*. She prefers to be called *Maame Yaa* or *Obaa Yaa*. *T'es l'amour de ma vie* (You are the love of my life). Trained as Certified Nursing Assistant; but a woman of many parts, with interests in trading and decoration. She has a passion for children and draws satisfaction from taking care of children in the Children's Ministry in the local church. Our marriage was celebrated at the Church of Pentecost-Madina Central Sanctuary on March 20, 2005. My appreciation goes to the officiating minister and guest ministers, presbyteries of the Church of Pentecost in Madina and the Chicago districts.

We are thankful to our families for their active involvement. Our special thanks go to the supporting congregation and invited guests, *inter alia* including the following: **first**, Elder and Mrs. Adomako-Bonsu (Chairman), Mr. Forson Asiedu, Mr. and Mrs. Alfred Williams, Ms. Elizabeth Abla Jiagge, Madam Ernestina Nyarkoh, Elder John Osei Akowuah, Elder Freeman and family, the Church of Pentecost-SSNIT Flats Assembly-Elmina, Ewe Assembly of Madina, Elder and Mrs. Appiah Mensah, Mr. and Mrs. Anim, District Youth Ministry-Madina, Mr. and Mrs. Ayivoh, and the Women's Ministry-Madina Central.

Second, Elder and Mrs. Armah Kesse, Elder and Mrs. C.K Wiredu, Elder and Mrs. Wilson Mawuli Dovia, Sychar Assembly, Elder and Mrs. Yeboah, Mr. and Mrs. Akwasi Nyame, Madam Mary Damashie, Elder and Mrs. Richard Asamoah, Elder and Mrs. Napoleon Annan, Deacon Jacob Kpogo, Madam Victoria Bia, Shirley and Dede (Study mates), Ms. Aisha Tiwaa Gyasi, Elder and Mrs. Agyemang Dugbatse, and Madina West assembly. **Third**, Elder and Mrs. Richard Alugchaab, Elder and Mrs. Dwomoh Amaniampong, Elder E.O. Kissi and family, Elder Asamoah Manu, Elder and Mrs. Jonas Yakah, Reverend and

Mrs. Nicholas Darkoh, Mr. and Mrs. Essuman, Elder and Mrs. Adu-Gyamfi, I.P.S. Assembly, Elder and Mrs. Obeng Boateng, and Madina Central Assembly. **Fourth**, Elder and Mrs. Jacob Tetteh, Sister Dora Ayimah Yeboah, Mr. and Mrs. Nolasco Nyidu, Elder Osei Kwaku (Commander-Mampong), Elder and Mrs. Ofori Adarkwah, Nana Yaa Achiaa, Dr. Frank and Dr (Mrs.) Rita E. Baiden, Elder David Mensah, Elder and Mrs. Emmanuel Asante, Ishmail et al.(CTI-Tech), Mr. Joshua Hlordjie, Elder and Mrs. Kwakye, Mr. and Mrs. Adrian Sam (Sowutuom), **Lastly**, Mr. Robert Gyeke Darkoh, Mr. David and Mrs. Esther Ofantse (Study mate), Mr. and Mrs. Henry Acquah (study mate), Mr. Jacob Aidoo, Ms. Betty Vanderpuje, Mr. Johnson Koduah and Mr. Isaac Agyaaning, Anonymous, and Ms. Mabel Bakatue.

My testimonial is that: She is a good wife, who qualifies for the description of the virtuous woman mentioned in the Bible (Proverbs 31:10-31). I happen to be detail-oriented, principled, and not a fun of any of the following: picture-taking, publicity, and celebrations. We complement each other. She is generous, hard worker, compassionate, versatile and fond of children. The strengths include skillful driving, including trucks and forklifts. She looks forward to annual conventions and prepares adequately towards the Easter Season.

I remember the timely encouragement my wife offered me when I experienced a temporary discouragement in my doctoral education journey. Consequently, becoming my number one cheer-leader, making sacrifices to support me to succeed. She has made a lot of sacrifices towards my professional and academic pursuits in the United States of America.

I did not have a job during the financial meltdown. So, I spent considerable time preparing for my professional certification in accounting. Additionally, when I started my doctoral program, I was not initially working, couple with the fact that we had children to support. Nevertheless, she stood solidly behind me and supported me. I am very appreciative of all your help and love.

One of our church leaders once told me that your wife believes in you. I did not believe that until one day I was teaching in a class in Ghana and my wife called me on my cell phone. When I answered the call, she told me that she has had a flat tire on the *I-55* Express road in Bolingbrook, Illinois. Not quite long, one of our friends pull over to offer her help. I do not know exactly what she wanted me to do in the circumstance having regard to the distance between Ghana and the United States of America; but it gives credence to the fact that she felt I needed to know. She enjoys basketball and football.

We look forward to becoming "empty nesters" in the near future. As a result, we look forward to continuing our deeper relationship. My concept of marriage is based on decision rather than affection, cognitive, and behavioral considerations; because these considerations may change over time. As a result, a firm decision is what is required to hold the union.

Together, we have four amazing children- *Adwoa, Kwaku, Yaw,* and *Kwasi*; and two grand-children-*Adepa* and *Nhyira*.

CHILDREN

The basic information on my children is provided below:

EDITH

Adwoa (Monday born) is a thirty-two-year-old mother of two. She is happily married and currently working as an auditor in a national merchandising company. She attended the Saint Monica's High School and the University of Professional Studies. She read Business administration and her career interest is in Law and ultimately wants to be a lawyer. This is daddy's baby.

GEOPAT

The name of my first son is Kwaku (Wednesday born) and twenty-seven years of age. He attended the Romeoville High School and the Southern Illinois University of Edwardsville. He is pursuing a career in Computer Science. He enjoys computer games and designing.

ORGETIENCE

Yaw (Thursday born) is the third born and second son. He is twenty-four years old. He attended the Romeoville High School and the University of Illinois, Urbana-Champaign. His career interest is in Architecture and Management.

EMMANUEL

The name of my third son is Kwasi (Sunday born). He is twenty-two years old. He attended the Romeoville High School and the Northern Illinois University in Dekalb. His career direction is towards Occupational Therapy. He enjoys football and basketball.

FURTHER INSIGHTS

The foundation of our family ethos is anchored on-(1) Spirituality, (2) Knowledge, (3) Integrity, and (4) Service. The acronyms (SISK, ISKS, KISS) are the values that drive our life pursuits. I sought answers to the following questions from my children: *(i) Can you give a brief background of yourself? (ii) What are your aspirations and interests in life? (iii) What are you thankful for? How have you confronted life challenges?*

(iv) What lessons have been learned in life? In response to these questions, **ORGETIENCE** offered as follows:

My name is Orgetience Yaw Appiah-Sokye and I am aspiring to become a licensed architect. I chose to pursue architecture because I recognized the need and value of the profession. Out of the seven essential needs of mankind, proposed by Maslow – air, water, sleep, clothing, food, safety, and shelter - architecture is one of the few professions that addresses a multitude of these needs - safety, shelter, and sleep. From my perspective, this is the main reason why architecture is so foundational to the world and will continue to be an essential component to maintaining and sustaining our society.

INTEREST AND ASPIRATIONS- As of the writing of this book, I am a graduate student dual-majoring in Architecture and Management at the University of Illinois at Urbana-Champaign. My future goals and aspiration involve starting a not-for-profit architecture firm that designs houses for the impoverished people in developing nations with the resources and financial support of the wealthy. With an ever-increasing homeless population around the world, my hope is to join the fight to combat this social problem. By designing and building shelters, the goal would be to bring equity in the form of comfort, security, identity, and belonging, to the less fortunate.

This vision is a two-client system which involves working with both, the fortunate, and the less fortunate in society. One part involves building a network of philanthropists and humanitarians who see the need for increased shelters, and places of refuge for the people in developing nations. The other part involves meeting up with the individuals in need and ascertaining their needs, vision, and program requirement for their desired home. So, my job will be as a mediator and designer between two groups of people who can and are looking to make a difference. This is the vision that is currently driving and motivating my academic career.

In order to bring my vision to fruition, I will need the business planning acumen, marketing, and financial planning knowledge from my master's degree in Management, and my knowledge of design, sustainability, structures, and technical communication from my master's degree in Architecture. Till this appointed day comes, I plan to build upon my design understanding, and portfolio by accumulating merit and experience.

THANKFULNESS TO GOD- I am thankful to God for so many things. First and foremost, I am thankful for the lives of myself, my family, friends and loved ones. Additionally, I thank God for my great upbring in Ghana, living under the tutelage of my grandmother and other relatives. I know that the lessons and experiences of my childhood, have shaped me to be the man that I am today, and for that, I give thanks to God and my grandmother.

I am thankful for my life and the never-ending process of growth and the opportunity to chase after the Lord and strengthen my relationship with him. I am also thankful for all the people that I have met, who have impacted my life in some way shape or form, especially my friends. I am thankful and continue to be thankful for the many teachers in my life who continue to invest in me with their knowledge, time, and teachings, from spiritual leaders, to academic teachers, to friends, and of course to my parents, siblings and uncles. Lastly, I want to thank God for being faithful, loving and kind unto me for all these years.

CONFRONTING LIFE CHALLENGES- I personally do not like challenges in life, nor do I go looking for them, because often they are unplanned and can be chaotic. However, I believe that a life without challenges is lacking in opportunities to grow; while, a life with too many challenges is doomed to cause misery. Challenges overall, can mold you and teach you key lessons about perseverance, ingenuity, and focus. My process of confronting challenges involves many stages. It starts with me assessing the situation to see whether it's worth pursuing or leaving alone. From there, I start to assess myself by thinking about the things I am currently doing that are working and the things that are not working.

Then I try to brainstorm, new things that I can do to help me conquer the situation. When that does not work, I present my challenge before the people that God has put in my life, my friends and family, to see if they have an alternate perceptive on my challenge. From there I evaluate their advice and apply the knowledge best suited for the challenge. Often times, this is where the process ends for me; however, if all else fails I turn to God knowing that I have done all I humanly can and need his divine help. But I always make sure that I evaluate the situation and press into the challenge and discomfort in order to see it through. Sometimes it does not go my way but in the end, I always learn something new about the challenge and about myself. **LESSONS LEARNED IN LIFE**- Similarly, I have learned many lessons in my 24 years on this earth. I have learned that, in this journey we call life, applicable knowledge can come and will come from everywhere. However, it is up to you, to open up, soak it in and apply it. Always be kind and gentle because you never know the power of your words and actions. Do not, and I repeat, do not, let fear hold you back from exploring your interests.

Our minds are powerful and capable of many things, including the ability to fabricate the most unrealistic conclusions to hold you back from reaching your full potential. Lean into what the Lord is teaching you and what the Lord is calling you to do. For he will neither leave you nor forsake you if you abide under his teachings. Lastly, do not forget the importance of community and family because they will support you, counsel you, be a source of strength in your time of need.

CONCLUSION- Although, I have a long way to go before reaching my goals in life, I have faith that the Lord who started me on this journey will bring it all to a glorious end. In the meantime, I plan to continue learning and applying what I have learned throughout the years in my life. Never stop pursuing knowledge and never stop growing.

DEDE

Under this item, I will discuss Dede (means first born daughter), who has become a member of my IFM. She is now happily married. I consider her as a gift from God to my family. The search for somebody to help us began in earnest after my nephew had secured a full-time job after graduation and had to leave us. *First*, one of the elders of the SSNIT flat assembly of the Church of Pentecost introduced me to a family in one of the villages surrounding Elmina in the Central region of Ghana. When the Elder and I arrived at the village, the two brothers under consideration were playing football (soccer) on a field and the boys run to welcome us. I made my preference known to the Elder before we entered the house.

During our conversation, the Elder mentioned my choice to the couple, but they were insisting on offering the elder one. When I persisted in my selection of the younger one, the father was silent for a moment and told us that, there was a problem. I encouraged him to share his concerns and he intimated that the younger one had a medical condition that does not heal so he does not want to give him to me. I suspected either a dermatological or diabetes problem. So, I requested the family to take the boy to the hospital for evaluation at my cost, with a view to seeing if the situation can be cured. Unfortunately, the family never showed interest and we decided not to follow-up again.

Second, after the first effort did not work, one of our aunties invited me to *Bosuso* in the Eastern region of Ghana. She was the headmistress of one of the local schools and a leader of the Bible Study and Prayer Group of the Presbyterian Church of Ghana. She had had a conversation with an elder of the Church of Pentecost in the town, who had offered to allow his daughter to stay with us. I responded to the invitation to Bosuso one Saturday. When I arrived at the town in the morning, the two of us decided to visit the Elder's house to let him know of my arrival. We met the wife and the daughter in question at home but the man had gone to the farm and he was expected to be back soon.

During our conversation, it turned out that both the wife and the daughter were not aware of the arrangement with the man of the house. We came back to my auntie's house awaiting the arrival of the man from the farm. At about 2:00 pm, the elder and another man came to see us at the auntie's house to inform us that the daughter was not willing to stay with anybody again. I got to know that the young lady aged about 16 had stayed with two prominent women leaders in Accra, Ghana. My auntie was disappointed in the man for not having a conversation with the family before asking me to come down to the village. I returned to Accra.

Lastly, the same auntie invited me a second time that she had finally gotten a girl of 15 years for me and that girl was Dede. At the time she came to stay with us she had dropped out of school at Class or stage 5. Born in a farming community near Begoro in the Eastern region of Ghana. The parents gave her to us without charging us but requested as to take her as one of our own and help her with a livelihood. Initially, we wanted to enroll her at the Dr. R. P. Baffoe's Elementary School at Elmina but her interest was in dressmaking. She followed us from Cape Coast to Accra; then, accompanied the children to Kumasi in the Ashanti region and back to Accra (all in Ghana) spanning over a decade.

She knew what to do at every point in time and I never had to devote as much time on domestic issues of the household. I thank God that she completed her apprenticeship in dressmaking and *Tie and dye* or Batik making; as well as, getting married before she left us to her matrimonial home. I appreciate the contribution of Dede for assisting my family. Dede agreed to continue to stay with us and to assist us with domestic and household chores. I was very surprise that Dede turned down a marriage proposal because she could not in good conscience leave her brothers to go and marry. This was huge for me! I thank God for reserving the man for her in His own time. I am asking my family to continue to show kindness to her and her family.

DEPENDENTS

I have supported and stayed with some of the children of my sisters, as follows:

JOHNNY

Kwasi is my nephew and the third born and second son of my elder sister-Auntie Adwoa. I am grateful to my sister and the late husband for allowing him to stay with us in Cape Coast in the Central region of Ghana. Johnny offered us a good support during his stay with us and left when he completed his tertiary education at the Cape Coast Polytechnic (now Technical University) and was employed as an accountant of a Cocoa Purchasing Company in Kade and Nkawkaw in the Eastern region of Ghana. I was privilege to visit him at the two stations. I am forever thankful to my good friend- Charles, who made this possible. I am grateful to Johnny and his late wife for naming their first-born son after me. By this gesture, his son-*Kingsley Appiah-Sokye* (Paa Kay), who bears my name takes over the place of his father in my Integrated Family Model discussed in this chapter.

HANNAH

At a point in time, while Rebecca and two of my sons were in Kumasi, one of my nieces by name Hannah joined me in Accra to stay with me until she gained admission to a Training College on the Akwapim-ridge of the Eastern region of Ghana. She took up a teaching appointment and also got married and remained on the Akwapim range. I appreciate her service during this period.

BEATRICE

The late Beatrice Essah-Mensah (Awura Adwoa) was the last relative to stay with me. She was the last born of my elder sister-Auntie Adwoa, meaning that she is a brother of Johnny (my nephew mentioned above). She came to replace Hannah, when she went to the training college. Her stay was rather short because I was about to travel. I sent her to Kumasi to work on her grades when I was traveling. The next time I met her was at my mother's funeral, where she told me that she had not been able to get the desired grades and that she wanted to learn a particular trade and requested for assistance for the purpose. I sent the money for that purpose but before she could apply the funds, she passed away. I am grateful for her assistance and May her memory be a blessing!

ANALYSIS OF TERMINAL REPORTS

I perform *analysis* and *evaluation* of the terminal reports of my children while in the elementary school; utilizing trend analysis and analysis of percentages. I reproduce excerpts of one of such analysis based on class mark (30%), examination mark (70%), total score (100%), average mark, position in subject and in class, and attendance below: **Class score**- Exceeded the 20/30 standard in the class in all subjects.

There is however room for improvement in Ghanaian Language and Social studies. The English Language score was the best in the class.

Examination score-Exceeded the 50/70 standard in the examination score. Performance in Environmental studies and Ghanaian Language was particularly good. However, performance in Examinations regarding Mathematics, English Language, and Social studies should be improved. **Total score**-This is highly impressive for the period and must be sustained; **average mark**-The average mark of 70 percent was obtained in Environmental studies and social studies but could not meet the average in English, Mathematics, and Ghanaian Language. **Subject position**-The standard set is 10th in all subjects but failed to meet this in all subjects but one and narrowly missed one.

Observation-The observations include the following:(i) The number in class has been rising, giving an average number of 53.4 pupils; (ii) the position in class averaged 13.4th instead of standard of 10th; (iii) The average expected attendance for the period was 58.8 out of which 58 was achieved. This is not bad at all. (iv) The 8th position in Environmental studies is difficult to accept because a constant position has been maintained for four consecutive terms without any variation; (v) My observation is that the class is a strong one to which my son belongs. The marks level vis-à-vis the positions in class and in subjects attest to the strength of the class. This gives the opportunity to be the best or among the best.

Recommendation-The recommendations are two-fold: (1) Reading habit should be inculcated; and (2) To be praised where strengths are and cautioned for lapses. Likewise, prizes to be awarded for achieved standards, backed by encouragement, love, care, and concern, as well as logistical support. **Conclusion**-There is sudden improvement in the performance in association with previous evaluation, overcoming predicaments.

I recently reviewed the school reports of all my children from the

Kindergarten to the elementary school level and compared my findings to their college and career level pursuits and observed as follows: **One**, a nursery teacher of one of my children scored him average of *B* for each of the following-creativity, drawing, coloring, paintwork, clay and sand work. I find that this is incongruous with his abilities at a higher level of education.

Two, all teachers of one of my children have recorded *reading* as his interest. While this finding may be true because the teachers may be comparing children in the class; I know that of all my children, this is the one who does not like reading.

Three, I find that the following conduct listed over the years is accurate-respectful, calm, very good, good, excellent, quite good, studious, and serviceable. The attitude recorded included the following- honest, serviceable, brilliant, industrious, well organized, enthusiastic, imaginative, and motivated. Similarly, the teacher's comments-excellent performance, active in class, excellent work, impressive performance; as well as backup in Environmental Science was a true reflection of this child.

Four, I find that the remarks of the headteachers did not add value to the development of the children- "An encouraging performance but needs improvement". While this comment appears relevant, it loses its weight when the same comments is written for all students and for all terms. **Five**, one of my children met the standard for reading but was below the standard for mathematics because of the following: (i) the grades were affected by missing and late work; (ii) lack of effort in reading; (iii) bright but just needed to apply himself. Later on, the teacher remarked that there has been marked improvement in getting work done on time; but requested for a continued help with his homework, especially in reading and mathematics. For that reason, the teacher elaborated that the student has a lot of potential but just needs extra support to reach full success, through keeping writing and reading, and practicing mathematics.

Six, the conduct recorded for another child encompassed the following-respectful, well behaved, very good, excellent, quite good, good, obedient, friendly, acceptable behavior, calm, gentle, and satisfactory. The interests identified by teachers covered the following-very good in reading, likes working mathematics, telling stories, football (soccer), and drawing. **Seven**, the attitudes were: imaginative, sincere, active, affable, respectful, obedient, active, and very good. I find the interest in soccer very surprising.

Eight, some of the comments from the teachers were as follows: exceptional performance, needs improvement in writing, *brainy child but needs motivation*, quite encouraging, backup in French, *should keep books tidy, relaxed in class during the term*, was slow (not attentive in class) and not serious in class, and a good performance. I find some of the teachers' comments very helpful and diagnosis for success.

REFLECTION

Upon reflection, I want to state as follows:

Appreciation to Mrs. Yorke (an educationist and mother of Dr. Paa Kwasi Nduom)- I want to register my sincerest thanks to Mrs. York, the founder of Saint Monica's Smiling Faces in Elmina in the Central region of Ghana, for the special accommodation she made for two of my children in her school. The school was set up as Kindergarten and at the time we did not have a babysitter, she wholeheartedly made babies courts to accommodate our babies and that of another nurse in her own house. This gesture allowed us to attend to our full-time jobs during the workweek.

Grandmothers' Support-The contributions of grandmothers towards the education of our children is acknowledged because of some circumstances beyond our control, some of our children had to stay with their grandmothers to continue their education. We place on record our eternal gratefulness to grandmothers.

***Breakdown of School Bus at Adenta Estates*-**Two of our children were attending a private school in Accra, Ghana. One day, while I was in town around Abeka-Lapaz area in Accra-Ghana, I bought a few baskets of fruits and put them in my vehicle but initially, I did not know the motivation for doing so. Not quite long, I received a phone call from one of my children about the breakdown of the school bus after school at the Adenta Estates. When I went through the hectic traffic to the Adenta Estate around about 4:00pm, I met a disserted- school children in the school bus all by themselves. I was told the driver has gone out to look for a mechanic to fix the problem. Likewise, there was no staff available to attend to the children.

As soon as the children saw me as a parent, they run to me to complain of hunger. Then, I provided the fruits I bought to the pupils on the bus and after taking the fruits, they started opening up conversation with me. I became the father of all the students at that particular time. With the help of a passer-by, who called the numbers of parents of children with *024* numbers; I called parents with *020* numbers. Interestingly, the children could provide phone numbers of their mothers and not fathers. One pupil told me of his absentee-father, who is seen once or twice a week. Finally, as parents begun arriving, we arranged for them to transport other children in their locality with consents from their parents until all the children made it home. The driver had not returned after about 6:30pm when we were departing. The following day, I made a formal complaint to the Director of the school and I pull out of the school bus transportation arrangement.

CONCLUSION

I thank God for my family and I am privileged to be called the head of this family. Each member of the family brings uniqueness in natural endowments and peculiarities to the union. Yes, it is not a perfect one; yet it is an excellent one. I am not ashamed to be identified with this family unit. The skills and abilities and capabilities complement each other. In actuality, from the systems theory, the whole has been greater than the sum of its parts (gestalt). The embedded qualities weaves into a holistic union. The journey thus far has not been easy but has been wonderful. Hurdles involving mountains and valleys have been surmounted. To God Be the Glory!

CHAPTER 28

LESSONS LEARNED

THIS IS THE PROCESS THAT can be encouraged throughout life, and establishing this practice at university can be a particularly powerful way of further engaging students with their discipline, with their peer group and with themselves and the confidence to believe that these stories might matter in the world beyond their writing journals and university lectures (Moriarty, & Adamson, 2019). Reverend Father Anyimadu-Bona observed that *"God is the author of life. Religion is just one dimension of life"* (1995, pp.65-68); nevertheless, *"Intangible free gifts of God encompass: (i) life, (ii) health, (iii) time, and (iv) weather, and (v) etc."* (Boateng, 2010, p.56).

Writing on *10 Universal Principles you find in the lives of truly successful people* in 2004, Albert Ocran offered **10 Commandments of Success**, as follows: Thou shalt: (1) Know how to walk with God; (2) Have a clear sense of purpose; (3) Be fruitful and multiply; (4) Understand personal management and self-discipline; (5) Have faith backed by desire; (6) Seek knowledge and wisdom; (7) Be diligent and persistent; (8) Cultivate and maintain right relationships; (9) Develop character and integrity; and (10) Make healthy choices. Ocran (2004) elaborated:

> *"It is imperative that we surround ourselves with counselors who are not shallow, but deeply grounded in principles. We must incline our ears towards friends who care enough to tell us when and where we are wrong. Everyone needs someone who can correct him/her when they err. Where do you incline your ears? It could be good indicator of the kind of future that awaits you"*(p.176).

Key and Spencer (2008) have illuminated insight into how the average person lives in the second half of life. The authors refer to age 40 as the first half and life after 40 as second half of life or midlifers. At this crucial phase of life, people are consumed with the needs of children such as education and property (residential and commercial) to provide protection to the next generation. The quest to leave a legacy tends to engage the attention of people in this group to the extent that all their lifestyle is focused on providing the needs of the family. Likewise, the demands of employers become manifest because such people tend to be in the middle or close to the top of the career path and the related burden and responsibility become weighty for the midlifers. Similarly, the responsibility of meeting the needs of surviving parents becomes enormous.

In African societies, some people invite parents to live with them; but in the Western world, several parents are sent to Nursing home for the needed care. When enough financial resources cannot be made available by the parent; then, the burden of maintenance fall on the children and the government. The demands on the time and talents of the midlifers in the church also grows because of the experience that comes with age. The roles played becomes highly visible. It is typical to have midlifers holding key offices and responsibilities in the church.

Once upon a time, my presiding elder in the 1990s told me of an instance where he returned from a church meeting close to midnight only to come home to meet his doors left open by his children, who were deeply asleep.

A few midlifers also forget to take good care of their own bodies. Instead, they feed on junk food and often get glued to the Television set. In 2008, Key and Spencer asserted:

> *"We midlifers get pulled in lots of directions. We do and do and do for our kids, our parents, our bosses. Many of us move from one sitting position to another, all day, every day,*

eating junk or nothing at all. And if ever we do get a little time to ourselves, about the only thing we can manage is to shlump in front of a mind-numbering TV show with a stiff drink in hand. It's no way to live–like I need to tell you"(Key & Spencer, 2008, p. xvi).

In this section of the book, I will discuss pertinent lessons I have learned in life over time, including the following:

HARDWORK PAYS

The Biblical admonition in Proverbs 6:6-7 speaks volumes of the plight of lazy living. Hard work can be profitable because labor is included as a factor of production in Economics 101. Laziness can lead people into abject poverty. However, Pastor Mensah Onumah Otabil in February 2020 asserted that success is not imparted by laying-on of hands and cautioned persons who go to see men of God for them to lay hands on them to excel in their endeavors.

ASSIDUITY

Many people do not achieve their God-given dreams because they lack focus and want to be at all places at the same time. Approaching your duties with assiduity is powerful such that attention is brought to bear on the situation. Multi-tasking is very helpful in getting a lot of things done at the same time, but each task receives dedicated attention at a period of time and that is the essence of assiduity.

TENACITY OF PURPOSE

The most important aspect of life is to be driven by purpose because it is the best sustainer of vision. A sense of purpose is needed to fuel one's passion. For me, passion without a purpose is inadequate but a purpose with a passion is desirable. The central part of human endeavors is driven by purpose. Consequently, finding your purpose in life is like discovering mineral deposits in a hidden place and marshalling all resources to extract the resource. I would encourage young people to approach knowledge with the understanding that there is a proper alignment with purpose.

POWER OF RESILIENCE

Resilience is very powerful because several life activities and events are rooted in repetition. In some cases, the same acts have to be done repeatedly before success can be achieved and without resilience; discouragement can set into thwart efforts directed at failure. I see resilience as a driving force or power that enables things to be done for the high achiever. Successful people tend to attribute their achievements to the power of resilience.

SELF-CONTROL

Self-control is a very important virtue in the life of a person. A lot of prominent people have been disgraced in one way or the other because of their inability to control themselves. The irony is that human beings are capable of controlling huge machines and equipment but are not able to control the human body. It takes discipline to bring one's body into subjection. There is also the issue of *arousal-reduction* tendencies that can present a cause-and-effect relationship. While men are attracted by sight, women tend to be attracted by what they hear. As a *cause*, anytime someone is aroused in one way or the other, the body moves into a state of disequilibrium until reduction is sought and achieved to bring the body back into equilibrium.

This is so with sexual attraction, answering nature's call, responding to hunger, and so on. As an *effect*, what we see and hear can become vehicles of arousal, which might invariably lead to reduction or the actual committing of an act. The lives of several young people have been destroyed because of drug abuse, alcoholism, sexual promiscuity, smoking and many more. My advice to the younger generation is to hold your bodies in check in order to avoid scandals and unnecessary headlines.

CREATIVITY

Man is a creative being with the capacity to create from creation. The instruction from God to man in the creation story contemplates creativity. For example, "Be fruitful and multiple", "subdue the earth", "have dominion over the birds of the air and creeping animals" All the keywords-dominion, fruitfulness, multiplication, and subduing point to creativity. Most problems have been tackled through human ingenuity and creativity, leading to inventions and solutions to human problems. In recent times, the world has been plagued with the COVID-19 Pandemic, but mankind responded with creativity to meet the dictates of the new normal. As a result, most businesses and educational institutions deployed technological interventions that allowed for employees to work from home and learning instructions to be deployed to students through technology modes.

POSITIVE MINDSET

Having a mindset is not the same as having a positive mindset. It is the mind that controls what man can accomplish. When people feed their minds with negative thoughts, the outcome is anyone's guess. When a person takes a positive philosophy of things and holds on to positive confessions, a lot can be achieved. A lot of political slogans are built on positive confessions to endanger positive mindset. Positive mindset does not suggest that everything will be positive but even during failure, hope is kept alive to turn things around for the better. Consequently, I do not have in my dictionary "It is not possible."

I interpret this to mean a limiting factor on what man is capable of accomplishing. The question is: *Why place a limitation on yourself?*

HONESTY

Honesty is priceless and it is one of the virtues that is fading with modernization because people want to get rich overnight and honesty is considered as an "enemy of progress" In the past, honesty was assumed but in recent times, honesty has become undesirable burden on people. As a result, people who demonstrate honesty are considered as unwise; yet, when it suits them, the same people want to entrust their valuable property to honest people. I am calling on society to inculcate honesty in the younger ones as the American society has done. The educational system should revisit the internalization of honesty in the pupils as American society has done in raising their children to be honest.

TRUSTWORTHINESS

The ability to know that God is developing you for a bigger purpose will show the way to success. One of the virtues that is fast eroding is that of trust. To the extent that even married couples do not trust one another. The question that arises for determination is: *Where is the first love?* There has been competition among married couples, culminating into losses on both sides. Intimate friendship has become a mere lip service to say the least.

I have observed that partnerships are not common in Ghana; instead, private companies limited by shares abound. I have come across business leaders lacking basic competences but are occupying positions by virtue of blood associations. There is power in co-operation and collaboration as I have mentioned elsewhere in this book. No human being is self-sufficient, but we do play complementary roles. For that reason, if there is anything that can be done through collaboration, we should not hesitate to get it done. If we insist that others cannot be trusted; then, we cannot be trusted either.

DEPENDABILITY

Good stewards are dependable but people who are not dependable cannot be good stewards. Implicit in stewardship function is dependability. Therefore, dependability is at the core of the stewardship conundrum. In life a lot of things can be achieved through the involvement of other people but if such people cannot be considered to be dependable; then, the system will crumble to the ground. Such people let others down in every step of the way.

Entrusting valuable things to the care of people viewed as less dependable is setting oneself for failure. When you assign dependable people task, you literary to sleep because you know when it all said and done, nothing will go wrong. Nevertheless, a delegation to a person viewed as non-dependable is a border because you have to be monitoring constantly to avoid going off track.

.ENDURANCE

Endurance is the virtue that enables the best to come out of people. To be tried and tested is to have met the standard of endurance. Typically, people who have gone through painful experiences tend to develop inner capacity of endurance to withstand what life throws at them. Such people are not easily broken by events of life but are able to respond appropriately, utilizing the past experiences as the pivot upon which the wheels of endurance rotates. At times, when the names of successful are mentioned, their stories are not told to permit an appreciation of what has sharpened their personae.

I have observed that a closer interaction with successful personalities can reveal the processes that have molded them. If you want to be associated with the success of any personality, be ready to be identified with their life experiences.

PERSEVERANCE

Perseverance is the ability to respond with consistency even in the teeth of opposition or failure. The innate ability that enables a person to be persistent at something. In most cases, it is the combination of *passion, determination, purpose*, and the *mental adroitness* to succeed.

Per Pastor Otabil, many people like to skip the process of learning and toil to succeed simply because they had been blessed by anointed men of God (Otabil, February 2020). Two Biblical cases were used to buttress the point as follows: **One**, *Elisha*, studied under Elijah for twenty years, implying twenty years of training; and **Two**, *Joshua*, followed Moses for 40 years from Egypt to the time Moses was taken away (Otabil, February 2020). Perseverance is part of the processes of life to build us up for good works.

AFFABILITY

A noble trait to develop is teachability or affability. There is no human being above teaching or learning. There is always a teaching moment in everything we do as human beings. I want to encourage all readers to be humble enough to be taught. In spite of our abilities and accomplishments, there are always new things to be learned. I have recounted the story my professor told us about the "Village University

Graduate" who disappointed the elderly man for his inability to read and translate a letter written in German to him.

I have argued that societal expectation of university graduates is very high; So, graduates cannot afford to let society down. Afterall, society supported the education of the graduate. Yes, you might find this burden unreasonable but that does not negate the fact that education is a lifelong adventure and continuous education is implied. Anybody can teach you something new. As a teacher, I have had the opportunity of learning from my students all the time.

HUMILITY

Humility or humbleness is the mental attitude of not holding yourself highly than your real value because the value you hold about yourself may be on the higher side. It pays to be humble. While humility can be rewarding, the lack of it can be expensive. The tendency is for people to be arrogant by virtue of some unique stature we have attained unto but bear in mind that situations are not permanent because old age and death make the things, we hold dear "vanity" If you have been placed in a position of trust, keep in mind that the position is temporal and your ascension into that office is to fulfill a specific purpose within the stipulated time. Beyond that period your relevance will be diminished. You will soon be referred to as the "former" or "ex" Just respect your fellow human being as the creation of God, whom God has placed in your path for a purpose.

PATIENCE

I have told the young people I have encountered to learn to be patient; especially, in the United States of America, where most things are done in real time and online. Most of the young people have come to know that everything is instant and so do not have capacity to wait for anything. Yes, understandably so but life is not programed in an instant fashion. Most of life decisions come with the passage of time and not until the younger generation comes to appreciate this fact of life, they may have to learn it the hard way. Life is a process to be understood and internalized.

Per Bishop Dag Howard-Mills (August 2017), snakes are masters at hiding and silence is a powerful weapon that allows you to truly *hide, flourish*, and *prosper*. As a result, (i) serpents are wise because they hide and flourish (Ecclesiastes 5:2-3); (ii) silence, quietness, hiding and flourishing (Isaiah 45:15NASB); (iii) quietness and silence will cause you to command respect of outsiders (I Thessalonians 4:11-12NIV); (iv) hiding and flourishing will protect you from premature exposure in the ministry (John 7:7-9-Howard-Mills, August 2017). Comparatively, a lion makes people aware of its existence in an area because of the noise it makes but hardly does anyone hear the noise of a snake because it chooses to live in silence, rarely disturbing anyone (Howard-Mills, August 2017).

Major decisions of life such as career choices and life partner choices, come with preparation and patience. As a result, I recommend these two important life pillars to the younger generation. The laying-on of hands in the two cases (Elisha and Joshua) can best be describes as graduation; and as a result, people should be patient to be groomed and also respect the process (Otabil, February 2020).

TIME MANAGEMENT

Time is the resource that is equally available to all mankind but the extent to which it is managed makes all the difference. We all have 24 hours in a day and 7 days in the week but different people achieve different feats because of how they manage this important resource.

The most important characteristic of time is that once past it cannot be regained and appointed time is now. Every resource needs to be managed properly for desired impact.

BALANCING ACTS

I draw lessons from the double-entry principle in accounting that provides two sides to a situation. The coin has a *head* and a *tail*. So, life issues should be viewed through the lenses of duality. Major decisions should not be made from only one perspective, rather other sides of the issue should be considered for maximum effect. Dr. Yaw Osei Adutwum in November 2019 counseled the youth to build careers for themselves before pursuing partisan politics; because politics must not be seen as an end in itself but a means to an end and that all who seek to be in politics should be motivated by a desire to better the lot of society (Adutwum, November 2019).

OTHER LESSONS

In addition to the above, add modesty, show genuine love and affection, speak the truth, be outspoken when things are getting out of hand, be faithful, be measured in temperaments, and be enthusiastic in giving to support the needy and the work of ministry.

VALUE YOU BODY

My counsel to the younger generation is to avoid alcohol and smoking completely because of both the Spiritual and health costs. Another admonition is to avoid excessive sex; especially abstinence before marriage and doing everything in moderation in marriage.

LIFE LESSONS

I have come to understand that God's silence is also an answer and for that reason, failure is a state of mind but God's provisions are timely and often misunderstood. I call on you dear reader, to accept assignments you can discharge with excellence and allowing others to be fruitful by taking on assignments we know we cannot discharge well. I call for a strong moral and ethical standard in all our inter-personal relationships to produce a deeper appreciation of life experiences. Likewise, unusual sense of humor can be an asset to people around us; for that reason, instead of self-centeredness, the focus should be on problem-centeredness; as well as, spontaneity in thoughts based on the perception of reality. Similarly, learn to tolerate uncertainty and show concern for welfare of humanity by looking at life with objective lenses.

CHAPTER 29

REFLECTION

THERE IS A LONG TRADITION of including autobiographies as empirical data in qualitative research, particularly within the fields of anthropology, sociology, and literature studies (Hanssen, 2019, p312). Once upon a time in every person's life, there is the need for reflection on the past, present, and the future because the past and present can provide the foundation for confronting the future. While the future is unknown, the decisions we take and choices we make can affect the outcomes of critical issues of life. Historically, organizations have responded to this approach through stocktaking and the conduct of retreats.

In stocktaking, the business owner compares items issued out to the items received. I have received the gift of life, Christian training, parental ethos and upbring, life-long education and training, and many more. I have given back in different forms, as discussed in this textbook. From time to time, individuals and organizations conduct retreats with a view to appreciating progress made, challenges to be surmounted, and legacies to bequeath to the next generation. A balance has to be struck between the resources bestowed us and the responsiveness towards society.

I seek to do just that in this book project. So, the process should be as honest as possible; and as a result, the *input-output* connection should result in the fulfillment of purpose.

MY PURPOSE vs. GOD'S PURPOSE

My father wanted me in the *full-time* ministry. Perhaps, he would have wished to be a minister himself but for his age. As I shared with you, I was interested in the foreign service as an ambassador; probably, influenced by the message delivered on II Corinthians 5:20 by Deacon Aggrey, an Inspector of Ghana Police Service at the time. I made attempts by applying to the School of International Relations of the International University of Japan and another in Switzerland.

My desire of becoming an ambassador never materialized because I could not secure the much-needed sponsorship for the program. At this same time, my call into accountancy became evident; yet, I received it with a pinch of salt. I rejected this purpose because it did not align with my self-identified purpose. I remember sharing this story with Dr. Albert Osei of Chicago in the State of Illinois and he told me that it takes a President of a country to appoint an ambassador.

LAW AND ACCOUNTING PROFESSIONS

My interest in the law profession begun from my adolescent stage, when I paid regular visits to the Courts in Mampong-Ashanti (Ghana). Later on, I gained some law experience from my Business Law courses in both academic and professional education; as well as, a protracted family litigation that lasted from January 13, 1987(Original action) to January 25, 1996 (Court of Appeal Judgment). A detailed discussion of this case has been treated in Chapter 23 of this book under the sub-theme-Litigating to possess your possessions on the main challenges theme.

Some members of my extended family would have wished that I consider the *Krontihene* stool of Asante Mampong because the stool had gone to another gate to restore family fortunes. One of our grandfathers is in contention and another uncle has shown interest. I wish them well but I am not interested.

SERVICE TO GOD AND CHURCH

The Church has benefited from my services in varied roles and responsibilities. While some of the roles relate to the past; several responsibilities are current and ongoing. "In the Church of Pentecost, it has come to be accepted that once a presiding elder always a presiding elder. This assumption cannot always hold" (Amponsah, 2009, p.47). I consider these responsibilities as part of my ministry to God.

Specifically, the following are worth noting:

1. *Elder of the Church of Pentecost-ordained in January 1994 by Apostle Rigwell Ato-Addison*
2. *Registrar of the Pentecost Biblical Seminary(PBS)-July 2020*
3. *Member, National Audit Committee-Appointed in February 2015 and Re-appointed upon review of first term in February 2019 by the National Executive Council*
4. *Member, Chicago Regional Executive Committee-Elected in Minnesota in January 2020*
5. *Chairman, Chicago Regional Audit Committee-January 2019*
6. *Member, Chicago Regional Audit Committee-January 2013*
7. *Secretary, National Retirement Trends Committee (adhoc) in June 2014*
8. *Member, District Executive Committee-Romeoville District-August 2014 to December 2018*
9. *Member, District Executive Committee-Chicago District-December 2013 to August 2014.*
10. *District Finance Committee, Church of Pentecost, Ghana. 1994-1996*
11. *Dean, School of Ministry, Romeoville District*

12. *Facilitator, Romeoville District–Mount of Transfiguration*

13. *Coordinator, McKeown Worship Center (MWC) Special Communities Project*

14. *Secretary, Marriage Committee from December 2012 to March 2019*

15. *Bible Study Teacher*

16. *Front and Back Office Co-Ordinator (Membership, Welcome, and Attendance)*

17. *Member, Local Finance Committee from August 2014 to December 2018*

18. *Coordinator, Security, Parking, and Transportation Team– McKeown Worship Center (MWC)*

19. *Chairman, Dedication Planning Committee, June to July 2014*

20. *Presiding Elder, Pentecost International Worship Center (PIWC), Chicago–January 2008 to August 2009*

21. *Elder for Special Duties, Madina District, Ghana*

22. *Chairman, Local Welfare Committee–Madina West, Ghana*

23. *Chairman, Local Welfare Committee–Madina Central, Ghana*

24. *Local Secretary, Madina West from 1997 to 2002*

25. *Secretary, Foundation Stone Committee–Madina West*

26. *Member, District Estates Committee, Madina District*

27. *Secretary, History Committee, Dedication of Sanctuary Committee, Madina Central*

28. *Bible Study Teacher, Ebenezer Temple*

29. *Sunday School Teacher, Ebenezer Temple, Madina*

30. *Assistant District Pentecost Youth and Evangelistic Ministry (PENTYEM) Leader–Elmina District*

31. *Assistant District Financial Secretary–Elmina District*

32. *Local Financial Secretary, SSNIT Flats Assembly, Elmina*

33. *Timothy Class Preparatory Class, SSNIT Flat Assembly, Elmina.*

34. *Sunday School Teacher, Mampong Central*

35. *PENSA Core Team, Mampong Central*

36. *Training the Trainers, Mampong District Children's Movement (Ministry).*
37. *Patron, Sophia McKeown Singers, Chicago*
38. *Counseling Ministry–Romeoville District*
39. *Chaplaincy Ministry–Romeoville District*
40. *and many more*

CREDIT UNION DIMENSION

I offer reflection regarding my active involvement in the credit union system in Ghana covering a period of 8 years, as follows: *first*, I am grateful for this life changing experience of championing the course of the credit union by leading two separate credit unions; *albeit*, from the same organization from scratch. I spent the entire period at the primary (society) level as chairman of the Board of Directors. It is refreshing to know that the credit union that I was instrumental in starting as a small society has grown to become a very big and robust society and continuing to help in the financial upliftment of workers.

Second, I was elected unto the Supervisory committee of the Ghana Co-operative Credit Union Association (CUA) Limited on three occasions and three different biennial conferences at *Legon, Tamale,* and *Bunso* and I ended at *Ho* in the Volta region of Ghana; covering a period of 6 years. While I was elected as an *observer* in both the Legon and Bunso Biennials, I was elected as a *delegate* in Tamale because I served on the Central Regional Chapter Board. I am grateful to the Biennial conferences for the confidence reposed in me and giving me the opportunity to serve humanity.

Third, I have benefited from the enormous amount of training from the credit union system, especially, those sponsored by CCA. The knowledge acquired over time has served me very well in life. I have been exposed to principles of management, auditing, and financial management in my academic and professional training but the exposure I have received through CUA on lobbying and strategic planning (practical aspects) have been game-changing experience for me.

Four, I have had the opportunity to learn from the system. Specifically, Mr. Akwasi A. Ankomah, whom I served with on the Supervisory committee from 1992 to 1996, affected me positively on the skill of rightly interpreting *bye-laws* and *constitutional* documents because of his experience as a Registrar of the Chieftaincy Secretariat of Ghana.

The name of Mrs. Victoria Erskine of Crop Research Institute of Ghana (CRIG) Credit Union in Kumasi cannot be spared mentioning. Auntie Vick was very excited about my involvement in the credit union system as a young man. She voluntarily offered me insight into the approach she followed to get her property developed in Kumasi. I paid a visit to Kumasi and took the opportunity to see at firsthand, her success story.

I remember in one instance, when I have finished delivering my report in Ho in the Volta region as the Chairman of the Supervisory Committee of CUA to the applause and administration of a lot of people, an elderly co-operator called me aside; congratulated me and pointed out to me that I did great on the presentation but just to let me know that the law I quoted-The Ghana Co-operative Decree (1967), NRCD 252 should be the NLCD 252 because Ghana did not have the NRC in 1967 but that was after 1972. While the acronym NLC means National Liberation Council, on the contrary, NRC is National Redemption Council, both Military regimes in Ghana, yet different time horizons. I thank the *elderly* co-operator for this teaching moment.

The IRS Co-operative Credit Union Limited-Greater Accra sent the following delegation to the Ho Biennial Conference: Messrs-. G.K Segbaya, A.K. Yankson, and Mrs. Margaret Aryeetey (Education Committee, IRS Newsletter, June 2000, 1(3), pp.1-2). *Lastly*, the relationships built from the credit union association have grown over time. For example, Board Member X, one of the people I worked with on the Board of the IRS Employees Co-operative Credit Union Limited had these words of comfort for me when I lost my mother:

> "... *Be consoled by one thing that she has passed the biblical mandatory 70 and optional 80. She has paid her due in life and I know, if only it were possible for us to see, that she would be smiling in her death for having mothered a man called GEORGE, very astute in character, persevering in industry, versatile in all spheres of human engagements and very patient and enduring in very trying and challenging times and moments and above all, a man very humane and abundant in humour.*
>
> *George, I am proud of you. It was a great experience for me to have been associated with you and I learnt so much from you. Thank you so very much...*" (Board Member X, Personal Communication, July 7, 2016).

REGRETS

I have recounted how my plans of working in the foreign service as an ambassador and also going to the Ghana Law School to become a lawyer never came to fruition in the sections above; but I do not have any regrets at all. I have not taken family vacations as I would have love to but this would be revisited in the coming days. I have spent over thirty years of my life educating and investing in myself.

LIKES

The few things I like doing include traveling, writing, reading, listening to music, and social work. I like teaching and my students continue to motivate me through the constant feedback I receive from them. One cannot be a good teacher without the habit of reading, researching and writing. These are required for teaching and learning. I like traveling but so far, my travels have been restricted to road and air travel, with few rail travels. I have never travel by sea partly due to the fact that I do not know how to swim. As a result, I am not a fun of water.

DISLIKES

I have observed over time that I do not like some things, including the following:(a) *Publicity*, I have not liked publicity. I have adjusted to publicity relating to my calling as an elder and a teacher. (b) *Photos*, I generally do not like taking pictures (photos). I have pictures for some occasions but I do not fancy the taking of pictures on routine basis. (c) *Parties*, There are individual differences. I do not have any problem with those who want to organize parties to celebrate graduation below High School level and age below 70. I enjoy parties associated with key milestones in life, especially, those relating to age 70+ and graduation above High School. I consider those below 70+ years and graduation parties below High School as family affair. Please, that is my opinion.

I like pointing people to the long-range goals. (d) I used to like dancing but my zeal for dancing dwindled from the year 2000. I dance occasionally but not as frequently as I used to in the past. I do not dance because somebody is dancing but I am usually moved by the import of the song.

CONTRIBUTIONS OF OTHERS

Several people have made different impression on my mind; including the following: The first person to have taught me human temperament was Elder Dorgbadzi. Later on, I read Apostle Professor Opoku Onyinah's *Are two persons the same?* On the concept of marriage, Nancy Van Pelt (1982) discusses singleness very well, the names of the following cannot be left out- Reverend Dr. Kissiedu, Reverend Anyane Boadum (Courtship), Opanin Kwadwo Kyere, and Elder Joshua Adjebeng.

Similarly, Apostle (Lt. Col) Kumi-Woode (Concept of Time), Elder Dr. Chris Ampadu (Samaritan Strategy) based on "And the child grew..." (Acts 2: 42, 52). Others include: T.L. Osborne (The Gospel According to T.L. and Daisy Osborne), Derrick Prince (my teacher); free Christian literature from Evangelist Jimmy Swaggart, Oral Roberts, Kenneth Copeland, John Wimber, Richard Leadon, Wiglesworth; as well as 'Bible for others' Ministry (Free Bible).

SHARED RESPONSIBILITY

There is a genuine source of contentment in sharing but we need to assume responsibility for our actions instead of overstretching the grace of God (Romans 6:1). Trust in God with all your might but do not stockpile because the race is not for the swift but God rules in the affairs of men (Daniel 4:17; Proverbs 3:8). The current crop of leaders should impact the future generation with **intentionality**; through the building of bridges and relationships, teaching and learning, and praying and allowing them to lead so mistakes can be corrected now.

My generation of leaders in the church was developed through *observation*. Initially, we just followed the patterns we saw our 'fathers' utilize in ministry as a guide. Less or no questions asked. With time, things have changed. The current generation (youth) demand answers to questions and concerns; and so, the church has to respond to meet this need.

I have drawn inspiration from the following quotations: *"Fulfil your purpose else people will employ you to fulfil theirs"* (Robert Mugabe);*"Where there is a will, there is a way"* (Anonymous); *"identifying your objective is like identifying the Morning star;… fixing your compass on it to bring you back on track"* (Anonymous);*"Doing a little but helping a lot"* (Pens and Plastics Company Limited, Ghana); *"One step ahead of progress"* (Neoplan Ghana Limited); *"Make yourself relevant so you cannot be ignored"* (Dr. Donkor, UDS); *"The work of the opposition is to oppose"* (Mr. Drah, Political Scientist);*"Don't weaken the hands of power bearers"* (Professor Gyampoh). I present these 30 life lessons below:

1. *All human beings are selfish (seeking individual self-interest)*
2. *Better preparations lead to victories in future*
3. *Consider the lone voice of dissent*
4. *Delay is not necessarily denial*
5. *Don't be discouraged if your dreams take long to mature*
6. *Each life experience presents a new lesson*
7. *Education should be combined with Spirituality*
8. *Endurance through waiting is priceless*
9. *Equipping the younger generation unleashes the potential in them*
10. *Events of yesterday can shape actions of today*
11. *Failure is mindset*
12. *Faith determines accomplishments*
13. *Identify your purpose in life to stay on course*
14. *Investment in yourself through education can be rewarding*
15. *Learning is a journey and life-long*
16. *Life is a process to be cherished and observed*
17. *Life is bittersweet*
18. *Life is of no value unless shared*

19. *Losses can be countered in numbers*

20. *Past victories can be springboards of success*

21. *Peoples' skills are all about relationship*

22. *Positive environments breed positive outcomes*

23. *Service to humanity is service to God*

24. *Strive to become relevant and indispensable*

25. *Success can be contagious*

26. *Success should be managed because of the pressure that comes with it*

27. *There is hope for the tree (Job 1:6)*

28. *Time is capable of solving a lot of problems*

29. *We are stewards of grace*

30. *Where there is a will, there is a way.*

CHAPTER 30

ACKNOWLEDGEMENT

THERE ARE SEVERAL PERSONALITIES WHO were helpful to me, but it would virtually be impossible to acknowledge with thanks, their individual contribution and help. I would attempt to identify or mention some of those who contributed in diverse ways in bringing about this work. I would like to identify some key individuals and organizations for their contribution to the success story of this textbook. In pursuit of a daunting task of this magnitude, diverse and several personalities were helpful; otherwise, it would have been impracticable to achieve the desired outcome without their individual contribution and help.

I thank Apostle Mbanyane Socrates Mhango (PhD-President, Pentecost Biblical Seminary, Wayne, New Jersey) for writing the foreword of this book. I thank Mama Phyllis (*Nyame Ye*-God is Good) for the support she has given my friend in life and ministry.

In approaching this work, I have referred to numerous literatures and I would like to recognize the contribution to these works especially the pioneering works of many authors. I owe a debt of gratitude to my parents for proper upbringing and also providing a stable home for me to flourish. It was in the course of this project that I learned more of the immense sacrifices they made towards my education. I am eternally grateful to them.

I thank my eight siblings and their offsprings. I appreciate the services rendered to me and my family at different times by Mr. John Essah-Mensah, Hannah E. Koduah, and Beatrice Essah-Mensah (deceased).

I thank my Sunday School teachers-Apostle Johnson Agyemang-

Badu and Elder George Owusu for providing me spiritual instructions in my childhood days. I thank all my teachers, ministers, classmates and school mates; as well as, my professional and academic colleagues.

I appreciate the Spiritual nourishment received from our fathers- **Apostles**-John O. Amaniampong, B.K. Swanzy (deceased), J.A. Mensah (rtd), E.K. Apeah (rtd), Nicholas Y. Siaw, B. K. Barabu (rtd), Moses Ladejo (rtd), Rigwell Ato Addison (rtd), Ofosu, Albert Amoah, Dr. Emmanuel A. and Mrs. Patience Owusu, Michael and Mrs. Sheila (Mama Shee) Agyemang Amoako, Samuel K. and Mrs. Mary Arthur, Andy D. and Mrs. Evelyn Donkor, and Sampson Ofori and Mrs. Millicent Yiadom.

Prophets-James O. Amaniampong, J.E. Ameyaw (rtd), Appiah-Agyekum (rtd), and J.K. Appiah-Kubi (rtd). **Pastors**-Isaac K.A. Mensah, S. Opoku-Adipah, F.T. Obuobi, A.K Awuah, Asamoah, E. Davidson, M.N. Wiredu. The rest are Pastors- Maxwell Kofi and Mrs. Mary Kusi (Grandpa, deceased), Benjamin and Mrs. Sarah Dankyi and Isaac K. and Mrs. Sarah Ameyaw. There is no space to contain names of all ministers and fellow elders I have labored with in the Lord's vineyard. To them I say a very big *Thank You.*

Specifically, I thank Messrs.-Alex Cofie, Evans Boakye and wife Beatrice, Opoku Mensah, Richard Boamah, John Osei Akowuah, Osei (former Bursar of NKWASCO), Kwame Osei Sarfo, Kwaku Konadu, Kwame Asafo Agyei; Samuel Obeng, Elder Isaac and Deaconess Christina Nyarkoh, Elder Dr. Albert A. and Mrs. Francisca Buabeng, Elder Dr. Nana and Mrs. Doris Appah-Dankyi, Mr. Kyei-Mensah, Mr. Kenneth Oppong-Kyekyeku. The Larbi and Albert Nsiah families.

Similarly, the names of the following people cannot be spared mentioning: Willie Adjetey-Solomon (Esq), Joseph Bernard Appeah (PENTAX), Dr. Joseph Siaw and Cynthia Agyapong (Jospong Group of Companies), Rosemond Ako-Asante (GTZ), J. C. Akosah, Gifty Andoh Appiah, Willy S. Morny, Group Captain A. A. Awusima, Isaac

Quaye (KPMG), Emmanuel K. Nyamordey, Aisha Tiwaa Gyasi (PKF), Bartholomew Darko (ADB), William Kyei (formerly of Techno Serve), Paul Amponsah (Ernst and Young), and Patrick Acheampong.

I thank God for the lives of Evangelist Paula Mondisa, Mr. Edward Owusu, Ms. Michelle Gyamerah, Mr. Ernest and Mrs. Charlotte Nkpeh, Pastor Aaron Kyei, Mrs. Ernestina Koomson, Elder and Mrs. Kwasi Ofori Tano, Mr. and Mrs. Bernard Nana and Mrs. Hilda Bonsu, Mr. and Mrs. Isaac Obeng, Mr. and Dr. (Mrs.) Ware, Mr. and Mrs. Sarpong, Mr. and Mrs. Afreh, Elder and Nana Robinson.

I am grateful to the Vice Chancellor and staff of the Ghana Institute of Professional Studies (now University of Professional Studies, Accra-UPSA) for their continued effort in advancing the course of professional education in Ghana. Likewise, I am grateful to the UPSA for giving me the opportunity to teach students across the spectrum of the tertiary education divide-professional, undergraduate, and graduate levels. The over 1,000 students I taught have been a source of inspiration to me. I am appreciative of their motivation.

All-in-all, I recognize the help and contribution of those who contributed in diverse ways towards the completion of this task, but for the sake of space would not permit their names to be mentioned. To all my friends, your encouragement has made this dream possible- Your support is acknowledged.

I thank my wife for the love, care, concern, and support she has shown me. I salute my children for their genuine love, sacrifices, affection, and understanding towards me. May the Good Lord bless them richly. Above all, I am grateful to the Almighty God for bringing me this far because in Him I live and have my being. I take full responsibility for errors-omission and commission.

To God be the glory!

EPILOGUE

LIFE-WRITING SERVES TO DEMONSTRATE TO readers the whole process of the author's cognitive development (Dadashova, 2018). This book-*Enough to be shared: A purpose driven name-A vivid life story application of George Appiah-Sokye* is an autobiography (Aurell, September 2019; Beard, September 2019; Jensen, September 2019; Pihlainen, September 2019); written in response to the overwhelming requests from young people especially those in accountancy for mentorship. I have provided my knowledge and experiences, involving *bitter-sweet* life lessons surrounding a mixture of challenges, blessings, bitterness, failures, disappointments, frustrations; as well as, failed promises and unmet expectations.

By virtue of my purpose-driven name, I am convinced God has endowed me with enough lessons in life that are worth sharing. My name is characterized by good virtues- Appiah-*Sokye* (bearer of responsibility or literally *hat carrier*, or *enough to be shared*). It has been established without doubt that names depict the identity, personality, and character of persons.

I have enjoyed a long-run upward growth and trend in life. The Latin maxim-*"Nemo dat non quid habet"*-means "you cannot give what you do not have" Suggesting that I cannot through this autobiographic process give out what I have not experienced or learned in life. Beyond that, life experiences should be relevant in order to be shared.

In this book, I provide the reader with my life story as a foundation upon which useful lessons could be drawn. I deem my personal experiences as the minimum towards the provision of purpose-driven lessons to be shared with all.

I have been influenced by a management framework-*Johari Window*, which is rooted in self-disclosure and feedback. I have made genuine efforts to tell most of my life story to the best of my ability against the backdrop of memory decay that comes with age. I have observed that my rate of recollection of events was good but the recollection of names has been the most challenging. I have realized that I am not as fast at recollection as I used to be when I was young. If you find your name omitted from any of the accounts, do not be offended because it was not intentional.

A lot of young people in the accounting profession and in the Christian community, as well as those in colleges have reached out to me for mentorship. For that reason, the writing of this book will provide me with the opportunity to share my life with a wider target of interest. To them, this is from me to you.

I also deem the writing of this book as a way of giving back to society because of the investment society has made into my life. I have benefited from varied sponsorship across the educational spectrum such as free education, free tuition, educational loans and subsidies. Likewise, numerous people have supported me in one way or the other. I thank all of them.

Unlike a biography, which is written in third person pronoun-*s(he)* by another, I have used the first-person pronoun (I) required for an autobiography in this book. Nevertheless, I do not place the emphasis on myself. By virtue of my name, I have the responsibility to share my life experiences with all through the writing of this book.

I have decided to document my life journey to commemorate my 57th birthday in written format in order not to forget them in my very old age. I may be enabled to update this story with time if need be. I have thus far lived a fulfilling life and I give the glory to God for His divine selection and protection. *I owe it all to Him.* I take responsibility for better-or-for-worse of the contents of the book.

TO GOD BE THE GLORY

ABOUT THE AUTHOR

DR. GEORGE APPIAH-SOKYE
(DBA, CA, CICA, FCIT, CPA)

DR. GEORGE APPIAH-SOKYE HAS OVER thirty-five years of exposure as an accounting professional, academic, adjunct professor, and author; with experience in auditing, accounting, teaching, property management, taxation and fiscal policy, and many more. He has worked in various capacities and organizations in Ghana and USA. Currently, he works for the Youth Connection Charter School (YCCS) in Chicago as fiscal compliance auditor in charge of the following funds: SBB/Non-SBB, Facility Supplement, Supplemental Aid for the eighteen affiliate campuses.

An Adjunct faculty for the Graduate School of Southern New Hampshire University (SNHU). He has departmental approval to teach the finance and accounting courses. The courses encompass: Managerial accounting, Advanced auditing, Federal taxation of individuals, Tax research methodology: Practice and procedure, and Capital budgeting and financing.

Dr. George Appiah-Sokye holds Doctor of Business Administration (DBA) degree in Advanced Accounting (2016) from the Northcentral University in Arizona (USA); Master of Business Administration (MBA) and Bachelor of Science (BSc) degrees with concentration in Accounting from the University of Ghana, School of Business Administration in 2001 and 1989 respectively. In-between these academic qualifications, he completed the final certificate in Taxation and was admitted into membership of the Chartered Institute of Taxation, Ghana in 1995 and subsequently, awarded fellowship in August 2011.

George finished his professional examinations in Accounting with the Institute of Chartered Accountants, Ghana in November 2006 and was admitted into membership in 2008. Similarly, he was admitted into membership of the Institute for Internal Controls in USA in 2009, as well as, completed and passed the Certified Public Accountant (CPA) examinations with the Illinois Board of Examiners in September 2010. He is a member of the American Institute of Certified Public Accountants (AICPA) in USA and a registered CPA in the State of Illinois, USA.

He worked with the Ghana Institute of Professional Studies (now University of Professional Studies, Accra) from January 2004 to January 2012, where he taught: Public Sector Accounting and Taxation (undergraduate); Taxation and Advanced Tax Planning and Fiscal Policy, Corporate Reporting Strategy (ICAG); Corporate Financial Management (ICSA), Performance Management (ACCA), Financial Accounting Fundamentals (CIMA); and Advanced Taxation and Fiscal Policy (Graduate). Additionally, he was the Head of the Accounting Department in the Accounting Faculty and the ACCA Course Head.

He has served on a number of Statutory, and *ad hoc* committees in the Ghana Institute of Professional Studies, as follows: Member, Academic Board; Member, Time Table Committee; Member, Admissions Committee; Chairman, Student Hostel Outsourcing Committee; Chairman, Provident Fund Drafting Committee; Member, Oversight Committee of Business Development Centre; Member, Academic Planning Committee; Member, IPS-NAPTEX Course Project on Accounting and Finance; Member, Convocation; Member, Senior Members Disciplinary Committee; Member, Committee on IPSTA joining UTAG; Member, Accounting Faculty Board; Member, Sub-committees on Research and Conferences, and Exemption from Professional Bodies, etc.

Dr. Appiah-Sokye has attended several courses, conferences, workshops, seminars on: Securities Industry, Principles of Management, Strategic Management, Financial Management, Lobbying, Taxation, Oil and Gas Accounting, Christian Leadership, Theology, Shelby, etc.

He has been involved in the Credit Union Concept from the primary level to the national level; and for that reason, he served as Chairman, Board of Directors of the Internal Revenue Service (now Ghana Revenue Authority-GRA) Employees Co-operative Credit Union in Cape Coast and the Greater Accra. In addition, he also served as a Member, Secretary, and Chairman of the Supervisory (internal auditing) Committee of the Ghana Co-operative Credit Unions Association (CUA) Limited, Ghana for six years. He was Secretary to the National Service Personnel Association in 1985.

Dr. Appiah-Sokye's professional interests cover: Accounting, Finance, Taxation, Auditing, and General Management. Above all, enjoys reading, writing, travelling, researching, some driving, listening to music, social work, and correspondence.

He is married with three sons and a daughter. An Elder of the Church of Pentecost both in Ghana and USA, and has served the church in various capacities, including: Member, National Audit Committee; Registrar, Pentecost Biblical Seminary (PBS); Member, Chicago Regional Executive Committee; Chairman, Regional Audit Committee; Member, District Executive Committee (Chicago and Romeoville); Presiding Elder, PIWC-Chicago, Local Secretary; Member, District Finance Committee; Assistant District PENTYEM Leader, Assistant District Financial Secretary, Elder for Special Duties, Bible Study Teacher, Cell Groups Co-Ordinator, and Sunday School Teacher, and many more.

Currently, focused on developing a new crop of Christian leaders through blended (in-class and online) teaching format; as well as, ensuring effective financial stewardship over the resources of the church. Dr. Appiah-Sokye has mentored a lot of students and accountants and looks forward to having a meaningful and purposeful interaction with you.

TO GOD BE THE GLORY

REFERENCES

Abarry, A. S. (December 1991). The significance of names in Ghanaian drama. *Journal of Black Studies, 22*(2), 157-167.Sages Publications, Inc.

Aboagye, A. A. (June 2018). *Gender and accounting education in Ghana.* University of Ghana. Thesis (MPhil.).

Abraham, W. E. (1962). *The mind of Africa.* Chicago University Press.

Adjaye, J. K. (1990). Asantehene Agyemang Prempeh I, Asante History, and the Historian. *History in Africa,17,*1-29. Cambridge University Press. Retrieved from https://www.jstor.org/stable/3171803. doi:10.2307/3171803.

Adutwum, O. Y. (November 2019). *Build a career before entering politics.* Retrieved from http://wwwpeacefmonline.com -accessed on 02/13/2020

Aheto, J. B. K. (February, 2020). *Your reputation more important than your stomach.* Retrieved from http://www.classfmonline.com -accessed on 02/27/2020

Akyeampong, E. (n.d.). Northern Factors in Asante History. Diversity and tolerance in the Islam of West Africa. A Digital Library of Peaceful Muslim Practices.

Amponsah, G. K. (2009). *I am a church elder.* Cantonments, Accra-Ghana: Advocate/Excellent Printing Press.

Anderson, A. (2004). Writing the Pentecostal history of Africa, Asia, and Latin America. *Journal of Beliefs & Values, 25*(2),139-151. doi:10.1080/1361767042000251564

Anonymous (1994). *Planning.* CUA Workshop on Planning in Management Handout.

Anyane-Ntow, K. (1992). Accounting education and certification in Ghana. *International Handbook of Accounting Education and Certification-Published in Association with the International Association for Accounting Education and Research,*55-69. doi:10.1016/B978-0-08-041372-3-50012-3

Anyimadu-Bona, G. (Rev. Fr.,1995). *Life is common to all.* pp. 68. ISBN:9988-7649-0-1

Appiah-Sokye, G. (April 2016). *Church History.* This paper was presented to the Leadership School of Ministry organized by the Romeoville District of the Church of Pentecost for lay leader of the church.

Ashimolowo, M. (1997). *It's not over 'til it's over-Keeping your dreams alive.* Shippensburg, PA: Destiny Image Publishers, Inc. USA.

Assenso-Okofo, O.; Ali, M. J.; & Ahmed, K. (December 2011). The development of accounting and reporting in Ghana. *The International Journal of Accounting,*46(4),459-480. doi:10.1016/j. intacc.2011.09.010(MPhil.).

Aurell, J. (September 2019). History and autobiography: The logics of a convergence. *Life Writing,* 16(4),503-511.doi: 10.1080/14484528.2019.1648198

Aurell, J., & Davis, R. G. (2019). History and autobiography: The logics of a convergence. *Life Writing,*16(4), 503-511.doi:10.1080/1448 4528.2019.164819

Awiaga, J. Y.; Onumah, J. M.; & Tsamenyi, M. (2010). Knowledge and skills development of accounting graduates: The perceptions of graduates and employers. *Accounting Education,*1-2,139-158. doi:10.1080/09639280902903523

Beard, L. J. (September 2019). 'Accurate history and facts' or memoir? Unraveling the weave of history and life narrative in the Black Hills. *Life Writing,16*(4).

Boateng, K. (Rev.Prof-2010). *Oracles of God-For Good success in business and work.* BenchMac Services. p.123.

Bock, J. D. (February 2000). Doing the right thing: Single mother's by choice and the struggle for legitimacy. *Gender and Society, 14*(1), px. doi:10.1177/089124300014001005

Bowden, H. W. (2004). Minutes of the annual meeting of the American Society of Church history. *Church History, 73*(2), 458.

Bowling, S. (June 2019). How we successfully implemented AI in audit. *Journal of Accountancy, June 2019,* pp.27-28

Burial, Memorial. and Thanksgiving Service for the Late Patience Olivia Appiah-Sokye (Alias "PAT"). Aged 35. Accra, Ghana: Jospong Printing Press

Celebration of life of the Late Mr. Lawrence Larbi (1958-2020).

Center for Audit Quality (January 2019). *Audit Quality Disclosure Framework.* Retrieved from http:www.the caq.org -accessed on 01/18/2019.

Central Finance Facility Internal Regulations,1974; Ghana Co-operative Credit Unions Association (CUA) Limited. Amended and Approved at Tamale, April 1996.

Leonard, C. (1989). *A giant in Ghana.* New Wine Press, Chichester, England

Da Rocha, B. J., Hans, C., & Lodoh, K. (n.d.). *Ghana Land Law and Conveyancing.*

Dadashova, S. (2018). Power and representation in women's autobiographies. *Lithuanian Academy of Sciences, 29*(4), 230-238.

Darko, E. O. (2002). *The reality of life–How to get yourself out of poverty* (Credit Union in Perspective). ISBN:9988-585-36-5

Dr. Brons (Chief Learning Officer). *Express Coaching* (Retrieved from www.ajournettojoy.com –accessed on 05/30/2020).

Drabent, W. (1992). What is failure? or: Constructive negation by fail answers. *Proceedings. ICCI-Fourth International Conference o*n 62-66-1992

Drew, J. (June 2019). What's critical for CPAs to learn in an AI-powered world. *Journal of Accountancy, June 2019*, 20-24.

Duarte, L. (November 2016). *How important is education?* American International School Den Hag. Retrieved from http://www.quora.com –accesses on 04/08/2020

Ediger, R. M. (2005). History of an institution as factor for predicting church. *Eastern European Quarterly,39*(5), 299

Edward A. Ulzen Memorial Foundation (February 1,2018). *February 1, 1896: Exiled Prempeh I and his retinue arrive at Cape Coast Castle.* Retrieved from eaumf.org/ejm-blog/2018/2/1/February-1-1896-exiled-prempeh-1-and-his-retinue-arrive-at-cape-coast-castle -accessed on 02/24/2020 at 4:52pm.

Eichsteller, M. (2019). There is more than one way-a study of mixed analytical methods in biographical narrative research. *Contemporary Social Research,14*(3-4),447-462. doi:10.1080/21582041-2017.1417626

En.wikipedia.org -accessed on 02/24/2020

Enderstein, A. M.; Boonzaier, F. (October 2015). Narratives of young South African Fathers; Redefining masculinity through fatherhood. *Journal of Gender Studies,24*(5), 512-527.doi:10.10 80/09589236.2013.856751

Notes from G. E. Appiah-Sokye's Daily Dairy or Journal: January 1, 1982 to May 17, 1985

Galardi, D. E. (2015, 2006). *Corrective church discipline–What every Christian should know about the Third Mark of the Church.* Owosswo, MI: Community EPC, p.265.

Gaston, E. (2014, 2013). *William J Seymour and the origins of global Pentecostalism: A biography and documentary history.* Durban, Duke University Press. p436.

Ghana Co-operative Credit Unions Association (CUA) Limited (February 2020). *The Credit Union Concept.* Retrieved from http://www.cuagh.com/credit-union/concepts -accessed on 02/15/2020.

Ghartey, A. (December 1988). *Antecedents and significance of accountancy in development: The case of Ghana.* Ghana Universities Press.pps. 319.

Ghartey, B. J. (1992). Evolution, problem, and challenges of accountancy education and certification in Ghana. Edited by Kwabena Anyane-Ntow, In *International Handbook of Accountancy Education and Certification-*Published in Association with the International Association for Accounting Education and Research. Pergamon Press Limited, New York, Oxford, Seoul, Tokyo.

Glenn, J. C., & Florescu, E. (n.d.). *Global future studies and research.* The Millennium Project (Retrieve from http://www.millenium-project.org -accessed on 09/29/2020).

Hammond, T. A. (2002). *A white-collar profession–African American Certified Public Accountants since 1921.* Chapel Hill and London: The University of North Carolina Press.

Hanson S. (2002). *A History of Pentecostalism in Ghana: 1900-2002*. Accra: Ghana

Hanssen, J. K. (2019). The researcher-initiated autobiography's work as an actant in producing knowledge about the social. *Qualitative Research,19*(3),311-322.doi:10.1177/1468794118760748

Hayfron vs. Egyir (1984-86). Possession, Title, and Ownership, GLRD 79, pp.51-54

Hayfron, D.N. (2018). *Come up higher* (1st,2nd,3rd Editions). ISBN: 9988437552

Heitzenrater, R. P. (2011). Inventing church history. *Church History, 80*(4), 737. doi:10.1017/s0009640711001193

Honnesey, J. (1997). Church and state in the modern age. A documentary history. *The Catholic Historical Review, 83*(2), 290.

Howard-Mills, D. (August 2017). *A leader is a master of hiding and flourishing*. Retrieved from http://wwwghanaweb.com -accessed on 02/13/2020

Iuliu-Marius, M. (2019). Self-development and autobiography. *Journal for the study of Religions and Ideologies,18*(54),218-222. ISSN:1583-0039

Jaffee, S. R.; Moffitt, T. E.; Caspi, A.; &Taylor, A. (February 2003). Life with (or without) father: The benefits of living with two biological parents depends on the father's antisocial behavior. *Child Development,74*(1), 109-126. doi:10.1111/1467-8624-t01-1-00524

Jensen, B. E. (September 2019). Exploring human subjectivity: Barbara Taylor's autobiographies. *Life Writing,16*(4).

Jeshion, R. (August 2009). The significance of names. Mind & Language Names Conference. *Institute of Philosophy in London, 24*(4). Doi: 10.1111/j.1468-0017.2009.01367.x

Kavita, D. (2007). "In the eyes of a child, a father is everything": Changing constructions of the fatherhood in urban Botswana? In *Women's Studies International Forum,30*(2), 97-113.doi:10.1016/j. wsif.2007.01.005

Key, S., & Spencer, P.(2008). *50 ways to leave your 40: Living it up in life's second half.* Novato, California: New World Library, p.xvi

Kiran, D. R. (2017). *Failure modes and effects analysis.* Total Quality Management.

Koduah, A. (2013). *Preparing for the ultimate journey-The need to develop a new attitude towards death.* Accra, Ghana: Cobby Kay Enterprise.pp.114-130.

Koninklinjke B. & Leiden N.O. (2003). Review of Professor Kingsley Larbi's PHD dissertation, *Journal of Religion in Africa, 33*(4)

Kreol International Magazine (June 4, 2012). *The exile of Prempeh in the Seychelles: Separated by water but united by culture* -accessed on 02/24/2020.

Lafuente, E.,Viailant, Y., Vendrell-Herrero, F., & Gomes, E. (October 2019). Bouncing back from failure: Entrepreneurial resilience and the Internationalization of subsequent ventures created by serial entrepreneurs. *Applied Psychology: An International Review,68*(4),658-694.

Larbi, E. K. (2001). *Pentecostalism-The Eddies of Ghanaian Christianity.* Accra, Ghana: Center for Pentecostal and Charismatic Studies. pp.517.

Larson, L. (June 2020). Maturing over time. *The Evangelist, 54*(6), pp.38-38-39.

Lovat, S. (2019). Whose life is it anyway? Practice-based research into performed fictional-autobiography and the paradox of fiction.

Journal of Writing in Creative Practice,12(1&2).doi:10.1386/ jwcp.12.1-2.61_1

Manalo, E., & Kapur, M. (December 2019). The role of failure in promoting thinking skills and creativity: New findings and insights about how failure can be beneficial for learning. *Thinking Skills and Creativity,30,*1-6. ISSN:1871-1871(Print).

Manson, M. (n.d.) *10 reasons why you fail* (Retrieved from www. markmanso.net -accessed on 05/30/2020).

Meyer, B. (2004). Christianity in Africa: From African independent to Pentecostal-Charismatic churches. *Annual Review of Anthropology, 33*, 447-474. doi:10.1146/ annurev.anthro.33.070203.143835

Meyer, M. (February 2020). *Fatherless daughters: How growing up without a dad affects women.* Retrieved from http://www.wehavekids. com -accessed on 08/24/2020

Ministry of Youth and Sports-Accessed on 02/24/2020

Minutes of Joint Meeting Between the Family of the Late Mrs. Patience Appiah-Sokye and the Presbytery, The Church of Pentecost, Madina West Assembly held on Friday, August 11, 2000 to Plan the Funeral of Our Late Dear Sister.

Mohr, A. (2011). Capitalism, chaos, and Christian healing: Faith Tabernacle Congregation in Southern Colonial Ghana, 1918-1926. *Journal of African History, 51*, 63-83.

Moriarty, J., & Adamson, R. (2019). 'Storying the self': Autobiography as pedagogy in undergraduate creative writing teaching. *Journal of Writing in Creative Practice, 12*(1&2), 91-107.doi:10.1386/ jwcp.12.1-2.91_1

National Fatherhood Initiative (n.d.). Retrieved from http://www. fatherhood.org; store.fatherhood.org;cdn2.hubspot.net -accessed on 08/24/2020.

Ocran, A. (2004). *10 Commandments of success (10 universal principles you will find in the lives of truly successful people).* Accra, Ghana: Combert Impressions.

Ogbukalu (2008). African Pentecostalism. Reviewed by Baldwin Lewis V. Ojo, M. A. (2001). A history of the church in Africa. *Church History, 70*(4), 807.

Onumah, J. M.; Gariba, F.; Packeys, A.; & Agyapong, R. A. (n.d.). *The banking industry requirements of accounting graduates in Ghana.* Accounting in Africa.

Onyinah, O. (2004). *The pressure of success.* Rock Publicity.pp.32.

Onyinah, O. (2013). *Fanning the Pentecostal fire to impact the generations* (Retrieved from http://www.thecophq.org

Opanin Kwaku Duah Agyemang Vs. Akua Kontoh (Suite Number LC8/87). Record of Proceedings. Exhibits 1-10,Index 1-55, Pages 1-80.

Otabil, O. M. (February 2020). *Success is not imparted by laying-on of hands.* Retrieved from http://wwwghanaweb.com -accessed on 02/13/2020

Owusu, G. Y. (2017). *In pursuit of Jubilee-A true story of the first major oil discovery in Ghana* (1st Edition). Printed in the United States of America. Library of Congress

Pabel, H. M. (2000). Retelling the history of the early church: Erasmus' paraphrase on acts. *Church History, 69*(1), 63.

Pihlainen, K. (September 2019). Experience, materiality and the rule of past writing: Interrogating references. *Life Writing,16*(4).

Quartey-Papafio, A. (1913). The use of names among the Gas or Accra people of the Gold Coast. *Journal of the African Society, 13*, 167-182.

Retrieved from http://www.guidedbiblestudies.com/library/azusastreet_revival.htm

Retrieved from http://www.thetheologynetwork.org/historical-theology/a-complete-churchHistory.htm

Sampath, M., Sengupta, S., Lafortune, S., Sinnamohideen, K., Teneketzis, D. C. (March 1996). Failure diagnosis using discrete event models. *IEEE Transactions on Controls Technology, 4*(2), 105-124. doi:10.1109/87.486338

Shryock, H. (n.d.). *Happiness for husbands and wives.* An International flavor on Mastering Moods (Chapter 11). Review and Herald Publishing Association, pp.138-139.

Simpson, S. N. Y.; Onumah, J. M.; Oppong-Nkrumah, A. (2016). Ethics education and accounting programmes in Ghana: Does university ownership and affiliation status matter? *International Journal of Ethics Education, 1*, 43-56.doi:10.1007/s40889-015-0005-4

Sjastad, H., Baumeister, R., Ent, M. (May 2020). Greener grass or sour grapes? How people value future goals after initial failure. *Journal of Experimental Social Psychology, 88*.doi: 10.1016/j.jesp2020 103965

Stortz, G. J. (2013). A history of Canadian Catholics: Gallicanism, Romanism, and ...*Theological Studies, 64*(20), 417.

Swaggart, J. (2018). Amazing grace-An autobiography. Baton Rouge, Louisiana: Jimmy Swaggart Ministries.

Taylor, A. A. (February, 2016). *Sam Jonah and the remaking of Ashanti.* Legon-Accra, Ghana: Sub-Saharan Publishers, p.302.

The Church of Pentecost (2007). *Tell the next generation-Lecture notes on the annual themes of the Church of Pentecost* (1998-2002). Volume 1.Compiled by the Literature Committee, Accra-Ghana.

The consequences of the absent dad (Retrieved from http://www.allprodad. com -accessed on 08/24/2020)

The devastating effects of the absent father(June 24,2015-Retrievd from www.thefathercode.com -accessed on 08/24/2020).

The Institute of Chartered Accountants (Ghana). *2018 Annual Report and Financial Statements*. Retrieved from http://www.icagh. com -accessed on 02/27/2020

The Institute of Chartered Accountants (Ghana). *List of licensed firms for 2019 that have fulfilled all the prescribed requirements of the Institute*. Retrieved from http://www.icagh.com -accessed on 02/27/2020

The Village of Romeoville: Parks and Recreation Department-2020 Fall Edition. pp.2-55.

Unger's Bible Handbook-A Best-selling Guide to Understand the Bible (1966). The Moody Bible Institute of Chicago (1st Edition). pp.685-691

Vickery, B. G. (1968). *Principles and Practice of Book-keeping and Accounts.* pp.958.

Waller, M. R. (2002). *My baby's father: Unmarried parents and paternal responsibilities*. Cornell University Press. Ithaca and London.

Wendebour, D. (1997). "Pseudomorphosis" A theological judgment as an axiom for research in the history of church and theology. *The Greek Orthodox Theology Review,42*(3-4), 321-342.doi:10.4102/ ids.v49i1/98

Werner, D. (2004, 1993, 1970). *Where there is no doctor-A Village Health Care Handbook for Africa* (Revised Edition) With

Carol Thuman, Jane Maxwell, and Andrew Pearson. United Kingdom: McMillian Education. TALC. Hesperian Health Guides, USA. pages 512.

White, P. & Niemandt, C. J. P. (2015). The missional role of the Holy Spirit: Ghanaian Pentecostals' view and practice. *In die skriflig, 49*(1).doi:10.4102/ids.v49:1:1987

Wood, S. A. (2013). Fundamentalism, perspectives on a contested history.

www. Pfsr.org/history-of-seychelles -accessed on 02/24/2020.

www.expresscoaching.net -accessed on 05/30/2020

www.sucess.com -accessed on 05/30/2020

Yiadom, S. O. (2019). *The meaning of life.* Springfield, VA: Naberm Publications.

Yirenkyi-Smart, J. (2017.). *Pentecost: From Jerusalem to Asamankese– The Journey of Pentecost and the Untold Story of James McKeown and The Church of Pentecost 1937-1982.* Accra, Ghana: Pentecost Press Limited.

Yong, A. & Alexander, E.Y. (2011). Afro-Pentecostalism: Black Pentecostal…

Printed in the United States
by Baker & Taylor Publisher Services